ArtScroll
Mesorah Publications, ltd.

By
Rochel Istrin, RN • Michal Eisikowitz, MA, CCC-SLP
Suri Brand • Miriam Zakon

Illustrations by
Chani Judowitz

Published by
ARTSCROLL® Mesorah Publications, ltd

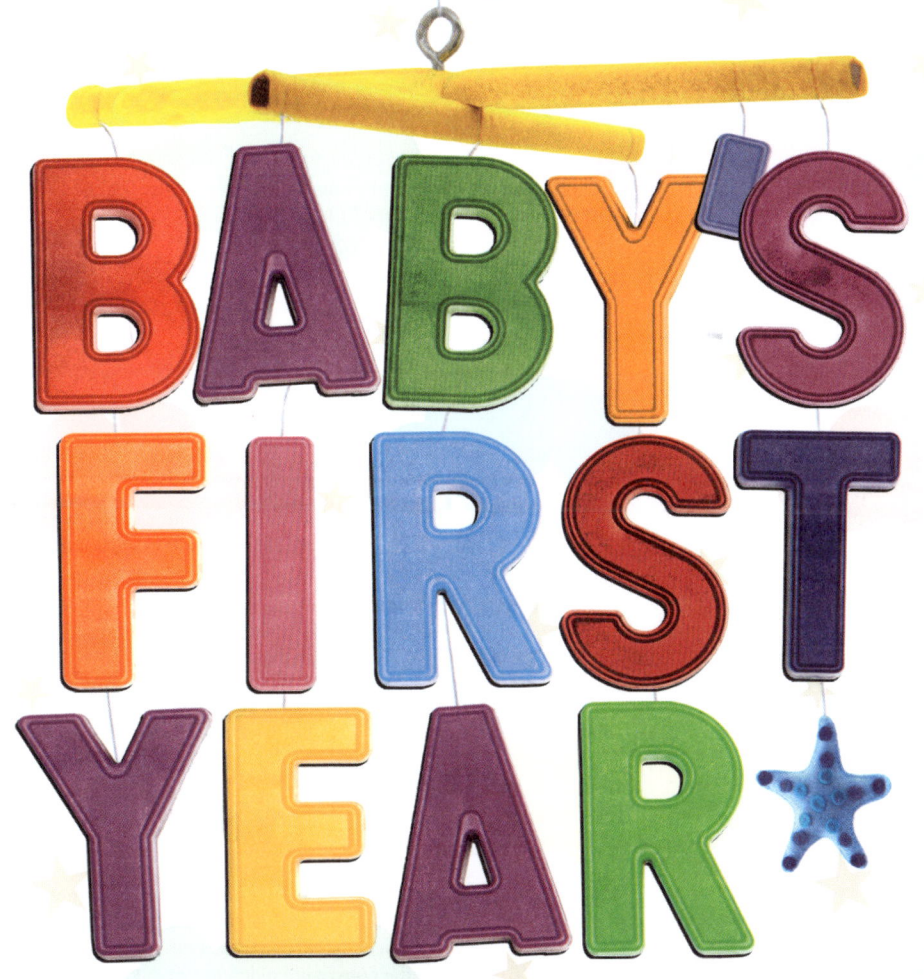

BABY'S FIRST YEAR

THE JEWISH MOTHER'S GUIDE

FIRST EDITION
First Impression … November 2016

Published and Distributed by
MESORAH PUBLICATIONS, LTD.
4401 Second Avenue / Brooklyn, N.Y 11232

Distributed in Europe by
LEHMANNS
Unit E, Viking Business Park
Rolling Mill Road
Jarow, Tyne & Wear, NE32 3DP
England

Distributed in Australia and New Zealand
by **GOLDS WORLDS OF JUDAICA**
3-13 William Street
Balaclava, Melbourne 3183   Victoria,
Australia

Distributed in Israel by
SIFRIATI / A. GITLER — BOOKS
Moshav Magshimim
Israel

Distributed in South Africa by
KOLLEL BOOKSHOP
Northfield Centre, 17 Northfield Avenue
Glenhazel 2192, Johannesburg, South Africa

ARTSCROLL® SERIES
BABY'S FIRST YEAR
© Copyright 2016, by MESORAH PUBLICATIONS, Ltd.
4401 Second Avenue / Brooklyn, N.Y. 11232 / (718) 921-9000 / www.artscroll.com

---

ALL RIGHTS RESERVED
*The text, prefatory and associated textual contents and introductions
— including the typographic layout, cover artwork and ornamental graphics —
have been designed, edited and revised as to content, form and style.*

No part of this book may be reproduced
IN ANY FORM, PHOTOCOPYING, DIGITAL, OR COMPUTER RETRIEVAL SYSTEMS
— even for personal use without written permission from
the copyright holder, Mesorah Publications Ltd.
*except by a reviewer who wishes to quote brief passages
in connection with a review written for inclusion in magazines or newspapers.*

THE RIGHTS OF THE COPYRIGHT HOLDER WILL BE STRICTLY ENFORCED.

ISBN 10: 1-4226-1836-6 / ISBN 13: 978-1-4226-1836-3

Typography by CompuScribe at ArtScroll Studios, Ltd.
Printed in the United States of America by Noble Book Press
Bound by Sefercraft, Quality Bookbinders, Ltd., Brooklyn N.Y. 11232

This book gives parents an overview of infant and baby care, development, and medical issues. It is meant solely for informational purposes, and does not in any way substitute for the advice and diagnosis of trained medical practitioners. This book should not be used for diagnosis or as a treatment plan. A pediatrician or other medical professional should be consulted whenever an infant shows any unusual symptoms or signs of illness, or unexpected behavioral changes.

This volume is dedicated
to the memory of
Benjamin and Irene Lowy ז״ל
בנימן בן רפאל הלוי ז״ל
נפ׳ כ״א תמוז תשס״ח

אסתר בת יקותיאל יהודה ע״ה
נפ׳ ז׳ אייר תשע״ה

After surviving concentration camps and all the horrors of the Holocaust, they came to America, where they married and built a new life. She lost virtually everyone; he lost most of his close family. All their lives they strove to emulate their revered parents and always remained proud of their origins — he from Bardejov and she from Chust. They never wavered in their *emunah* despite the many challenges they faced in their lives.

They shared in everyone's *simchah*, and projected dignity and *yiras Shamayim* wherever they were. Though they had no children of their own, they found joy and satisfaction in the accomplishments of — and were beloved by — their many nephews and nieces, cousins, and children of their extended family, as well as all Jewish children.

It is fitting, therefore, that this volume should be dedicated to such a distinguished couple. As it guides Jewish mothers and fathers in raising Hashem's precious gift — the gift of a healthy baby — Mr. and Mrs. Lowy in their World of Truth will forever share in the *nachas* of the parents and the children of Hashem whose growth will be guided thanks to this volume.

Table of Contents

About the Authors — 13
Acknowledgments — 15
Introduction — 17

Part One: Welcome, Newborn

Chapter 1   The First Days — 21

The First Hours — 23
Rooming-In or Nursery? — 25
In the Nursery — 27
Your Newborn's Appearance — 29
What to Expect from a Newborn — 33
Burping a Baby — 37
Crying — 39
Spitting Up and "GER" — 40
Newborn Bowel Movements — 41
Your Baby's Reflexes — 43
Some Primary Reflexes in Healthy Newborns — 44
Is Your Baby Getting Enough Milk? — 45
Your Baby's Weight — 47
Going Home from the Hospital — 48
Carrying a Newborn — 50
Dressing Your Baby — 52
Baby's Basic Wardrobe — 52

Chapter 2 Getting Acquainted — 58

- Getting to Know Your Baby — 61
- Safe Sleeping — 62
- Back or Tummy? — 63
- Giving Yourself Time to Recover — 64
- Sleep Deprivation — 68
- Developing a Schedule — 69
- "Baby Blues" and PPD — 70
- Visitors — 72
- Trust Yourself — 73
- What about Daddy/Tatty/Abba/Papa? — 74
- The Fine Art of Diapering — 75
- Diaper Changing Step-by-Step — 77
- Surprise! — Stuff You May Find in Your Baby's Diaper — 78
- Caring for the Umbilical Cord — 81
- Bathing Your Baby Step-by-Step — 85

Chapter 3 Welcoming Your Jewish Neshama'leh to the World — 89

- Mazel Tov, It's a Girl! — 90
- Mazel Tov, It's a Boy! — 92

Chapter 4 Baby Essentials — 111

- The Essentials List — 113
- Furnishing Your Nursery — 121
- Car Seats — 125
- The Best Stroller Money Can Buy — 126
- "Wearing Your Baby": All About Baby Carriers — 131

Chapter 5 To Your Baby's Good Health! — 136

- Choosing a Pediatrician — 136
- Well-Baby Checkups — 139
- Fever — 142

When Baby Is Sick	146
Administering Medication	152

Part Two: Feeding Your Baby

Chapter 6   Making the Right Choice for Your Baby — and You ... 157

Breastfeeding or Bottle Feeding	159
The Benefits of Breastfeeding	160
The Advantages of Formula Feeding	163
When It's Not Working	164

Chapter 7   Mommy, I'm Hungry! ... 167

Let's Get Started!	167
The First Days After Birth	174
The Hormones of Breastfeeding	180
Establishing Your Milk Supply	182
How Long to Nurse	182
How Much Should Baby Eat?	183
Scheduling Feeds	184
Increasing Your Milk Supply	186
Nursing and Diet (and Dieting)	188
Nutritional Needs	189
Staying Hydrated	190
Food Sensitivities	191
Dieting	192

Chapter 8   Common Nursing Problems ... 195

Failure to Latch On	195
Inadequate Weight Gain	196
Flat or Inverted Nipples	197
Leaking	198
Nipple Pain	198

Cracked or Bleeding Nipples	200
Engorgement	201
Mastitis	202
Abscess	203
Blebs and Blocked Ducts	204
Thrush	205

Chapter 9 Mom 2 Mom: Real Mothers, Real Experiences — 207

Chapter 10 Nursing to Go! — 214

Expressing and Pumping Milk	214
Manual vs. Electric Pumps	217

Chapter 11 A Guide to Formula Feeding — 219

Before You Begin	220
Keeping the Equipment Clean	224
Formula Preparation	225
The Feeding	226

Part Three: Watch Me Grow!

One to Three Months

Chapter 12 Smiling, Crying, Moving, Seeing... — 234

The First Smile	235
Oh, the Sights There Are to See!	236
Hands and Feet: Getting to Know Them	236
Look Who's Talking!	238
Trimming Baby's Fingernails and Toenails	238
Choosing a Babysitter	240
Why Is Baby Crying?	243
Self-Soothers: Pacifier vs. Thumb	246

Four to Six Months

Chapter 13 Teething, Sleeping, Moving, Playing... 254

- The Tooth Fairy Arrives — 254
- Dental Development and Care — 256
- The Mystery of the Disappearing Sleep — 258
- Seeing Eye-to-Eye — 260
- Feeding Fixes — 261
- Baby's on a Roll — 261
- Tummy Time — 262
- Diaperless Babe on the Loose — 264
- Baby's Up for Grabs — 265
- Making Sense of Baby's Senses — 265
- Baby Massage: A How-To Guide — 267
- King of the Burble — 271
- Play = Learning — 272
- Building Lifelong Bonds — 274
- Toy Story — 275

Seven to Nine Months

Chapter 14 Your Emerging Social Butterfly 280

- Play with Me! — 280
- Separation Anxiety — 284
- Finger Play — 284
- Say Hello to Sippy Cups — 285
- Toy Story — 286
- Sitting Pretty — 287
- Creepy Crawlers — 287
- Is Crawling Essential? — 290
- Stand-Up Comedy — 291
- Baby-Proofing Your Home — 292
- Dreaming About...a Good Night's Sleep — 301

Your Baby's Personality 305
Building Your Family by Building Yourself 310

Chapter 15 Feeding Time: Moving Up to Solids 313

When to Start 314
Prep for Success 316
Best Beginner Foods 316
Foods to Avoid 318
Gastronomic Gear 322
Moving Forward 324
Abort Mission? 326
I Can Feed Myself! 328
The Scoop on Supplements 329
A Diet for My Darling? 331

Ten to Twelve Months

Chapter 16 Walking, Thinking, Talking, Feeling... 336

Just Cruisin' Along 336
Walk the Walk: Getting on Two Feet 338
Goody Two-Shoes: Baby's First Shoes 339
Bye-Bye Butterfingers? 340
Brain Builders 343
Speak Up 344
Baby Has Feelings Too 346

Chapter 17 Weaning: Making the Break 348

Child-Led Weaning 348
Mother-Led Weaning 349
No-Go Weaning 352
Cold-Turkey Weaning 352
Help! Baby Got Sick 353
Extended Breastfeeding 353

Chapter 18   Everyone Loves Baby — 355

    Abba Attachments — 355
    Skeptical Siblings — 357
    Grandparent Goodness — 363
    It Takes a Village — 369
    Older Siblings — 370

    Afterword — 371

Appendix I   Selected Halachos of Baby Care — 373

    Selected Laws of Shabbos — 373
    Selected Laws Concerning Soiled Diapers — 388
    Selected Laws of Kashrus — 389
    Selected Laws of Yom Tov — 390

Appendix II   Tefillos and Techinos — 393

    A Prayer Said on Behalf of a Woman in Labor — 393
    A Prayer Said by a Woman Going into Labor — 394
    A Prayer of Thanksgiving Said by a Mother After Childbirth — 395
    A Prayer Said by a Mother Just Before Her Son's Circumcision — 395
    The Shelah's Prayer for Children to Go in the Way of Torah — 396

Appendix III   Medical Care — 401

    Center for Disease Control Recommended Vaccination Schedule — 401
    Vaccine-Preventable Diseases and Vaccines — 402
    Fahrenheit and Celsius Temperature Chart — 405
    World Health Organization Growth Charts — 406
    CPR for Infants — 410

Index — 413

About the Authors

Rochel Istrin, RN, received her nursing degree from Laniado Hospital in Netanya. She worked in the newborn nursery at Mayanei HaYeshua Medical Center in Bnei Brak (where they average one thousand Jewish births a month, *bli ayin hara!*) for eleven years before transferring to the Emergency Medicine GYN department. Her responsibilities in the nursery included receiving newborns straight from the delivery room, overseeing their care during the mother's hospitalization, and discharging the mothers home when they were ready. She developed workshops for first-time mothers on baby care, and was available to advise parents about caring for healthy infants, breastfeeding, and explaining problems and the proper care of infants with health issues. Before becoming a nurse, she worked as a teacher and parent trainer at a center for autistic children.

She is also an accomplished writer, whose published works include the novels *Searching* (Targum Press) and *Hidden* (ArtScroll) as well as articles and short stories in many periodicals.

She is, *baruch Hashem,* the mother of a large family and delights in many grandchildren, who give her even more "on the job experience" with babies.

Michal Eisikowitz, MA, CCC-SLP, is a speech-language pathologist and writer originally from Brooklyn, New York. The mother of a boisterous crew — her most challenging role by far — she wishes she'd owned a book like this before she became a mommy! She enjoys merging her knowledge of child development with a passion for powerful prose, empowering bewildered moms and dads with support, reassurance, and guidance. On a typical day, she can be found treating language-delayed children, producing magazine features and personal essays, creating compelling copy for marketing firms, and wiping runny noses.

Suri Brand has worked in Jewish book publishing for more than twenty years as an editor, translator, writer, and proofreader. She created and teaches a course on copyediting for the Jewish market. She has also worked in magazine and newspaper editing, most notably as an editor for *Hamodia* and for *Horizons* magazine. But her real labor of love is her eight children, *bli ayin hara*, the youngest of whom just turned a year old. She has enjoyed seeing **Baby's First Year** grow along with her baby!

Miriam Zakon has more than three decades of experience in the world of Jewish publishing. She often says that the writing, editing, and publishing process is a lot like pregnancy and childbirth. In this book, she feels she worked as the doula, helping an outstanding team give birth to an important, readable, and confidence-inspiring book. She looks forward to much *nachas* from **Baby's First Year.**

Acknowledgments

t takes a lot of people, a lot of talent, and a lot of dedication to create a book like this.

The team thanks:
- The fantastic ArtScroll editorial and proofreading team: **Judi Dick, Felice Eisner,** and **Esther Feierstein**
- **Shmuel Blitz**, a bulwark of good judgment and encouragement
- **Mendy Herzberg**, for patiently pulling everything together
- **Dr. Eli Eilenberg, MD, FAACP**, for reviewing and commenting on the manuscript
- **Rabbi Pinchas Waldman** and **Rabbi Avrohom Biderman** in consultation with *poskim*, for their scrupulous review of the halachos section
- **Devorah Cohen**, for an amazing job of design
- **Chani Judowitz**, for her great pictures
- **Eli Kroen**, for still another magnificent cover

Rochel Istrin thanks:
- First I have to thank **Hashem**, of course.
- All **the wonderful staff** and **new mothers** (and their newborns!) **at Mayanei HaYeshua Medical Center** over the years

- » The most wonderful writing partner in the world, **Millie Samson**
- » My friend **Judy Arev**, who never fails to encourage me no matter what I write
- » **My children and grandchildren** (I won't list all the names because that would fill another book!)

Michal Eisikowitz thanks:
- » My husband, **R' Dovid Yoel**, whose advice and perspective consistently prove invaluable
- » **My children**, who've gifted me with the hardest, most gratifying work assignment yet
- » **My mother**, who's taught me more about motherhood than any book ever will
- » **My friends from Targum**, who gave me the confidence and skills to embrace a profession I love
- » **Hashem**, for a life filled with blessings

Suri Brand thanks:
- » My husband, **Hershel**, who supports me in all that I do
- » **My wonderful children**, who never (well, hardly ever) complain when supper is late so I can "just finish this chapter"
- » **My students**, who keep me on my toes
- » **My mentors** — I've been lucky enough to learn from the best
- » **Hashem**, Who gives me everything

Miriam Zakon thanks:
- » **The Team**, for making working on this project such a pleasure
- » My husband, **Rabbi Nachman Zakon**, for great advice and for putting up with all the venting
- » My sons, **Moshe** and **David**, for making everything worthwhile
- » My daughter-in-law, **Tamar**, for being such a fantastic mother, and for her invaluable 21st-century input on baby care issues
- » **My grandchildren**, just for being
- » **Hashem**, for all of the above, plus so much more

Introduction

Mazel Tov!

Mere words are insufficient to express your joy and wonder as you look upon your newborn baby. As a brand new mommy you've traveled a long road to reach this defining moment, no doubt with ups and downs and unexpected turns along the way. At last, you gaze lovingly at the precious new life nestled in your arms and feel overwhelmed with gratitude to the Ribbono shel Olam for this miracle.

At the same time you become fully aware for the first time of the awesome responsibility you've been given. How helpless a newborn is! How totally dependent on others for everything! Deep inside, you may well ask yourself, "How will I ever manage?"

The Torah teaches us that there are three partners in the creation of a baby, and you can be sure that Hashem will be with both of you, Mommy and Daddy, every step of the way, as He has always been for the Jewish nation. Remember that He chose this precious *neshamah* precisely for you because He trusts you, and He knows that for this child's needs you both are the best possible parents.

This book has been lovingly designed for you, to help you on this wondrous journey. Our intention in writing **Baby's First Year** is to be there for new parents all through the first year of their precious baby's life. Our goal was to anticipate the questions and concerns of any new mommy or daddy, and then present the solutions to common problems, as well as to share tips and suggestions for getting through the ups and downs of this special time as smoothly and as enjoyably as possible.

There are many approaches to different aspects of baby care, and much ongoing research on what works best for our little ones. In addition — an important truth to remember as you become a parent — every baby is an individual, with his or her own needs and wants. And guess what? Mommies and daddies are also individuals, with their own family dynamics, social and economic situations, backgrounds, strengths and weaknesses. In this book, we have attempted not to "push" the agenda of any one childrearing expert or approach. We respect our readers enough to give them information on many different kinds of parenting approaches, empowering them to choose what works best for their child.

Even experienced parents will discover new information in these pages. No matter how many children you've been blessed with, it never hurts to have a reference for practical guidance with a Torah *hashkafah*.

Baby's First Year offers guidance on caring for a healthy newborn from the day of birth to the day of the first birthday. Issues relating to multiple births, premature babies, and handicapped or congenitally sick infants are beyond the scope of this book.

May you, the readers of **Baby's First Year**, merit *siyatta d'Shmaya* in raising healthy, happy children to become fine, upstanding Jews who serve *the Ribbono shel Olam* with devotion and joy.

Part One

Welcome, Newborn

Chapter One

The First Days

You're a mommy! Can you believe it? That tiny, perfect baby cradled in your arms is really yours. May you have abundant *siyatta d'Shmaya* to raise this precious *neshamah* to Torah, *chuppah*, and *ma'asim tovim*!

The spectrum of emotions a new mother feels when she hears her precious baby's first cries to the joyful background of "Mazel tov!" varies widely. Whatever you feel is perfectly normal. For some, it's love at first sight; other new mothers need time to gradually develop a relationship with their newborn.

Devory

It took a while to comprehend that the birth was finally over. I heard the baby cry, and I felt his wet little body as the nurse gently laid him on my stomach. I stroked him a little, but I was glad when she took him away to be weighed and washed and whisked to the neonatal nursery. I wasn't feeling well and I just wanted to sleep. The next day when I felt better, I was ready to meet my son and get to know him.

Malky

I didn't feel anything in the beginning. There wasn't any automatic connection between this red-faced, wailing infant and the baby I'd imagined during the months we were waiting and dreaming. I was so sure I would love him immediately that I was afraid something was terribly wrong with me when it didn't happen the way I'd expected. Then the midwife placed the baby in my arms and helped him begin to nurse. Out of the blue, the most incredible rush of love flowed through me, much greater than I ever could have imagined!

Chaya

I reached out my arms for her as soon as she cried. I whispered in her ear how happy I was to be able to hold her at last, and I told her how much we love her. She stopped crying and gave a little sneeze and blinked. Words cannot describe how totally connected to her I felt at that moment. I was over the moon!

Rikki

I was frightened. I was afraid to even hold him, terrified that I might drop him or damage something by doing it wrong. I wanted my mother beside me with her experienced hands. I felt totally lost and inadequate for most of the first weeks of his life.

Yael

I couldn't take my eyes off her. I kept counting her fingers and toes and stroking her downy cheeks. I couldn't bear the thought of them taking her away to the nursery. I thanked Hashem over and over. Such a miracle!

Leah

She looked so helpless, I just wanted to hold her close and reassure her that I would be with her and protect her always. I was suddenly aware of the great responsibility a mother has. I felt awe for my own mother, who had been through childbirth ten times!

The First Hours

It can be a shock to realize that newly born infants rarely look like the adorable pictures you see in magazine advertisements. In the first seconds of life, most babies' skin is more blue than pink because oxygen is what gives the baby's skin that healthy-looking pink hue and the newborn is still somewhat oxygen deprived right after delivery. A new baby's skin may be mottled or wrinkled or even hairy, depending on what week of pregnancy he was born in.

In the first moments of life the direction of blood flow in the baby's heart completely reverses direction. As a fetus, the blood flowed from right to left and at birth, with the first lusty cry, blood begins flowing from left to right. At this time some babies respond to being held by calming down and burrowing instinctively into Mommy's arms, turning their tiny heads from side to side as they search for the comfort of her milk. Less commonly, a perfectly normal infant may refuse nursing overtures and cry inconsolably until finally falling into a deep sleep.

Typically, a newborn is alert for the first hour or so, blinking or closing his eyes tightly to shut out the brightness of the room. A newborn's vision is fuzzy and he is nearsighted, but he can see about ten inches in front of him — and yes, your new baby can see you! His eyes may be puffy from his arduous entry into the world; don't worry. This is common. Within a few days, you will see him open his eyes wide to gaze at the wonder of his new and unfamiliar surroundings.

THE APGAR SCORE

The pediatrician or midwife assesses the baby's well-being the moment it's born. Since 1952 the Apgar test has been universally used to evaluate the medical state of newborn infants. The evaluation is done at one minute and then again at five minutes after birth. The five criteria below form an acronym that spells "Apgar" (which, by the way, is the name of the doctor who initiated the innovative test: Dr. Virginia Apgar).

Appearance

What color is the baby's skin?
- 0 = Blue or pale white
- 1 = Normal pinkish body color, even if the extremities are still a little bluish
- 2 = Normal pinkish color over the entire body

Pulse

How is the baby's heart rate?
- 0 = Absent, no heartbeat
- 1 = Less than 100 beats per minute
- 2 = Normal, over 100 beats per minute

Grimace Response

How does the baby respond to stimulus?
- 0 = No response
- 1 = The baby's facial expression shows a frown or scowl, but the body doesn't respond
- 2 = When stimulated, the baby pulls away, cries, sneezes, or coughs

Activity

How is the baby's muscle tone?
- 0 = Unmoving, floppy, limp
- 1 = Baby holds arms and legs bent near body, with little or no movement (some flexion: extremities are drawn close to body)
- 2 = Spontaneous movement of head and limbs (active motion)

Respiration

How is the baby's breathing?
- 0 = Baby is not breathing
- 1 = Baby is crying weakly, taking slow and irregular breaths
- 2 = Effortless strong cry, normal rate of breathing

The Apgar score is checked twice, at one minute after birth and again at five minutes. The highest possible score is 10. Healthy newborns usually score 9 out of 10 on the first assessment since their color is still partially bluish, and 10 of 10 on the second.

Rooming-In or Nursery?

Most hospitals today encourage new mothers to choose the option of rooming-in, where the healthy newborn baby stays with its mother from birth until discharge. Nurses will come in from time to time to check that baby and Mommy are managing well together. If Mommy is feeling well, this is generally the best option. During the first few days, nearly all babies sleep most of the time anyway, so caring for them is usually not difficult.

Some women prefer not to have full-time rooming-in because they want to use the time in the hospital to rest and recuperate from giving birth (which is known as "labor" for very good reasons!). But even if a baby spends most of his time in the nursery, resting is usually not a realistic expectation on a maternity ward. It's not the babies who disturb the mothers; in fact, most mothers sleep more peacefully when their little one is close by. A mother of a large family or a woman following a difficult birth may opt for the nursery if she feels a need for more time to recuperate.

As a rule, nurseries schedule feedings once every three or four hours. It may take an hour or longer to nurse on this schedule because babies are very sleepy during their first days of life and reluctant to wake up to nurse when it doesn't synchronize with their biological needs. (For more on breastfeeding, see Chapter 6.)

Aside from being called frequently for feedings, new mothers usually have a lot of visitors. Though they are welcome, visitors can leave her exhausted — not to mention the frequent interruptions by lab technicians wishing to take blood samples and medical staff coming in to record the mother's temperature and blood pressure.

Many women do not readily fall asleep in an unfamiliar bed, especially if they are accustomed to a quiet, darkened bedroom at home. A maternity ward is anything but quiet. Cell phones ring at all hours — your own or the phones of your roommates. Doors open and close; curtains are drawn back and then closed again

ADVANTAGES OF ROOMING-IN

- » Babies tend to cry less when they sense their mother's presence.
- » Babies settle better into sleep-wake cycles when their needs are met without delay. (In the nursery caregivers do their best, but it is impossible to respond immediately to each baby when there are many infants and only one nurse!)
- » Nursing is more smoothly established when baby is given small, frequent feedings from the very beginning, something that is difficult to do if the baby spends all his time in the nursery. Mommy's milk will come in significantly earlier, and the possibility of engorgement is greatly reduced (see Chapter 7, p. 182).
- » Many nurses and *mohelim* note that babies who remain with their mother are less likely to have abnormally high bilirubin levels (the cause of newborn jaundice that may cause a bris to be delayed [see Chapter 3, pp. 96-97]), most likely as a result of frequent small feedings that do not overburden the newborn's still immature digestive system and allow it to efficiently excrete excess bilirubin.
- » It prevents separation anxiety for both mother and infant. (You have been so close for nine long months and sudden separation can be emotionally wrenching.)
- » Ironically, the new mother often gets more rest because she doesn't worry about whether the baby is crying or hungry or needs a clean diaper.
- » With rooming-in, Mommy knows that her wishes are being followed (such as whether or not to use a pacifier, how often diapers are changed, which position to place a sleeping baby, or whether to supplement breastfeeding with formula).
- » When the baby is continually by her side, the mother can note any problem that arises regarding the baby's behavior or care and can turn to the professional personnel who are available for advice and guidance. By the time she is discharged from the hospital, the rooming-in mommy has already gained some experience and confidence, and her baby is no longer a stranger.

by staff or visitors searching for someone else. Nearby conversations are often loud (and often just when you've finally managed to fall asleep!). None of this is especially conducive to rest and recuperation.

Sometimes there are medical reasons to leave the baby in the hospital nursery for treatment or observation. And of course, some mothers feel emotionally more secure having their baby taken care of by experienced nurses, or feel they will recuperate better after the birth without rooming-in, and therefore choose the hospital nursery. When that is the case, you can take comfort in knowing that nurses who choose to work with infants are usually warm and caring individuals who give the babies the best care they possibly can. When an infant is in the nursery, the pediatricians and the most advanced medical equipment are at hand, and the baby is under the supervision of experienced nurses trained to respond quickly and efficiently to every potential problem.

In the Nursery

A newborn is routinely given two injections shortly after birth:

Vitamin K

Vitamin K is necessary for the body to activate the factors in the blood that help form blood clots. Vitamin K does not cross the placenta, which means that newborns are born with little or no reserves. The baby's body only begins to produce vitamin K at the age of eight days (the day the Torah mandates a Jewish boy to have his bris). In the presence of a severe vitamin K deficiency during the first week of life, spontaneous bleeding can occur without warning. Since HDN (hemorrhagic disease of the newborn) is known to cause severe brain damage, the routine injection of vitamin K at birth has proven to be an effective prevention treatment since the 1940s. It has been found to be safe and harmless for the infant.

Hepatitis B Vaccine

Hepatitis B is a contagious and potentially serious disease that damages the liver and can lead to hepatic cancer. Hepatitis B carriers are initially asymptomatic (until the disease has progressed to a point requiring hospitalization).

There is disagreement regarding this vaccine. Proponents, including many major health organizations, claim that the hepatitis B vaccine is both safe and effective. Receiving the first injection within twelve hours of birth serves as a safety net to protect an infant from exposure to any person carrying the virus who may come in contact with the baby.

The vaccine is given in three doses. The first injection is administered within twelve hours after birth. The second dose is scheduled between four and eight weeks of age, and the last dose is given at the age of six months. No serious side effects to this vaccine are known.

However, there are others, including pediatricians and other health care professionals, who oppose giving the vaccine to all newborns, rather than just to newborns in specific high-risk populations. Their position is that since hepatitis B is a sexually transmitted disease, or transmitted through blood transfusions or tattooing, it is unnecessary to vaccinate an infant born into a population where these are rare, unless there is close family contact with people who might be carriers.

Mothers should make an informed decision after consulting with their doctors.

Antibiotic Eye Ointment

Aside from the vitamin K and hepatitis B injections, the American Academy of Pediatrics, the American Academy of Family Physicians, the Centers for Disease Control and Prevention, and the World Health Organization all recommend that newborns receive a single application of antibiotic eye ointment to prevent infection from contagious eye diseases that may be contracted in the birth canal. The only known side effects are temporary blurriness and occasional mild irritation for a day or so after application, and these are rare.

Examinations

Every newborn is examined shortly after birth. The baby's weight and head circumference are recorded, birthmarks or irregularities are noted, and reflexes are checked. The doctor will fold the baby's knees and rotate her legs to rule out hip dysplasia (a hip misalignment). A vision screening test is performed (called "red reflex") and before discharge a simple BAER will test the baby's hearing.

Your Newborn's Appearance

Baby's Head

Depending on how long it took the baby to traverse the birth canal, the infant's head may resemble a cone more than the smooth, symmetrical shape of older babies, and you may feel ridges when you brush your hand over your newborn baby's scalp. Don't be alarmed: This is the manifestation of the skull bones overlapping to fit through the birth canal, and it will correct itself within a few days.

The ability of a baby's skull to be molded during delivery is one of the miracles of childbirth. An infant's cranium is made up of five bony plates held together by fibrous material known as sutures. These sutures serve as expansion joints, enabling the skull bones to shift during the birth process. The spaces between the bones are called "fontanels" and can be felt if you gently explore the top of your baby's head with your fingers.

The biggest fontanel, often referred to as the "soft spot," is on the top of the baby's head at the junction between the front and side bony plates. When there is sufficient lighting, this area appears to throb with the baby's pulse. If the baby doesn't have a

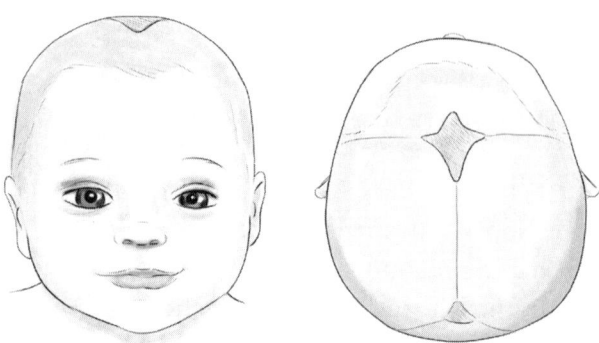

Location of anterior (front) and posterior (rear) fontanels on a newborn's head

lot of hair, you can even see his tiny veins and arteries there. This soft place gradually closes and will be completely gone sometime between eighteen and twenty-four months after birth, though at times it closes even earlier, between three and six months.

The second, smaller fontanel is on the crown on the back of the baby's head and closes during the first months of life. These fontanels are very important because if the sutures would fuse prematurely, the brain would not be able to grow properly.

The skin of the fontanel looks fragile, but you can safely touch it when you wash or hold your baby because his brain is securely covered by a fibrous, protective membrane that is similar to canvas. Sometimes when a baby cries, coughs, vomits, or fills his diaper the fontanel bulges slightly and then returns to normal. This is not a cause for concern.

The fontanel may also indicate the condition of your child's health. During the first year of life, a very sunken fontanel is a sign of dehydration, while an obviously bulging fontanel may be a symptom of meningitis or another serious illness (though this can also be harmless). Any unusual appearance should be reported to your pediatrician.

In contrast to a baby born via the birth canal, the head of a baby born via Caesarean section is usually round since it was not molded in the birth canal. In addition, these babies tend to spit up far more amniotic fluid after birth than those born naturally, probably because the water in their lungs was not gradually pressed out by the pressure of contractions during delivery.

A mild complication of childbirth occurs when the baby is pulled forcefully through the birth canal. This might happen when the obstetrician must use forceps or a vacuum extraction to safely deliver the baby. These procedures sometimes cause tiny veins under the scalp to rupture and bleed (hemorrhage), which results in a discernible swelling at the back of the baby's head near the top. Squishy to the touch, this is known as "caput succedaneum" and takes two to three weeks to resolve, as the blood is reabsorbed.

Baby's Skin and Hair

The appearance of a new baby's skin often causes anxiety to new parents. In the beginning the skin may be covered with a white, waxy substance called "vernix." Within a few days, many babies develop painless red bumps that look like pimples (and you thought babies were too young to get acne!). Sometimes they also have peeling skin. For the most part, these skin conditions are normal and harmless.

Before birth, every fetus is coated with vernix to protect the skin from its watery amniotic environment. Vernix is gradually absorbed by the baby's skin as pregnancy advances, so that a forty-week baby has only a bit of residue in the folds of his skin while an early baby may be totally covered with vernix. (In previous generations, vernix was valued as a cosmetic by women who used it as a moisturizing cream to keep their skin soft and supple.) Even after the midwife carefully rubs our newborn clean with a towel, vernix is often visible on parts of his body, especially if gestation was less than thirty-seven weeks.

Some studies attribute immunological benefits to amniotic fluid and vernix, similar to what is known about the advantages of breastfeeding. Parents may request the hospital staff to delay the infant's first bath for a day, or at least a few hours, in order to allow their baby's skin to absorb some of the vernix.

Within a few days, the infant's outer layer of skin dries and begins to flake and peel, especially at the wrists and ankles. This is perfectly normal and requires no special treatment, though use of a gentle, unscented moisturizer is fine. The underlying skin will be pink and healthy. A newborn's skin is delicate and sensitive. Avoid scrubbing to remove dry skin, and don't apply scented baby lotion because this can cause unnecessary irritation.

The red pimply rash that some infants develop on their face and body ("erythema toxicum") during the first days is due to maternal hormones still circulating in the newborn's body. It is harmless and does not require treatment. Old-time grandmothers used to recommend wiping the baby's face with a few drops of mother's milk, and guess what? It often works! No cream or lotion should be applied.

Most parents are prepared to see their new baby with a head full of soft, downy hair, completely bald, or some variation between. Few anticipate discovering that the baby's face, back, and shoulders will be covered with hair. This is characteristic of many babies, especially those born a few weeks earlier than their due date since this hair gradually sloughs off during the last weeks of pregnancy. Like the fuzz on a peach, this hair, known as "lanugo," protects the baby's skin. Some experts suggest that lanugo plays a role in regulating fetal temperature before birth as well. This phenomenon is temporary, and the hair sheds on its own within a few weeks.

Birthmarks

Birthmarks are pigmented areas of the skin, and they may be found anywhere on the baby's body. Some are already visible at birth, while others appear during the baby's first few weeks.

Though it may seem scary, don't panic! Many birthmarks typically vanish over the course of time (months through years) without treatment, and most others will disappear with proper treatment. Show any birthmark to your pediatrician to ascertain if it should be monitored.

Hemangiomas (sometimes called "strawberry marks") are red birthmarks caused by irregularly formed blood vessels. This type of birthmark, which is fairly common, usually fades with time. In a small percentage of cases, your doctor will want to monitor and sometimes treat the birthmark.

The most common vascular birthmarks are called "macular stains" and appear mostly on the baby's face, especially the eyelids. They range in color from pale pink to red and usually disappear spontaneously within the first year.

Another type of birthmark is a colored stain of indeterminate shape caused by excess melanin cells. It may be light brown or darker and typically doesn't require any treatment. It may fade and disappear as the baby gets older, or actually become darker. If it becomes darker, consult with your physician regarding whether or not to treat it (usually with laser therapy).

Infants whose parents have dark complexions are sometimes born with a large bluish-gray stain across the area of the buttocks, lower back, or thighs. This is known as a "Mongolian spot," and it typically (though not always) disappears by the time the child is between two and four years old.

What to Expect from a Newborn

Babies are born with special qualities that make us want to love them: big, round eyes, plump cheeks, incredibly soft skin, and a delicious baby smell; not to mention their need to nuzzle and their utter dependence on you, their one and only mommy.

A newborn's behavior changes from day to day.

During the first hour after birth, neonates are typically alert to their environment, but shortly afterward they fall into a very deep sleep. During the first day most normal-weight infants do not appear to be hungry even though they may nurse for long periods. At this stage mothers typically feel they have no milk yet; they do have small volumes of colostrum (see below, p. 36). Baby

SWADDLING

Before your baby was born, he grew in a small, warm, closed place. Now that he is big enough to be in the world, firm (but not too tight) swaddling can recreate the familiar and secure feeling he knew before birth, and it's a very effective way to calm newborns during the first weeks of life. Use a soft receiving blanket, preferably one made of a stretchy material.

(See illustrations on facing pages.)

Once baby is swaddled correctly, his trunk and limbs will be strong and stable. If the swaddling is too loose it will upset the baby, but take care that the hips are not bound uncomfortably tight.

You know you've done it right when the baby opens his eyes wide and appears relaxed.

After he is well wrapped, grasp your baby securely on each side and lift him. Try slowly raising and lowering the precious bundle in your hands, and you will be amazed to see him open his eyes wide and gaze around in calm wonder. Even babies who have held their eyes tightly shut since birth will relax and look around when swaddled. If baby is very hungry or in pain, swaddling will only help temporarily, but if he's clean and satisfied, the swaddled baby will eventually fall into a deep sleep until he's ready to eat again. (For the first three weeks, if baby is sleeping deeply, wake him after three hours to feed, to ensure adequate feedings and growth.)

Note: *At this age, do not put a swaddled baby on his tummy. There is some disagreement on when a baby should no longer be swaddled: some say by three to four months, others up until six months. But once a baby can roll over he should not be swaddled, to avoid risk of suffocation.*

Take a thin baby blanket and spread on a surface (bed, changing table, etc.). Place baby in the middle of the blanket with his head above the top edge of the shorter side of the blanket (there should be enough blanket beneath the baby's feet to bring it up at least to his waist later).

Holding baby's arms in a natural position close to his body (either alongside the body or folded across the baby's chest), wrap first one side and then the other around the baby's body, tucking it in beneath him.

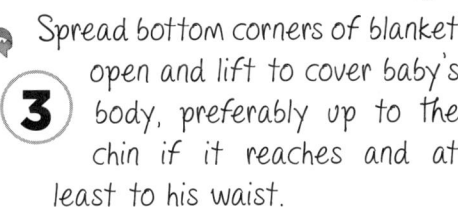

Spread bottom corners of blanket open and lift to cover baby's body, preferably up to the chin if it reaches and at least to his waist.

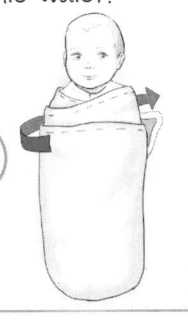

Wrap one corner and then the other around the baby's body, tucking it in under previous folds.

drinks only a spoonful per feeding, as he learns to coordinate suck, swallow, and breathe, as he nurses.

During the initial twenty-four hours, newborns typically retch and disgorge a significant amount of fluid. Most commonly, the liquid they regurgitate is transparent and bubbly, like thickened water. This is amniotic fluid that was swallowed before birth. The baby feels nauseated until he spits it out or until it makes its way out through the digestive tract.

When a baby spits blood on the first day, it can be very frightening to the inexperienced mother. If the blood is black it indicates that it is her own blood swallowed during the birth process and partially digested by the baby. If it is red, she should report it to the doctor, but most often this is the mother's own blood, sucked from a cracked nipple during nursing even if she hasn't noticed any sign of injury.

Before a mother's milk comes in, she produces colostrum, a thick liquid that is golden yellow in color. Since it contains a combination of vitamins and minerals, including immune and growth factors, colostrum is extremely important for your baby's health (see Chapter 7, p. 177). So even though it doesn't seem like the baby is getting much nourishment those first few days before you begin to feel fullness, the colostrum he does ingest is providing essential nutritious benefits.

A newborn needs a day or so to learn the important skill of breathing. A common occurrence on the first day is for the baby to spit up and inhale at the same time. Any nearby nurse will recognize that all too characteristic sound before Mommy even realizes what is happening and quickly scoop the little one out of her arms. The nurse will examine his expression and breathing, and if necessary tip him almost upside down for a few moments to let the fluid in his mouth drain out while rubbing or patting his back. The startled infant typically wails in protest, but his color will return to normal right away.

If a nurse isn't close at hand, you will probably instinctively do the same thing she would have. At any rate, report this to the pediatrician and be careful not to leave the baby lying on his back without supervision. Experienced nurses recommend laying a newborn on his side, supported by a rolled up towel behind his back if necessary, so that the offending fluid will automatically be ejected out of the baby's mouth when he spits up.

After the first day, babies are less likely to vomit without an apparent reason. Of course, most babies will still tend to spit up a little milk from time to time. This is to be expected, though it can be minimized by ensuring a good latch, where baby's lips form a seal on your breast. When switching sides and after nursing, burping the baby can release the bubbles of air that he swallowed and are trapped in his tummy, making him uncomfortable. Most babies outgrow the need for burping after a few months, when they learn to eat more efficiently and can turn over on their own.

Burping a Baby

There is more than one way to help an infant release a bubble of air that is bothering him. With experience, you will find the one your baby prefers. When burping the baby, it is recommended to position a diaper, receiving blanket, or bib over your clothing as protection in case the baby spits up when he belches. Here are some ways babies like being burped:

Over the Shoulder — Gently hold the baby against your chest or shoulder. With one hand, hold his bottom against you and with the other rub or pat the baby's back. Be sure the baby's face is not pressed into your body, which can cut off his air passages. You can check the baby's position in the mirror if it's hard to see his face.

Sitting down — Sit the baby on your lap, facing away from you. Support his chest with the palm of one hand (take care not to press on his throat with your fingers) and lean the baby forward slightly, using the other hand to rub or pat his back.

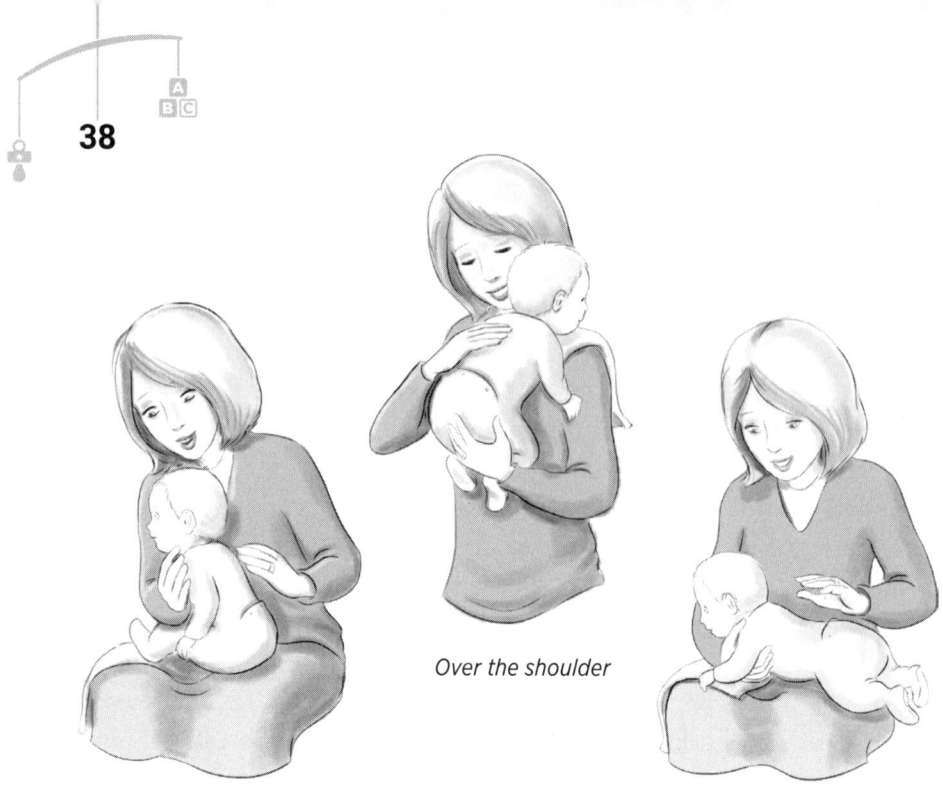

Sitting down *Over the shoulder* *On the tummy*

On the tummy — Lay the baby on her tummy across your knees. Make sure to support her head with one of your hands so it stays on the same plane as her body while gently patting or rubbing her back with the other hand.

New mothers often express alarm at the frequency of hiccupping in newborns. It has been suggested that hiccups may result from stimulation of the vagus nerve in the diaphragm when thick milk stretches the esophagus. It may be helpful for nursing mothers to increase their fluid intake. As the baby's nervous system matures this problem disappears.

Sneezing is another source of worry to inexperienced mothers, but it doesn't mean that the infant has contracted a cold. For one thing, it takes some time for the cold virus to incubate, and the baby has not been in the world for that long yet! It's possible that the presence of a tiny amount of amniotic fluid in the nasal passages is causing the sneezes. If there is no thick yellowish mucal discharge, sneezing is a perfectly normal phenomenon; it is the baby's way of clearing the nasal passages. (Should the discharge be yellow or green, report it to the doctor.)

Crying

In the early days, a baby's sole means of verbal communication is crying, which can understandably be very distressing for the new mother. The best way to handle a crying baby is to try to find the source of the baby's discomfort. Never leave a baby alone to cry for long periods. If she is still crying after ten minutes, that is too long. (After the age of two to three weeks many babies have periods of inconsolable crying known as colic. This will be discussed in Chapter 12, p. 244.)

A baby might cry because he is hungry and needs to be fed. Crying after a feeding may mean that a baby is unsatisfied and needs more to eat, but it can also mean he has eaten too much and his tummy hurts!

Other reasons for crying include discomfort before he moves his bowels, discomfort from the way he's being held, or clothing or a diaper that's not comfortable. Sometimes crying is just a way for an infant to discharge excess energy before falling asleep.

One of the most frustrating problems with tiny babies is not knowing exactly what the reason is for their crying. Ask yourself: Is she hungry? If she ate well, not long ago, then it's probably not that. (Crying before eating is a late sign of distress, beyond hunger. You can prevent this by responding to early feeding cues: Is baby licking her lips, rubbing her face, trying to put her hand into her mouth? Time to eat!) Even if it hasn't been very long since you last fed her, you can try nursing again — your milk is digested in just about 90 minutes!

She may be uncomfortable if her diaper is soiled. Check her diaper and change it if necessary. Run your hands over her clothing and bedding to be sure she's not lying on anything, including bunched material, that might be disturbing her. Check for threads or hair tangled around tiny fingers or toes — is circulation being cut off?

If that doesn't help, try to coax out another burp. Change her position and see if that makes her feel better. Perhaps she is dressed too warmly, or not warmly enough for the temperature in the room? Is there elastic pressing on her sensitive skin? (Babies may not appreciate pressure on their heads — wait for the pretty headbands and ribbons until she is older.) Does she calm down when you pick her up? Maybe she just wants to be held and snuggled for comfort and security.

She may be tired and is having a hard time settling. Try nursing, rocking her gently, singing to her, or chanting softly until she settles down.

Spitting Up and "GER"

A significant percentage of infants spit up. This happens because the muscle intended to serve as a tight valve between the stomach and the esophagus is immature at birth and incapable of closing tightly enough to keep down the contents of the baby's stomach. As a result, some of those contents back up instead of continuing through the digestive system, especially if baby is placed on his back soon after feeding.

As the neonate nurses, his stomach becomes full, which can create uncomfortable pressure against the undeveloped sphincter valve. Naturally the baby will become fussy. Since liquids spill more easily than solids, both breast-fed and formula-fed infants tend to spit up part of their meal until they begin to eat solid food. Keeping him upright after feeding may help.

During the first weeks, when your baby spits up it may come out of her nose as well as her mouth. Don't be alarmed when this happens. You might try to reduce such incidents by holding her in an upright position for a while after feedings.

Babies who spit up a lot may be suffering from GER (gastroesophageal reflux), which is similar to acid reflux in adults.

SYMPTOMS OF GER IN INFANTS

1. Baby arches back often, especially when feeding
2. Baby cries before, during, and after every feeding
3. Swallowing is noisy and painful and adjusting the latch doesn't help
4. Baby appears uncomfortable during and after feeding
5. Excessive amount of milk is forcefully spit up (in simple spitting up the liquid spills out)
6. Excessive frequency of actively spitting up

TREATMENT FOR GER IN INFANTS

- Hold the little one upright or place him in an upright position in an infant chair for a half hour after feedings. This allows gravity to assist the weak valve in keeping stomach contents down.
- Always gently burp the baby before laying him in a horizontal position.
- Avoid infant clothing with elastic bands that put pressure on the baby's tummy.
- Feed your baby smaller meals at shorter intervals.
- With your pediatrician's permission, try adding baby cereal to infant formula to make it thicker and easier to retain.
- If reflux continues, your pediatrician may prescribe an acid suppressor to make it less painful for the baby.

Newborn Bowel Movements

In the beginning, babies seem to have bowel movements every time they eat. If you change your baby's diaper before a feeding, it's likely you'll have to change it again afterward as well. Although frequent diaper changes keep you on your toes (literally) in the early days, be comforted that it's a sign of a well-nourished baby.

The first few bowel movements produce greenish-black shiny stools the consistency of tar. This substance is called "meconium," and was already present in the baby's intestines before birth. Meconium is sticky and rather difficult to wash off, but the task can be made easier for the next time by applying ointment or baby oil to the diaper area after each diaper change.

Formula-fed babies usually settle into about four soiled diapers a day (though some will have more, up to ten a day). Fully breast-fed infants follow a different pattern. From day three to six weeks, expect at least three mushy yellow dirty diapers every 24 hours. After six weeks this often changes abruptly to only a few dirty diapers in a week, or even no soiled diapers for up to two weeks. You may be concerned that all those soiled diapers in the beginning are a sign of diarrhea or that the sudden change to fewer dirty diapers means constipation, but this is just the typical way breast-fed infants move their bowels.

Don't be alarmed if the colors of a breast-fed baby's stools change from one diaper change to another. Depending on the food the mother eats, the stool will be some shade of yellow or light brown, but it often takes on a greenish hue. These stools are normally of a soft, almost liquid consistency, and do not have an unpleasant smell. The bowel movements of a formula-fed baby are usually the same color and consistency every time.

Atypical colors, such as black, white, or green, or texture such as fat globules, threads of blood or mucous, or a pungent, unpleasant odor may be signs of an intestinal problem. Report any unusual change in the frequency of bowel movements or appearance of the stools to your pediatrician.

Your Baby's Reflexes

Labor is over, and mother and baby are about to meet for the first time. The obstetrician or midwife places the newly born infant on Mommy's tummy. The baby lifts his head slightly and turns his face from side to side as if searching for something. The mother helps her baby find what he is looking for, and when his cheek brushes against the nipple, his little mouth opens wide, and he begins to suck. Soon he is contentedly nursing in Mommy's arms.

For most mothers, this is a defining experience of bonding with their new baby. For many fathers, the intense feeling of connection comes the first time he touches his newborn's palm and feels the infant's strong grasp on his finger. These wonderful moments are the result of inborn reflexes that help newborns survive outside the womb, where previously all their needs were automatically met. Some of the baby's reflexes are relevant to eating or protection from harm, while the purpose of others is less obvious. The presence or absence of neonatal reflexes is a significant factor in assessing the health of a baby's neurological development.

The Moro reflex can be intimidating to the inexperienced mother, especially because it happens quite frequently at the beginning. Mom finally gets her baby settled down for a nap after spending hours changing, dressing, and feeding only to have the baby wake, startled from his sleep, his arms flailing about, because a truck went by outside or someone slammed a door somewhere in the vicinity. Don't worry; the baby will probably calm down and go back to sleep quickly with a little soothing.

It's not the reflex itself that wakes the baby, but rather the sensation of having his arms flail about. Swaddling will reduce the movement that disturbs him and allow him to sleep better in spite of any background noise.

Some Primary Reflexes in Healthy Newborns

REFLEX	STIMULUS	RESPONSE	AGE WHEN REFLEX DISAPPEARS
Grasping	Touch baby's palm	Baby catches onto finger and grips tightly	Begins to weaken around 3 months of age, becoming voluntary between 4 and 5 months of age
Rooting	Lightly stroke baby's cheek	Baby turns toward you, opens her mouth wide, and searches for nipple	Between 1 and 2 months of age
Sucking	Touch roof of baby's mouth with your finger or breast	Baby sucks energetically	Between 3 and 4 months of age
Biting	Lightly touch baby's gums or tongue	Baby opens and closes her mouth	Becomes voluntary between 3 and 5 months of age
Blinking	Blow gently or shine a light onto baby's face	Baby closes both eyes	This is an enduring reflex for life
Stepping	Support baby in an upright position, his feet touching a flat surface	Baby will raise his knees alternately as if to walk	Between 3 and 4 months of age
Moro startle reflex	Any loud noise or sudden change of baby's position	Baby startles, throws out both arms with open fingers, and then brings them back tensely embracing body	Between 5 and 6 months of age

Tonic neck reflex	Place baby on his back on a flat surface and turn his head to one side	Baby's arm on the opposite side stretches out and bends at the elbow	Between 5 and 7 months of age
Swimming	Support baby in a horizontal position over the crib	Baby will "swim" with his arms and legs and lift his head up and down	Appears at 3-4 days until around 4 months of age
Crawling	Place baby face down on his tummy on a flat surface	Baby will raise his head off the surface and creep forward with arms and legs	Between 3 and 4 months of age
Babkin reflex	Apply medium pressure to baby's palm	Baby will open his mouth and close his eyes	Between 2 and 4 months of age
Babinski reflex	Stroke the sole of baby's foot	Baby's big toe will lift up and the others will splay open	Between 9 and 12 months old
Plantar grasp	Touch the sole of baby's foot	Baby's toes will curl under to grasp your finger	Between 9 and 12 months old

Is Your Baby Getting Enough Milk?

On their first day, normal-weight infants usually show little interest in eating, and like Jewish mothers everywhere, new mothers worry whether their babies are eating enough. Mothers who try supplementing with formula in soft-nipple bottles that spill the milk into the baby's mouth soon discover that most of the liquid is promptly regurgitated. With the possible exception of the brief period of alertness immediately following birth, neonates just want to sleep for the first twenty-four hours of their lives. Remember: Hashem made your milk to perfectly match your newborn's needs. Newborn stomachs are tiny; they drink a spoonful of colostrum per feeding that first day — perfect for small tummies. (See Chapter 7 for more detailed information and advice about breast and formula feeding.)

On the second day, neonates are generally more alert and ready to practice feeding. Many continue sucking industriously even when appearing to sleep, and they wake and cry when returned to the bassinet. At first the new mother is relieved, comparing today to yesterday when she could hardly entice him to wake up. Then she often begins to worry whether the frequent nursing now means she hasn't enough milk. Before forty-eight hours after birth, few first-time mothers are able to sense the reassuring physical changes indicating that sufficient milk is being produced for her hungry infant. But Mommy doesn't have to worry: nursing frequently is telling her body to make more milk: about an ounce per feeding by day 3! And by then, baby has had lots of practice coordinating sucking and swallowing (which he did in utero) with his brand-new skill of breathing!

On the third day of life, things change again. First-time mothers may be puzzled to find that the baby appears to eat less than on the previous day. She will wonder if she should wake the sleeping baby so he will continue nursing; her milk has definitely come in, and she feels heavy and full. If she had IV fluid, she may feel even more engorged. The explanation for the change in the baby's behavior on the third day is that Mommy now has so much milk that he received his fill in a much shorter feeding. If it took him a half hour or more to nurse on the second day, he may be satiated after just five minutes on the third because there is more milk due to all that "practice" he did yesterday.

At this juncture, nursing at least every two hours can relieve the pressure and ensure that baby continues filling dirty diapers. Three stools the size of a quarter are expected every twenty-four hours by the end of day 3 until about six weeks.

To remove any doubt, you can weigh your three-day-old infant before and after a feeding. Use a scale that is accurate to two grams. The difference between the two weights is the quantity of milk consumed. On average, a normal-weight newborn (between five and a half to ten pounds) drinks an ounce per feeding on day 3, 1.5 ounces on day 7, and two ounces by day 10. This amount gradually increases as the baby grows. From one month until baby begins solids, usually at about six months, babies drink three to four ounces per feeding. Amazingly, mother's milk changes to exactly meet her baby's needs as she grows.

Most babies learn to nurse well and most mothers work out any initial difficulties, but there are many reasons why a mother may choose to feed her baby formula. Well-meaning but insensitive people may criticize her, but no woman should be made to feel like a bad mother for this decision. She may have tried her very best and used all the resources available, and she may be deeply disappointed that breastfeeding didn't work for her. There may be medical, emotional, or many other reasons why she can't breastfeed her baby. It is certainly better to use formula than stubbornly insist on nursing when it doesn't work out for either Mommy or baby. As International Board-Certified Lactation consultants say: Rule #1 is: Feed the baby! The definition of a good mother does not depend on her ability to produce breastmilk, but on the love and care she gives her infant.

A tried-and-true indication that your baby is receiving sufficient nourishment is the number of dirty diapers. If by day 3 a baby is producing at least 3 stools the size of an American quarter, and the urine is clear or very pale yellow, then his intake is satisfactory. By day 5 babies wet diapers at least five times in 24 hours, when they are drinking a greater volume.

Your Baby's Weight

Babies are born with extra fluid and tend to lose weight for the first few days. They reach their birth weight by two weeks, then gain about an ounce a day for the first four months. Though there are several reasons why a baby might fail to gain weight, the most obvious one is that he is not getting enough nutrition. For the first few weeks a breast-fed firstborn infant should be weighed weekly or at least once in two weeks, until it is clear that nursing is successfully established. (A mother with experience in breastfeeding will generally know if the nursing is going well or not.) By the age of one month the new mother should have amassed enough experience and confidence to feed and care for her baby with competence and confidence.

Babies are known to have growth spurts — periods of rapid growth. This can happen at any stage, but usually occurs at predictable intervals. Growth spurts are most common between one week and two weeks of age, around six weeks, at four months, and again at six months.

During a growth spurt, your baby seems hungrier than usual and wants to eat more often and for longer than he usually does. Responding with more frequent feedings will cause the supply of breastmilk to increase until it satisfies the baby's increased need. In bottle-fed babies, the physician will prescribe an increase in formula quantity at these times.

Going Home from the Hospital

The day you take your newborn home from the hospital is one of the most exciting days of your life, but don't be surprised if you experience mixed feelings. This fragile little person who has suddenly taken over your life represents a new and uncharted world. Until now, you had the reassuring guidance of the nurses to help you care for your baby. You know that when you step through your front door with your baby in your arms, your baby's care is in your hands, and that can be scary. Even if you anticipated the ups and downs, the reality of parenthood is intimidating and presents unexpected challenges.

Take a deep breath and relax. You've been davening for this day for so long, and it's finally here. Take your time and enjoy every moment!

BUBBY TIP

WHAT TO WEAR HOME

Unless you are one of those rare women who return to prepregnancy size by the time they leave the hospital, you probably don't yet fit into your prepregnancy clothing. Plan on wearing a skirt with an elastic waistband or in a larger size than you wore before you became pregnant.

Before you and your baby are discharged, the hospital gynecologist will examine you to determine that your recovery from the birth is going well. The doctor will provide information regarding the nursing mother's dietary intake, and include supplementary vitamins and minerals if needed. In addition, you will be given instructions on how to soothe any discomfort from stitches you may have received in the course of the birth.

On the day that the baby is discharged from the hospital nursery, the pediatrician does a thorough physical examination before the new parents are summoned to take their child. Seeing your baby without clothing for the first time since he was born can be vaguely unsettling. He appears so fragile! Many infants fuss when undressed because the sensation of being unrestricted makes them feel insecure. He will be calm again as soon as he is dressed.

Take note of your baby's identity bracelets, which should be identical to your own. These were attached immediately after birth, and you will remove them only once you are at home. Generally, the hospital security guards must verify that this baby belongs to you, so they will need to compare your identity bracelets when you leave. Besides, your mother probably saved yours, and you may want to keep your baby's as a keepsake as well. One day you may show it to this baby's children!

Carrying a Newborn

The first time an inexperienced mother picks up her newborn can be intimidating. She seems so helpless and fragile! Don't worry, it's not as difficult as you imagine, and you'll soon be doing it naturally and with confidence. Babies are warm and soft, and when held they snuggle right into your arms.

Before she was born your baby was held securely within the womb, gently rocked by the movements of Mommy's body. She will experience that feeling of security again when held firmly close to your heart. In the first weeks, try not to make sudden or jerky movements when holding your baby.

The first time you hold your newborn might be less stressful if you are seated and someone hands you the baby to hold. If she starts to whimper, calm her with gentle rocking motions. Most people naturally settle a baby into the crook of their arm, so that the infant's head is supported by the top of the arm, and the little one is settled comfortably on the inside of the elbow; you'll probably find that the most comfortable way to hold your baby as well. You can hold her with either one or both arms in the beginning. As she becomes heavier, you'll need the support of your other arm as well.

An alternative way to hold an infant, especially when she's old enough to begin to look around, is upright facing your body. Rest her head on your shoulder or against your chest under your chin. Use one hand to support her bottom, and hold her upper back, neck, and head with the other hand. Make sure her face is turned to the side so her breathing is not obstructed.

Before lifting your baby from the bed or changing table, slide one hand under her head and the other under her hips so that you are lifting her whole body at the same time. When you return your baby to her crib, place her down gently, maintaining head support until your hand is touching the mattress.

The First Days **51**

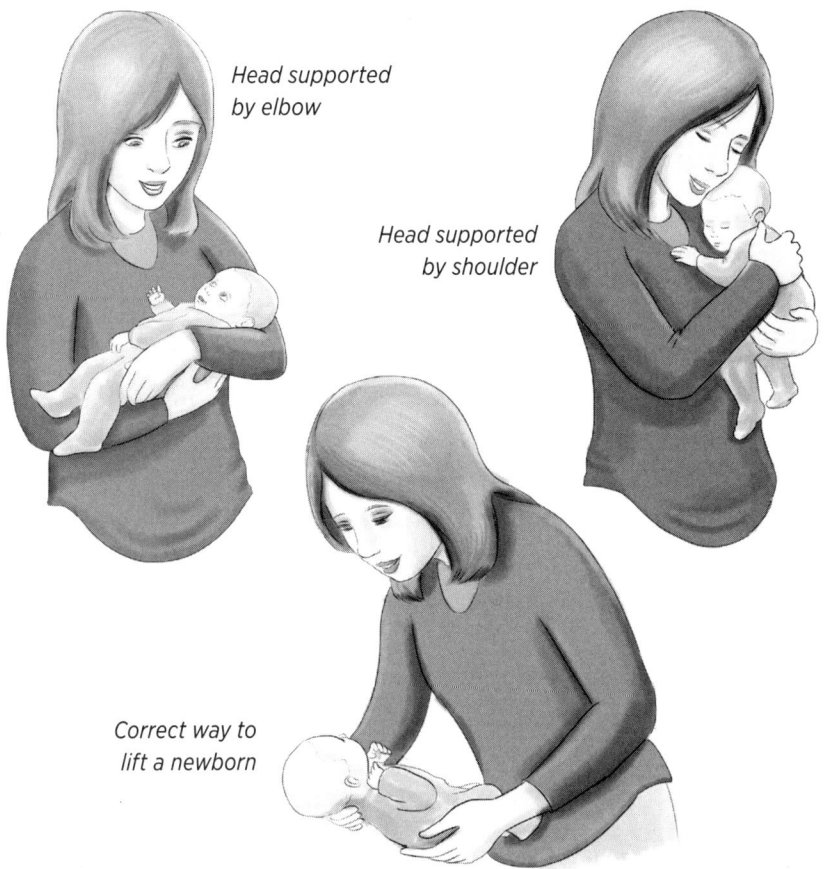

Head supported by elbow

Head supported by shoulder

Correct way to lift a newborn

A newborn's head feels large and heavy in proportion to her little body (because it is!), so always take care to cup your palm behind her head when you lift her, and hold her head securely against your body so the head doesn't wobble while you hold her. Move slowly so that she isn't startled by the change in position. Experienced mothers often slip their hands under the baby's arms, supporting his head and neck with their fingers, before lifting a newborn.

Some babies are fussy and want to be held all the time, while others are content to be wherever you put them. If your baby needs to be held, don't be afraid of spoiling her. Infants thrive on physical contact. Hold your sweetheart while you can, because it won't be long before she is an active and independent toddler with little time for cuddling.

If your little one protests vociferously when she is not being held, using a baby sling (see p. 135) will make your baby happy while freeing your hands to get on with other things you want or need to do.

Dressing Your Baby

While you are in the hospital, baby clothes are provided by the hospital. For discharge you should bring at least two undergarments (onesies or undershirts), a simple stretchie, an outer outfit (a jacket or sweater, according to the season and weather), a hat, and at least one blanket. It is understandable that you want beautiful photographs on this special occasion, but simplicity is a virtue in dressing infants. A comfortable stretchie is much simpler to deal with than a frilly two- or three-piece outfit bedecked with ribbons and ruffles. Take into consideration that the baby will be strapped into a car seat on the way home. She'll have a buckle between her legs and a strap over her shoulders. Too many frills and accessories on her clothing can be very uncomfortable for a baby.

Some parents put thin cotton mittens on their baby's hands to prevent him scratching his face until those long, sharp fingernails detach. The fingernails usually begin to detach by themselves within a few days of birth, and it is generally advisable to wait for them to fall off by themselves, since it's not easy to clip a newborn's nails. (For more on clipping nails, see p. 239.)

Baby's Basic Wardrobe

Infants often must be changed several times a day. Despite the fact that they will quickly outgrow their outfits, a fairly large wardrobe is required. Here are the items a baby needs in the first weeks of life:

Newborn's Basic Wardrobe

- ☐ 4-8 undershirts or onesies (those with snaps at the neckline are recommended to make it easier to get over the head)
- ☐ 5-7 stretchies
- ☐ 5-7 leggings (useful when diapers are soiled so you can just put on a new one instead of changing the whole outfit; some parents prefer pull-on pants with snaps on the inside of the legs)
- ☐ 1 front-fastening sweater or jacket (because babies dislike having clothing pulled over their heads)
- ☐ 4-7 pairs of pajamas (avoid complicated snaps) with feet
- ☐ 2-3 fleece or cotton kimono-sleepers (to keep baby warm at night or in cool weather)
- ☐ 1 one-piece hooded snowsuit or stroller sack (for winter babies)
- ☐ 2 Shabbos outfits (avoid excessive trimmings or lacy frills; check laundering instructions, since many are only hand washable)
- ☐ Socks and booties (to keep the baby's feet warm)
- ☐ 1-3 baby bonnets (including a wide-brimmed hat for sunny days; soft, warm hat for winter)

At the beginning (until about six to eight weeks or when the baby weighs ten pounds), newborns don't have the ability to regulate their own temperatures, so they should be dressed warmly even in the summer (rule of thumb: one layer more than you are

DRESSING YOUR BABY

» *Newborn-size clothing is not practical for long because they are outgrown so quickly. Size 0–3 months is the recommended size for normal-weight infants. Even so, it is nice to have one or two that fit well even if they'll be outgrown before the month is over.*

» *New baby clothing should be washed, if possible with an extra rinse, before it is worn because manufacturers use chemicals that may be harsh on baby's sensitive skin. Either wash by hand or use the gentle cycle on your washing machine for special, delicate outfits, as they are easily ruined. White undergarments of sturdy cotton material can be washed in the hottest cycle. (It's usually best to dress a newborn in layers according to the season and weather. When the environment is warm, you can remove a layer and when it is cold you simply add another layer.)*

» *Make sure that the outfit is comfortable. It should be made of soft, not rough, material. Check that it is not too tight at the wrists, ankles, or waist. Lacy decorations and ruffles may bother newborns.*

» *Avoid cords and ties. Buttons, ribbons, and other decorations must be securely attached to prevent a choking hazard.*

wearing). How do you know if your baby is warm enough? Some grandmothers touch the baby's nose or hands and then conclude that the baby is cold, but this is not a reliable indication. Due to their immature circulatory system, it's normal for a neonate to have cold extremities. A more trustworthy test would be to slide a

- » A newborn's head is floppy. To make it easier to pull a shirt over his head, choose tops with relatively wide openings at the neck. Outfits that are closed with snaps or Velcro are easy to fit over a baby's head. Zippers can be uncomfortable for the baby to lie on if the tab presses into his delicate skin.
- » Pushing an infant's hand into an open sleeve becomes complicated if his grasping reflex is activated and he grabs the sleeve from the inside somewhere in the middle. Prevent this by gathering up the sleeve and sliding it over the baby's hands just like you slide tights over your foot. Take care not to bend his arm in an unnatural position (dolls never complain, but babies do). Check that all five fingers come through the sleeve and are free of stray threads. It is also possible to reach your fingers through the sleeve from the outside to catch the baby's hands and feet and pull them through.
- » Undershirts that snap closed under the diaper area ensure that the material doesn't wrinkle or roll up beneath the outer garment.
- » If you have to pull the material to close a snap, the garment is too small. Replace with a larger size.
- » It's usually easier to dress and undress the baby on a changing table. Never leave a baby unattended on the changing table or any other surface.

hand under your baby's undershirt and feel his chest and tummy. If they are toasty warm, then the baby is warm enough.

Approximately 18 percent of a newborn's surface area is his disproportionately large head. This means that infants are in danger of hypothermia (abnormally low body temperature) when exposed to cool air, and wearing a hat outside is imperative until the baby has gained enough weight to provide insulation, at about two months of age

A baby who is cold may show signs of failing to thrive and his health will be affected. The blood of an infant exposed to cold temperatures releases glucose. In a short time, this can result in low blood sugar, or hypoglycemia. There are no outward indications when a baby's blood sugar drops, although he may seem either jittery or very sleepy. (In extreme cases, low blood sugar causes convulsions.) Hypoglycemia can be reversed by feeding the baby, but obviously prevention is preferable.

On the other hand, too much warmth can also be a problem. Since an infant's internal temperature depends on his surroundings, his temperature drops if the room is cold and rises if it's too hot. Elevations in temperature may be caused by nursing difficulties (insufficient fluid intake), a room that is overheated, a crib placed too close to a source of heat such as a radiator or direct sunlight, or being overdressed.

Insufficient fluid intake results in dry diapers, often accompanied by a dry, pinkish, powdery residue. This can be the first sign of hyperthermia (abnormally high body temperature), and mothers should be alert to this possibility. At home it is recommended to set the thermostat between 68 and 72°F, depending on the season and your own comfort level.

As the nurse dresses your baby for the first time, you will watch in wonder. Be sure to have a spare outfit in reserve in case he spits up or soils his diaper before leaving the hospital. As she dresses the baby, the nurse will explain what she is doing; she will answer questions and reiterate any special instructions. Make

BUBBY TIP

MAKE IT EASIER TO GO HOME

The day you are released from the hospital will go much more smoothly if you manage to send the extra things home a day earlier. This includes flower arrangements, soiled laundry and clothing you won't be wearing, treats you won't be eating, and the assortment of cards and balloons left by visitors.

sure you address the issues you feel unsure about, and find out when to schedule your baby's first visit to his pediatrician. Once you have signed the hospital release forms, it's time to take your baby home!

You'll receive baby presents and complimentary items during your hospital stay. As a result, you can expect to take home more than you brought to the hospital. Let your husband or whoever is accompanying you home schlep your bags and suitcases to the car once you've been discharged. Your body has just been through a physically taxing experience, and it's normal to expect that you will need a few more weeks until you are able to do all the things you used to do. Walk as slowly as you need, and don't try to juggle anything else while you carry your precious baby. The driver should maneuver the car as close to the hospital exit as possible.

Take good care of your baby! Whether you're going home in a taxi or a car, make sure you put him into a safety-approved infant car seat. Many hospitals will not discharge your baby unless you have a car seat. For more on choosing, and using, the safest car seat, see p. 125.

Chapter Two

Getting Acquainted

You're home! If this is your first child, you're no longer just a young couple — now you're a family. If this is your second, fifth, or even your eighth — you know that every baby brings something very unique into the home.

You and your husband and baby have a lot to learn about each other in the next few weeks, and if you have patience for the process, it's going to be a wonderful journey to self-discovery, appreciation, and fulfillment. The most helpful attitude is not to expect perfection from anyone, and that includes yourself, your spouse — and your new baby.

Esty

In the beginning I just felt lost and kind of scared when the front door of my house closed and I was alone with my husband and baby for the first time. Dovid and I looked at each other and I could see how he was trying hard to act natural and in control, then we both began laughing and a lot of the tension dissipated. Mercifully our baby slept for the first two hours, which gave us time to settle into the new world we'd landed in.

Moshe

I wouldn't admit it, but I was terrified. The first few days I just touched his cheek and let him hold my finger when he was in someone else's arms. Finally Malky insisted that I pick up the baby. My hands were shaking, but I'm brave, so I scooped him up. Now, I'm a strong guy, I can easily pick up heavy cartons of books or canned goods, but that seven-pound newborn was almost too much for me. I panicked and tried to hand him to my shvigger, but she laughed and backed away. When I saw there was no escape, I stood up straight and looked deep into his eyes. "I'm your tatty," I introduced myself, and he smiled! I know he was too little to smile, but it seems we men understand each other.

Michal

Being the oldest of ten, I thought I already knew everything. I had helped my mother with my younger siblings since I was eight years old, and I was an experienced babysitter in our neighborhood from the age of fourteen. What was left to learn? Ha! I learned that when it's your baby it's a whole different planet! I was on the phone every day — "Ma, help!" — with questions I had never imagined in my life before. But things settled down into a routine, and by the first month everyone said I was born to be the mother of a dozen children at least.

Mindy

All the time I was in the hospital I couldn't wait to get home and begin life as a real mother, but when the moment came, I felt like running back to the safe maternity ward where there was always someone experienced to help me learn how to care for my baby and to tell me what it meant when she cried or slept too much! Little Sari began squalling the minute we walked in the door, and nothing I did seemed to help, which didn't help my wavering confidence. Jonathan dialed my mother and she took a car service to come as fast as she could. As soon as Mommy walked into the door Sari yawned and fell asleep. "That's children for you," she told us, and we relaxed. My mother stayed for the first week, and it made all the difference for me. Though it was a bit hard on Jonathan, he was good about it. After she left I felt much more confident, especially knowing she was just a phone call away.

Naama

Shoshi was a good baby, eating her fill and sleeping well between meals. My younger sisters were delighted to come by after school to see their first niece and to help me with shopping and laundry and housecleaning. It was so much fun dressing her (like playing with a real live doll!) and hearing the compliments. It was all much easier and more natural than I had imagined it would be.

Batya

During my pregnancy I read every book and article as if this information was going to be included on a Regents exam. I could quote the opinions of all the eminent doctors and baby specialists, and I felt confident and ready. From the beginning, baby Chaim didn't fit the mold. He had trouble latching on until we realized he was tongue-tied and the doctor fixed it in his office. He almost didn't sleep; whenever I looked at him, his huge blue eyes were staring thoughtfully into the distance. He gained weight steadily but in very small increments. It took a few weeks to understand his likes and dislikes, what bothered him and what calmed him; after that, everything went smoothly. I think I should write another book on all the things that weren't in those I studied so assiduously!

Gila

We were still in our first year and living in Eretz Yisrael. My Hebrew was pretty limited, and not many of our neighbors spoke fluent English. I was in tears within the first fifteen minutes after we came home with the baby, feeling utterly unqualified to cope with the responsibility of being this precious baby's mommy. While I was sobbing, the doorbell rang and the first neighbor arrived bearing a heavenly smelling casserole. Her smile didn't need any translation, and I felt a little better. Then another neighbor knocked and came in with a carton of food trays to put in the freezer. Her admiration of my new baby boy filled my heart with nachas. And so it continued, until the counters and table in the kitchen were full, the refrigerator was stocked, and I felt so cared about and special!

Getting to Know Your Baby

Even if you've set up a separate room for your baby's nursery, it's best that in the beginning she spend most of her time in your room near you. Babies benefit from stimulation to all their senses — hearing your voice, feeling your touch, recognizing your scent, and tasting your milk.

Since the baby's sight is still developing, visual input has an especially positive effect on the baby's neurological development. She's still very little, but it's not too early to hang a mobile over her crib or bassinet. Newborns like to look at pictures with patterns, especially in black and white, because their vision is still blurry and the sharp contrast between black and white is easier to focus on. The more opportunities a baby has to concentrate on a picture, the more neurological connections are created to develop the visual center in her brain.

Certain babies are highly sensitive and startle very easily in the first weeks of life. If your baby does this, try swaddling (see p. 31), and keep the noise level soft and light levels low. This behavior is temporary; she will soon become accustomed to normal levels of stimulation. However, it's not a good idea to keep the environment perfectly quiet because a baby needs to become accustomed to normal levels of noise if possible.

In the beginning, you'll find that your newborn will probably sleep up to eighteen hours a day, but there will be periods when your baby will be alert and interested in her surroundings. Use the times when she is awake and alert to spend time with her and stimulate her. Infants love sounds, so talk to her and sing. She will stare at you in total concentration, and maybe even wiggle or gurgle in response!

If you need to wake your baby for a feeding or a diaper change, try tickling her feet or stroking a cheek. Never, ever shake a baby — vigorous shaking can cause internal bleeding — and don't allow anyone to play roughly with the baby or to bounce her up and down.

The head of a newborn is proportionately large and heavy in comparison to her body. When held upright or when lying on her tummy, your baby will try to hold her head straight, but you'll notice that it wobbles. Until she is old enough to hold it steady, be careful to cradle her head and neck with the palm of your hand when you lift her or lay her down (see p. 50 for tips on holding baby).

It's normal for newborns to lose weight during the first days after birth. Losing up to 10 percent of the birth weight in the first week should not be a cause for worry. Babies are born with a lot of extra fluids, and it's natural that their weight goes down as these fluids are eliminated. Most babies regain their birth weight within a week to ten days, and some regain it even sooner.

In the first two weeks, the rhythm of breastfeeding gradually becomes routine. In the event that feedings don't proceed smoothly or pain persists during nursing, consult with an expert. Don't wait to see if things work out. Most problems are much easier to solve before nursing habits have already become firmly established.

Common problems include a baby with a "tied tongue," which is easily corrected by an office visit to a pediatrician, oral surgeon or ENT, or incorrect positioning, a technical issue that can be quickly rectified (see Chapters 7-10 on breastfeeding). You can also contact your local La Leche League or friends to get a referral for an experienced lactation consultant to help you diagnose any problems and offer solutions.

Safe Sleeping

In October 2016, the American Academy of Pediatrics (AAP) released new sleep recommendations for children. Among the recommendations for safe sleeping are for infants to sleep in their parents' room — but not in bed with parents — for at least 6 months, and preferably up to a year. Infants should never be placed to sleep on couches, armchairs or soft surfaces.

The guidelines also state that an infant should sleep on his back, on a firm mattress with no pillow, bumper guard, blanket or plush toys in the crib. (You can put the baby in a sleeper to keep him warm.) Obviously adult beds were not designed for infant safety.

Recently manufacturers have begun offering co-sleeper bassinets. These can be set up in close proximity to a parent's bed, allowing the infant to sleep on a separate mattress in safe conditions while Mommy can still reach out and easily touch her baby.

Back or Tummy?

The United States National Institutes of Health, the American Academy of Pediatrics, and many other medical associations recommend that babies up to the age of one year should be put to sleep on their backs. They cite statistical studies showing that sleeping on the back significantly reduces the risk of SIDS (Sudden Infant Death Syndrome) and that babies who sleep on their backs are less likely to get fevers, stuffy noses, and ear infections. In their recommendations, they add that if a baby turns over onto his tummy during the night, and he is capable of rolling over — back to tummy, tummy to back — there is no need to move him onto his back.

It must be noted that some respected pediatricians feel that this recommendation is flawed. These doctors point out that sleeping on the back is not best for the baby's development. It can cause a stiff neck, poor coordination, and poor core strength. They feel this policy is causing children to need physical and occupational therapy as they grow older, and can also lead to a need for developmental early intervention. Parents should make informed choices, after speaking to their pediatrician.

If you do choose to let the baby sleep on his back only, make sure to be even more careful that he gets enough "tummy time" in order to give him the developmental boost he needs. (For more on "tummy time," see p. 262.)

Giving Yourself Time to Recover

After giving birth, it often comes as a shock for a first-time mother to discover that she's no longer the same person she used to be. She may be very emotional, dissolving into tears when she never did before. Lack of sleep may make her cranky and cause her to sometimes say words that she regrets immediately. She may feel weak and unable to do all the things she used to do without a thought. Ideally, her close family understands the importance of giving the new mother help and emotional support during this period, until she recovers from the aftereffects of childbirth.

Time needed for recovery is individual. Even if you feel fit and ready to face the world just a few days after birth, try to take things slowly. Doctors estimate that it requires six weeks for the body to return to the physiological state it was in before pregnancy. Some women need longer, especially if they have other little ones at home. Use this time to nurture yourself — eat nutritious meals (after the first few days, you'll find yourself feeling hungry all the time if you're breastfeeding; try to make healthy choices to keep your strength up), get sleep when you can grab it, and accept help when offered.

Even if you are naturally organized, a newborn in the house is a big change. It will take time to learn how to adjust your schedule to accommodate feedings, fewer hours of sleep, and diaper changes along with the usual household tasks like washing dishes and preparing suppers. Resist the temptation to overexert yourself. Getting another hour of sleep and eating properly must take priority over vacuuming and dusting, at the least until your milk comes in and nursing is successfully established. Look for shortcuts whenever possible and consider temporarily lowering your

> ## HELPING A NEW MOTHER IN THE FIRST WEEKS
>
> Your family and friends will probably be eager to give a hand after your baby is born. Here are some ways to take advantage of this wonderful resource, without letting it get in the way of bonding with your baby:
>
> » New mothers don't have enough time or energy to prepare meals at first. This is to be expected. Ask family and friends if they want to help stock the refrigerator, freezer, and cabinets with healthy, ready-to-eat meals and snacks before you come home from the hospital so that everything will be waiting for you when you get home.
>
> » Accept offers of help with shopping, washing dishes, cooking, laundry, babysitting for the other children, and housekeeping.
>
> » If experienced mothers offer to help take care of the baby for you, politely decline. You will probably start comparing yourself to them and will feel even more inadequate and less able to manage. Remember: Others can do the dishes or wash the floors for you, but no one else can be your baby's mommy!
>
> » Everyone offers free advice, but you must be the main caretaker for your new baby. Thank everyone, but don't feel obligated to follow their advice. All the decisions on how to raise your child belong to you and your husband, so accept advice that fits while quietly ignoring advice that doesn't feel right for you.
>
> » Surround yourself with positive people who reassure you, and try to avoid people who are critical and insensitive to your needs. You need to rest a lot after childbirth, so if a difficult person comes to visit, just plead exhaustion and go to your room and close the door. If there is someone around who makes you feel bad about yourself or your mothering skills, and it's difficult to avoid the person, discuss it with your husband. As the man of the house, he bears responsibility for protecting the welfare of his wife and baby, and he may have the unpleasant duty of limiting visits from certain people.

POSTPARTUM DOULA

Most mothers need several weeks of support after childbirth until their strength returns and it becomes possible to resume their normal lifestyle. In recent years it has become popular to employ a postpartum doula or a baby nurse (often a licensed practical nurse) to assist during the transition period after a new baby is born. The fee is usually reckoned by the hour, and not every family can afford this luxury, but friends or extended family can pool their resources to employ a postpartum doula for a few days a week as an invaluable gift in honor of the new arrival's birth.

The postpartum doula's main goal is to help the mother adjust and gain confidence in her new role, so much of her job is about education. She offers services in lactation counseling, emotional support, and advice to aid in physical recovery. She may also do light housekeeping, shopping and errands, and simple meal preparation. The postpartum doula is trained to assist the new mother in diapering, bathing, feeding, and soothing her new baby. When there are older siblings, she helps with such babysitting tasks as making supper, bathing, getting the children into pajamas, and putting them to sleep so that the new mother can rest or concentrate on her newborn.

The postpartum doula's role may change from day to day, according to the needs of the family. She also offers information about local resources, such as available parenting support groups, pediatricians, and relevant *gemachim*.

Health service clinics and leaders of childbirth preparation classes can recommend experienced postpartum doulas. It's also possible to locate a doula online through the DONA organization (Doulas of North America).

When you contact a prospective doula, be sure to communicate your expectations about which services you need, verify her fees, and ask for references from people she has worked with in the past.

balebusta standards. This is not the time for three-course meals, a spotless kitchen, closets with clothes lined up in perfect military order, or ironing the linens. And tuna on bagel can make a very nice dinner!

Don't be embarrassed to accept help. No matter how independent and self-sufficient you were before, now is the time to keep your priorities straight, and that means recovering your health and meeting the needs of your baby. Remember to eat well and drink plenty of fluids. At this time, carbohydrates and fats are important to increase energy and, if you are nursing, your milk supply; right now, proteins are less important.

There is no reason to feel guilty if you want to do nothing but sit and hold your little one close. This feeling is called bonding and contributes both to the baby's emotional growth and his physical development. Even more: When a mother holds her baby close she is teaching lessons in *emunah* and *bitachon*: The child, no matter how young, is learning that his mother — and HaKadosh Baruch Hu — will always be there to help him. Children thrive on unconditional love. Being held makes your baby feel safe and secure. If your baby is crying or you feel exhausted, leave those

---

NIGHT BABY NURSE

Hiring a night baby nurse is an option to relieve sleep deprivation. Baby nurses are not necessarily RNs, but they are professionally trained to care for newborns.

A night nurse shift is usually between 8 p.m. and 9 p.m. until the following morning. Unlike a postpartum doula, she does not offer any service beyond baby care. She changes the baby's diapers, handles formula feedings, and settles the newborn to sleep. In the morning she reports on what transpired during the night, leaves the baby clean and dressed, and answers your questions about his care.

A night baby nurse is an especially good investment if you've had twins, and you are likely to feel overwhelmed. If you're lucky, it's possible your mother or mother-in-law will be able to fill this role at no cost to you.

THINK AHEAD

Keep a list of telephone numbers that you'll need (you or someone else can prepare this before you give birth) and hang it on the fridge or keep it near your bed. These should include emergency numbers, pediatrician, gynecologist, postpartum doula, hospital, pharmacy, lactation consultant, and the phone numbers of family, friends, or volunteers for assistance.

dishes in the sink and the laundry unfolded. They'll still be there until there is time to deal with them.

Exercise is also important to your recovery, but take it easy at the beginning. When you feel strong enough, start with a daily ten-minute walk. Not only will it help you recover physically, but it will help you find new energy and recharge your emotional batteries.

Sleep Deprivation

A breast-fed newborn usually nurses for up to half an hour (ten to twenty minutes on each side, with ten minutes of burping in between!) every two and a half hours; formula-fed infants eat every three to four hours. The laundry also suddenly starts to pile up, since newborns tend to spit up and soil their clothes faster than you can change them. And if you're using cloth diapers, the pile of soiled and wet diapers soon becomes a mountain. Between all the diaper changes, feedings, and the need to soothe baby when he seems to be crying for no reason, new mothers quickly become sleep deprived.

Don't expect to keep to the routine you knew before the baby was born. Try to flow with your little one's needs and sleep when he sleeps, even in the daytime. It will be a few months before you can sleep straight through the night, so now you must fill your need for sleep in short naps whenever the baby is calm or sleeping.

Keep his bassinet near your bed to make it easy to respond quickly when he wakes. If you attend to him before he is crying hard, then he will settle back to sleep much faster afterward.

Part of this difficult adjustment period is getting the baby to follow a schedule. The optimum time when infants are receptive to establishing patterns of eating and sleeping begins between two and three months of age. As soon as you establish a schedule, it will all become much easier. Remember that babies are excellent barometers of their mothers' feelings: If you're calm and relaxed, then often your baby will mirror your mood.

The time it takes to establish a routine is very individual, depending on the nature of the baby and the personality of the mother as well as the circumstances surrounding them. Don't forget the importance of *siyatta d'Shmaya*; slip a few coins into the *pushkah* with a heartfelt request for Divine help.

Finally, be patient. This, too, will pass.

Developing a Schedule

It's not easy to establish a sleep routine in the first weeks, up to about three months, because new babies need frequent feedings to fuel their rapid growth. Most healthy newborns are unable to sleep more than two to three hours at a stretch before they wake up to eat again. If you are able to reset your own biological clock by resting during the times your little one is napping, you will find it much easier to cope with baby's irregular schedule of sleep and eating.

As she grows older, pay attention to your baby's behavior. When tired, some babies pull on their ears, yawn, suck their thumbs or rub their eyes. Getting her settled soon after you observe her sleepy sign will help her fall asleep calmly. The wails of a baby who is overtired increase stress and make the whole process more difficult.

Experienced mothers report that following a consistent bedtime routine helps babies — even tiny infants — make the transition from wakefulness to sleep. Examples include bath time before bed, saying *Shema* and singing *HaMalach HaGoel*, or closing the shades and dimming the lights.

Remember that when a baby becomes accustomed to sleeping in a hushed house, his sensitivity to noise may make him unable to fall asleep unless everything is quiet. If this is your first baby, and the house tends to be quiet at bedtime, you might want to listen to a *shiur* or play some gentle music, so baby learns to sleep with some ambient noise.

Most babies settle into a schedule, even when they're being breast-fed on demand. Writing down the times and length of time your baby eats over a few days will show you the emerging pattern. Within a few weeks you will notice that once a day he sleeps longer, perhaps skipping a feeding altogether. If he gives you this extra time in the daytime it's not to be expected that he will repeat it at night when you need your sleep. Wake him after three hours (if this is his usual schedule) during the day to make it more likely that he will give you the longer sleep time during the night.

"Baby Blues" and PPD

The physical discomfort of those first weeks after the birth is compounded by uncontrollable hormonal changes. There may be times when a new father fears that his wife is no longer the woman he married. One moment she will be all smiles and the next finds her dissolving in tears. Although every experienced mother will reassure you that these unpredictable and shifting moods are normal, it can be a challenge to cope with them in the beginning.

On the third or fourth day after giving birth, many women find themselves feeling sad for no apparent reason. This condition, known as "the baby blues," is characterized by irritability, problems with sleeping, and a decrease in the ability to concentrate, as well as apparently unexplainable mood swings. This appears to be the normal reaction to the abrupt drop in hormones after delivery. The euphoria of the birth cannot be sustained endlessly, so don't worry if this happens to you. Expect your moods to stabilize over the next week or two as you gradually get back to yourself.

In the event that these bouts of sadness continue for more than three weeks, and especially if you find yourself repressing thoughts of harming yourself or your newborn, you may be suffering from postpartum depression (PPD) and you should seek medical attention immediately.

Postpartum depression affects up to 16 percent of new mothers. It begins like the baby blues, but the symptoms worsen and last longer, until the woman is no longer able to function. These symptoms include loss of appetite, withdrawal from family and friends, insomnia, extreme fatigue, feelings of shame, guilt, or anger. She may feel that her head is cloudy and her life is out of control, and at the extreme, she may have thoughts of hurting herself or the baby.

Postpartum depression is not a character flaw. It is a complication of childbirth. Prompt medical treatment can restore the mother's joy in life and help her manage the symptoms until the condition passes. Untreated postpartum depression may continue for months and can develop into a psychological emergency requiring expert medical help and medications, and, rarely, even hospitalization.

If you think you are suffering from PPD, remember that you are not alone! Most communities have PPD organizations that will help with referrals, hotlines, support groups, and information to help you recover. The main thing to remember is: If you suspect that you — or someone you love — has PPD, GET HELP AS SOON AS POSSIBLE.

Visitors

Having a baby is such an exciting event that some friends and relatives find it difficult to stay away. You will probably welcome short visits — who doesn't get *nachas* from having others ooh and aah over their baby? — but now is not the time to entertain company.

Keep visits to a minimum during the first weeks because not everyone is sensitive to the new mother's need for rest or the baby's need for a reliable routine. Inexperienced parents often find it difficult to place reasonable restrictions on visitors, and the inevitable result is an exhausted mommy and a hysterical infant.

After showing off his progeny to the visitors, the new *tatty* should politely but firmly excuse his wife, and she should retire to her room with the baby, closing the door behind her. If you are at home for your baby's *shalom zachar*, there is no need for you to entertain women who stop by to say mazel tov, and the baby does not need to be on display.

Another reason to keep visitors to a minimum during these first weeks is that everyone will want to hold the infant, often passing the baby back and forth between adoring aunts and cousins. Exposing your baby to so many people at this stage leaves him vulnerable to infections since a baby is born with an immature immune system.

In the first weeks, your baby's immunity comes from his mother's milk, but that's not always adequate when he is exposed to germs. RSV (respiratory syncytial virus infection) is a common virus that presents in adults as a simple cold, but can be serious in infants. Request that visitors look, but don't touch, and after a few minutes return the baby to the safety of his crib.

Remember that your baby is completely dependent on you. Protect his health, even if setting limits makes you uncomfortable. Be firm, even if someone complains or tries to convince you that it's unnecessary. Your pediatrician will confirm the importance of being careful.

Anyone who does hold the baby should make sure to wash his hands with soap and water and avoid putting his finger in the baby's mouth.

Trust Yourself

Well-meaning visitors often feel obligated to share advice about the proper way to raise children. This is very nice, but can be confusing. How is a new mother to know what to do when Tante Henya's lecture on the proper way to dress a baby is later contradicted by Aunt Malka, who insists the baby is dressed all wrong? Everyone has an opinion, and they are often very different!

You will have to sort out many issues. Most of the time there is no right and wrong. Does a good *balebusta* roll out her challah dough on a wooden kneading board, the marble countertop, or on the kitchen table — or (gasp!) does she use a bread maker? There is no one right answer. People are different, and the final decision rests on the specific mother's situation and personality. The same applies when it comes to caring for your baby.

One new mother might want to dress her baby girl in the most stylish frilly dresses and tights from the very beginning, while another prefers simple, interchangeable tricot tops and bottoms for weekday wear. Will you feed your baby according to a schedule like they did in the hospital nursery, or do you want to let her nurse whenever she cries? Will your baby sleep in the room with you or in a different room? Will you leave a light on at night or do you want her to become accustomed to sleeping in the dark? Will you go to her as soon as she seems restless, or wait until she begins to cry?

If you can't settle down and fall asleep because your baby is grunting in his sleep, it may be necessary to move the crib elsewhere. If you can't relax because you worry constantly whether she is breathing, doesn't it make more sense for the baby's bed to be near yours?

How will you decide what to do? Use logic and your intuition (and, of course, this book) and be open to revising your decision. Some mothers like to research all sides of the question; others simply turn to their pediatrician for guidance.

In the end, it's your baby and you must choose what feels best to you. Hashem gave you this precious child. He trusts you to be the best possible parent. Shouldn't you trust yourself?

What about Daddy/Tatty/Abba/Papa?

It's not uncommon for new fathers to feel left out at first. After all, Mommy got to spend the first few days with her baby almost constantly and had a chance to get used to holding and caring for the baby. In addition, most of the baby's needs involve breastfeeding. Even if the baby is bottle-fed, women are usually more comfortable with child care from their experience as older sisters or babysitters before marriage, while new fathers are often quite terrified of their newborn infants.

Establishing a relationship is no less important for a first-time Daddy than for Mommy, and he should be encouraged to help care for his baby too. Abba can also give bottle feedings, change diapers, bathe and cuddle and soothe a newborn. No one loves that baby more than he does, and he will become more confident with practice.

The Fine Art of Diapering

Your baby will need diapering about ten times a day during the first month. Be sure you have all the supplies you will need at hand before you begin, because you must never leave an infant unattended on the changing table or other unprotected surface even for a minute while you go to retrieve something you need. Always keep at least one hand on him while you are changing the diaper, because even seemingly helpless newborns have been known to wriggle their way to the edge, especially when crying.

Here is the paraphernalia you will want to keep at hand near the diaper-changing area:

- ☐ Clean diapers in the appropriate size. (Disposable diapers are produced in sizes according to weight. A diaper that is too large will leak, and a diaper that is too small pinches the baby's skin when closed.)
- ☐ Baby wipes
- ☐ Ointment for diaper rash
- ☐ Spray bottle filled with water for diaper changing if you don't use wipes on Shabbos (for more on baby care on Shabbos, see Appendix I, pp. 373)
- ☐ Pail with a lid for soiled wipes and diapers
- ☐ Hamper for soiled clothing until they are washed
- ☐ A clean change of clothes to replace soiled ones

It's generally more convenient to clean a baby's soiled bottom with baby wipes, but some babies are hypersensitive and develop sore, inflamed skin from the chemicals in the wipes. Hypoallergenic wipes that do not contain alcohol are recommended, or you can hold the infant over a sink or tub with one hand and wash him under running water from the tap (taking care it's not too hot or too cold) with the other hand. Another option is to prepare a small container of warm water with a soft cloth in advance to wash the diaper area.

CLOTH OR DISPOSABLE?

A few generations ago mothers had to fold cloth diapers so that the thickest part was correctly positioned to absorb the most wetness. Cloth diapers were secured with large safety pins, and the only way to prevent or limit leaks was with nylon or rubber panties pulled over the diaper under the baby's clothes.

Disposable diapers were hailed as a great breakthrough, both for baby's comfort and Mommy's convenience. Nowadays, though, there has been a movement among some mothers to go back to cloth diapers.

Today's cloth diapers (often called "pocket diapers") come in soft materials such as terry cloth, cotton, or flannel, are preshaped to fit a baby's body, and close with snaps or Velcro strips. Removable inserts (you put them into the "pocket") make changing cloth diapers as simple as using disposables, but since most disposable diapers are super-absorbent, cloth diapers must be changed more frequently. Like many issues in childrearing, there is no right or wrong way, with advantages and disadvantages to both. Choose what works best for you and your baby!

And remember: The longer wet or soiled diapers of either type are in contact with baby's skin, the greater the risk of diaper rash.

So why use cloth diapers? For one thing, babies often feel more comfortable in softer cloth diapers because the chemicals, dyes, and gels in disposable diapers may cause an allergic reaction on delicate sensitive skin.

> Economics is also a factor. Cloth diapers can be bought with the firstborn child and subsequently handed down to siblings, or they can be rented from a diaper service. Though washing cloth diapers takes time and uses water and electricity, it is about half the cost of buying disposable diapers.
>
> In addition, disposable diapers wind up in landfills and are only partially biodegradable, so cloth diapers are more ecologically friendly.
>
> Also, many mothers relate that it's easier to potty-train babies accustomed to cloth diapers because the toddlers are immediately aware when the diaper is wet; the ultra-absorbency of disposable diapers keeps baby from feeling the discomfort of a wet diaper.
>
> On the other hand, disposable diapers are very convenient. They're easy to change, come with liners that wick wetness away from baby's skin, lessening the risk of rashes, and usually don't leak. Negative aspects to throwaway diapers include the ongoing expense, running out of diapers when stores are closed, or mistakenly pulling too hard on a tab, causing it to detach and wasting a diaper.
>
> Even if you choose to primarily use cloth diapers, you will probably prefer disposable diapers for traveling or day care due to the inconvenience of schlepping soiled, smelly diapers back and forth.

Diaper Changing Step-by-Step

1. Put the baby on his back and undress the lower part of his body.
2. Unfasten the tabs of the soiled diaper.
3. Grasp both of the baby's ankles with one of your hands and lift above the changing surface, or roll him to the side or onto his tummy, so you can clean the baby's bottom with your other hand.
4. Use a clean wipe or cloth to clean the genital area.
    » To avoid urinary infections, always wipe a baby girl from front to back. Gently separate and clean the skin beneath and between the genital lips.

» Always carefully clean under and around a baby boy's genitals, since feces remaining in the folds can cause painful irritation.

5. Remove the soiled diaper and set aside, all the while keeping one hand on the baby.

6. With one hand gently lift the baby's feet to raise his body from the changing surface while positioning a clean diaper under his bottom with the other hand.

7. Apply a thin smear of baby cream or ointment to the diaper area, if needed.

8. Fasten the sticky tabs securely but not so tight that it pinches. (At the beginning, you may have to fold over the front of the diaper to avoid rubbing against the umbilical cord stump.)

9. For newborns, some doctors recommend applying alcohol around the umbilical cord stump at each diaper change. This should be done until the dried cord stump falls off and continued for one more day; afterward the navel is considered healed. Other doctors say it will heal faster without alcohol, and to just clean it with water and keep it dry. Check with your pediatrician.

10. Place the baby securely in his crib or infant seat, and thoroughly wash your hands with soap and water.

Surprise! — Stuff You May Find in Your Baby's Diaper

Even if you've changed a baby's diapers before, you may feel intimidated by the experience of changing your newborn's diapers in these first weeks. The baby seems so helpless and may cry every time you open his diaper, making you wonder if you're doing something wrong or if he's in pain. (Actually, this is most likely due more to the fact that newborns feel insecure when exposed.) It helps to change the diaper quickly and get him

> **DIAPER RASH PREVENTION**
>
> » Change your baby's diaper frequently during the day, as soon as possible after he moves his bowels.
> » It's recommended to apply creams or ointments that contain zinc oxide because of their moisture-resistant properties. Ask your physician for recommendations.
> » Exposure to air heals diaper rash, whereas prolonged exposure to a wet or soiled diaper exacerbates it. If your baby has diaper rash, try leaving him on his tummy on an absorbent pad without a diaper for a while. A baby lying on his abdomen should not be left without supervision.
> » If the rash doesn't improve within three days, or if the condition becomes worse, this may indicate a fungal infection. Contact your pediatrician for appropriate treatment.

covered up again as soon as possible. When he is older, he will like the sensation of freedom and then you'll have to struggle to get him into a clean diaper and dressed again!

In the beginning, you never know what you will find when you open up your baby's diaper. Mothers occasionally discover blood in the diaper of a baby girl during her first week of life. There is no reason for alarm if this happens. The transfer of maternal hormones to the fetus before birth temporarily activates the infant's ovaries, causing a bloody vaginal discharge. This needs no medical treatment, and the bleeding terminates, generally within five days. If it continues beyond a week or involves a significant amount of blood, your pediatrician should be consulted. (Maternal hormones are also cited as the reason one occasionally sees swollen breasts in both male and female infants. This situation passes within a short time, since the baby is no longer exposed to these hormones.)

In the days after birth, you may have occasion to notice a small orange stain in your baby's diaper, especially in male infants. This

UNDESCENDED TESTICLES

The part of a baby boy's anatomy beneath the *ever habris* is called the scrotum. The scrotum shelters two glands known as testes that are vital for fertility, similar to the ovaries in a female. During pregnancy the testes form in the fetal abdomen and gradually descend into the scrotum before birth, where they can be felt when touched. About 2 to 4 percent of male infants (30 percent of premature baby boys) are born with undescended testicles, which means that one or both testes have not yet descended into the scrotum. This causes no pain and there are no symptoms. Testes almost always move into place by the age of six months without medical intervention. In the rare case that they do not, the child will be referred to a specialist who may correct the problem with a simple surgical procedure when the baby reaches twelve to fourteen months.

HYDROCELE

Congenital hydrocele is the medical term describing a balloon-like collection of fluid in one or both testicles, caused by improper drainage from the scrotum. Hydrocele usually resolves without treatment, but if it persists then a minor surgical repair will be done between the ages of twelve and eighteen months. There are no long-term effects.

is not blood. The atypical color comes from crystal sediment in the baby's urinary tract. Since it can be a sign of dehydration, consult with your pediatrician if it recurs because it could mean that your baby is not receiving adequate fluid, and increase his fluid intake through nursing, formula, or water.

It also happens that a baby's genitals appear swollen. This is a common condition, partly due to maternal hormones and partly because newborns are born with extra fluid that collects in areas like the face and genitalia. It is normal for babies to lose up to 10 percent of their birth weight as this fluid is excreted.

Breech babies often have swollen testicles due to the trauma of their birth presentation. This problem soon subsides.

By the time your baby is two weeks old, you will be an old hand at diaper changing, and the effects of the birth will have disappeared (not to mention the bris will have healed and the umbilical cord will have fallen off).

Caring for the Umbilical Cord

Many new mothers feel squeamish about touching or even looking at the stump of the umbilical cord that is still attached to the baby's navel. The umbilical cord provided oxygen and nutrients to the unborn baby, but after birth it no longer serves any purpose. The midwife, obstetrician, or maternity nurse clamps the cord a few inches from the baby's abdomen before cutting him free of his former life support. This procedure is painless for the newborn because there are no pain-sensitive nerves in the umbilical cord.

At first glimpse, the umbilical cord resembles a soft, moist, bluish-white rope. Forty-eight hours later, after the clamp is removed, the umbilical cord is dried and shriveled, looking rather like a dry banana stem. It continues to dry up until it falls off. When that happens, most likely you will discover the stump in the baby's diaper or clothing.

The baby's diaper should be kept folded away from the umbilical cord because it is important to keep the area clean and dry until the stump detaches. Expect the process to occur gradually over the first two weeks. Don't pull the stump off, even when it is barely connected by a last thread of dried skin.

Some doctors recommend wiping the area of the stump with alcohol with every diaper change, while others prefer leaving it alone unless the area has become soiled or odorous and must be cleaned. Your pediatrician will advise you about the best way to treat your baby's navel.

It may happen that you notice a few drops of dried blood on the baby's diaper or clothing after the stump has fallen off. This happens occasionally when the baby's clothes rub the freshly healed site and doesn't signify anything to worry about. The process of the stump healing is nearly always smooth and natural. Less common signs to consult your pediatrician about include redness or swelling around the navel, especially if it feels warm to the touch, discharge from the navel resembling pus or an extremely unpleasant odor, or real bleeding. Prompt treatment at the first indication of infection can prevent it from becoming more serious.

NEWBORN JAUNDICE

Newborn jaundice often appears in the early days after birth. Though it can be alarming to inexperienced parents, this phenomenon is quite natural. Your doctor will explain that newborn jaundice is not a disease, and it is not contagious. The majority of cases require no treatment whatsoever.

What causes neonatal jaundice?

A fetus is totally dependent on its mother for its supply of oxygen. But an unborn baby can't pant to increase oxygen intake during physical exertion, like we do, so how does it kick and somersault for hours (remember those sleepless nights during pregnancy)?

The answer is part of the *nifla'os haBorei* — fetal blood has more branches for oxygen than are needed outside the womb. After birth, these unnecessary cells are broken down by the baby's spleen and recycled into cells with a normal number of oxygen connectors. The extra components are then further dismantled by the liver and gradually expelled with other waste from the body.

One of the components to be dismantled is bilirubin, a fatty molecule that collects in the bloodstream. After two or three days, the immature liver of a newborn can become overwhelmed by the steadily increasing quantity of bilirubin to be broken down.

Untreated bilirubin accumulates in the bloodstream, and the baby begins to have a yellowish tinge. You may also find that the jaundiced newborn's urine is dark colored and his stools have an unusual whitish color — that's from those extra cell components that the baby's body is expelling after birth.

The first place that jaundice is noticeable is the whites of the eyes, which is the area with the highest concentration of blood vessels. The next stage is the face. If you withdraw your finger quickly after pressing gently on a baby's forehead, the skin will blanch and the presence of jaundice can be seen clearly. Gradually the yellowish color spreads down to the body and the arms and legs.

When all the fetal blood has been broken down and recycled, the liver recovers and the jaundice disappears. By the end of the first week (in time for the bris!), the yellow tinge has receded and your baby will be a healthy pink.

In certain situations, newborn jaundice begins shortly after birth and reaches unacceptably high levels. The most common reason for this is ABO incompatibility — where the mother has type O blood and the baby has inherited the father's A, B, or AB type of blood. (A more serious form of this kind of incompatibility occurs if the mother has Rh-negative blood and the baby is Rh-positive. For this reason, all mothers with Rh-negative blood must receive an anti-D injection within seventy-two hours after birth to prevent the production of antigens that will affect future pregnancies.)

Before a baby is born, there is no direct contact between fetal blood and the maternal blood, but during childbirth this can happen. The response of a type O immune system to this exposure is the production of antigens that pass through the placenta and begin breaking down the baby's blood, releasing bilirubin and causing early jaundice. Early-onset jaundice may take longer to pass, and it can be necessary to give the infant treatment under an ultra-blue light to help break down the bilirubin through the baby's skin.

Generally, newborn jaundice passes without harm to the baby, but sometimes the condition can be more serious. That's why, though most people associate jaundice as being a reason to postpone a bris, it's important to regard jaundice just as seriously for girls as for boys. If the medical staff in the hospital nursery determines that your baby's bilirubin levels are too high, they will treat it before it becomes a problem.

The degree of jaundice depends on various factors, including your baby's gestational age and birth weight. A two-hour-old infant with a bilirubin level of 4 milligrams per deciliter (mg/dL) requires treatment, while a three-day-old baby with 4 mg/dL is not considered to be jaundiced.

To assess bilirubin level, a wand known as a transcutaneous bilirubinometer is pressed against the baby's forehead to give a bilirubin reading that is generally reliable. If that reading is high, a more accurate lab test will be done by pricking the baby's heel to measure the level of bilirubin in the blood serum.

Interestingly, there are two seemingly contradictory pieces of advice that the mother of a baby with high bilirubin may be given. Many doctors and *mohelim* advise mothers to temporarily cease breastfeeding (usually for up to forty-eight hours) until the bilirubin level goes down. A break in breastfeeding generally improves a baby with jaundice, and does so relatively quickly. There seems to be something in the breastmilk that connects to the bilirubin and prevents it from being excreted. Though this has been proven effective, it can be the most emotionally traumatic part of the neonatal jaundice experience for the mother. If stopping temporarily is recommended, continue to pump in order to build up and maintain your milk supply.

On the other hand, since bilirubin leaves the body through the waste, it also makes sense to feed a yellowish baby more often, so that he will have more bowel movements. If your baby is jaundiced before breastfeeding is successfully established, he may not be receiving enough milk to pass the bilirubin out of his system. You might consider temporarily adding a little formula until your supply increases. A nurse will weigh the baby before and after nursing in order to calculate the correct amount of formula to add after nursing, if possible.

If you are continuing to breastfeed, make sure the baby gets frequent small feedings. When the baby gets lots of milk at a feeding, it makes more work for his immature liver, which is trying hard to break down the bilirubin that causes jaundice.

As always, if you must make a decision on whether to take a temporary stop in breastfeeding or breastfeed even more, consult with a medical professional or *mohel* that you trust, making sure the professional has all the pertinent information.

The most common treatment for neonatal jaundice is phototherapy, which is noninvasive and painless. This blue light helps the baby's overworked liver break down bilirubin via his skin. A soft mask protects his eyes from the strong light. Since he wears only a diaper under the light (to allow maximum exposure to the light source), his body temperature will be monitored during the treatment.

Phototherapy is much harder on mothers than on infants. New mommies may find themselves in tears due to the enforced separation and imagined fears and worries. Also, babies with jaundice tend to be drowsy and sleep more than usual, which makes it hard to wake them for feedings. A solution to this problem is to express your milk and feed the baby from a bottle without removing him from the ultraviolet light.

When the bilirubin level drops, it usually continues decreasing gradually. Even if your little one is still a little yellowish at discharge from the hospital, don't worry. If necessary, you will be instructed to continue monitoring his lab work from home until he is completely recovered. In most cases, neonatal jaundice is the easiest problem you will ever have to cope with!

Bathing Your Baby Step-by-Step

There are varying opinions about how frequently a baby should be bathed. It depends on the season your baby was born, your family habits, and the baby's physical needs. Consult your pediatrician for his recommendation. Sponge baths may be

recommended during the first two weeks until the umbilical cord (and bris) has healed. (After the circumcision, the *mohel* should instruct you in how best to care for your baby until the bris heals. See p. 96 for more on the bris.) If the navel gets wet before it's completely healed, don't panic. Simply dry it carefully with a clean, absorbent cloth.

Older babies love to splash and play in the water, but newborns feel insecure when undressed. A new baby may cry in protest from the beginning to the end of the experience, so it's best to keep baths brief and gentle. Covering baby's torso with a dry washcloth as you wash his head, arms, and legs can help him stay calmer.

A small plastic tub that fits into a safety stand that holds the tub at waist level is convenient in the early stage of infancy. If you have the kind of baby bathtub that fits into the regular family tub, it might be more comfortable to use it when set on a tabletop so you won't need to bend over it, especially while you are still recovering from childbirth.

Parents might want to purchase a special slanted plastic device to support the baby in the water, which is available in stores selling baby products and furniture. It fits onto the bottom of the bathtub with suction cups and has a raised bump between the baby's legs to prevent the baby from slipping under the water.

Here are some guidelines for bathing baby step-by-step:

1. Be sure the room is warm and draft-free and everything is at hand before you begin.

> You will need the following:
> - ☐ A soft, absorbent infant-size towel, preferably with a hood
> - ☐ An infant bathtub filled with a few inches of warm water (check the temperature of the water against the inside of your wrist or forearm — it should be comfortably warm but never hot).
> - ☐ A washcloth or soft baby sponge
> - ☐ Baby soap and shampoo (mild and unscented)
> - ☐ A very soft baby hairbrush
> - ☐ A clean diaper and a change of clothes

2. Undress your baby and wrap him in a towel while you carry him to the bathtub. Slip him into the water immediately to prevent him from becoming chilled, and cover exposed parts with a washcloth to keep him warm.

3. Supporting the baby's head and shoulders in the crook of your elbow, use your other hand to dip a clean washcloth or soft baby sponge into the warm water. Wring it out and then use it to gently wash the baby's face. Hold the baby's head well above the water.

4. Start with the inner corner of one eye and wipe toward the outer corner. Use a different corner of the washcloth to repeat this procedure with the other eye.

5. Clean the baby's nose and ears.

6. Wet the baby's head. Using a few drops of baby shampoo, lather and wash his head and hair, gently massaging his scalp with the tips of your fingers.

7. Incline the baby's head slightly backward into the bathwater with your supporting hand and cup your other hand over the baby's forehead to protect his eyes as you dip his head into the water to rinse off the shampoo. Speak gently and soothingly as you work to keep baby feeling calm and secure.

8. Apply a few drops of baby soap (baby shampoo works fine too!) to the wet washcloth or soft baby sponge and guide it over his body and limbs to wash them. Pay special attention to the creases and folds around his neck, under his arms, and in the crotch area.

9. Immediately drape the baby with a towel after the bath, including his head, to keep him warm.

A baby may **never** be left alone in a bath even for a moment, even if there is only an inch of water in the tub. If you absolutely must leave the bath to attend to something urgent (like your toddler taking a fall; phone calls and knocks on the door can wait), first wrap the baby in a towel and take him with you or put him safely in his crib until you return.

Chapter Three

Welcoming Your Jewish Neshama'leh to the World[1]

Whether it's the parent's first child or the tenth, bringing a Jewish child into the world is a cause for celebration, and the Torah gives plenty of opportunity to celebrate. Nothing can match the frenetic excitement of preparing a *simchah* in just eight days, or the ecstatic joy of a *kiddush* to ooh and aah over your darling daughter along with friends and family.

---

1. This chapter offers an overview of halachos and *minhagim* marking the birth of a new Jewish baby. Information here should not be used for *piskei halachah*; questions of halachah and *minhag* should be brought to a rabbinic authority.

Mazel Tov, It's a Girl!

At the birth of a newborn daughter, Ashkenazim have the custom of reciting the *berachah* of *shehecheyanu*. The blessing should be recited as soon as possible after the birth, and it is normally said by both the father and the mother. If the father was not present at the birth, he says the *berachah* upon the news of his daughter's birth. Sephardim generally do not follow this custom.

The first public celebration of the birth of a baby girl is during the special *MiShebeirach* recited when the father is called up during the public Torah reading. This is a prayer for the new mother's health and an announcement of the baby's name, as well as a prayer that this new baby grow into a wise and discerning Jewish woman. Some families have a tradition to do this at the first opportunity after the birth, whether on Monday, Thursday, or Shabbos (the days when there is a Torah reading). Others wait until the Shabbos after the birth in order that more people will be present to enhance the joy. Among some Chassidic groups the practice is to wait until the second Shabbos after the birth to name the baby girl.

Sephardim celebrate a baby girl's birth with a ceremony known as *Zeved HaBat* on the sixth night after she was born.

Among Ashkenazim it has become widely accepted to make a *kiddush* after the birth of a daughter, though the parents are not obligated to do so.

The main purpose of both the Sephardic *Zeved HaBat* and the Ashkenazic *kiddush* is to express thanksgiving to Hashem for this new *neshamah*. Some believe that the significance goes even deeper, as illustrated by the possibly apocryphal story attributed to several different *gedolim* about the father of an older unmarried daughter who had not made a *kiddush* when the girl was born. The *rav* instructed the father to make the *kiddush* even though she was nearly thirty years old, and shortly thereafter the young woman became a *kallah*. Apparently, because her father had never made a *kiddush*, the girl had not received the blessings for a *zivug* typically given by guests to the parents and their newborn daughter.

Regarding whether, who, and when the *hagomel* blessing should be recited, there are various customs. Each family should consult its *rav* or follow its established custom. This blessing parallels the *todah* sacrifice offered in the Beis HaMikdash in gratitude for being saved from mortal danger.

Elisheva

My mom is a party planner, and there was no question we would have a lavish kiddush after Tehilla's birth. I was still quite overwhelmed from the birth, and the only thing I remember about the occasion are the beautiful berachos we received from the guests for nachas and siyatta d'Shmaya in raising her. Baruch Hashem, she is a delightful child and our greatest pleasure.

Suraleh

It worked out best for us to make a modest kiddush at home. My husband brought a minyan of friends to our house after the davening, and we served simple refreshments. The highlight of our daughter's kiddush was the divrei Torah spoken and the heartfelt blessings everyone showered on us.

Mindy

Our little Chaya Sarah was born while we were in Israel during the first year after our marriage. We were on a shoestring budget, and most of the family lived far away. The rebbetzin suggested that my husband contribute to the cost of the kugels at the shul kiddush on the Shabbos that the baby was named and that's what we did. I didn't even leave the house.

> **Michal**
> My husband named the baby during the Torah reading on Monday, the morning after she was born. We had already agreed on a name beforehand, so at the hour I knew they were reading the Torah at shul I announced the baby's name to my roommates in the hospital. Afterward Gedalya served crackers, herring, and schnapps to the men in shul, and everyone was happy. I was especially grateful that I didn't have any stress about organizing or preparing a Shabbos kiddush such a short time after giving birth.

> **Hanni**
> Our extended families live quite a distance from our shul. Since we really wanted their participation we made a small kiddush on Shabbos morning after the naming, and then everyone came to celebrate with us at a melaveh malkah on motza'ei Shabbos.

> **Lakey**
> My parents and my in-laws planned and organized a beautiful kiddush. Gitty is the first granddaughter on both sides after a lot of boys, so there was a lot to celebrate!

Mazel Tov, It's a Boy!

Upon the birth of a baby boy, the baby's parents recite the blessing of *hatov v'hameitiv*.

The *Shalom Zachar*

On the first Friday night after the birth of a son, the Ashkenazic custom is to welcome the baby to the community with a *shalom zachar*, where friends and relatives drop in to visit and partake of light refreshments. It is often held in the home, but if this is inconvenient the *shalom zachar* may be celebrated in shul, or wherever it is convenient to receive guests. Often it is the grandparents who host the *shalom zachar*. If possible, it is appropriate to make the *shalom zachar* in the place where the baby is staying. However, the baby does not need to participate in the festivities and can stay in a quiet room with his mother.

If the mother and baby are still in the hospital or are in a convalescent home, or if the newborn is not well and it is clear the bris will be delayed, the *shalom zachar* still takes place on that first Friday night.

Among other reasons cited for this practice is that people come to comfort the infant on his loss; before he was born, an angel taught him the entire Torah, which he forgot at birth. When guests come to speak words of Torah on his first Shabbos, the *neshamah* of the baby is consoled. This is one reason that the occasion is called a *"shalom zachar."* The word *zachar* means "male" in *lashon hakodesh*, but it also means "remember." This refers to

---

SOME REASONS WHY THE *SHALOM ZACHAR* IS HELD ON FRIDAY NIGHT

1. The Midrash states (*Emor*) that Shabbos has a central role because when the child experiences his first Shabbos he has not as yet had a *bris milah*.

2. The *Terumas HaDeshen* explains that Shabbos is the most practical time, because people are free to come to the *shalom zachar* after their *seudah*.

3. The *sefer Bris Avos* states that the infant is regarded as a pure tzaddik, and it is appropriate to greet a tzaddik on Shabbos.

4. The *Bris Efraim*, citing Rav Shlomo Zalman Auerbach, *zt"l*, says that we celebrate the *shalom zachar* to demonstrate that the uncircumcised infant also has a portion in the holy Shabbos.

5. Rav Moshe Sternbuch, *shlita*, citing the *Zohar*, explains that having the *shalom zachar* on Shabbos demonstrates that Shabbos is the source of all the blessings we experience during the week.

> ## SHALOM ZACHAR ARBES
>
> 1. Place 2 cups of dried chickpeas in enough water to cover by several inches. Cover with a towel and soak overnight. (Optional: You can add 1 teaspoon of baking soda to assist in the soaking process.) The chickpeas will grow approximately double in size.
> 2. Drain, check, rinse, and cook in boiling salted water for an hour or more (you can taste one to check that they are soft).
> 3. Drain in a colander and place on a clean tablecloth or towel (to absorb any remaining water).
> 4. Add salt and freshly ground pepper.
> 5. Mazel tov — they're ready for the *shalom zachar*!
>
> This will yield approximately 4 cups. Adjust the measurements, depending on how many guests you are expecting.

the memory of the Torah that was lost; it may also be a reminder of the oath a *neshamah* makes to the angel in the moment before birth, promising that he will be a tzaddik and not a *rasha*.

In ancient times lentils were served at a *shalom zachar* because this was a traditional food of mourning, as the baby is "mourning" the loss of the Torah he learned. Today most families fulfill the custom by serving *arbes*, cooked chickpeas.

Some serve an assortment of other foods so that guests can make as many *berachos* as possible: wine for *borei pri hagafen*; cakes, or other baked delicacies for *mezonos*; olives or fruit for *ha'eitz*; *arbes*, pickles, or a vegetable platter for *ha'adamah*; and soft drinks for *shehakol*. These blessings are made as a *zechus* for the baby and the mother.

It is appropriate for family and guests to share a few words about the *parashah* or the halachos of *bris milah* in honor of the occasion.

Miri

Did you know there are gemachim for arbes? I had just come home from the hospital and didn't have the faintest idea what to do with the bag of chickpeas on the kitchen counter. I called our nearest neighbor to ask for a recipe, and she told me about the gemach. Many of our friends and neighbors contributed cakes and kugels. The whole shalom zachar only took an hour or so, but it left us with such a warm, happy feeling because so many people shared our simchah.

Blima

My first child was born in the afternoon on the Friday before Pesach. We didn't even tell my mother-in-law that I was in labor, so when she got the mazel tov it was a bit unexpected. My shvigger is the organized type, and she had already finished cleaning her dining room for Pesach, but with only three hours left before Shabbos she offered to host the shalom zachar! And then she cleaned the dining room for Pesach again on motza'ei Shabbos! To this day, I'm touched by her amazing kindness.

The Night Before the *Bris Milah*

In the Sephardic tradition, a *Brit Yitzchak* is observed on the night before the *bris milah*. A minyan of men gather in the house to recite passages from the *Zohar*, to protect the newborn from evil influence.

Among Chassidim, it is customary for the father and other close relatives to spend the night before the bris learning Torah in the house of the infant. This is known as the *vachtnacht* — literally, a "night of watching."

There is a widely observed custom among both Sephardic and Ashkenazic Jews for children to recite *Krias Shema* in the baby's presence on the evening before his bris. According to the Netziv, the tradition of reciting the *Shema* before the newborn baby is to protect him from evil influences and increase his potential for spiritual development. Afterward the children are customarily rewarded with *pekelach* (bags of sweets) or another treat.

Gitty
I became engaged two days after my older sister gave birth to the first grandson in our family. At work I was bubbling over with the news about my vort and my new nephew's vachtnacht. The secretary at our office typed up an invitation cordially inviting everyone to attend "Gitty's vachtnacht"!

Miriam
My husband and my brothers stayed up all night learning together the night before the bris. Every time the baby woke up, he seemed to be listening to them. From my bedroom we could hear the Gemara niggun and it was so beautiful!

Ruchi
I think that one of the best parts of having a baby boy is when the cheder children come to say Krias Shema beside the baby's crib. Their pure little voices and sparkling eyes always bring tears to my eyes. Ashreinu mah tov chelkeinu!

Hanni
Here's what I think about treats for the children after saying Krias Shema before the bris: Please, people, keep it small and simple! At times my kids come home from a vachtnacht with huge hauls. In my opinion, this is thoughtless. Who wants to give their kids an armload of candy right before bedtime? A pekele should be a token thank you to the children for saying Shema with the baby, not a month's worth of sugar packed into one bag!

The *Bris Milah*

The Torah commands that every Jewish father circumcise his newborn son on the eighth day after birth. Unless the father is a qualified *mohel*, he fulfills this obligation by appointing a *mohel* to carry out the procedure in his stead. (Some intrepid fathers actually study under a *mohel* so they can perform the bris on their son!) For any number of health considerations, a *bris milah*

may be temporarily postponed, until the baby is well enough to have one. The decision of whether to postpone a bris, and when a bris should be performed if there are health issues, is made by an experienced *mohel*, in conjunction with medical professionals.

A baby born naturally on Shabbos has his bris on Shabbos, but babies born by Caesarean section on Shabbos are circumcised on the ninth day (i.e., Sunday). Similarly, if the eighth day after a Caesarean birth is Yom Tov, then the bris is postponed until the next day as well.

The bris is performed anytime between sunrise and sunset on the eighth day, although it is commendable to make the bris as early as possible. For this reason, many *brisos* are performed in the morning, right after *Shacharis*. The circumcision ceremony is followed by a *seudas mitzvah* that may be held wherever is most convenient, in shul or at home or in a catering hall. Friends and family should be informed of the time and place, but should not be formally invited.

Libby

I spent the day of the bris alternating between crying and worrying. My baby seemed to feel my nerves, and he was uncharacteristically fussy. After I fed him for the last time before the bris, he spit it all up in a huge puddle. I was sure something was wrong, and I informed my husband darkly that in the future I wanted only girls! In the end, the bris passed with no complications at all, and I was sorry that I had been so fretful that I missed the magic of the day, the beauty and joy of bringing a son into Klal Yisrael.

Hodaya

As soon as the mohel began the bris, my baby had a bowel movement. I didn't know it until the kvatter brought him to me afterward and I saw the suspicious stain on the bris pillow. When I realized what had happened, I was so embarrassed that I didn't know where to hide, but later the mohel told me it's a common occurrence. In the first weeks babies usually move their bowels after a meal, and I had fed him a short time before the bris. Next time I will take the mohel's instructions more seriously, and the last feeding will be an hour before the ceremony!

> **Tzipi**
> Our bris was handled by a bris gemach. We only paid the cost price of the food, and everything else was taken care of by the local ladies who volunteer for the gemach. It's fabulous — every community should have one!

> **Judy**
> When Rav Chaim Kanievsky agreed to be the sandak for our son, we were absolutely thrilled! The only problem was that we live in Yerushalayim, and Rav Chaim does not leave Bnei Brak for sandakaus anymore. So we made the bris at the Lederman shul next to his house. The mohel drove my husband and me with the baby to Bnei Brak in the morning. People who came to daven were happy to serve as kvatters. After the bris, we returned to Yerushalayim and hosted an afternoon seudah in our house.

Choosing a *Mohel*

Jewish circumcision is much more than a medical procedure, and a *mohel* is much more than a pediatrician or a surgeon who knows how to circumcise a baby.

The *mohel* should be contacted as soon as possible after the birth of a healthy baby boy. Delay can result in disappointment if the *mohel* you prefer is previously engaged. If you don't know whom to call, ask the people close to you (family, friends, your *rav*, other congregants in your shul) for their experience and recommendations. (Be cautious regarding social network advertising.) If a *mohel* is not available near where you live, contact the nearest Orthodox rabbi for referrals to *mohelim* in other vicinities. For an out-of-town *mohel*, be prepared to pay for his traveling expenses in addition to the accepted fee.

Welcoming Your Jewish Neshama'leh to the World

Many extended families have one *mohel* who has been performing the *brisos* for the babies in their family for a generation or more, or he may be the son of the *mohel* who did this for the previous generation. If you don't have a family *mohel*, here are tips to find the best *mohel* for your baby on this momentous occasion:

The first requirement is that a *mohel* must be a *yarei Shamayim*, a G-d-fearing Jew, who is an expert in the halachos of performing *bris milah* and will perform the bris with the proper intentions. This is important because the spiritual aspects of circumcision will have a continuing impact on your baby for his entire life.

The *mohel's* formal background must include training and apprenticeship under a skilled professional *mohel* to learn circumcision techniques; in Israel and western Europe, *mohelim* are licensed and certified. (In Israel, a *mohel* without certification may not perform a bris or advertise his services in a hospital.)

When you speak with the *mohel*, feel free to request the following information:

- » Testimonials from couples who have used his services
- » Recommendations from professionals (*rabbanim* and doctors) who are familiar with his skills
- » His backup plan if something prevents him from performing the bris — for example, if your baby's bris is unavoidably delayed, and by the time it is rescheduled this *mohel* is no longer available
- » His fee (if the *mohel* does not ask for a specific amount, discuss the appropriate payment with your rabbi)
- » When he plans to first see the baby (most *mohelim* visit during the days before the bris to ascertain that the child is strong and healthy)
- » When the baby should be fed the last feeding before the bris

What to Bring to the Bris

Make sure you have the following items with you at the bris. (At times the *mohel* supplies these items; nowadays most *mohelim* supply you with a list of all the items required. Please refer to his list and follow his instructions. The list may contain some or all of the following.)

- ☐ Several disposable diapers

- ☐ Bris pillow – the pillow on which the baby is placed during the bris, which is often embroidered with fancy decorations and has straps to tie around the baby. Many communities have a bris pillow gemach, and sometimes the mohel supplies it.

- ☐ Baby wipes

- ☐ Cloth diapers

- ☐ Pacifier (if baby is using one)

- ☐ A bottle of sweet wine and a Kiddush cup

What You Should Expect After the Bris

Each *mohel* has his own methods for helping the baby recover afterward. He will show you how to diaper the baby for maximum comfort, and he may advise you to wash the baby only with sponge baths for a few days to allow the bris to heal, or give you

oil, cream, or medicinal powder to apply to the area to facilitate healing.

He will also visit the baby soon after the bris to be sure that it is healing properly and that there are no complications — if the bris was in the morning, he might drop by your house that evening, or he might visit the next day, but a post-bris visit is generally part of his service.

Honoring Others at the Bris

Just attending a bris is considered an honor since Eliyahu HaNavi is said to attend every bris, but certain roles are offered to specific guests as special honors:

1. ***Kvatter* and *kvatterin*:**

    This privilege is generally reserved for a married couple. After the initial preparations by the *mohel* are complete, and it's time to perform the bris, the baby is placed on a beautiful white bris pillow and passed from his mother (if she is attending the bris) to the woman who is serving as *kvatterin*. She carries the baby on the pillow to the *mechitzah* and passes him to her husband, the *kvatter*, who accepts the baby and brings him to the area where the procedure will take place.

    Serving as a *kvatter* is a known *segulah* for having G-d-fearing children. It is often offered to a couple who don't yet have children of their own. Speak with the couple in advance to be sure they are planning to attend and that it is halachically permissible for them to serve as *kvatter* on that day, and explain that they have to come on time! Remember, not every childless couple feels comfortable being in the spotlight. Many regard this as a *segulah* and are happy to be honored with it; others prefer not to be singled out. Use your sensitivity.

2. ***L'kisei shel Eliyahu* — to Elijah's chair:**

    A special chair is set aside and designated as the *kisei shel Eliyahu*. The *kvatter* may take the baby directly to the *kisei shel Eliyahu*, the "chair of Eliyahu," where the bris will take place, or he may pass the infant to another man whom the family wishes to honor. If there are other guests that should be given recognition, this procedure can be repeated as necessary until the last honoree places the child on the elevated chair designated for the bris.

3. *Mekisei shel Eliyahu* — **from Elijah's chair**

    A different honoree brings the baby from the chair of Eliyahu to the *sandak*.

4. *Sandak*

    The role of *sandak* is considered comparable to offering incense in the Beis HaMikdash. It is generally reserved for the baby's grandfather, the father's *rav*, or a much esteemed scholar, although the father of the baby himself can also serve as *sandak*.

    The *sandak* positions the baby, who is lying face up on the pillow, over his knees during the performance of the bris. In some communities, after the bris is completed, the *sandak* gives personal blessings to those who request them.

5. **Blessings recited at the bris**

    After the bris has been performed, blessings are recited, and also a prayer during which the baby is named. Generally, these honors are given to two different people. Occasionally, one person is honored with saying the blessings and giving the name, and another person holds the baby during both the blessings and the prayer.

6. **Holding the baby during the blessings**

    This person honored with holding the baby takes him from the *sandak* and holds him while the blessings are recited. A second person takes the baby and holds him while the baby's name is given.

    After the ceremony, the infant is returned to the *kvatter*, who passes the baby to the *kvatterin*. She then returns the baby to his mother.

Choosing a Name

A daughter is named during the public Torah reading, and a son receives his name at his *bris milah*. In Jewish thought, a person's name has profound spiritual implications, expressing both the essence of the child and his or her potential.

Even though it is written that parents of a newborn are granted some measure of prophecy when choosing the name of this precious *neshamah* entrusted into their care, it sometimes can be difficult for parents to agree on the best choice.

Names indicate our hopes for the baby's future, but they also connect the child to his past. It is the Ashkenazic custom to name a newborn after someone, most often a relative who is no longer living. This honors the *niftar*, keeping his memory alive, while creating a metaphysical bond between the baby's soul and the person for whom he or she is named. The mitzvos the child will perform in life will continue to elevate the soul of the *niftar*, and the child is inspired to live up to the legacy of his forebears (see *Noam Elimelech, Bamidbar*).

AFTER THE BRIS

After the bris, everyone wants to say mazel tov and ooh and aah over the baby and his new name. But your newly named little boy needs his quiet — and his mommy. Find a quiet room where you can feed and cuddle your brave little boy, and leave the hostessing and mazel tovs to your husband, parents, in-laws, relatives, and friends. Don't forget to ask one of them to bring you a bagel or some other goodies to your room!

A complication arises when there are living relatives with the same name that the parents wish to bestow on their newborn. According to Ashkenazic tradition, a baby should not be given the same name as either of his living parents, grandparents, or siblings; giving the same name as living uncles, aunts, cousins, nieces, or nephews is permitted.

The Sephardic custom is to name children after either living or deceased relatives. In Sephardic families, it is considered a special honor for the parents to name their newborn for a living grandparent.

The practice in many Jewish communities is for the mother to choose (or veto) the name for her firstborn while the father has first rights to name the second child. This order continues alternately for subsequent births. However, each parent should consider the other's personal feelings about any specific name, and special circumstances such as a recent death in the family or a close relative who has no child named for him yet.

One of the conflicts that may arise in choosing a baby's name is calling the newborn after a relative with an unusual or unfashionable name. It is said that the Chazon Ish and the Steipler Gaon advised parents not to use a name that might cause the child embarrassment as she grows older. Think this over well before you choose a rarely used or old-fashioned name for your baby. Be aware, however, that it is your own response to a name that will reverberate among others. If you feel confident and are proud to use the name, it is likely that your child and all of her acquaintances will feel the same way.

Sometimes there are expectations by the extended family that the baby will be given a certain name. Perhaps a beloved relative was *niftar* within the past year, or there is a grandparent whose name has never yet been given to a great-grandchild and your *shvigger's* dearest desire is to finally have a grandchild with her father's name, or every single married sibling of your spouse called their first daughter for the *alte bubby* who was a great

tzaddeikes. As the baby's parents, the decision is yours. No one should be forced to give their baby a name they would prefer not to give, but take exceeding care not to cause a *machlokes* in the family for the sake of a name. Whenever there is a question of *shalom bayis* or *kibbud av va'eim*, a reliable *posek* should be consulted.

The bottom line is to bear in mind that avoiding conflict is the biggest *zechus* for a deceased relative. He/she is in the *Olam HaEmes* — the World of Truth — and knows without doubt that having a child bear his/her name pales in comparison to having peace reign supreme among the family members. Likewise, if giving a particular name will bring joy to the family and prevent *machlokes*, the parents' willingness to yield will be a *zechus* for them and for their baby.

One should never name a child for a wicked person. If there is pressure to name your baby for a member of the family who was not a role model for your child, the problem can be resolved by having in mind a tzaddik with the same name at the time the name is given. For example, instead of the nonobservant relative named Joshua, have in mind that your son will be like Yehoshua ben Nun, who led the Jewish people after Moshe Rabbeinu.

What to do if you don't like the name that your spouse (or your families) desperately want this baby to have? One solution is to give the baby two names and use the one you prefer. You can also use a nickname you like: Miri for Miriam, Zalmy for Zalman, or Shevy for Batsheva.

Additional compromises include using the Hebrew translation of a Yiddish name, such as Adina for someone named Aidel, or Zev for a male named Wolf; in this instance consult with a *rav* who is experienced in names. You can also choose a name that expresses the dominant character trait of the person you want to memorialize: Tova for one known for her good heart, Aryeh for a man who was brave as a lion. Another possibility is to choose a name that uses the same initials or has a similar pronunciation.

Some people choose names based on the *parashah* of that week or an admired figure in Jewish history. According to the *Midrash Tanchuma* (*Ha'azinu*), the inner dimension of a name creates a spiritual connection that can enable a child grow to be a tzaddik. For example, the name Avraham inclines him toward the trait of *chesed*; the name Yosef is associated with resisting temptation.

Connecting the name to the nearest Yom Tov is another traditional source for naming a baby. Boys born in Adar are often called Mordechai, and girls, Esther or Hadassah. A son born around Shavuos time can be named after David HaMelech and a daughter for Rus or Naomi.

Names may also be chosen to express meaningful messages, such as the hope for consolation when a baby born on Tishah B'Av is named Menachem or Nechama, or Nesanel to express appreciation for the gift from Hashem that this baby represents.

To minimize discord, it is prudent not to discuss your final choice with anyone except your spouse. Hopefully, the overwhelming joy of the new baby will soon smooth any ruffled feathers and effectively put off controversy — at least until the next baby is born.

If you wish to name your child for someone of the opposite gender, keep as close to the original as possible — calling your son Dan for a dear aunt named Dina, or naming your daughter Bracha for a grandfather whose name was Baruch. Rav Moshe Feinstein, *zt"l*, said that the name Ahuvah could be used to memorialize someone named Avraham, since Ahuvah has three letters that appear in Avraham.

Although one of the reasons we were redeemed from Egypt was that we did not change our Hebrew names, people living outside of Israel often give names that can be used interchangeably in English such as Sarah or Abigail, Michael or Jonathan. Although it was a source of merit in Egypt, it is not a halachic requirement. In fact, in many countries, Orthodox Jews use non-Jewish names.

Rav Moshe Feinstein recommended that a name be altered by using a different spelling — for example, adding or omitting a letter — if a baby is named after someone who passed away young or unnaturally. A more common practice in such a case is to add another name.

Pidyon Haben

The Torah commands every father who is not a Kohen or a Levi to redeem a firstborn son through a ceremony called "*pidyon haben*." The commandment does not apply if the mother of the baby is from a family of Kohanim or Levi'im.

The reason for this obligation is that during the redemption of *Bnei Yisrael* from Egypt, the Egyptian firstborns perished. At that time firstborn Jewish sons had a degree of *kedushah* that entitled them to serve in the priesthood. After the sin of the golden calf in the desert, Hashem took this unique privilege from the firstborn who had worshiped the graven image and awarded it to the tribe of Levi for their loyalty.

Due to the following reasons the *pidyon haben* ceremony is relatively uncommon:

1. It must be the mother's first birth, since firstborn status is conferred by the mother. A man with children from a different marriage is required to conduct a *pidyon haben* for his son if the newborn is the first for the child's mother.
2. The birth must be natural (not by Caesarean section).
3. The mother is not the daughter of a Kohen or a Levi.
4. The mother never had a miscarriage before this birth.[2]
5. In a multiple birth, only the first infant to emerge is considered the firstborn. If twins are born, for example, and the first is a girl followed by a boy, there is no *pidyon haben*.

---

2. If a woman had a previous miscarriage, a *posek* should be consulted. Whether or not there will be a *pidyon haben* depends on certain circumstances, such as the week of pregnancy when the miscarriage occurred.

The mitzvah to redeem a firstborn son belongs to the father. If for any reason this is not an option, a *posek* should be consulted. If a firstborn child was not redeemed as an infant, he must redeem himself as an adult.

After the birth of the child, a father should search for a Kohen with a strong family tradition affirming as far as possible that he is a descendant of Aharon HaKohen and arrange for his participation in his son's *pidyon haben*. If this is difficult, an Orthodox rabbi should be consulted to help locate a Kohen.

The *pidyon haben* ceremony takes place when a firstborn son is fully thirty days old. If that day is Shabbos or Yom Tov, it is delayed until *motza'ei Shabbos* or *motza'ei Yom Tov*.

Sephardim make the *pidyon* immediately after *Maariv* — upon the arrival of the thirty-first day. Ashkenazim make it at the end of the afternoon of the thirtieth day.

The *pidyon haben* is a festive occasion. The parents don their Shabbos finery, and the baby is dressed like a royal prince. Before the infant is brought to the Kohen, he is placed on a large silver tray and the women guests attach their jewelry to the baby's clothing with safety pins or place it on the tray beside him.

It is customary to prepare tiny packets containing sugar cubes and cloves of garlic and tuck them around the baby. The reason for this appears to be that partaking of the *seudah* has great spiritual significance, equivalent to fasting eighty-four fasts. These packets are distributed to the guests, who take them home and use them to flavor other foods, thus spreading this unique blessing to as many people as possible. (You can put them in your Shabbos soup or cholent — a delicious way to share the *simchah* with your Shabbos guests!) Also, garlic may be a *segulah* for health or fertility, and sugar illustrates the sweetness of the mitzvah.

The guests wash, make *hamotzi*, and begin the *seudah* before the *pidyon haben* ceremony. The Kohen generally is seated at the head table with the baby's family and distinguished guests.

Welcoming Your Jewish Neshama'leh to the World

When the ceremony begins, the father of the baby brings the infant on the silver tray to the Kohen and declares that his son is a firstborn and requires redemption.

The Kohen inquires in Aramaic whether the father prefers five silver *sela'im* (ancient coins) or his child, and the father declares that he is prepared to pay in order to redeem his son. The father then makes the blessing on the mitzvah, recites the *shehecheyanu* blessing, and places the money in the right hand of the Kohen.

The payment given to the Kohen from the baby's father is the equivalent of five silver *sela'im*, which according to the Chazon Ish is ninety-six grams of silver. The father must give the Kohen an object with inherent value; a check or an IOU are not acceptable. Therefore, most halachic authorities do not permit using modern currency because the bills and coins have no intrinsic value; rather, the payment should be in silver coins. The Kohen may have pure silver coins in his possession, and he sells them to the father before the *pidyon*. It is permissible to buy those coins with cash, a check, or a money order. The Kohen is entitled to either keep or return the money to the father, but the accepted practice is not to return it.

The Kohen then waves the coins over the baby's head while reciting the priestly blessing and other words of blessing. The ceremony is completed by the Kohen reciting *borei pri hagafen* over wine. The infant is returned to his mother, and the guests resume their *seudas mitzvah*, celebratory meal.

Shoshanna

After the ceremony, the guests took all the little bags of sugar and garlic. I had promised my parents back in London to send them a little memento, but by the time I got my baby back there was nothing left. I was so sad, but then my wise and thoughtful mother-in-law calmly lifted the baby off the tray and showed me where she had hidden five little bags under the pad he was lying on. My shvigger had experience!

Yocheved

My son's pidyon haben was the most beautiful thing in the world. During the ceremony he kept silent for a full ten minutes, when he had never stopped wailing at the top of his lungs since the day he was born! He was so good that I was almost afraid that the Kohen would want to keep him, but a minute after the Kohen made the berachah on the wine, my son resumed his screams and I was busy nursing him until the guests had all left.

Batya

My son's pidyon haben was especially poignant because the Kohen was his own great-grandfather. (Obviously I'm not a bas Kohen, or there wouldn't have been a pidyon haben! The Kohen's daughter, my grandmother, married a Yisrael, so my father, also, is not a Kohen.) The alte zeide was understandably emotional. His tears rained down on the baby, who was happily kicking all the little pekelach of garlic and sugar off the silver tray. At the back of everyone's minds was the knowledge that our zeide is a survivor. During the Holocaust, his worst fear was that after him his family name would be obliterated.

Chapter Four

Baby Essentials

"You don't need a special baby bathtub. Just wash him off in the kitchen sink (clear out the dishes first!)."

"If there's one major purchase you'll never regret, it's a rocking chair to sit in while nursing. It's the best thing I ever bought!"

"I ordered a bassinet, a crib, and a Pack 'n Play. I want to make sure I've covered all the bases."

"Are you getting the stroller with or without the car seat attachment?"

hile you were in the hospital, everything was provided for you. Your baby was in a bassinet on wheels that doubled as both a bed and stroller. He had baby clothes, diapers, bedding, bottles, and formula if necessary. Now that you're home, you've suddenly realized that there are a whole lot of essentials you need to purchase in order to properly care for your baby.

> **READY, SET...SHOP:**
> **WHEN TO MAKE YOUR PURCHASES**
>
> Many of us have the *minhag* to wait until after the baby is born to make any purchases for the new arrival. That's not easy, when you know that you'll be bringing home a newborn who needs clothes and a place to sleep.
>
> If this is your *minhag*, you can still do your research before the baby is born and choose which stroller, crib, or changing table you'll want. Then, during your hospital stay, your husband or parents can buy them so that they'll be there when you come home.
>
> Remember: You don't need everything the first day. A stroller, a changing table, and even a crib can wait a week or so, or sometimes even longer, until you've had a chance to get settled. In the meantime, you can borrow a bassinet or portable crib and change the baby on the bed (put a pad underneath to protect the mattress!).
>
> Waiting a little before buying has some advantages. Once the baby is born, you'll find it easier to know what is essential and what you don't need. The only item you will certainly want to have when you're discharged from the hospital is an infant car seat so that you will be able to transport your precious cargo home.
>
> Another reason not to rush: Chances are you'll get baby clothes and even some of the equipment as gifts from friends and family, especially if this is your first child. So wait, relax, and allow yourself time to gather what you need.

Baruch Hashem, the equipment and products available nowadays are abundant. On the other hand, the equipment and products nowadays are...abundant. How in the world do you decide what you need?

Do you really need a nursing pillow to support your baby while nursing? Is a baby swing necessary for your baby's developmental health — or is it just something to take up space in your crowded living room? Will you need to buy another house to store the stroller that comes with four attachments and seven accessories?

Although it's wonderful that there are so many goods available for your precious darling, the truth is that some are essential — like, you do need a place for your baby to sleep — and some are extras that totally depend on your individual needs.

Let's talk essentials.

The Essentials List

Here is a list of things you don't want to be without. Below, we'll expand on some of the essential equipment and advise you on what you need to know to make wise purchases. (Obviously, if space or financial considerations don't allow you to get all of the equipment listed below, there are creative and safe ways to substitute. And remember: Beautiful furniture and accessories are fine, but care, concern, and love — and, of course, *tefillah* — are the true mommy/baby essentials!)

Furniture and Equipment

- **Crib** or **bassinet with a waterproof mattress**
- **Changing table** and **dresser**
- **Carriage** or **stroller**
- **Infant car seat**

Clothing, Linen, and Accessories

- **Clothing** (for a detailed list of baby clothing, as well as tips on dressing baby, see pp. 52-53)
- **Waterproof mattress protectors** for the crib (and for your own bed, especially if you are co-sleeping), for when baby wets through his clothing — at least two
- **Crib/bassinet sheets** — at least three
- **Baby blankets, "sleep sacks,"** and **"wearable blankets"** — The American Academy of Pediatrics recommends not

putting baby blankets in the crib until the baby is twelve months old, because of suffocation risk. Instead, put baby into a "sleep sack" or "wearable blanket" — garments made of cotton or fleece that keep baby warm without the suffocation risk of a loose blanket. If you plan on taking baby outside in cold weather, though, you might want a blanket over her warm clothing. There are linings available for strollers and car seats that eliminate the need for blankets and keep baby cozy warm outside or in the car — but if using them in your car make sure they are "crash tested" or they may actually inhibit the effectiveness of a car seat in a crash.

» **Receiving blankets** — These all-purpose lightweight blankets are made of light materials such as flannel or cotton and can be wrapped around your newborn as a swaddling cloth to keep him warm, or they can be used as a summer blanket; they're also handy as burp cloths, to cover Mommy while nursing, to give baby a clean surface to lay on, to shade baby in the stroller or car seat, or, in a pinch, to use as a changing pad.

» **Pacifiers** — two or three (for more on pacifier use, see pp. 246-249)

Diapering Supplies

» **Pad** for the changing area

» **Diapers** — ten to twelve daily (for more on diapering baby, see p. 75); newborn-size disposable diapers are available, but if your baby was born on the larger side of the scale (seven pounds or more), you may want to skip to size 1 so that the baby doesn't outgrow his diapers so quickly

» **Cloth diapers** and **inserts** — three dozen if you are diapering baby exclusively in cloth diapers, or one dozen if you are using disposable diapers as well (for more on cloth diapering, see p. 76)

- » **Diaper liners** — If you're using cloth diapers, these flushable liners are optional, for easier cleanup. They generally come in rolls.
- » **Diaper bag**, when leaving the house — most come with their own changing pad
- » **Baby wipes**
- » **Diaper ointment** — Changing a baby often will prevent diaper rash, but if you see signs of redness or rash, don't wait until the baby gets uncomfortable.

Bath Time

- » **Baby bathtub** — There are different kinds of bathtubs designed especially for babies (see p. 85 for bathing instructions), but this isn't strictly essential; you can use the sink (cleaned well!) or a plastic basin at the beginning and then switch to the regular bathtub when the baby gets a little older.
- » **Infant bath ramp** — If you do want to use your regular bathtub, or even your kitchen sink, from the beginning, this item comes in very handy for the first six months. A soapy baby is a slippery baby, so you want to be as careful as you can be! Since the ramp safely supports the baby, it leaves both your hands free, and the reclining position keeps the baby's head out of the water. Note that you should ***never leave the baby unattended in the bath, even if he is secured in a bath ramp,*** not even for a second.
- » **Washcloths** or **soft bath mitt**
- » **Soft infant-size towels** (those with hoods are best) — at least two
- » **Baby shampoo**
- » **Baby soap**
- » **Baby brush** and **comb**

Feeding Supplies

If you're using formula exclusively, supplementing, or expressing breastmilk, you'll need the following paraphernalia:

- **Bottles** and **nipples** — if you are only bottle feeding, six to twelve; if you're feeding expressed milk or supplementing, two to three will suffice
- **Large bottle brush** for cleaning bottles
- **Small bottle brush** for cleaning nipples
- **Burp cloths** (about a dozen)

Your Medicine Cabinet

- **Thermometer** (for more on thermometers and measuring temperature, see p. 143)
- **Vaseline** or **lubricating jelly,** for lubricating rectal thermometers
- **Nasal bulb** or **aspirator**, for suctioning mucus when the baby gets congested (for use of bulb, see p. 149)
- **Saline nose drops** for moving mucus to the front of the nose and making it easier to remove with the nasal bulb (saltwater and a medicine dropper work just as well)
- **Safety nail scissors** and **nail clippers** — Babies grow fast, including their nails; you'll find that soon enough, baby's nails need to be clipped at least once a week. Some parents prefer a nail file, if cutting nails is difficult. (For instructions on cutting a baby's nails, see p. 239.)
- **Baby pain relievers** (such as infant Tylenol) — syrup or suppositories
- **Medicine dropper** or **syringe** for administering medication — Over-the-counter medication may come with one of these.

- » **Antibiotic cream** or **ointment** — This will especially be needed right away if your baby is having a bris; ask your *mohel* or doctor for a recommendation.
- » **Baby sunscreen** — The American Academy of Pediatrics says sunscreen is safe even for infants, but use it sparingly, only on skin that is not covered by clothing. Look for sunscreen specifically for babies. It should be "broad spectrum" (providing protection against both UVA and UVB rays), with an SPF of 30 to 50. Check the ingredients, and don't use sunscreen that contains DEET.
- » **Alcohol 70%** — for cleaning thermometers
- » **Hydrogen peroxide** — for disinfecting wounds
- » **Band-Aids** and **gauze pads**

The Extras

Here is a list of equipment and accessories that are nice to have, but you don't absolutely need them. They are available to make your life more comfortable, but *you* may not find it necessary or more comfortable, or you might just not have room, or the budget, for all this stuff! Take a look and decide for yourself what's essential for you.

- » **Mommy's chair** — a comfortable rocking chair or glider for nighttime feedings and also just for snuggling; some chairs come with a footrest as well (ah, a touch of Gan Eden at the end of a long day!). Many mothers find their living room sofa works just as well: Just sit in a comfortable position, put the baby tummy down on your chest, and relax as gravity bonds baby to your body.
- » **Nursing pillow** — a U-shaped pillow that you rest on your lap to support your newborn. This elevates the baby, enabling you to nurse while avoiding an aching back. Some mothers find themselves leaning forward to reach the pillow, so try

the "laid back" position on your couch (see above) before buying a pillow.

- » **Bibs** — A little bib protects your baby's clothing when she spits up or drools; just be careful that it doesn't present a choking hazard; infants should never sleep with bibs.
- » **Baby sling** or **baby carrier** — There are so many kinds, it's hard to choose one! See below, p. 135, for more information.
- » **Baby swing** — This piece of equipment can be a lifesaver when Mommy needs a break; many babies calm down when settled in a baby swing. Look for safety features (such as a three- or five-point harness), a wide, sturdy frame, easy-to-clean parts, and adjustable head support. Keep in mind that once your baby starts to get more active, rolling over or pushing himself up (around five or six months), the baby can upend the swing, so follow the manufacturer's recommendations for weight and age. Swings are available in both full size and portable models. The downside of a portable swing is that you have to crouch to put the baby in and out, but you can take the swing with you when traveling or move it from room to room, and it takes up much less space than a full size. Whatever you choose, never leave the baby unattended in a swing.
- » **Baby gym** and **activity mat** — Your baby might not be able to move much yet, but that doesn't mean he's not developing and learning about the world around him. Give him colorful objects to look at and play with (when he learns how to use his arms and hands!) — and get a baby gym. Many baby gyms come with play mats on which the baby can lie and are made from cloth and foldable parts. The baby gym unfolds into padded arches that you place over the baby. From the arches hang brightly colored plush animals, much like a mobile; some play music and have flashing lights. Baby gyms can keep babies entertained from newborn till about

ten months. What's great about them is that they allow the baby to get plenty of tummy and back time while keeping him entertained. (If you have toddlers around, keep an eye out that they don't try to join in the fun!)

» **Mobile for the crib** — Much like the baby gym, you can attach a mobile that plays lullabies while soft furry animals swing round and round. Some mobiles are available in black, white, and red, the colors that a newborn sees most easily after birth. Mobiles entertain babies till they are about six months old; once the baby starts sitting up she can pull the mobile down, which may present a hazard, so it's time to take it down.

» **Playpen** or **play yard** (such as a Pack 'n Play) — These lightweight, portable cribs are great if you're traveling. A playpen should fold easily, lock securely when open, and not be too heavy. For more on playpens, see below.

» **Baby monitor** — This is essentially an intercom that allows you to hear your baby from another room; one part is placed in the room with your baby to pick up any sounds of stirring or crying, and the other is placed where you are to relay those sounds. Some models even come with a video screen, allowing you to see your baby as well. It's worthwhile to select a monitor with two receivers so you can keep one in your bedroom at night and the other one in the kitchen or living room during the day. Be aware that some baby monitors interfere with cellular phone frequencies, and you might have to exchange it. Be sure to keep the cord well away from the baby, or use a wireless monitor.

» **Night-light** — A small light fixture that plugs into an electric outlet or a lamp with a dimmer, this low-intensity light will make nighttime changing and feeding much easier. It should not be placed within the baby's reach. For Shabbos, there are special lamps that can be turned "on" and "off" by turning a cover that covers or reveals the light. Again, keep out of reach of the crib — and any of the baby's mischievous little siblings.

» **Infant seat** or **bouncer** — Babies need stimulation and lying in the crib or stroller all the time won't do the trick. Besides, in areas where there isn't room for the stroller (and you obviously won't be lugging your crib all over the house), you need other options. The baby swing is one (see above); an infant seat or bouncer is another. Easily portable, this gives the baby another view of the world. Some bouncers come with their own entertainment system: music, lights, and hanging toys. Note that flashing lights may be overstimulating; it's best to avoid flashing lights before the age of one. Or you can just place a baby gym (see above) over the infant seat and the baby will have toys to look at and play with. But as we mentioned before, make sure to also give your baby plenty of supervised tummy time; babies who spend too much time in infant chairs or lying on their backs in the crib may be slower to roll over and develop their arm and neck muscles.

» **Diaper pail** — a special diaper pail for soiled diapers. To contain unpleasant smells, a pail with a tight-fitting lid is essential, and it's convenient to have one with a foot pedal that opens the lid. Line it with a garbage bag that can be transferred when the trash is emptied. Do *not* keep a diaper pail filled with water for soaking cloth diapers; it's a breeding ground for bacteria. (For that matter, don't keep a pail of water around the house ever — it's a drowning hazard.) There are several brands of diaper pails that include odor-cutting filters and other features; if you want a perfectly odor-free and keep-your-hands-free-from-dirty-diapers environment, you can check them out.

» **"Wet bags"** — If you are using cloth diapers, you may want to invest in a few "wet bags" — reusable, washable, waterproof bags with zippers to keep odors and moisture from leaking out. Wet bags come in different sizes; you can line your diaper pail with them, and carry a small one in your diaper bag if you don't want to use disposable diapers even on the road. For those who use disposable diapers, a small wet bag is useful when traveling, since babies tend to make lots of their clothing smelly and wet! You can also use Ziploc bags, but wet bags are more economical and better for the environment.

Furnishing Your Nursery

When you're expecting, there's nothing more fun than browsing the baby department and imagining which nursery set you'll choose for the baby's room when he's born. Whether you're planning on having a fully furnished nursery, or you're just in the market for a good crib, here is some information on choosing these major purchases.

Rock-a-Bye Baby: Bassinets, Cribs, and Play Yards

Does your *bubby* also tell the story about how they couldn't afford a crib in those days and the newborn slept in the dresser drawer for the first couple of months until they could scrape together the funds to get a bassinet?

It's a little hard to imagine today, when there are so many affordable sleeping options available for your baby. Even if you can't afford a new crib, you can purchase one secondhand for a reasonable price (just make sure the crib complies with the latest safety guidelines — see the box below).

It's not just about cribs either; there are so many options to choose from. You may start out with the baby sleeping in a bassinet (which is similar to a cradle, but on wheels), then switch to a full-size crib. You may start with a crib from the beginning, but it can convert to a toddler bed. There's also the "co-sleeper" — a special bassinet that's open on one side. This way, the baby can sleep right next to you without the risk of your rolling onto the baby, *chas v'shalom*.

Let's take a look at what's out there:

» **Bassinet** — Most newborns get fussy in an expansive crib. They like to feel snug, and a bassinet, which is so much smaller than a crib and usually comes with a hood (some even have an entire canopy) makes the baby feel snug! Most bassinets are easily portable, so you can move them from your room to another whenever you'd like. Besides, during those first few months, when the baby will probably be sleeping in your room, it's more convenient to have a bassinet, which takes up a lot less space in your bedroom than the standard-size crib. Some bassinets double as gliders or rockers, so you can rock your baby to sleep, even if you've only got one eye open!

» **Co-sleeper** — Some bassinets are made with one side open. You place the open side right next to your bed, which makes it easier to reach for your newborn. This allows you to sleep "with" your baby without the danger of rolling over onto him. But the co-sleeper is only good for the first few months. As soon as your baby begins to roll over, at the age of around four to five months, you'll have to move him to a proper crib.

» **Convertible crib** — Some cribs convert into toddler beds, or even proper twin-size beds. These cribs usually allow you to remove the sides, leaving a headboard and footboard. They may also come with a toddler rail, protecting your toddler — new to beds — from falling off in his sleep.

» **Playpens** or **play yards** (Pack 'n Play) — These fold-up, portable "cribs" are so convenient if you're traveling. They come in an assortment of sizes and colors. Most are tailored for the older baby who is already sitting and standing up

CRIBS: SAFETY FIRST

As soon as we become parents, the worry begins (okay, let's be honest: it begins even before the baby makes his appearance...). We constantly daven that Hashem should keep our children safe at each and every moment, and we do our *hishtadlus* to keep them safe. This begins at the very beginning: We transport our babies in car seats, handle them with care, and make sure their environment is secure.

The baby will be spending a lot of time in his crib. Make sure it complies with the safety guidelines of the American Academy of Pediatrics:

» The bars of the crib should be spaced no more than 2⅜ inches apart.
» The mattress should be firm and it should not sag under the baby's weight. It should fit snugly, and there should not be any space between the mattress and the crib walls. If you can get more than two fingers between the mattress and the crib wall, the mattress is too small for the crib frame.
» The top of the crib rail should be at least 26 inches from the top of the mattress.
» The headboards and footboards should be solid, with no sharp corners. Corner posts should be no more than 1/16 inch high.
» Cribs with drop rails are not safe; babies can get stuck between the rail and the mattress if the rail comes loose. (Sales of cribs with drop rails have been banned by many countries, including the United States.)
» Don't use crib bumpers. They don't protect the baby from injuries and could pose a risk of suffocation. Older babies may use them to help them climb out of the crib.
» Don't keep large toys or stuffed animals in the crib. The baby might use them to stand on and this will enable him to climb out. Toys in a newborn's sleep space are a suffocation hazard.
» Don't use pillows or bulky comforters; babies can smother under them.
» Set up the crib in a safe place: away from direct sunlight or drafts, and where there are no cords, curtains, or drapes that can wrap around the baby's neck.
» When the child reaches three feet in height, transfer him to a bed.

— they come with high walls and plenty of room for the baby to play and maneuver.

» **Crib mattress** — The mattress should be firm, not soft, and it should remain flat when pressed. Foam mattresses come in various thicknesses and are less expensive and lighter than spring mattresses. Quality is determined by thickness; the denser the mattress, the better it is. If the information is not listed on the packaging, compare the relative weight of mattresses the same size and choose the heavier one. If you prefer a spring mattress, choose a firm mattress with at least 150 coils.

Dresser and Changing Table

Changing tables come in a variety of sizes and colors. Buy one to match your crib in a set, or get a stand-alone. A changing table may include drawers or shelves for stowing baby's clothes and accessories. For the budget conscious, a sturdy chest of drawers with a changing pad on top can serve just as well as a changing table, and when the baby is out of diapers (yes, it will happen!) the changing pad can be removed and the chest of drawers will serve as a dresser.

When making your purchase, check for stability. Drawers should slide smoothly when opened and closed. If you're buying a dresser and changing table in one, check that the height is comfortable for you and your husband. You'll be changing a lot of diapers in the next couple of years, so give a thought to your back.

The changing pad should be easy to wash and nonslip. Some pads come with straps to buckle the baby into place, but they can never substitute for an adult standing next to the baby, making sure she doesn't slip, and many parents find the straps unwieldy. You can also get a changing pad that's contoured rather than flat, so that the baby can't slide around so easily.

Rocking Chair or Glider

There's nothing like snuggling with your sweet-smelling newborn in a comfortable armchair or glider at the end of a long day. With a newborn, that comfortable rocking chair may be the only vacation you'll have for the next few months!

All kidding aside, if you have the space, a rocking chair, glider, or armchair may be the best purchase you've ever made. You can even get one to match the rest of your nursery set. Some gliders come with a footrest, so you can put up your feet while you're feeding the baby. Your back will also thank you!

Place the armchair in the nursery, close to the crib, so that if your baby falls asleep while he's feeding, you can transfer him gently without waking him.

Car Seats

Car safety is a serious responsibility. In most countries, including the United States and Israel, it is illegal for any infant to travel in a private vehicle unless the baby is securely strapped into a weight-appropriate car seat. The rear-facing seat is used from birth until about two years of age, but must never be positioned in the front seat unless the car's airbag has been disabled.

Federal expiration dates on car seats depend on technological development, design, installation, and the strength of the materials used for construction. Expiry is determined by the estimated performance of the infant seat in a crash.

Using a secondhand or borrowed car seat is discouraged unless you know without a doubt that the infant seat has never been in a crash. Determine that all the original parts and accessories are still correctly attached. Check that labels with instructions for proper use are affixed. You should also verify that this type of seat was not involved in a manufacturer's recall.

Keep the original user's guide. In addition to the expiration date, there are recommendations for cleaning the infant seat, how to thread the harness, and instructions for correct installation.

New parents may find it easier to first strap the infant into the car seat before strapping the car seat into the car. (Tatty should practice fitting the car seat into the car before coming to the hospital to pick up Mommy and baby.)

Don't cover the baby with a blanket after you have strapped him into the infant safety seat — he can kick it up over his face. Never put a blanket between the baby and the strap of the car seat, since the loosened straps may not contain the baby in case of a crash.

All car seats should be destroyed after their expiration date. The correct method of disposal is to cut off the straps, slash the seat cover, and remove or blot out the serial number and the date of manufacture. Before discarding, mark the seat with the words "Do not use" in large, clear letters.

Laws on the use of car seats and boosters for older children vary from state to state and country to country. To ensure your child is safe (and to avoid costly tickets and points on your license!) be aware of the laws in your area and in the area where you are driving.

Remember: A properly fitted car seat can save your child's life!

The Best Stroller Money Can Buy

There are so many kinds of strollers available — those with removable bassinets and those without, with car seat attachments and without, single, double, lightweight, heavy-duty... The dazzling array of choices can be overwhelming.

Which Should You Choose?

There's no one right answer to this. The kind of stroller you need depends on your lifestyle, your budget, and your family's

needs. But let's make it a little easier for you. Here's what you need to know about purchasing a stroller:

Durability

Strollers are a major purchase, and chances are that *im yirtzeh Hashem* the stroller will be passed on to children you have in the future, so you want a stroller that will last.

If you don't anticipate carting the stroller around too much, and it will spend more time in your garage than on the road, then it may not matter if the material isn't durable or shows every speck of dirt. But if that stroller will be seeing a lot of use, check that the material is waterproof, washes easily, and doesn't show too much dirt.

If you don't drive, the stroller will have to be able to withstand being taken on and off buses and trains, so choose a carriage that folds up easily and will not get easily scratched.

Size and Weight

Strollers take up space. Some take up a lot of space (especially if you buy one that comes with all the accessories — more on that below). Some strollers fold compactly; others are nearly the same size when folded. Consider how much space you have to store a stroller before you make your purchase.

The weight of the stroller may also make a difference to you, especially if you have lots of steps to navigate. Have in mind that babies do grow (*baruch Hashem!*), and you have to take the baby's weight into account when you decide to buy a hefty stroller. Not to mention a diaper bag filled with all the amenities you'll need when you go out, and anything you choose to stick in the basket underneath. All that can add up to a lot of schlepping. If that's an issue for you, there are well-made lightweight strollers that are also durable. Some companies specialize in producing lightweight strollers, so those are the ones you should consider when making your purchase.

ONE LUMP OF SUGAR OR TWO?

No one will deny that babies are sweet as sugar, so two babies are surely sweeter than one! Whether you have multiples or this is baby number two, you may decide that the purchase of a double stroller is in order.

Instead of the standard side-by-side, you can get a tandem stroller (AKA the "bus") where one baby sits behind the other in single-file style. These may be easier to maneuver on narrow sidewalks. In some models, the seat flips so that the babies can face each other and keep each other entertained.

Cost

The most expensive stroller must be the best, right? Why buy a four-door sedan to transport your precious darling if you can get the Lamborghini of strollers?

Be aware that the most expensive carriage isn't necessarily the most durable, or the right one for you and your lifestyle. The carriage may be too large to fit in your car trunk or hallway, or may not last in your neighborhood's hilly terrain (Yerushalayim, anyone?). While it's probably true that the cheapest carriages are made of cheaper materials, there are scores of midrange strollers that are both durable and gorgeous, so don't automatically rule them out.

Brand Name

If you're like most pregnant women, you've been eyeing strollers for months, and you've noticed that certain brand names are

quite popular. There may be a good reason for that: It's a good stroller, so everyone wants to get it. On the other hand, it may be that everyone else has it simply because...everyone else has it.

Every company that produces strollers has its pros and cons. Some are known for the beauty of their products and the variety of colors available. Others are known for producing well-made but affordable strollers, while others simply produce the best quality strollers made with the best — and the most expensive — materials.

Do your research. Ask your friends who already have babies what they like about their strollers and what they don't like. You may realize that the most popular stroller is not the right one for you, or you may decide to throw in the towel with the rest of them and buy the same stroller as everyone else on your block. There's nothing wrong with that — just make sure you don't take home your friend's stroller by mistake!

Color and Material

You will be spending a lot of time with this carriage. You'll want to feel good wheeling your beautiful baby around, and you don't want to be the weird mother in the park with *that* odd carriage. Just as with a clothing purchase, choose a color and pattern that suits your personality and makes you happy.

However, before you choose that adorable pink carriage with the leopard pattern, consider that usually a carriage lasts through at least three children and your next baby might be a boy. As lovely as that pink color is, are you prepared to constantly hear what an adorable girl your Yanky is?

Accessories

Strollers today come with lots of accessories. In a way, this makes your decision easier. You don't have to decide between a baby carriage with a bassinet or the stroller that isn't quite right for the newborn. Many strollers come with both! If a stroller with all the accessories appeals to you, then go ahead and get it all.

If your budget or space is limited, you can buy a stroller that will still be good as your baby grows from newborn into a toddler; many of these strollers are just as convenient.

Here's a breakdown of some accessories that come with or may be purchased to enhance many strollers:

- » **Basket** — Almost every carriage has a basket underneath to store things; some are bigger than others, so purchase according to your needs.

- » **Bassinet** — Some strollers have an option for a bassinet suitable for newborns, which looks like a baby cot with a cover canopy and foot cover; the bassinet may come as an attachment that can be removed and replaced with a regular stroller seat for when the baby can sit up. What's nice is that these removable seats can be placed with the baby facing you or away from you. It's quite convenient to be able to see if your newborn is sleeping or is ready for action while you're strolling with your stroller. Then, once your baby gets older and can sit up, you can turn him around to face the world. He'll find the sights interesting and stay entertained while you do your shopping.

- » **Rain hood** — A rain hood is a basic necessity. It will protect your infant from rain and also from the cold and wind; if you are getting a stroller with bassinet and stroller seat attachments, make sure you have a rain hood for each.

- » **Car seat** — There are many possibilities for women who want to combine their car seats with their strollers. You can get a "travel system" — a stroller frame that you can place your car seat into. If you opt for this, make sure you first find out which car seats the frame will safely hold. Another innovation is a car seat integrated with a stroller — you take it out of the car, pull down the wheels, flip up the handle and, voila, you've got a stroller!

- » **Diaper bag** — Some carriages come with matching diaper bags in the same material and color as the carriage.
- » **Stroller hooks** — These are just like what they sound, hooks that you can attach to the handle of your stroller to hang a diaper bag or shopping purchases; what's a carriage for if not to carry stuff! Check your stroller instruction manual to see if your stroller can balance well with bags on the handles.
- » **Tray** — Some strollers come with a removable tray on which you can place a toy or a snack and drink for an older baby. And some even have a tray at the top for Mommy's iced coffee!
- » **Handle grips** — You can buy handle grips that wrap around your stroller handle in a variety of colors for comfort and durability.
- » **Stroller toys** — It might be hard to believe now, but in just a few months your baby will not be content just to lay still in the carriage; once your baby turns about three months old, you may want to get a toy that attaches to the stroller to keep baby stimulated and occupied.

As you can see, strollers have gotten pretty complicated. Before your first outing, make sure you know how each piece attaches and detaches, how to fold the stroller, and how to strap and unstrap your baby. Otherwise, you may find yourself alone with a bawling newborn and a stroller you have no idea how to unfold in the middle of the mall parking lot (yes, it's happened!).

"Wearing Your Baby": All About Baby Carriers

It's becoming more and more common to see a mommy strolling happily down the street with her baby carried snugly in a carrier or sling. Wearing your baby in a carrier makes it easier for Mommy to make a quick run to the grocery, get some exercise (with the baby adding weight for good measure — what a fabulous core workout!), fold laundry, or have her hands free to hold her toddler's hand.

They're also convenient for Daddy: He can rock the baby to sleep as he *shuckles* while learning, or while working at his desk.

And baby absolutely adores the feeling of closeness that a carrier brings!

You'll want a carrier or sling to be able to support the weight of your baby safely while protecting your back. If budget is a concern, there are many quality baby carriers that are made to last and are affordable.

Here's what to consider when making this purchase:

Comfort

When you carry a baby in a carrier or sling, your back and shoulders, rather than your arms, carry the weight. Find a baby carrier that is comfortable for you. Some carriers also distribute some of baby's weight to your hips, taking some of the burden off your back. The straps should be wide and padded so that they are comfortable on your shoulders or back.

Make sure your baby fits comfortably in the carrier as well. The leg holes shouldn't be so small as to be too tight, nor should they be so large that the baby slips down. Some carriers also come with a headrest to give your baby extra support.

There are carriers that can be worn in the front or in the back. Back carriers are usually for older babies, since they require a baby to be able to hold his head up.

Some carriers are easier to nurse in, while others make nursing almost impossible. Be sure to check before accidentally choosing a "daddy carrier."

Size

Carriers come with age limits — not for you, but for your baby. Check how much weight the carrier can hold and have that in mind when making your purchase. Some are only good until the

WHAT DO YOU PACK IN YOUR DIAPER BAG?

There are some snazzy diaper bags available today; many come with matching changing pads, a special waterproof, insulated pouch to store a baby bottle, and another one to place a soiled diaper until you can dispose of it. Some strollers come with diaper bags that match the color and material, which you might prefer, or you may find another kind of diaper bag more durable and functional.

You'll be carrying that diaper bag around often, especially if you enjoy taking your baby out for a breath of fresh air, so you'll want one that's both convenient and stylish.

It's a good idea to keep your diaper bag stocked and ready so that you can just grab it when you need to go out. Here's a list of things to keep in your diaper bag:

» Diapers — two or three, depending how long you'll be out
» Diaper changing pad
» Baby wipes
» Diaper ointment
» Disposable bag for soiled diapers
» Hand sanitizer
» Baby bottle and formula (if you're not breastfeeding)
» Extra pacifier (if you're using one)
» Change of baby clothes
» Baby acetaminophen and any medications baby needs, either routinely or for emergencies
» Burp cloth
» Tissues
» Rattles or other toys, when the baby gets a little older

Restock as soon as you return home so that your bag will be ready to go when you're going out again. When your baby outgrows his diapers and you switch to a new size, don't forget to switch the diapers in the diaper bag too.

baby is about six months, while others can carry a baby up to 35 or 45 pounds. Sizes go according to weight because a baby who is a lightweight at ten months can still use a carrier that a heavy six-month-old has outgrown.

Some carriers "grow" with your baby, and can be adjusted for an older baby as he gets bigger.

Durability

Make sure the carrier is well stitched, that the material is sturdy, and the straps and buckles are of good quality. It should also be easy to clean and the material shouldn't fade after just a few washings.

Style

There are a variety of baby carriers that will cater to every mother's needs and personality. Some are black and sleek, while others are neutral or come in bright patterns. Essentially you'll be "wearing" the carrier on you, so make sure it's a style that you like. Needless to say, you don't want to sacrifice comfort or your baby's safety for style, but there is a wide enough assortment that you should be able to have both.

Babywearing Safety Tips

» The baby should always be well secured and not be able to slip. Make sure the newborn's head is well supported and his back is naturally curved but not slumped.

» On hot, sunny days, smear baby's hands and face, which will be peeking out of the carrier, with sunscreen (make sure it's safe for use on babies and follow instructions on how to apply), and cover his head with a hat. Dress him warmly in the winter but realize that you are sharing body heat, so don't overdress either him or you.

» Watch for signs that the baby is becoming overheated or dehydrated. A baby who is feeling snug in a carrier may

LET'S WRAP IT UP

If you're most concerned about comfort and size, a sling or wrap may be the answer.

A **sling** is a wide piece of material worn across the back, chest, and shoulder. It can come padded or unpadded.

A **wrap** is essentially like a huge scarf that wraps over both shoulders. Some find it more comfortable than a sling.

These carriers are usually made of 100% cotton, or 95% cotton and 5% spandex (to give it a stretchy feel). They're lightweight, versatile, and can usually be adjusted for your baby's size.

Another advantage is that you can use it to cover yourself up when nursing the baby. If the baby falls asleep while feeding, he's already snug and comfy.

Here are some pointers when purchasing a wrap or sling:

» Make sure that the wrap is long enough to wrap comfortably around you and your baby.

» The material should be easy to wash and lightweight. If the material is too heavy, it will become uncomfortable on hot, sunny days and your baby might also become overheated.

» The wrap should be, well, easy to wrap. The point of the baby carrier is to allow you to take your baby to go. You don't want to spend fifteen minutes every time wrapping your baby.

» You can usually adjust the wrap or sling to carry your baby on your side or hip. This may be more comfortable than carrying the baby's weight with your back and shoulders.

tend to sleep more and may not demand to be fed as often, and being wrapped up could make him overly warm. If baby nuzzles your chest, it's time to feed.

» Make sure the baby's face is always visible and isn't pressed up to the fabric, in a way that would cover his nose and mouth. His chin should be two fingers away from his chest to keep his airway open.

Chapter Five

To Your Baby's Good Health!

Choosing a Pediatrician

For your baby's healthy development, it's important to have a doctor who specializes in the care of infants and children. During routine well-baby visits the pediatrician evaluates the baby's growth and development and administers immunizations at the proper intervals. The doctor also provides you with the information you need for the nutrition and care of your child as he grows. The pediatrician diagnoses common childhood illnesses and detects potential health problems before they become serious, prescribing appropriate medication and making referrals to specialists when necessary.

It's a good idea to choose a pediatrician during the second trimester of pregnancy; once the baby is born, there will be little time for the task of finding the best doctor. Begin by asking neighbors, relatives, friends, and coworkers for names to consider. You can also ask your obstetrician for her recommendation and request referrals from the hospital where you plan to give birth. Names of certified pediatric practitioners are available from the American Academy of Pediatrics as well.

Choosing a doctor is very individual. The same pediatrician can be perfect for one family and completely unsuitable for another. One mother might prefer a young female doctor, while another feels more secure with a grandfatherly type. It may be reassuring to know that the doctor understands your issues not only professionally but also because he is a father of young children, or you might prefer the style of a career professional whose family has long since grown up.

Once you have a list of possible candidates, do your homework. Find out if the doctor you are considering is accepting new patients at this time. Verify that his office accepts your health insurance plan and that he is on the most updated list of pediatricians covered by your policy. It is prudent to contact your state's medical board to be sure there is no record of discipline because of malpractice, negligence, or misconduct.

Now go over your list and delete those with inconvenient locations or office hours that don't fit into your schedule. Also, check: Is there access by public transportation and/or sufficient parking space near the office?

UNDERSTANDING CREDENTIALS

If the doctor is "board certified," that means the doctor has done a three-year residency program in pediatrics after completing medical school and has successfully passed a series of rigorous exams that require routine retesting.

A doctor who belongs to the American Academy of Pediatrics (AAP) follows the guidelines and standards of that organization.

An FAAP listing indicates that the doctor is both board certified and belongs to the AAP.

The next step is a personal visit. Call and schedule an introductory meeting. There may be a reasonable fee for this; check to see if your insurance will cover it.

Try to arrive at the office a few minutes early and look around. Ask other parents in the waiting room whether they are satisfied. Are there books and toys to distract children until their appointment? Are there separate rooms for well-baby visits and sick children? Is the waiting room clean and pleasant? How long is the usual wait for the doctor to receive patients? Do his young patients like their doctor? Are the members of the doctor's staff patient and helpful? What is the general atmosphere like?

During the interview with the pediatrician you want an impression of how this doctor relates to his patients.

The following suggested questions are intended to help you get more information:

- » Which hospitals is the doctor affiliated with?
- » How does the doctor keep up-to-date about the latest medical advances?
- » What is the protocol if there is a medical question outside of office hours — will the doctor be on call, or someone else?
- » Does the doctor welcome questions and will he or she be available to hear your concerns and discuss solutions?
- » Does the doctor belong to a group practice? Will you always have access to your doctor or are there circumstances where you will be transferred to another member of the group without notice?
- » Will the doctor first see your newborn in the hospital or at an office visit?
- » How are telephone inquiries handled?
- » Discuss subjects that are important to you such as breastfeeding, vaccinations, returning to work after birth, SIDS, pacifier use, etc. Are you and the doctor on the same

page on issues that are of prime importance to you as a parent?
- » Does the doctor have additional specialties besides pediatrics?
- » How does the office handle billing, lab charges, and insurance claims?
- » Look around the office. If it's full of formula-branded products and posters, that may mean the practice is more likely to suggest supplementation instead of solving breastfeeding issues or referring to lactation specialists. (On the other hand, it may just mean the secretaries liked the pictures on the posters!) If breastfeeding is a very important issue for you, consider checking with other patients on how strongly the doctor encourages it.

Take note of the doctor's manner. The right one will not be judgmental or condescending. He will have patience and be willing to explain things to your satisfaction.

Also consider: Is it important to you to be included in the decision-making process? One type of doctor will give you options while another may give precise instructions. Hopefully you will feel a "click" with the doctor who is most suitable for you and your new baby.

Of course, it's always possible to change your mind if it doesn't work out after a few visits. As with everything in life, we must daven for *siyatta d'Shmaya* in making the right choices!

Well-Baby Checkups

Your newborn will be carefully examined by a pediatrician within a short time after birth. Another checkup will be done before the two of you are discharged from the hospital, with instructions to schedule a well-baby checkup with the pediatrician you've chosen.

By now you should have done your homework and chosen a pediatrician or clinic for your baby. Most doctors recommend a schedule of regular visits during the first year. This may differ from one pediatrician to another, but usually includes visits at the ages of one month, two months, four months, six months, nine months, and twelve months. Following this schedule will ensure that any problems are caught early, when they are most treatable, and that you will have access to professionals for the questions that arise naturally at each stage of development. Also, at these visits, your baby will be given vaccinations, and it's important they be administered at recommended intervals.

What Happens at a Well-Baby Visit?

Usually a nurse will see your baby first to weigh her, measure her height and head circumference, and record this information on her personal growth chart. You will be asked to undress your baby completely (including her diaper) for the weighing, since at this age the weight is measured down to the ounce and this will ensure an accurate reading.

Your baby's growth chart follows your baby's development and allows you to see how she is doing in comparison to most infants her age. Remember that it's not a scorecard! It doesn't make any real difference whether your little one is in the tenth or ninetieth percentile. The important thing is that her rate of growth remains stable over time.

The doctor will now check your baby's physical development. Using a stethoscope, he listens to her heart rhythm and breathing. Then, starting at the top of the baby's head, he will check that the fontanels (soft spots — see pp. 29-30) are gradually fusing as expected and that the shape of her skull is normal. He looks into her eyes to rule out problems such as congenital eye conditions, blocked tear ducts, or discharge. If you're concerned about your baby's vision, mention this to the doctor and he will check the alignment of her eyes and her ability to move them.

The baby's ears will be checked for signs of infection, and the doctor will observe how she responds to your voice and other sounds.

The doctor will look into your baby's mouth, examining the oral anatomy and ruling out thrush (yeast infection common to infants) and tongue-tie.

He will check the baby's muscle tone and reflexes, and note birthmarks and signs of rash or jaundice.

He will press your baby's tummy to rule out enlarged abdominal organs or a hernia, and examine the navel to be sure it is healing well after the umbilical stump detached.

The diaper area is checked for signs of rash, redness, or infection. Male genitals will be examined to verify that the baby's testes are properly placed (see pp. 80-81) and that the bris has healed completely.

Your baby's legs will be gently rotated to rule out congenital problems with her hip joints.

Your doctor will ask questions to determine that your baby's development is proceeding as it should and will record the social and physical milestones she reaches. Be prepared to describe her sleeping and digestive patterns. This is an excellent time for you to express your own questions and need for clarifications.

If the doctor notices anything that needs treatment, including such common problems as cradle cap, baby acne, diaper rash, and spitting up, he will advise you on the steps to take. Your pediatrician will compare the information you supply with the baby's growth pattern and offer recommendations for changes as necessary.

Your baby will also receive any vaccinations she is scheduled to receive. The pediatrician will explain what to expect after the vaccinations and how to relieve her discomfort if she is feverish or cranky.

The doctor may also ask about your well-being to see how you are coping with the new baby. If you are finding it difficult to

> ## VACCINATIONS: WHEN AND WHAT
>
> Your baby will usually get his second injection of the hepatitis B vaccine at his first- or second-month visit to the pediatrician (the first was given in the hospital; for more on hepatitis B vaccinations see p. 28). There are no known side effects to this vaccination. The third and final shot of the series will be scheduled when your baby is between six and eighteen months old.
>
> At the two-month, four-month, and six-month appointments, your baby will receive two vaccinations, if they are appropriate. Vaccinations are carried out with parental consent after an explanation of the benefits and risks. Each vaccination will be given in a thigh, where it is least painful. These include the pneumococcal, DTP, Hib, and polio vaccines. He'll also get a few drops of the oral vaccine to protect him from rotavirus, and if it's flu season and he is past six months he may also get a flu shot.
>
> If your little one has missed any immunizations, they will be made up on his nine-month visit. The second-year vaccinations include Hib, pneumococcal, varicella (chicken pox), MMR (measles, mumps, and rubella), and hepatitis A in two or three shots.

cope, speak to the doctor about ways to alleviate the stress. He may want to screen you for symptoms of postpartum depression (see p. 70) and will be able to offer advice for prevention or treatment, if necessary.

For a full chart of vaccinations, see Appendix III, p. 401.

Fever

What Do You Do If Your Baby Has a Fever Over 100.4°F?

To begin with, stay calm. Even if your little one has flushed cheeks and feels hot to your touch, it's probably not an emergency. A rise in body temperature is a healthy immune response

to the presence of invading bacteria or viral infections, or in reaction to immunizations. Fever by itself causes no harm; it is only a symptom. (The exception is fever in newborns up to six weeks or ten pounds; see below.)

Don't rely on touch. Use a thermometer for accuracy! Body temperature can be measured rectally, orally (in the mouth under the tongue, but not before the age of four years), temporally (on the forehead), or under the armpit (not before three months of age). The most accurate reading of the child's core temperature is from the rectum, and the least accurate is under the arm, which may be two degrees off the real temperature.

Always follow the manufacturer's instructions for the thermometer you use. Clean it both before and after each use, gently

WHICH TYPE OF THERMOMETER IS BEST?

» Digital multiuse thermometers are inexpensive and easy to use. They give a clear reading within a short time and can be designated for either oral, rectal, or axillary (armpit) use.

» Specially designed digital rectal thermometers are made with a flexible tip and a handle wide enough to prevent accidentally inserting them too deeply.

» Ear thermometers use an infrared ray to measure the temperature in the ear canal, although ear wax or a curved ear canal make them less dependable.

» Forehead thermometers measure the temperature of the temporal artery with an infrared scanner when swiped across the forehead midway between the eyebrows and the hairline. These thermometers can be used even when the baby is sleeping.

» Readings from fever strips that change color or digital pacifiers are not reliable.

» An old-fashioned glass liquid-filled thermometer, if available, is a good Shabbos option. Take care not to drop it because these thermometers break easily.

rubbing the tip with soap or alcohol and rinsing with cool water. Don't use the same thermometer for both rectal and oral measurements — label each thermometer according to its purpose. Never leave a child unattended while the thermometer is in his mouth.

When measuring temperature rectally, coat the tip with a dab of petroleum jelly to make it easier to slide inside. Put the baby on her back in the position she is accustomed to for diaper changing. Gently insert the tip of the thermometer to a depth between three-quarters to one inch (any deeper carries the risk of perforation). It will calm her to see your face and listen to your voice.

Push the button on the digital thermometer to activate it. It will beep when the reading is complete. Be aware: It's fairly common for infants to move their bowels after having their temperature taken rectally.

Just like adults, an infant's body temperature is not always exactly 98.6°F. A warm bath, layers of warm clothing, or physical exertion can elevate the core temperature several degrees. Only a reading of 100.4°F or higher is actually considered a fever. (For a Fahrenheit and Celsius chart of body temperature, see Appendix III, p. 405.)

Fevers caused by viral infections are much less serious than a fever from a bacterial infection. The common cold and the flu are examples of illness caused by a virus. They usually last between three and seven days and are not responsive to antibiotics. Ear infections and pneumonia can be either bacterial or viral. Examples of bacterial infections include urinary tract infections and strep throat. These are less common than viral infections, but they require antibiotics and will continue for a lengthy period unless treated. In general, if your baby has a fever of over 100.4°F for longer than three days you should turn to your pediatrician.

Bringing the Fever Down

Doctors and experienced mothers know that the main symptom of a sick child is not the fever, but the behavior. A cranky baby

> ### FEVER IN NEWBORNS: CAUTION!
>
> During the first six weeks, and up to three months of life, colds don't cause a fever. If there is a rectal temperature of over 100.4°F, it may be serious and your pediatrician should be contacted immediately. *Be sure to mention to the pediatrician or emergency clinic that the baby is less than three months old.* If your doctor is unavailable, you should take the baby to the hospital immediately. In order not to mask any symptoms before he can be seen by the doctor, don't use fever-reducing medication that you have in the house unless advised to do this by your pediatrician.
>
> The reason behind the urgency in this case is that bacterial infections in the first three months don't show the typical symptoms of serious infection before the situation becomes life-threatening. Since it's not possible to distinguish between a dangerous bacterial infection and an ordinary viral infection (which, of course, it also may be) according to the baby's symptoms, it is necessary to run complete blood and urine tests, and sometimes a spinal tap is necessary to rule out meningitis.

with a 101°F temperature who appears tired and needs to be held much more than usual is much sicker than a content and responsive baby with a temperature of 103°F! The main signs of a sick baby are listlessness, fatigue, and poor feeding.

There are medications to bring down a fever and help a child feel better, but they must be used judiciously. Before treating the fever with medicine, try an old-fashioned sponge bath. Dip a cloth or sponge in lukewarm water (85 to 90°F), wring it out, and then wipe down the baby's skin. A damp cloth on her forehead or in her armpits is especially effective. If this doesn't help and the baby still seems uncomfortable, ask your pediatrician about using medication to reduce her fever. If she falls asleep, don't wake her up just to give her medicine to bring her temperature down.

Before giving any medication to your baby for the first time, check with your pediatrician. Babies are more likely than adults to have negative reactions to drugs. Using over-the-counter medication, including herbal remedies, may have adverse consequences. Any appearance of a rash or vomiting after medication may indicate an adverse reaction to the medicine, and your doctor should be contacted.

All medication must be kept safely out of reach. If you find an open medicine bottle near your baby, call your pediatrician or, if he is not available, Poison Control, for advice even though you don't know for sure whether the baby swallowed any of the contents. Keep your local Poison Control phone number on your refrigerator or other easily accessible place, together with other emergency numbers.

When Baby Is Sick

When your baby gets sick, your first instinct is to call the doctor, whatever the time of day or night (So what if it's two in the morning? This is an emergency!). He's so little, so vulnerable, and it can be worrying, even frightening, when your newborn is ill. As a parent, your child's well-being is entrusted to you and you do need to be alert for signs that all isn't well. But not every sniffle and rise in temperature calls for a doctor's visit.

So when do you call the doctor?

Coughing

If the baby is coughing due to a common cold, that usually isn't cause for concern. Keep in mind that coughing typically worsens during the night. Setting up a humidifier in the baby's room can ease the discomfort of a little one who is miserable and unable to sleep because of a cold and coughing. You can also raise the mattress crib under her head a little, but make sure it's not so high that she might slip down.

If your baby wakes up in the middle of the night with a harsh cough similar to a seal's bark, it's probably croup. You can bring him into a bathroom full of steam (turn on the hot water in the

shower). Alternatively, you can take him outside into the cool night air (bundle up!). Both are effective ways of dealing with croup (but don't try both — you shouldn't take the baby from a hot environment to a cold one). The baby will probably be able to fall asleep afterward. Call your doctor in the morning to report what happened.

If you witness signs of respiratory distress (grunting, flaring of the nostrils, observable sinking between the ribs every time the baby inhales), or if your baby's skin is turning blue, call 911 or a local rescue service such as Hatzalah without delay.

Vomiting

Vomiting multiple times, even after nothing remains in the stomach to throw up, is an emergency, especially if the vomit shoots out forcefully from the baby's mouth (projectile vomiting). Contact your doctor immediately and describe the frequency, color, and consistency of the vomit and whether or not it contains blood. A baby with persistent vomiting may have ingested something poisonous, there may be an intestinal obstruction that needs immediate attention, or it might be a stomach virus.

Diarrhea

Though unpleasant, diarrhea in and of itself (fewer than seven incidents in twenty-four hours) is not usually a cause for concern. Bloody diarrhea can indicate a serious condition and should be reported to the pediatrician as soon as possible. The danger of diarrhea is dehydration. If you suspect dehydration, seek medical care immediately. Signs of dehydration include diapers that aren't wet, sunken eyes or fontanel, a dry mouth or tongue, fever, weakness, paleness, no tears, lethargy, and poor feeding.

Upper Respiratory Infection (AKA the Common Cold)

Infants and babies tend to "catch colds" even more often than the rest of us (especially those in daycare, who are exposed to

AVOIDING DEHYDRATION

To avoid dehydration when baby has diarrhea, give him frequent fluids (breastmilk for nursing babies; Pedialyte or other electrolyte solution for formula-fed babies). Avoid fruit juices, though diluted applesauce can sometimes be tolerated. If he is eating solids, try to encourage him to eat, but stay away from fruits and dairy products. Foods known to bind diarrhea include white rice and rice cereal, cooked apples or carrots. Older children can eat salty crackers or pretzels. And, of course, there's that old standby, mashed banana. To avoid diaper rash, change baby's diaper whenever it is soiled and be generous with the ointment!

far more children), because they haven't yet built up immunity against the hundreds of viruses out there. Symptoms will be similar to those we've all suffered through: runny nose, coughing and sneezing, nasal congestion, sometimes fever and loss of appetite. You can alleviate symptoms by using a humidifier in baby's room. If his nose is very stuffed, soften the mucus with normal saline nose drops (available over the counter) and, if necessary, suction the mucus with a nasal aspirator.

Petechiae

A feverish baby sometimes develops a dot-like rash under the skin known as "petechiae." This kind of rash cannot be felt by touch but it is visible to the eye. If you suspect petechiae, it is important to notify your doctor, since it can be a symptom of a bacterial infection, but do not panic: Petechiae can also be caused by repeated coughing or vomiting.

HOW TO SUCTION THE MUCUS FROM BABY'S NOSE WITH A NASAL ASPIRATOR.

Do not use the nasal aspirator more than three times each day, to avoid irritating the lining of baby's nose.

1. Squeeze the air out of the bulb.
2. Gently place the tip of the squeezed bulb into baby's nostril. Be careful not to push it in hard, and don't push it in too far. You might want to consider buying a nasal bulb aspirator that comes with special markings that indicates how deep to insert it. Some are manufactured in a way that makes it impossible to push them in too far.
3. Slowly release the bulb. As air comes back into the bulb, the mucus is pulled out of the nose and into the bulb.
4. Remove the bulb from the baby's nostril and squeeze the bulb to push the mucus out onto a tissue.
5. Repeat the procedure for the other nostril.
6. If mucus is very thick, thin it with saline nose drops before aspirating. Alternatively, you can sit with the baby in a bathroom full of steam for a few minutes. That will also help loosen up the mucus. Some mothers spray their milk into baby's nose for a gentle "wash" filled with antibodies.
7. Gently wipe the area around baby's nose, to clean away any remaining mucus.
8. It's very important to clean the nasal aspirator thoroughly, since it is full of germs, which can live for up to forty-eight hours. Squeeze the air out of the bulb. Then release the bulb to fill it with soapy water, then let it out. Repeat a few times. Let it air dry.

Falls and Fractures

Babies are very wiggly and active, and it takes a few months for them to learn to control their movements. Always buckle your baby into any seat or stroller to prevent falls. If your baby falls from the highchair, the changing table, or from your bed to the floor, you are right to be concerned. If the child is unconscious, call 911 (and local emergency services) and then your doctor. If he just cries and then calms down, contact your doctor. Even though a big lump on the forehead often looks much worse than it really is, if you are concerned, have him examined by a doctor.

Danger signs after a fall include drowsiness, disorientation, vomiting several times, or bleeding from the baby's nose or ear. Getting hurt on the bridge of the nose or either side of the head is more serious than bumping the rest of the skull. If your baby's head seems misshapen or pushed in, contact emergency services.

The pediatrician should be called immediately if a baby stops using one of his arms or legs. An x-ray will show if the limb is fractured or dislocated. Dislocation can be caused by lifting the child by an arm, causing the bone to slip out of the shoulder or elbow socket. This can be very painful and must be fixed by a skilled doctor.

Discharge from the Eye

When a baby has a cold, you may notice a goopy discharge from the tear ducts of one or both eyes. After a night's sleep, this sometimes dries into a crust that pastes his eyes shut.

Use a soft cloth dipped in warm water or your breastmilk to soak and soften the crust until he can open his eyes, and gently wipe away the remaining discharge. Be in touch with your pediatrician regarding further treatment. Discharge from the eye can also be a result of pinkeye (conjunctivitis). It is not an emergency, but consult with your pediatrician during office hours.

Middle Ear Inflammation (Otitis Media, AKA an Ear Infection)

Ear infections, as they are commonly called, are not always easy to spot. At times the baby will pull at his ear or run a slight fever, while sometimes there are hardly any symptoms at all. Often the ear infection follows a cold. If you suspect an ear infection,

BUBBY TIP

SALT AND EARACHES!

Another way to soothe a painful ear is to fill a sock with table salt. Knot it tightly, and place in the microwave for one minute. Make sure it's cozy warm, not hot, by putting it first next to your lips, and then place it near the baby's ear.

contact your pediatrician, who will check inside the ear for inflammation and fluid. Sometimes your pediatrician will suggest waiting a few days, since ear infections usually heal by themselves. In more severe cases, the doctor will prescribe antibiotics and, occasionally, ear drops. Until you can get medical help, try putting a warm (not hot) hot water bottle by the ear or use warm ear drops to soothe the pain.

Cradle Cap

The medical term for cradle cap is "infantile seborrheic dermatitis." If you notice the skin on your baby's scalp becoming flaky and scaly, it's probably cradle cap, also called "baby dandruff."

Cradle cap is a very common condition during the first months of life. There is no consensus among doctors about the cause of cradle cap. It appears to be a reaction of the skin to a temporary overproduction by the oil-producing (seborrheic) glands. It does not seem to be related to either poor hygiene or allergy, and cradle cap is not contagious. Even though it is unappealing, it's harmless and usually requires no special treatment.

To remove cradle cap, try tenderly massaging his head with your fingertips or using a soft baby hairbrush to loosen the flakes and then gently comb them out. Some mothers recommend applying natural olive oil. Don't leave the oil on the baby's head for more than fifteen to twenty minutes before washing it away because it can clog the pores and make the cradle cap worse.

Baby shampoos specifically designed to alleviate cradle cap are available. These may be used daily. Leaving the shampoo on the head for several minutes before rinsing is effective in cutting the excess oil produced by the pores, but don't neglect to thoroughly rinse away any residue afterward.

The pediatrician should be consulted if the baby's scalp bleeds or becomes inflamed. If necessary, your doctor will prescribe a topical antifungal medication or a cortisone cream.

Administering Medication

If a baby needs any medication, either prescription or over-the-counter, refer to the chart on the package for instructions. Proper dosages for infants are always determined by the baby's weight, and not according to age. Check the label before each use. To avoid overdosing, remember that infant drops are more concentrated than the same medication in liquid form for older children.

Medications to avoid:

- » Do not give ibuprofen to relieve a fever for infants younger than six months. Acetaminophen is the preferred option for babies under that age, and is FDA approved for infants. For children older than six months, both are accepted, though if a child is dehydrated, vomiting, or has abdominal pain, don't medicate without consulting your doctor.
- » Never use any medication without your pediatrician's approval. Do not give a baby a smaller dosage of adult medication; if no appropriate dosage is listed for your baby's weight and age, then do not use that medicine. Giving your baby prescription medication prescribed for another child or for a different condition will most likely be ineffective and may cause serious harm.

» Aspirin must never be given to infants or children. Don't assume that over-the-counter medication for children is aspirin-free — always read the label. Other names for aspirin include salicylate and acetylsalicylic acid.

> ## THE WELL-STOCKED MEDICINE CHEST
>
> Don't wait until your baby gets sick to stock your medicine cabinet. You'll want to make sure to have these items at hand, just in case, by the time you bring your baby home from the hospital after birth:
>
> » A digital thermometer (for more on choosing thermometers, see p. 143)
> » Liquid fever- and pain-reducing medicine (acetaminophen for babies under six months of age). These medications are often available in suppository form as well.
> » Syringe for measuring and administering liquid medication (sometimes this comes in the medicine package)
> » Sterilizing alcohol (for cleaning thermometer tip)
> » Water-soluble lubricant (such as petroleum jelly) for lubricating the tip of a rectal thermometer, if you will be using one
> » Saline drops to relieve a stuffy nose
> » A bulb syringe (nasal aspirator) designed to gently clear mucous from a stuffy nose (for instructions on how to aspirate mucus, see p. 149)
> » Lotion or cream for insect bites and rash (topical hydrocortisone or calamine)
> » Cotton swabs to apply cream or lotion
> » A first-aid reference manual for emergencies
> » The phone number for Poison Control (in the United States: 1-800-222-1222), the fire department, and the closest hospitals and emergency clinics in your area, as well as Hatzalah or other emergency responders. (Keep these numbers in other prominent places, such as the fridge or a phone, as well.)

- Over-the-counter cough suppressants are ineffective in infants, and an overdose can be dangerous. The American Academy of Pediatrics warns against side effects from cough medication, which may include drowsiness, upset stomach, rapid pulse, or convulsions.
- Anti-nausea medication is inappropriate for babies and may cause complications, such as dehydration. If your baby is vomiting repeatedly, contact your pediatrician.
- Both prescription and over-the-counter medications should be disposed of after their date of expiration. If a medication does not appear the same, i.e., color or consistency changed, as when it was bought, it should not be used. Medicine past its expiration date may not be effective and may be harmful.

Part Two
Feeding Your Baby

Chapter Six

Making the Right Choice for Your Baby — and You

Y ou've imagined this moment over and over. You've pictured the scene down to every detail:

You're holding your newborn baby in your arms for the first time. The lights are dim; the baby is warm and relaxed. She is making soft noises and nuzzling you, looking for her first drops of nourishment. You hold your baby against you, and naturally and happily the baby begins to nurse. A feeling of calm rushes over you. Everything is perfect...

Many women do enjoy this experience the first time they try breastfeeding. Perhaps they've imagined this scene so many times or have done sufficient research to know what to expect. Maybe they watched the women in their families caring for their newborns and now they are ready to follow easily in their footsteps.

But many new mothers are ambivalent or uncertain about how they will feed their babies. This section will dispel many myths and give you the facts to help you make an informed decision, and to do what's best for your precious new baby.

You might really want to nurse your baby, but you're afraid. You worry that you won't have enough milk, that it will hurt, that you will try but won't succeed, or that it will take over your life. Perhaps in your heart you believe that bottle feeding is the best choice for you, but you're anxious about what people will say. Does it mean that you're not a good mother if you give your baby a substitute for breastmilk?

Then there is all the well-meaning "advice" — much of it based on myths — you received even before the baby was born:

"If you don't breastfeed, you'll regret it for the rest of your life."

"All your friends are breastfeeding their babies. Why do you want to be different?"

"Your mother-in-law gave formula and see? Her children turned out just fine."

"How can you deprive your own baby? Nothing is better for his emotional and physical health than breastfeeding. It's important to nurse him from the very beginning."

"You don't have any milk during the first days anyway. Give the baby formula until your milk comes in."

"Never give a bottle! As soon as you give a bottle, your baby won't want to nurse anymore."

"Be practical. You have to go back to work in a few weeks. Just feed the baby with a bottle from the beginning."

"Leave the baby in the nursery. The nurses will give her a bottle until you feel stronger."

"Formula is poison! How can you even consider it?"

With all the conflicting advice, how is it possible to know which is the right decision?

You may certainly seek advice from lactation professionals, family, and friends you trust — but no one but you can know what fits your personal circumstances. It is your responsibility, as the mother of this sweet *neshamah* that Hashem has entrusted to your care, to assess all the pros and cons and then make the best decision for you and your baby. This chapter is intended to present the information you need to help you decide.

Breastfeeding or Bottle Feeding

Although breastfeeding is natural, like walking, it takes time to learn. Before the modern invention of human milk substitutes, the art of breastfeeding was passed down through the generations from mothers to daughters. After growing up around relatives and neighbors who were nursing mothers, young women generally experienced little difficulty when they married and were blessed with their own children.

Around the twentieth century, the wonders of technology created a loss of confidence in natural approaches. Breastfeeding was pronounced old-fashioned, and bottles with rubber nipples were promoted as freeing modern women from their supposed bondage. By the late 1950s and early 1960s, though, women began to wonder if breastfeeding wasn't the better option, both for themselves and for their babies, and slowly nursing came back as the method of choice for more and more mothers.

In developed countries today, breastfeeding is once again valued and encouraged as ideal for healthy mothers and infants. Most mothers hope and plan to nurse their newborns for as long as possible. International health organizations, as well as the American Academy of Pediatrics, recommend that healthy babies should be breastfed exclusively for the first six months of life, after which appropriate solid foods are introduced to complement the breastmilk for the growing child. (For information on baby's nutrition and when to introduce solids, see p. 316.)

The Benefits of Breastfeeding

Hashem created breastmilk as the next stage after pregnancy. Nursing mothers agree that breastfeeding provides a unique physical and emotional experience. This holds true for both the mother and her baby. Since breastfeeding is something only Mommy can do for her baby, it creates a unique and very powerful bond between them.

There are numerous additional benefits of breastfeeding for both baby and mother:

For Infants

» **Health advantages** — Many childhood illnesses, including the common cold, ear infections, and gastrointestinal infections, are less common in breastfed infants than in formula-fed infants, and less severe when they do occur. Nursing infants may have fewer hospitalizations and fewer visits to the doctor than babies fed on formula. Breastfed babies may also have a lower risk of developing allergies.

» **Digestion** — Since breastmilk was created specifically for human babies, it is easily digested, and acts as baby's first immune system. Digestive upsets, such as colic, spitting up, gassiness, constipation, and intestinal illnesses, are less common than in formula-fed babies.

» **Future long-term protection** — Babies who were breastfed have statistically less risk for developing diabetes, celiac disease, Crohn's disease, high cholesterol, and asthma later in life. Research published in the *American Journal of Epidemiology* also showed that there may be progressively reduced risk for obesity the longer time a baby is breastfed.

- » **Protection from sudden infant death syndrome** — International studies associate breastfeeding with a significantly lower risk of SIDS. The U.S. Centers for Disease Control and Prevention recommend prolonging breastfeeding as long as possible as a way to reduce the risk of SIDS.
- » **Stronger immune systems** — Scientists suggest that the antibodies in breastmilk are responsible for improved immune systems.
- » **Increased IQ** — A direct correlation between breastfeeding and improved cognitive development is cited in many scientific studies. The longer an infant is breastfed, the higher the scores recorded on vocabulary testing in childhood.
- » **Orthodontics** — Bottle-fed babies must suck differently from breastfed babies. Not even the best scientifically designed bottle can match a mother's breast. This unnatural motion can lead to orthodontic problems later. The coordination of a baby's jaws, tongue, and lips during nursing results in optimal development as the infant's mouth grows, and may reduce the need for braces and speech therapy.

For Mothers

- » **Recovery after the birth** — Mothers who breastfeed heal better and have more rapid recoveries after childbirth due to the effects of the hormone oxytocin, which helps contract the womb and return it to a normal size. The postpartum hormones involved in milk production adjust gradually when a baby nurses, reducing the risk or severity of postpartum depression.
- » **Calcium** — Breastfeeding increases calcium absorption in the mother, which strengthens bones and lowers the risk of postmenopausal osteoporosis.
- » **Weight loss** — An ounce of breastmilk contains approximately twenty calories. Overall, breastfeeding can burn between

three hundred and five hundred calories a day. For some mothers, this loss of calories helps a mother lose weight after the birth. (For others, breastfeeding affects the metabolism, and they find that the weight doesn't come off — especially if they're noshing! — and they might even gain some weight until after the baby has been weaned.)

» **Lower risk of chronic illnesses** — Breastfeeding mothers have a lower risk for premenopausal breast and ovarian cancer, type 2 diabetes, rheumatoid arthritis, and cardiovascular disease. Breastfeeding has been linked to reduced risk of metabolic diseases like high blood pressure.

» **Postpartum depression** — Breastfeeding mothers have a lower risk of postpartum depression. The reason is the release of the hormone prolactin during nursing, which is associated with a peaceful, relaxing sensation. (Don't be surprised if you feel like nodding off every time you nurse your baby!)

» **Menstruation** — Breastfeeding exclusively on-cue by day and by night (without pacifier use when Mommy is home) can delay the return of menstrual periods. This is a natural form of contraception called "lactational amenorrhea" used up until the baby is six months old and begins eating solids. (However, if contraception is necessary one should not rely on this.)

» **Convenience** — If you're breastfeeding, you don't need all the paraphernalia of formula feeding. Mother's milk is much less expensive than formula, and nighttime nursing is much less disruptive because there's no need to get up to prepare a warm bottle of formula. When nursing, baby's food is always ready and completely sterile, and Mommy can just pick up her infant and go out of the house with minimal preparation.

New research on the benefits of breastfeeding are being published all the time. Even companies that manufacture formulas for infants admit that their products can't equal the benefits of

mother's milk, designed by the Creator as the source of nutrition meant for babies.

The Advantages of Formula Feeding

If most women find nursing to be the most rewarding and beneficial choice, why would anyone choose differently? There are many reasons.

Some of them include:

- » **Sharing** — Only Mommy can breastfeed, but Daddy (as well as grandparents, siblings, and other caregivers) can also feed the baby with a bottle.
- » **Independence** — A bottle can be held by anyone, so the mother isn't tied down to a nursing schedule and can resume working and other commitments more quickly.
- » **Intake control** — It's easy to calculate the amount of formula you need to prepare for a feeding and the quantity the baby ingests each time (especially important if the baby is not gaining weight as expected).
- » **A good night's sleep** — Someone other than Mommy can get up with the baby for the late-night feedings (on the other hand...that "lucky someone" has to get out of bed to prepare the formula!).
- » **Satiation** — Since infant formula takes longer to be digested than mother's milk, baby remains sated for longer periods and feedings are more widely spaced.
- » **Medication** — Nursing mothers are limited in the medications they can use because some chemicals harmful to babies may pass into her breastmilk.
- » **Contraception** — More options are available for mothers who are not breastfeeding (because of the contraindicated

chemicals they contain) when this is necessary for medical reasons.

- » **Health** — The quality and quantity of healthy food consumed by a nursing mother are partially depleted in the course of producing sufficient milk for her growing baby. If she does not adequately nurture herself, over time her well-being will be negatively affected.

- » **Marital relations** — There is sometimes discomfort (dryness, soreness, leaking) caused by hormones associated with breastfeeding. Some discomfort can be easily dealt with; talk to your gynecologist if you are experiencing problems.

When It's Not Working

Most women are prepared to breastfeed their newborns after birth, but some discontinue after a few days or weeks. Why would a new mother stop breastfeeding?

The main reasons include:

- » A lack of confidence regarding the quality or quantity of her milk
- » Physical difficulties in establishing breastfeeding during the days after birth (see below for details)
- » The baby experiences difficulty due to a physical problem with latching on or sucking
- » Insufficient emotional and technical support from relatives and hospital staff
- » A lack of information about the importance and advantages of breastfeeding
- » Psychological issues that present barriers to the physical act of nursing

Making the Right Choice for Your Baby — and You

> ## MOTHER'S MILK IN A BOTTLE
>
> Ideally a mother nurses her infant directly from her breast, but there are other options when necessary. She can express her milk and feed the baby from a cup, a bottle, a spoon, or a syringe. Some communities have local *gemachim* that provide mother's milk for mothers whose hormonal status cause them not to produce enough milk. Donor milk is available in certified milk banks (contact the Human Milk Banking Association of North America for the state licensed milk bank in your vicinity); however, these raise some halachic *shailos* and you should check with a *posek* before using their milk.

An important goal of this chapter is to support every mother who chooses breastfeeding and give her the tools to succeed so that she will nurse her baby joyfully and that her newborn will thrive and grow. Remember that nearly all healthy babies know instinctively how to suck without being taught and that they love to nurse!

Although rare, sometimes the decision of whether to breastfeed or formula feed is totally out of your hands.

There are some conditions that contraindicate breastfeeding:

» An infant is diagnosed with certain rare medical or nutritional conditions (such as galactosemia or phenylketonuria, rare metabolic disorders) and may require special formulas or a supplemental formula

» An infant is premature and may require supplements or expressed breastmilk until she reaches an appropriate stage of development

» Some physical or psychiatric conditions that require Mommy to take daily medication, which can preclude breastfeeding because the drug transfers to her milk and risks harm to the baby (for example, some kinds of epilepsy medication, chemotherapy agents, or radiation treatments). Most

medications are safe, but check with a doctor if you are taking medication regularly.

» If the mother suffers from an illness that can be transferred through her milk (such as tuberculosis or hepatitis)

The mother who is unable or unwilling to nurse, even if she has made a heroic but unsuccessful effort, should never consider herself a failure. Being a good mother is not determined by physical nourishment alone. On the contrary, by making the choice to formula feed because you can't breastfeed for whatever reason, you are making the best decision you can for your baby's benefit.

Chapter Seven

Mommy, I'm Hungry!

Let's Get Started!

hey call it "the magical hour": Within an hour (two hours, if you've been given pain medication), your newborn is ready to nurse. Baby's journey getting here is rough, and Mommy's warmth, her familiar heartbeat, and the taste of her sweet milk tells baby that the world she's been thrust into is good and her needs will be met.

It may take a little time to get the knack of breastfeeding, but newborns nurse frequently so you'll get lots of time to practice. Be assured that most mothers breastfeed successfully and happily, even if there were a few bumps along the way. The first time you put your baby to nurse, there will probably be someone available at the hospital who has professional experience to guide you. If you're on your own, here are some guidelines to help get you started successfully:

1. Babies are individuals right from the start, so be prepared. Even though your baby may not behave exactly according to

the script, she's still perfectly normal — she just may want to write her own script! Be sensitive to the signs your newborn gives that show she is hungry and wants to nurse — or not — and respond patiently and lovingly. Licking her lips, eating her hand, rubbing her face against whatever is near are all signs of being ready to eat. Crying is a sign of distress, and you should try to feed her before she cries.

- » If she is crying, don't rush. Just hold your newly born child close and try to comfort her with your voice and touch until she calms down. A crying baby won't latch, even if her mouth is open.
- » If she doesn't seem to respond at first, that's also fine. She might be overwhelmed by all the new sensations and unfamiliar stimuli. Give her as long as she needs to orient herself to her new surroundings, so different from the world she knew before birth! Placing her on your chest, covered with a receiving blanket, can sometimes help. She'll start bobbing her head as she chooses a side and may even latch on her own as you watch.
- » If you received pain relief during labor, such as Demerol or an epidural, some of the drugs will have passed through to your baby. It may take up to two hours after birth for the effects of the analgesia to wear off in your baby and for her to find the breast and latch on. Don't hurry her if she seems lethargic, and keep her close to watch those feeding cues.
- » Some babies are ready to nurse immediately after birth, while others need some adjustment time. When she is ready, your newborn will start rooting from side to side. She is searching for your nipple!

2. Positioning your baby comfortably: Hold your little one close so that she is facing you, her tummy against your body.

Support her shoulder at the base of her neck. Be careful not to hold the baby with her side against your body. This position forces the baby to turn her head sideways to eat, making it impossible to open her mouth wide enough to catch the nipple correctly. You may find it easier to correctly position the baby by placing a nursing pillow on your lap (see below in "Nursing Accessories," p. 175). Or try leaning back, with your hips forward, like your favorite position when you're chatting on the phone.

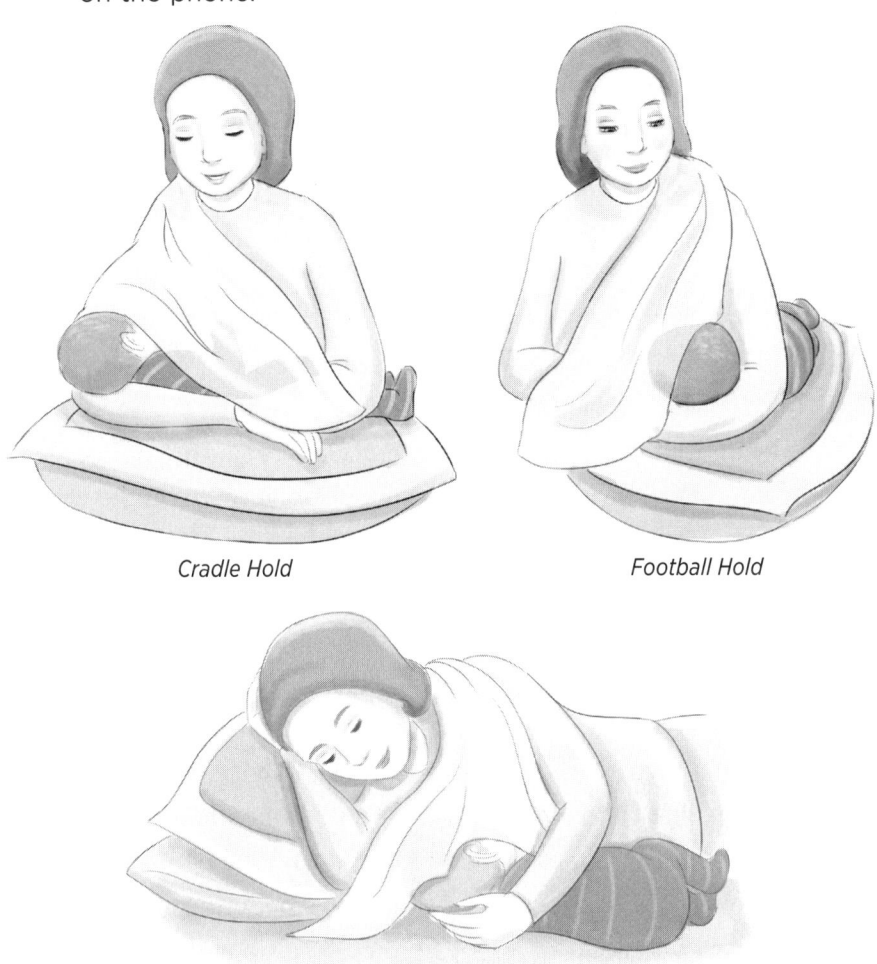

Cradle Hold *Football Hold*

Side-Lying Hold

> ## THOSE FIRST PRECIOUS MOMENTS
>
> Researchers have identified the following stages immediately after birth in healthy newborns who are placed on their mothers' abdomens immediately after birth:
>
> 1. Baby cries.
> 2. Baby relaxes.
> 3. Baby becomes alert, looks around.
> 4. Baby becomes active, moving his limbs.
> 5. Baby rests on his mother's tummy.
> 6. Baby makes crawling or sliding motions.
> 7. Baby orients himself to the nipple.
> 8. Baby sucks.
> 9. Baby sleeps.

3. The way the baby attaches to the breast is called "latching on." It's very important that her mouth opens wide enough to take in both the nipple and much of the areola (the dark area surrounding the nipple). Begin by positioning the nipple near the baby's nose so she'll "look up" to latch as you bring her toward your breast. Her chin should reach your breast first.

4. If she doesn't do so naturally, gently tilt your baby's head backward. Her chin should point toward you, and her nose should be sufficiently raised so that your breast does not block her breathing. To get this right, imagine someone eating a very thick sandwich — he must tilt his head backward so that his mouth can open wide enough to get a bite. If there is pressure against the back of the baby's head from Mommy's arm or a pillow, she will not be able to tilt her head correctly. You can keep your wrist behind the baby's neck; that will

support her head and allow your hand to snuggle baby tightly to your body.

5. Do not push your nipple into her mouth. Baby will latch on when she's ready and suck instinctively, with surprising strength.

6. The infant's lower lip and tongue connect with the breast before the top lip closes over it. The nipple should fill the upper half of the baby's mouth, against the palate, while her lips will seal her mouth onto the breast. When latched correctly, a baby's mouth appears off-center because more of the bottom of the areola is inside her mouth than the top.

7. Sometimes a baby is a little confused at the beginning. Try softly brushing her upper lip with your nipple. When she reflexively opens her mouth, gently pull her onto your breast as described above.

8. In the beginning, the baby sucks rapidly until the "letdown reflex" (when the milk is squeezed out into the milk ducts toward the nipple — see below) is activated, and only swallows after about eight sucks. During a feeding, the frequency of sucking changes according to the quantity of milk transmitted, with occasional periods of resting in between.

NURSING AFTER A CAESAREAN BIRTH

If you have a C-section, it is still possible to nurse immediately after birth. If the Caesarean was scheduled, be sure to tell the doctor before the birth that you would like to hold your baby immediately after birth. Even if the C-section was unscheduled, request that a nurse or staff member be nearby to help you hold the baby. As soon as you feel alert and fully conscious, you can start nursing! If you had anesthesia for a prolonged time before birth, both you and baby may need a little more time to get breastfeeding started, but generally in a short time you and baby will be ready.

9. It's perfectly normal to feel slightly sore during the first moments the baby begins to suck, since the nipple is very sensitive and is not yet accustomed to being nursed. Expect this discomfort to pass within a minute, replaced by a pleasant sensation as the feeding continues. After a couple of days, the nipples will have toughened up and you should not feel discomfort. (In the event that the pain and discomfort persist, consult with a lactation expert; continued soreness is very often the result of incorrect positioning, which can easily be corrected.)

    You may receive well-meaning advice to apply cream to your nipples during this stage. Refined lanolin will keep your skin supple and is not harmful to the baby, but perfumed lotions contain alcohol that dries the skin and often make the problem worse.

10. When a feeding is over, you will notice that your baby's body is relaxed. She lies quietly, her brow smooth, hands open and unclenched, arms floppy and toes curled. Often, especially at the beginning, babies fall asleep at the end of a feeding.

There is no feeling in the world like seeing your baby content and relaxed, sated and happy, after a feeding.

FEEDING POINTERS

» Baby's arms should be raised to embrace the breast, not held down across his body.

» Baby's hands should be free to naturally knead his mother's breast while nursing and not anchored by swaddling.

» Signs of incorrect latching: the mother's nipple is misshapen, cracked, bruised, or blanched from the baby's sucking. If this happens, gently detach the baby and give him another chance to latch on correctly. Your nipple reaches all the way back to the soft part of the baby's mouth. A shallow latch means the nipple will rub painfully on the ridgy part of the front of his mouth.

Yiska

It's funny, but the thing that gave me the most confidence in my ability to nurse was knowing that even though breastfeeding is the most natural thing in the world, for many women it doesn't come naturally! It can take time and effort to perfect, like learning to swim, ride a bicycle, or drive a car, but it is definitely worth it. In the beginning, you have to really concentrate, but once you get the hang of it, it becomes second nature and then you can just enjoy the ride.

Ruchy

I tried to nurse Batsheva as soon as she was born, but she just nuzzled me. The nurse insisted she should be nursing, and I felt under pressure even though in my heart I knew she was just understandably tired. One of the nurses gave me a syringe with sugar water to entice the baby to latch on. I requested a lactation consultant, but by the time she came, Batsheva was nursing beautifully and the consultant told me that I was doing fine and didn't need the sugar water.

Suri

I didn't have any problems getting started and have almost always found nursing to be soothing and relaxing. I think women who find it hard to sit still and relax have a harder time establishing breastfeeding because they don't know what to expect.

Miri

I remember being surprised right after birth that it didn't just go automatically, like it seemed to for my older sisters. A nurse helped me the first time or two, and from then on I was careful that the baby should get more of the bottom of the areola in her mouth as well as the nipple. There were no problems after that.

Bracha

Women who don't have difficulties should realize that this is less about what they're doing right and more that they've been granted an extra-special dose of siyatta d'Shmaya!

BE PREPARED

Prepare a bag or "nursing station" containing all the accessories you'll want close at hand while nursing:

- » *Refillable water bottle with a pop-top that you can open easily with one hand*
- » *High-energy snack*
- » *Newspaper, magazine, or book if you like to read*
- » *Cell phone (though don't spend all of this precious bonding time schmoozing with friends!)*
- » *Cloth diaper and/or a wipe to protect your clothes if baby spits up*

The First Days After Birth

Most newborns are extremely sleepy during the first twenty-four hours of life. Some sleep so deeply that they don't even wake for feedings, while others may start to nurse and promptly fall asleep again a few seconds later. In that case, if baby is still latched on, compress your breast to express colostrum into his mouth. If he starts sucking again, you'll know he wasn't done. If he's full, he'll unlatch himself.

If you are rooming-in, you will notice when your baby is ready to nurse. Visible hunger signs include sucking in his sleep, licking his fingers, bringing his fists to his mouth, rooting, or smacking his lips and extending the tip of his tongue. The final feeding signal is crying, but by then the baby is upset, and his immature system becomes so disorganized it can be difficult for him to

NURSING ACCESSORIES

Although breastfeeding is convenient and requires no equipment, there are a few things you may want to have to maximize your comfort and maintain modesty:

» **Nursing bra** — A quality nursing bra is essential, and it's a good idea to have at least one to bring with you to the hospital to wear as you begin nursing. These bras are designed to allow for comfortable nursing without removing the bra (with flaps that are fastened with hooks or Velcro) and are made to provide extra support. Look for a bra that is soft and flexible, with cups that open wide enough for your baby to nurse comfortably, with clasps that you can open with one hand (the other will probably be holding your baby). Make sure to get properly fitted since a tight bra can cause problems with breastfeeding, including mastitis and blocked ducts (see pp. 202-204). If you're buying a nursing bra before birth, wait until the last weeks of pregnancy, as your size may change after you give birth and nursing becomes well established. Or buy one with stretchable, adjustable cups and bands.

» **Nursing pillow** — This U-shaped pillow provides extra support to hold the baby's weight and keep the baby's body steady. This is especially helpful in those early days after birth while your body is still recovering and it may be uncomfortable to hold the baby against your stomach.

» **Nursing shawls** — From chic pashminas to handmade nursing aprons, these can be spread over your clothing and the baby, to keep things modest. Cover-ups designed for the nursing mother usually have a Velcro closure or a buckle at the neck, allowing you to see your baby while breastfeeding and adjust the airflow. Look for 100 percent cotton, and make sure the baby has plenty of ventilation under there!

» There are nursing shirts, dresses, and robes available that have strategically placed zippers or extra folds of fabric, allowing you to nurse while maintaining modesty. Some mothers layer their shirts, pulling one up and the other down to keep their sides and tummies covered while nursing.

BUBBY TIP

LEAKING

Especially in the first weeks of nursing, you may find yourself "leaking" milk from your breasts. To avoid embarrassing wet spots on your blouse, insert disposable or reusable breast-shaped nursing pads in your bra. Keep a supply of pads in your diaper bag, and change whenever they get moist.

Wet spots are less noticeable on dark-colored or print blouses — forget the beautiful white silk until your nursing is properly established.

And between leaks, baby saliva, and all the other moist things that babies tend to spit up on their doting mommies, you probably want to stay away from dry clean-only clothing until your baby has grown up a little!

nurse properly. Try to begin breastfeeding as soon as the baby indicates hunger instead of waiting until he is in distress. Generally, newborns like to feed at least every two or two and a half hours. Some nurse more often, so follow these cues to ensure your milk production grows with your growing baby. Keep note of how much time has elapsed between feedings to have an idea about when to expect these hunger signs to surface.

If the baby is in the hospital nursery, you may be expected to nurse him at scheduled times, which are not necessarily the times when he is hungry. Ask the staff to bring the baby when he shows hunger cues, and remember, soon you'll be discharged, and then you can feed your baby by either schedule or demand as you wish. And keep in mind: breastfeeding "early and often" establishes milk production!

Many first-time mothers worry about whether or not they have any milk at all. This thought brings them to wonder whether feeding with a bottle might not be better after all. A bottle is transparent and you can measure how much the baby eats, whereas with breastfeeding, especially at first, it's not immediately apparent that the baby is getting any nourishment. Don't worry! By late pregnancy the milk glands have already produced a small quantity of a golden liquid known as "colostrum," which happens to be exactly perfect for your newborn baby in both quantity and quality, so there's no need to worry if you "have milk."

Colostrum is measured in teaspoons, not in ounces. The small quantity is more than made up in quality. At birth, a baby's stomach is only about the size of a marble, and it doesn't stretch easily. If a newborn is fed more than five to seven milliliters of milk (about a teaspoon's worth), it will be spit up. By the third day, the baby's stomach capacity increases to just under an ounce, and by the age of one week it has grown to the size of a ping-pong ball.

WHAT IS COLOSTRUM?

Colostrum is also known as "newborn milk" or "first milk." It is yellow in color, or slightly orange, with a consistency that is thicker and stickier than the mature breastmilk that will appear a few days after birth.

Colostrum is higher in protein and lower in carbohydrates and lactose than mature milk. It also includes concentrated immune factors that protect the baby from infection until his own immune system develops.

In the womb, the nutritional needs of a fetus are met effortlessly, flowing directly into his bloodstream. After birth, food must be processed by the baby. There is no formula in existence that is better for a newborn than colostrum, designed by the Creator to be effortlessly digested and easily excreted afterward (especially important in helping baby excrete the sticky meconium that accumulated in his bowels before birth).

The best way to nourish infants and provide all their nutritional needs in the first weeks is with frequent, small feedings.

On the second day of life, most babies are more alert and want to nurse very often. It can seem to the mother that her baby is hungry, and she doesn't feel that her breasts are producing a significant amount of milk. Not to worry: The newborn's demand for long feedings at close intervals is the biological signal to your milk-making cells to increase milk production. On around the third day after birth, mother's milk will begin to replace the colostrum. Mommy goes to sleep as usual on the night of the second or third day, and wakes up full to bursting with milk early the next morning!

Day 3 is often an "all-day café," now that there is more milk after Day 2's practice time. Ironically, now that there is obviously lots of milk available, on the third day of life babies nurse less frequently than before. They often fall deeply asleep after only five or ten minutes of feeding and cannot be awakened to continue nursing. The reason behind this is that the milk literally pours into his mouth (you can hear him gulping to keep up with it!), and he quickly becomes satiated.

If you're still not sure whether the baby is getting enough to eat, watch his diapers. If he's had at least one bowel movement on day 1, two on day 2, and three on day 3, you'll know he's eating well.

Some little ones find the beginning hard. For whatever reason, they don't always latch on to the nipple correctly

YAWN!

During the first six weeks, when the baby sleeps, you sleep!

BUBBY TIP

HOW LONG BEFORE BABY IS FULL?

Watch your baby's hands as she nurses. Her little hands act as a "gas gauge." As her tummy fills her fists relax and her fingers spread open. She'll unlatch from the nipple when she's finished nursing that breast.

For mothers who like numbers, most babies are satisfied in about 15-20 minutes.

during the first few days and you and baby may become frustrated. Although it feels counterintuitive, try to relax and have confidence in your baby and her abilities. See it as a learning process; if latching is difficult or painful, you don't have to solve all the problems on your own. Lactation consultants and nurses are available in the hospital maternity ward and in the community when you return home. You can also get suggestions from experienced mothers you meet in the nursing lounge at the hospital or the *kimpeturin* home.

New mothers are commonly advised to nurse the baby from both breasts at every feeding. This is an effective way to stimulate milk production when necessary, but it can result in painful engorgement when done unnecessarily (for more on engorgement, see p. 201). Once a sufficient supply of milk is established, some women prefer switching breasts at each feeding, so that each side is emptied about once in six hours instead of both being emptied every three hours. The advantage of this is that there is always 50 percent extra for those times baby wants more. You won't find yourself empty after a feeding with a fussy, hungry baby.

REMEMBERING WHICH SIDE YOU NURSED FROM

Some mothers who choose to give one breast for each feeding fasten a safety pin, hair clip, or ribbon on the bra strap of the side the baby nursed from last to help remember which side to start with at the next feeding.

The Hormones of Breastfeeding

All the elements of Hashem's world work perfectly in concert to fill their purpose. This is certainly true of breastfeeding. A woman's body responds to nursing by releasing two hormones: oxytocin and prolactin.

Oxytocin is directly related to the bonding experience. Shortly after the baby begins to suck, you will suddenly feel an almost physical surge of love for your baby. At the same time, oxytocin causes the milk-making cells in the breast to contract and release milk into your milk ducts. This is known as the "letdown reflex" and is an important part of breastfeeding. Since exhaustion and stress are known to inhibit the letdown reflex, try to be as relaxed and get as comfortable as possible when nursing.

There are two types of breastmilk: the foremilk, which appears watery, tastes very sweet, and is bluish in color; and the white hind milk, which has a thicker texture and higher content of fat. Oxytocin causes the milk glands to contract simultaneously, causing the hind milk to mix with the foremilk, creating the most nutritious combination possible for your baby's needs.

If a baby appears hungry again an hour after eating, it's possible that he stopped nursing before he had a chance to get the hind milk. A diet of foremilk, with its high sugar content, causes infants to gain weight quickly, but without the rich cream from the hind milk, he won't feel satisfied and will cry from hunger soon after a feeding. Nursing from only one breast at a time for alternate feedings helps stimulate the letdown reflex to mix the thick hind milk with the foremilk and leave the baby satiated after eating.

On the other hand, recent research regarding the interplay between foremilk and hind milk and its impact on breastfeeding seems to indicate that while the fat content of the milk increases with the time spent breastfeeding, this increase is gradual and, when babies nurse frequently, some of the fat can remain in the foremilk of the next feeding. Babies who nurse for shorter times but more frequently seem to get the same amount of fat as those who breastfeed for longer periods of time. And frequent feeding from birth helps your body know how much milk to produce, since milk production is a "supply based on demand" — the more you nurse the more you have.

In the first days after birth, oxytocin has an additional role besides contracting the milk glands — it also causes the uterine muscles to contract to enable the uterus to shrink back to a normal size after childbirth.

BONDING TIME!

Try not to watch the clock while nursing. This is your special bonding time together, and you should be relaxed. Listen to music, read, or just close your eyes and enjoy this time with your precious bundle.

Shortly after delivery, these contractions, called "afterbirth contractions," are sometimes painful. During the first week or so, expect to feel contractions during nursing, along with temporarily increased bleeding. With your doctor's permission, take Advil or Tylenol every few hours until this stage passes. If afterbirth pains are especially painful, limit nursing to frequent short feeds until this uncomfortable stage passes.

Establishing Your Milk Supply

A mother's worry that her child is getting enough to eat starts from the very beginning (and never really stops...). When the milk comes in, three or four days after birth, it is common for engorgement to set in, where you feel uncomfortably full (see p. 201 below for treating engorgement). But then, several days later, it feels like you're completely empty and have nothing left to give.

Rest assured that you will produce enough milk for your baby's needs even as he grows in the coming months. Even though adjustments may have to be made in the beginning, once nursing is well established most mothers have no difficulty nourishing their babies solely on breastmilk for at least the first-half year of life.

Feeding your baby when he shows hunger cues is a very effective way of ensuring enough milk, especially in the first few weeks. Every mother has a different storage capacity — the length of time her breasts can be full before her body begins making less milk. A mother with a 90-minute storage capacity needs to nurse more often than one with a four-hour capacity, but both babies will get the same amount of milk over a 24-hour period. But if the "90-minute-mom" makes baby wait until it's "time to nurse," her body will produce less milk, not more.

How Long to Nurse

The rule is, the more often your baby nurses, the more milk is produced. Anytime it seems as if baby is not satisfied after a

feeding, the problem is naturally remedied by giving him more opportunities to nurse and longer feeds.

Taking into consideration the initial discomfort a new mother may feel from the afterbirth pains or sensitive nipples, give your little one as much practice as possible during the first days after birth. This will help him master the art of latching on and successfully nursing from the very beginning. When a baby is able to extract milk efficiently, feedings eventually take only around ten minutes. If the baby wants to nurse for longer than that, it may be the sign of a normal growth spurt, requiring production of more milk. It could also be a legitimate need for comfort and closeness.

Since most of the milk is consumed in the first ten minutes, be realistic about how long a feeding lasts. The general rule is that if you are both enjoying it, don't watch the clock. After about ten minutes, whenever one of you is ready to stop then it's time to stop. If you still feel uncomfortably full after a feeding, prevent engorgement by keeping to a reasonable length of nursing time (from twenty minutes to half an hour).

If Mommy is tired, not feeling well, or has important things to do, it is not always necessary to continue a feed just because the baby is still sucking and doesn't want to stop. He'll probably be just as happy with a pacifier. A baby who falls asleep while nursing is not really eating even if he continues to suck and should be taken off the breast to prevent sore or cracked nipples.

How Much Should Baby Eat?

The daily recommendation by doctors for a normal, healthy baby is two to three ounces of mother's milk or formula for every pound of body weight, with an upper limit of thirty-two ounces per day. A baby fed by bottle will drink 2–4 ounces if he is sitting up and has the bottle parallel to the floor. This "paced feeding" method allows baby to suck when he wants to eat, not just to swallow quickly, so he will recognize he is full even if the bottle isn't empty.

During the first three weeks, babies usually want to eat every two and a half to three hours. Using the above formula, a newborn weighing seven pounds should eat 14 to 21 ounces a day, or between 1.75 and 2.6 ounces of milk at each feeding. Between three months and half a year, the typical baby grows to about fourteen pounds and eats six times a day. By this time many babies begin sleeping longer between night feedings, so even though the average feeding has gone up to 4 to 6 ounces of milk or formula, the baby is naturally hungrier at the feedings before bedtime and upon waking in the morning.

Solid food generally is offered at about the age of six months (when baby weighs fourteen to sixteen pounds) (see Chapter 15, p. 313). By this time a baby will be taking in five to six ounces of milk five times a day. During this first year, solid food is only meant to complement the baby's main source of nourishment: breastmilk or formula.

Scheduling Feeds

When it comes to feeding schedules, you may hear contradictory advice:

> "Nurse on demand for as long and as often as the baby wishes."

> "Babies need to wait four hours between feedings."

> "The baby should eat no more than every three hours."

> "Your baby will never learn to sleep through the night if you don't put her on a schedule."

The truth is, this is not a simple mathematical equation because growing infants need different amounts of milk according to their stages of growth, and the "storage capacity" of mothers differ. Since breastmilk is perfectly designed for the needs of the baby, it is digested very easily and nursing infants usually need to eat at shorter intervals than formula-fed babies. Newborns normally nurse between ten to twelve times a day (at least every two hours), as opposed to bottle-fed babies who usually eat larger volumes on a regular three- or four-hour schedule.

During the first weeks babies grow so much! Most of your time is spent feeding your baby to power that growth. Each day is a little different as you gain experience and baby grows. In the beginning, her needs will determine the routine but around the end of her first month she will probably settle into a fairly predictable routine of eight to twelve feedings a day. To help recognize the emerging pattern, some mothers keep a notebook and pen beside a nursing chair and record the time and duration of each feeding. Everything becomes much easier as you master the technical details and become accustomed to the changes in your life.

Hannah

If you're a spontaneous type of person, can be flexible, and don't have problems with getting everything done on time, feed your baby on demand. It doesn't work for everyone, but undoubtedly that's the best piece of advice I got.

Naomi

The first three weeks my baby cried so much until finally I was desperate enough to call a lactation consultant. She told me, "There is no such thing as overfeeding a breastfed baby. Only formula can be overfed. Don't drive yourself and your baby crazy. Give him when he wants and you'll both be happier!" After that, everything worked out so well that I continued nursing for eighteen months, on demand, and never had another problem! Actually, he learned to eat on a decent schedule all by himself.

Increasing Your Milk Supply

Many inexperienced mothers have the perception that they do not have enough milk when they actually do. Weighing the baby before and after a feeding (on a scale accurate to 2 grams) can help ascertain whether there is really a problem.

Typically, new mothers believe that a fussy baby is hungry and a quiet baby is satisfied, but this is not always the case. A baby who is gaining weight and producing dirty diapers regularly is doing well even if he cries. On the other hand, a baby who is not getting enough to eat will conserve his energy by crying less and sleeping more. Dry diapers between feedings are a signal that the baby's fluid intake is not sufficient.

Low milk intake causes lowered energy, resulting in less vigorous sucking. Mommy's body responds to the diminished stimulation by producing less milk. A baby who is not getting sufficient milk does not gain and may even lose weight. This vicious cycle must be interrupted as soon as possible under medical supervision.

To increase your milk supply, begin by nursing more often, or pumping and hand-expressing your milk. (See Chapter 10, p. 214 for how to express and pump.) If a mother pumps less than baby needs, depending on his age, she should supplement with donor milk or formula until she is able to produce sufficient milk. She can contact a lactation consultant for individual support and guidance.

Adequate production of milk depends on several factors, including the "storage capacity" you are naturally endowed with (which has nothing to do with your bra size!). According to the ability of your body to store accumulated milk, you have more or less milk at any given time than your friends or sisters. That means baby will feed more or less often than anyone else's baby — so don't compare! Following his cues will ensure that he is eating enough.

To help your body produce milk efficiently, be sure to drink a sufficient quantity of liquids, six to twelve glasses a day. Preferably half of that should be water and half should be juice or milk. Make sure to get enough rest. Support from your spouse or family is critical, because an exhausted or tense mother can produce less milk.

Some natural practitioners recommend herbal remedies to increase milk production. Each woman's body responds differently so that what is helpful for one mother may not be equally effective for another. Avoid preparations labeled "not for nursing mothers" and be aware of possible side effects. It is always advisable to ask for your doctor's opinion before using any medication (including natural remedies) when nursing. Herbal teas may be used, either hot, iced, or mixed with apple juice.

The following are available in most health food stores:

- Lactation consultants often recommend Motherlove More Milk tincture. Use as directed on the bottle. It's better to take it with a glass of water because of the bitter taste.

- Ground fenugreek seeds are an ancient remedy for boosting milk supply. These are available in capsules or as tea. They are most effective when taken in combination with the herb called blessed thistle, but avoid fenugreek-thyme combinations. If there is no improvement within twenty-four hours, it's unlikely to be effective. Fenugreek has a distinct smell: When the dosage is sufficient, this scent is discernible on your skin. Fenugreek is contraindicated when thyroid or blood pressure are preexisting conditions.

- Mother's Milk tea is mildly effective at increasing milk supply. It tastes like licorice and contains honey and fenugreek. It's more effective at maintaining lactation than increasing milk supply.

- Some women find eating alfalfa sprouts increases milk supply (also available in capsules). Be aware of their laxative effect.

- » Brewer's yeast contains hops as well, but it's also known for causing weight gain.
- » Natural food options that increase lactation supply include oatmeal and moderate consumption of ginger. However, avoid sage and peppermint, which may decrease milk in some women.
- » Some women have been helped by the following herbs: spirulina, goat's rue, raspberry leaf, fennel, stinging nettle, and shatavari.
- » There are prescription medications known to increase breastmilk. These may be used only under medical supervision.

Nursing and Diet (and Dieting)

Perhaps you've heard that everything you eat passes through your milk to the baby. Or you've heard the horror stories of babies crying unendingly because a mother ate food that's too spicy. You may be wondering if you have to eat a special diet while you're nursing (just when you are no longer pregnant and thought you could eat whatever you want!).

Is it true? What should a nursing mother be eating — and what foods should she avoid?

Breastmilk, formed from nutrients in maternal blood, is essentially the same in all human mothers. This means that there are generally no *specific* foods that must be avoided when nursing. Current research says that changing diet does not generally change the quality of the milk, though it may change the flavor somewhat.

If you notice that the baby is colicky or fidgety and find that removing certain foods from your diet alleviates the distress, follow your instincts. (If there are known allergies in the family, consult with your doctor about avoiding those foods.) Milk quality remains fairly consistent no matter what or how much food you

eat in a day, as long as there is adequate consumption of carbohydrates, fats, and proteins. For the most part, a woman who is breastfeeding can continue eating any food she enjoys (some exceptions listed below), although beverages with caffeine or alcohol should be drunk in moderation.

Nutritional Needs

Nursing mothers need more energy — and that generally means burning more calories — than when they weren't breastfeeding. The amount of extra caloric intake varies with a woman's level of activity and amount of extra body fat, but the consensus seems to be that breastfeeding uses close to five hundred calories a day. More important is to make those calories count by eating right.

With a little attention, a nursing mother can follow the recommendation of most dieticians to decrease fat intake to about a quarter (or less) of their total caloric intake and increase proteins from forty-six to between sixty-five and seventy grams daily during the first six months (see list of protein-rich foods below). Be sure that your diet includes calcium-rich foods (see list of calcium-rich foods on next page), as well as fruits, vegetables, and whole grains. There is no evidence that a woman who is breastfeeding needs additional vitamin supplements, but if you feel weak or drained, try taking prenatal vitamins for a boost.

PROTEIN-RICH FOODS

- » Lean beef and veal
- » Turkey
- » Chicken
- » Cheese
- » Nuts and seeds
- » Eggs
- » Legumes
- » Milk and milk products
- » Tofu
- » Fish

> **RICH SOURCES OF CALCIUM**
>
> Though the following foods are usually good sources of calcium, always check the labels:
>
> - Dairy products, such as milk, yogurt, and cheeses
> - Soybean-based products, including fortified soy milk and tofu
> - Sardines and salmon (don't discard the bones of the fish, they are rich in calcium and highly beneficial)
> - Dark, leafy vegetables, such as kale, turnip greens, romaine lettuce, celery, cabbage, brussels sprouts, green beans, and asparagus
> - Fortified cereals such as oatmeal and Cheerios
> - Fortified fruit juices
> - Enriched grain products
> - Legumes such as black-eyed peas and beans (black, pinto, kidney, white)
> - Figs
> - Techina and sesame seeds
> - Almonds
> - Oranges (orange juice, too)
> - Blackstrap molasses

Staying Hydrated

It's important for a nursing mother to remain hydrated. Most nursing mothers naturally drink enough to alleviate their thirst (around twelve cups of water, juice, or milk each day; soup counts, too), but since summer temperatures and physical activity deplete the body's store of water it is important to be sensitive to your body's signals of thirst.

A common sign of inadequate hydration is constipation and urine that is darker than usual and has a strong smell. Keep a bottle of water beside you, especially while nursing, and sip from

time to time; it's not necessary to force yourself to drink if you're not thirsty.

Research shows that extra fluid intake does not increase milk production, and restriction of liquids is not effective in reducing engorgement (see p. 201 for information on engorgement). Take into consideration that fluids are also absorbed from many foods such as soups, cooked fruit, juices, and other beverages. Although you probably don't need the sugar and caffeine provided by cola drinks and coffee, they do contribute to your fluid intake.

Food Sensitivities

Most nursing mothers can continue eating their normal, healthy foods as usual. Occasionally mothers report that their babies react to particular foods they have eaten by excessive crying or with uncomfortable rashes in the diaper area. Individual babies may show sensitivity (cow's milk is a common one), but this does not automatically mean future siblings will react in the same way. In the case of a family history regarding a particular allergy, talk to your doctor about avoiding that food for the time being.

Strong flavors pass into breastmilk, but there is no medical reason to avoid them. Unborn babies swallow amniotic fluid, which carries the taste of the food in the mother's diet, so these flavors are already familiar to the baby. Enjoy! However, if you've never eaten a spicy dish that a considerate friend brought you after birth, you may want to save it for the freezer (or give it to your hungry husband!) for the first two weeks after birth.

Nursing mothers are sometimes warned against eating foods known to cause gas, such as beans, cabbage, broccoli, cauliflower, or carbonated drinks. However, although these types of foods release gas during digestion, and the mother herself may experience discomfort, it does not pass into her blood and is not usually the explanation for why her baby may be colicky. Nevertheless, if you find that restricting or eliminating any of these from your diet seems to alleviate your gassy symptoms and the baby is calmer,

> **FOODS SOMETIMES IMPLICATED IN INFANT REACTIONS (SUCH AS RASHES OR COLIC)**
>
> » Dairy products from cow's milk — this is the most common offender.
> » Citrus
> » Soy
> » Eggs
> » Chocolate
> » Wheat
> » Fish
> » Iron supplements (including multivitamins)
> » Beans
> » Raw garlic or onions
> » Melons
> » Leeks
> » Combinations of the above

do so. You don't *need* any of these foods to maintain maximum health, and not eating them for the duration of nursing will not be detrimental to your health and may very well be beneficial to the well-being of your baby.

Hinda

After my milk came in, my baby seemed to be crying a lot for no apparent reason. My mother-in-law suggested that it might be a reaction to something I ate, and I thought she might be right, so I began to use trial and error to identify the specific food causing my baby to cry. For two days I restricted my meals to safe foods like chicken, meat, bread, pasta, and rice. The baby seemed much more comfortable. After that I kept a food diary and added additional types of food to my meals one at a time. It didn't take long to identify that he couldn't tolerate oranges, tomatoes, and chocolate. I just didn't eat those foods anymore until he was weaned. No matter how much I loved those foods, it was not worth dealing with a screaming, suffering baby.

Dieting

After nine months of watching the numbers on the scales going up, it's understandable if you want to start a weight-loss program the moment you come home from the hospital. But don't even think of seriously restricting calories before breastfeeding is well established (after about three to four weeks when you have a plentiful supply and feel comfortable with nursing your baby). By nursing your baby you are burning close to five hundred calories each day, so if you're eating healthy, well-balanced meals, you're already on a weight-loss program! Experience shows that frequent feedings plus continuing to nurse after the baby is six months old results in natural maternal loss of weight in some mothers. (Occasionally a woman's metabolism seems programmed to maintain weight during nursing; in this case, the extra weight could be lost after weaning.)

Nursing is not a license for unlimited food consumption; eating over 2,200 calories a day will naturally result in weight gain instead of loss, especially if a number of those calories consist of sugary or high-fat foods. If increased hunger becomes a problem, plan three smaller regular meals each day and add healthy snacks such as fruit or raw vegetables in between. Nonessential caloric-laden foods such as pastries, sweets, fried foods, and sugary soft drinks should be cut out of the daily diet if you are trying to keep your weight down.

If you decide that you must lose weight after two months of nursing, don't be tempted by a quick-fix diet. Sudden drops in calories negatively affects the milk supply, as does dehydration from fasting, vomiting, medication, or heat exposure. Losing weight should be done gradually — one to two pounds a week (or six pounds a month). Reasonable dieting should not affect the quality of the milk, but eat at least 1,500 calories daily. Your body uses its own reserves to ensure nutritionally complete milk, so severely restricting calories is harmful to your health.

As for exercise, moderate workouts, preferably resistance exercises, burn fat while preserving muscles. When weather permits, twenty to forty minutes of daily walking sessions improves both your mood and physical well-being. And baby will love the outing!

Weight Watchers and Body for Life have programs designed specifically for nursing mothers. But avoid natural weight-loss

NURSING ON THE GO

Just because you're breastfeeding doesn't mean you can't leave home. If you're traveling and the baby gets hungry, first look for a nursing area. Many malls, airports, and restaurants have them.

Some traveling moms spread a large cloth diaper or receiving blanket over themselves to nurse discreetly, but there's also a huge variety of nursing covers, in many terrific patterns. Some mothers like an "apron-like nursing cover," which ties or buckles around the neck like, you guessed it, an apron, with a large cloth panel in front to keep things modest. Others wear layers, so they can pull up the top layer and pull down the bottom layer, with baby's head covering up everything that would show. Try nursing in front of a mirror at home; you'll be surprised by the way baby keeps you covered!

Others love the "nursing cape," which is like a poncho with a hole in it for your head. The cape covers Mommy in front and in back, so she doesn't have to worry about her shirt riding up, and it stays in place when her bubbly, bouncy baby decides to kick to show how much he's enjoying dinner! Nursing covers roll up and fit nicely in a large purse or your diaper bag. Have a good trip!

products containing ephedra (an herbal stimulant, also known as ma huang). The FDA has issued general warnings that ephedra increases the risks of serious side effects. (Energy drinks often contain ephedra.) In fact, natural weight-loss products often contain stimulants and herbal additives to repress appetite, energize, and increase metabolic rate that are untested and possibly unsafe. If you want more help or guidance, contact a nutritionist.

Chapter Eight

Common Nursing Problems

The first few days, breastfeeding may feel uncomfortable or unusual, as your body gets used to the new sensation: a slight tugging as baby drinks. Pain is not a normal side effect of breastfeeding; if you're in pain, speak to a lactation consultant, La Leche leader, or your doctor. It may be as simple to resolve as adjusting your baby's position, or you may be experiencing the onset of an infection, which will require antibiotics. Here are some common problems to be aware of and what you can do about them should they occur:

Failure to Latch On

Sometimes a baby has difficulty latching on. There could be several reasons for this. For one, if a mother's nipple is relatively large, it may be necessary to sandwich the breast between the thumb and fingers in order to help the baby catch it effectively; take care not to hold your fingers too close to the nipple, so baby's bottom jaw has room to open wide.

Sometimes a nipple is so small, flat, or even sunken into the surrounding areola, that a newborn has trouble finding where to suck. Rubbing the nipple gently between the thumb and forefinger before a feeding will usually cause it to stiffen enough for the baby to find it and latch on. A technique called Reverse Pressure Softening can also help. Press your fingers on your areola, on either side of the nipple, lean back and press. Hold your fingers there for 30–50 seconds and then rotate to another position. Repeat until your areola feels soft, like your lips, and not hard like your chin.

Inadequate Weight Gain

Newborns normally lose 7 to 10 percent of their weight between birth and your discharge from the hospital. Most of this weight loss is the excretion of surplus amniotic fluid or IV fluid received before birth. Exclusively breastfed babies often gain rapidly in the first three months (around an ounce daily) and then more slowly (around half an ounce a day from four months — see Appendix III, pp. 406-409, for tables on normal infant weight during the first year).

When a nursing baby loses weight or isn't gaining sufficiently, it may indicate a problem and a professional should be consulted. (Be sure your pediatrician uses the growth charts from the World Health Organization, which is recommended by the CDC and AAP.)

In most cases, changing positions during feedings or increasing milk production will resolve the issue. If the problem persists, it may be necessary to express breastmilk and feed the baby with a bottle, or even supplement with formula, until the baby has achieved satisfactory weight gain. At the same time, the mother may have to take measures to increase milk production (see above).

Flat or Inverted Nipples

The breast nipple doesn't have to resemble the shape of a bottle nipple in order for the baby to be able to nurse. A baby can nurse even if his mother has flat or inverted nipples.

Naturally flat nipples appear level with the surrounding tissue before birth; inverted nipples appear drawn back into the breast tissue. If the baby is able to compress the areola and draw the nipple into his mouth, it will be possible to nurse successfully in spite of flat nipples.

Flat nipples may be just a temporary condition. Sometimes a nipple may only seem flat because of breast engorgement; the mother should express enough milk to relieve the engorgement, making the area soft enough for the baby to draw the nipple into his mouth. Or flat nipples may be the result of using muscle relaxants during labor or edema brought about by excess fluids, and will pass after a few hours. Eating watermelon or grapes and massaging the breast toward the lymph nodes in the armpit will help remove the fluid more quickly.

If the mother has inverted nipples, they often change to an everted shape over time as a result of breastfeeding. The temporary use of a pump before nursing, or a nipple shield to change the nipple's shape, may help the mother and infant establish successful nursing, though long-term use may have negative ramifications for the milk supply. Silicone nursing shells worn inside the bra between feedings can help draw out inverted nipples.

Since infants who suck willingly at inverted nipples without drawing them out may be receiving inadequate nutrition (as evidenced by too few dirty diapers), a lactation consultant should be consulted at the earliest stage. These babies should be observed and weighed at regular intervals to avoid caloric deprivation (count 3+ dirty diapers daily from day 3 on to assess whether the baby is getting sufficient milk). One sign that a new baby is not getting enough nutrition, besides low weight gain, is apathy

— not waking to feed at least every two to three hours. Expressing milk with a pump to complement breastfeeding may be recommended if the baby is not receiving an adequate amount of milk at feedings.

Leaking

There are times, especially in the first weeks, when so much milk is produced that it leaks out and Mommy's clothes will get wet. You can purchase pad inserts to absorb this leakage, but avoid using these if you have a cracked nipple, and change the pads when wet — germs love warm, moist, and dark places and the nipple may become infected.

An alternative to nursing pads is to use double silicone collection kits, which fit over the breast; excess milk drips into them, keeping nipples clean and dry. Always discard this "drip milk" and wash the shield well between feedings.

Nipple Pain

In the beginning, there may be some discomfort during the first minute or two of a feeding because you aren't used to such pressure in this sensitive place. The sensation doesn't last long and usually ceases entirely after a few days.

If pain is more severe at the beginning and then subsides, watch carefully as the baby continues nursing to see if he changes his head or body position to get a better latch, then make sure the baby latches on correctly at the beginning of the next feeding. If he doesn't open his mouth wide enough to take in both the nipple and also the areola, it will hurt! The baby may even bite due to incorrect positioning. If this was the source of the problem, the pain will be resolved in the correct position. Many mothers find that leaning back comfortably with baby, tummy to tummy and nose to nipple, encourages baby's nursing instincts. He'll have room to drop his jaw to open wide, and gravity brings him deeply into your breast.

Another source of the discomfort may be caused when the mother unintentionally applies pressure to the back of the baby's head with her fingers, hand, or arm, causing him to pull away and stretch the nipple. Imagine how uncomfortable you'd be if someone pushed your head toward your fork, and you'll remember to support baby's neck and not his head.

If you feel pain during the entire feeding, this can be the result of a short frenulum of the upper lip, or a tongue tie, since a baby must be able to extend, elevate, and cup her tongue to suck properly. If this is the case, consult with your doctor or a lactation consultant. (See p. 62 for more information on a tongue-tie.)

Besides making sure that the baby is positioned properly, offer to feed your baby before he reaches the point of distress and begins to cry. Early signs that baby is ready to eat include rooting, sucking his tongue, smacking his lips, and putting fingers in his mouth (see also p. 174 above). If you nurse before the baby is starving, he will nurse more gently and you'll avoid nipple pain.

Sometimes there is no pain during the days the baby is receiving colostrum, but then the mother begins to feel pain and discomfort when the milk becomes abundant. This may be caused by the baby clamping down on the nipple to slow the rapid flow of milk into his mouth. The baby may also spit up large quantities of milk or act fussy after feedings. This problem can be remedied by assuming a posture that enables the baby to move his head freely when the milk is coming too fast for him to handle. Semi-reclining in an armchair or couch (think about how you sit on the phone for an hour!) or lying on your back with the baby's body tummy down supported on your tummy will let gravity keep the milk from flowing uncontrollably into the baby's mouth. He'll be above your breast, so he can collect milk in the front of his mouth and swallow a few times, instead of being flooded with a fast gush of milk right into his throat.

HELP FOR CRACKED NIPPLES

You don't need to buy expensive creams or ointments for sore nipples. After a feeding, express enough milk to smear it over the sore nipple and let it dry in the air for a minute or so before closing your bra again.

If your nipples are cracked, try holding your baby in different positions (for example, if you usually hold him against your stomach, try nursing him while he is lying along your side, using pillows to support him, with his feet behind you) until your nipple heals. This way the main pressure of his jaws will not be exactly on the same area where you are experiencing the most pain.

Olive oil can prevent and heal cracked nipples; some women even begin applying it in the ninth month to condition their nipples in advance.

If you find that your nipples are becoming sore and chafed, apply 100 percent refined lanolin oil, olive oil, or coconut oil between feedings. This can be very effective in preventing the dryness that causes nipple pain. You'll also have to fix baby's latch or they won't heal.

If the sources of nipple pain are not resolved right away, sometimes they lead to cracked or bleeding nipples.

Cracked or Bleeding Nipples

Some babies suck so strongly, or latch so shallowly, that the sensitive skin of the nipple can become injured. This should be

addressed right away, before the nipples become cracked or even bleed. Try to feed the baby before he is so hungry that he is screaming in distress. Change the point of pressure exerted by his jaws by rotating the baby's head to another position (for example, hold the infant across your stomach lengthwise, or against your side with his feet behind you) and apply refined lanolin cream between feedings to keep your nipples soft and pliable (do not wash nipples with soap because this dries out the natural lubricant secreted by the areola).

Cracked nipples can be very painful and if not treated may even lead to an infection, but you don't have to worry that swallowing some of the mother's blood from the cracked nipple will harm the baby.

To prevent cracked nipples, don't leave the baby on the breast after she falls asleep because she will inadvertently "chew" in her sleep and this may injure delicate tissue.

If the nipples do become cracked, avoid using absorbent pads to protect leakage, or make sure to change the pads as soon as they become wet, to avoid an infection.

Engorgement

In the first days, the supply of milk often goes from one extreme to the other. At first you may feel that there is not enough for one newborn, and then, when the milk comes in, you feel like you have more than enough for twins! Often mothers experience engorgement, a painful sensation of excessive fullness. This usually happens on days three to five, and is worse if the milk isn't removed often enough with efficient, frequent feedings.

Engorgement usually happens between two to four days after childbirth (later if the baby was delivered by Caesarean section). But it doesn't last long; as you both settle into a rhythm, your body will begin producing milk in exactly the quantity your baby needs. However, engorgement can recur if the baby skips feedings or is not nursing effectively (this can occur if the baby is ill, for example, or teething).

If you are experiencing engorgement, you can relieve the pain with analgesics, such as Tylenol or Advil (consult your doctor first). Cool compresses are often helpful as well. Some prefer very warm compresses right before nursing and icy cold between feedings — use whichever brings you relief. You can also relieve engorgement by standing in a hot shower and massaging the breasts.

Expressing a little of the milk can bring relief, but be careful. Take into consideration that this stimulation, especially if you aim to empty the breast, will result in increased milk supply and not less! This will lead to prolonged engorgement. If you do decide to express some of the milk, store it for a later time. Some mothers donate the milk to a milk bank.

With frequent feedings to keep the milk flowing and establish nursing, the pain and discomfort should subside, although it may take several days for engorgement to resolve completely. On the rare occasions when engorgement resolves in one breast, but the other remains swollen, this is not an issue of excess milk but rather of drainage of the lymph nodes on that side. Mild physical exercises to increase circulation (swinging your arms about, walking) plus gentle massage over the swollen area toward the armpit are usually successful in overcoming this. If you are still concerned, consult with your doctor or a lactation consultant.

Mastitis

Neglecting to treat engorgement can sometimes cause a medical condition known as mastitis, an infection of the breast tissue, which will probably require antibiotic treatment.

The mother with mastitis will experience local pain, redness, swelling, and heat in the area. If the mastitis progresses, it is accompanied by flu-like symptoms, including fever, and in rare cases an abscess can develop.

If you are experiencing these symptoms, seek prompt medical attention and get more rest. The worst solution is to stop breast-feeding, which makes the problem more severe.

Abscess

In this rare condition, a lump in the breast fills with pus. It is most often associated with untreated mastitis. The affected part of the breast is very tender, and pus may drain from the nipple. Diagnosis will be confirmed by fine needle aspiration, and the abscess is drained or surgically removed in an outpatient setting. The doctor will prescribe antibiotic therapy and anti-inflammatory medication to reduce fever.

There is usually no reason to discontinue nursing, but if the decision is made to cease nursing on the affected side, it should be done gradually — express milk if it is not possible to continue nursing the baby. Bed rest is very important, and breastfeeding should continue on the unaffected breast.

Ita

When I felt a lump in my breast I nearly panicked. The skin over it was reddened, and it was too tender to touch, but the lactation consultant reassured me that it was not dangerous. She explained that it was probably just a blocked milk duct and to keep nursing. To my relief, the lump moved down gradually, and a day later it disappeared.

Hanni

It was the funniest thing. When my baby cried, milk began to pour out all by itself! Later the same thing happened when it was time to nurse, even if she was still sleeping.

Kayla

It took two weeks before my nipples became accustomed to breastfeeding, but after that they never hurt again.

> **Dina**
>
> I felt sick and feverish. Part of the skin on one breast was an angry red and really hurt. My doctor prescribed anti-inflammatory drugs and antibiotics. She told me to update her, because if the treatment didn't work it might be serious, but, baruch Hashem, I was feeling better within twenty-four hours.

> **Esty**
>
> I noticed a pustule on the areola beside the nipple. It hurt a little when the baby nursed, but the lactation consultant identified it as only an infected hair follicle. She advised me that a doctor should see it and to be in touch if it became more painful or changed appearance. By the next day it was gone.

Blebs and Blocked Ducts

A bleb or "milk blister" is a blocked pore near the nipple opening and appears as a small, firm white spot. A bleb may be caused by constriction (bra too tight, pressure from an underwire in the bra, a bruise), hampering the breast from draining. It can also be caused by a blocked milk duct. The mother may experience nipple pain during nursing and also between feedings when anything touches the breast.

If this occurs, try changing nursing positions to one that is more comfortable. Soaking the breast in warm water before feeding may help to soften the bleb and make nursing easier. Sometimes it is possible to gently manipulate the bleb out of the nipple with your fingers. Gently rubbing a warm, wet washcloth on the bleb may remove the skin blocking the nipple pore to release the milk. Some mothers put a dab of olive oil on a cotton ball to "soak" their nipple when they are dressed.

In some cases, it may be necessary for the doctor to lance the skin covering the bleb; the milk behind it will be thick like cream cheese, and a few drops of blood are not unusual. Once the bleb and the milk underneath it are removed, there will be marked relief of the discomfort.

Thrush

Babies older than two weeks may contract a yeast infection known as thrush. You can identify it by white patches on the tongue, gums, and inside baby's cheeks. It looks like residue from spitting up milk, but doesn't rub off. Yeast infections often occur after mother or baby takes medication that disrupts the "good" bacteria.

Some babies with thrush find it painful to suck and become very fussy at feedings while others don't seem to notice the difference. Thrush occasionally spreads to the diaper area, causing an associated diaper rash. If the mother has cracked nipples, the infection can pass to her nipples and her breast will sting painfully when nursing. An antifungal ointment prescribed by your pediatrician will bring quick relief to both mother and baby. Rub it on baby's tongue and on your nipples between feedings. The doctor may also prescribe oral antifungal medications.

Another sign that the thrush infection has passed into the mother is excruciating shooting pain in the nipples after nursing in response to the change in temperature from warm to cold (for example, coming inside on a winter day) or wet to dry (after showering). She may not realize the cause is a yeast infection, since yeast infections do not cause the nipple to look white. If you experience these symptoms, consult your doctor or a lactation consultant for a proper diagnosis because it is very common for the nipple pain caused by incorrect latching to be misdiagnosed. If a yeast infection is the cause, your doctor will probably prescribe medication for relief. If the pain is felt inside the breast, it is more likely to be a bacterial infection than thrush, and antibiotic treatment will be needed.

However, treatment will not be effective unless bras, washable nursing pads, and breast pump parts are also thoroughly cleaned. If you have contracted a yeast infection, it is recommended to boil for twenty minutes any components that came in contact with your nipples. Also, keep in mind that freezing does not destroy yeast, so frozen milk that was pumped and stored while you had a thrush infection should be discarded.

Chapter Nine

Mom 2 Mom: Real Mothers, Real Experiences

What was the best advice you got when you were learning to breastfeed?

Yocheved
The best advice I got was to buy a nursing pillow. It helped me position the baby exactly at the right level and it supported my arms during her feedings.

Sarah
Guard your privacy! When nursing, make sure your voice mail is turned on, or turn your ringer off, so you won't be disturbed.

Alexandra
Read books about nursing before you give birth for inspiration and enthusiasm. Remember that when a mother nurses her baby, she is doing her best hishtadlus to protect their future, both physically and emotionally.

Ruth
Many times health insurance covers the cost of a lactation specialist. Even if it doesn't, paying a professional for a few visits is still cheaper than ending up on formula, even without figuring in all the long-term benefits to Mom and baby.

Ahuva
If nursing doesn't seem to be working, don't wait. Better to get help sooner than later. B'ezras Hashem, you will either get some much-needed validation for your efforts or get solutions to problems when they are small before they grow to become overwhelming.

Michal
I think the best advice is not to give up breastfeeding before you really try to make it work. Invest in this because there's nothing more amazing for you and your baby than breastfeeding. But if it's still stressful and difficult after six weeks, then reevaluate. Is it really feasible to continue in your situation? Who is paying the price for your desire to breastfeed? If you decide to give formula after you've tried your very best, then don't feel guilty!

Batya
Trust yourself! Conflicting advice is unavoidable, but don't let it disorient you. You won't be sorry if you just listen to your own intuition.

Malky
If it hurts, there is something wrong. Get help!

Leah
Even if your baby is a great full-time nurser, offer a bottle occasionally. A baby only used to nursing will refuse to switch to a bottle when you want to leave her with a babysitter or when you have to return to work.

Chaya
Best advice: Don't give up! Those early problems are temporary, and it all works out eventually. The bonding that comes from nursing is absolutely unique, and they grow so fast that the nursing stage is over before you know it.

What was the worst advice?

Ruchoma

The worst advice I was given was to take brewer's yeast to increase my milk. It worked, that's true, but it caused me to gain thirty pounds in six months! Later a rebbetzin told me, "As di vest nemen heiven, vesti voksen vi of heiven! — If you take yeast, you'll grow like yeast!"

Dassy

Here's the advice I didn't get! No one told me that I should alternate sides when I nurse, and somehow I fed more often from one side than the other. This resulted in an excess supply of milk on one side, and it made me look quite lopsided!

Miriam

Lots of people with the best intentions told me to put him on a schedule, and that became my biggest problem. I never knew just when to feed him. Should I wake him if he sleeps more than three hours? What should I do if he acts hungry but it's not time for him to eat yet? I remember standing at the foot of the cradle crying together with him, anxiously watching the hands of the clock until it reached the three-hour mark. Adhering to a strict schedule was the worst advice I got.

Mina

A friend told me to let the baby nurse whenever she wanted for as long as she wanted. This was terrible advice and very unrealistic. My baby was colicky and suffered from reflux, and she wanted to nurse even when she wasn't hungry because it soothed her.

Beily

One lactation consultant told me that my baby was tongue-tied and needed corrective surgery. My pediatrician didn't agree. She said my baby was not tongue-tied! Later I found out that that particular lactation consultant said the same thing to almost every mother, and she didn't know what she was talking about. Always get a doctor's opinion before you accept a medical diagnosis!

What was your biggest challenge in establishing breastfeeding?

Yehudit

The hardest part for my baby was learning how to latch on. I learned that it really makes a difference how you hold the baby. When you feed him on the right side, hold his neck in position with your left hand and use your right hand (the same side he's nursing from) to position the nipple so that it touches his lips. When he opens his mouth, quickly put the nipple into his mouth. This really helped my baby learn how to latch on effectively. Now that I'm experienced, this technique gives me a free hand to do something else, such as paint, type, or prepare dinner!

Devorah

With my first, the hardest was the feeling of isolation. My baby ate every two hours, so I had to leave everybody (my parents, in-laws, friends, and relatives) to nurse in the privacy of my own room and I felt left out. That was a long time ago. Now I'm nursing my sixth child, and today I relish the quiet time when I'm "forced" to escape to my room to feed the baby! It's the most wonderful opportunity to be together, just the two of us, and also it's a bit of calm and relaxation in the middle of my busy day. I've read many Jewish magazines and novels, cover to cover, in the bits of time I snatch for nursing.

Tzipi

Nursing in a tzniusdik manner is an art. I found that wearing a large-size t-shirt under my robe was ideal. You just have to unzip the robe partway and pull up the shirt, and everything stays covered. Nursing without showing anything is an acquired skill, so until you have experience, be sure to nurse someplace where you have privacy.

Liebe

I found myself nursing around the clock because my baby cried every hour. This was a very bad idea. A really amazing nursing consultant came to my house, and we tried all kinds of things until we worked it out. To be sure I had enough milk, she told me to pump 60 cc and feed my baby my milk from a bottle. When I couldn't express that much, I had to add formula and I thought my world would collapse. I felt so inadequate! I resented that bottle, as if it were taking over my motherliness. I even tried stopping in the middle and trying to nurse, as if I could force her to eat from me. Looking back, I understand that my extreme reaction was from hormones, which is normal after birth, but then my whole world felt black. After a period of pumping my milk, the supply grew and I was able to return to nursing full-time. I kept nursing for a year and a half!

Yael

I am very small and petite. When my daughter was born, my nipples were so small that the baby couldn't latch on. She was really frustrated, and one of the nurses advised me to use nipple shields, which helped. Soon she was feeding beautifully. The only drawback was that they had to be sterilized before every feeding. When she was a month old, I went out of town to my grandmother for Shabbos and accidentally forgot my nipple shields at home! My baby absolutely refused to nurse. She had gotten used to the shields, and she fussed and cried but she wouldn't nurse. I decided then that I was getting rid of those nipple shields entirely. Nursing is supposed to be convenient and easy, with no need for preparation. It was hard, but after that experience I weaned my baby off the shields. All my subsequent babies managed to nurse without using the nipple shields. It was harder in the beginning, and I needed a lot of patience, but it was really worth the trouble in the end.

How did you deal with the relatively common problem of your baby biting while nursing?

Atarah

Say no firmly, stop feeding them for a moment. Then they associate biting with no feeding. If they persistently bite during one feeding session, just take it as if they have finished eating and stop feeding them. The problem should stop quite quickly.

Esty

Definitely smoosh them into the breast. It stops the biting right away without hurting or startling the baby and he learns very quickly not to bite.

Nechama

Surprisingly enough, my children get their teeth and subsequently start biting as early as five months! I was told to lightly pat the baby on the nose or cheek each time he did this. Believe it or not, all it took was a couple of days for the baby to register and the biting stopped. I did however find the older babies — eight to ten months — more challenging, since at that age they were fully aware of what they were doing and got a kick out of it!

Yudit

My personal experience is that when my babies started biting me I would immediately stop nursing. It only took a couple of times and then they learned that it wasn't worth it. I've managed to nurse my babies until they were a year and a half old — with a full mouth of teeth.

Suri

Don't startle or shriek when they bite, especially with an older child. It will upset some children enough to scare them off eating fully, but with mine — he found it funny and promptly bit again to try and get a reaction. So it's important not to make an issue out of it — stay calm and firm.

Mom 2 Mom: Real Mothers, Real Experiences

Bella

Simply remove the baby from the breast and in as stern a voice as you can manage, tell the baby, "No. No biting Mommy." Keep it simple and to the point. Babies understand this much. Repeat a few times. This should be sufficient to teach the baby that the act of biting will cause a removal of the source of food.

Tova

Smoosh baby into your breast to get him to unlatch, then say, "No biting Mommy. Here's a teething toy. Do you want to bite or to nurse?" Also, biting usually happens toward the end of a feeding, when baby wants Mommy's attention. If you feel the suck starting to change, look for a gleam in baby's eyes and remind him, "No biting."

Shulamis

I learned this from my mom. Always works. Stop nursing abruptly when the baby bites. Say no and shake your finger at the baby and put baby back in crib or on the floor. Baby will begin to cry so resume nursing right away. Repeat if bitten again, saying, "I can't nurse you if you bite." I nursed eight kids this way...with teeth and while teething, till over a year, all of them.

Chapter Ten

Nursing to Go!

Expressing and Pumping Milk

here could be many reasons you'd want to express milk. You might want to increase your milk supply, your baby might not be able to breastfeed temporarily, or you may be returning to work or want to leave the baby with a sitter. You can express milk by hand or with a pump. Note: Many insurance companies will cover the cost of a breast pump, and many communities offer them through *gemachim*.

By Hand

It's possible to express milk by hand, especially if you are feeling full and uncomfortable:

1. Wash your hands well with soap and water before you start and have a sterile container prepared, preferably a wide-rimmed bowl or jar.

2. Make yourself comfortable in a place where you won't be disturbed. Massage your breast for about a minute, stroking downward gently.

3. Cup your four fingers beneath your breast (pinkie against your rib) and your thumb above and at the top of your breast. (The thumb and index finger should form a C shape.) Gently squeeze your thumb and forefinger together. Remember to feel for the firm texture indicating milk ducts inside your breast. Don't compress the nipple (which hurts and is not productive).
4. Release and repeat rhythmically until drops of breastmilk or colostrum appear on your nipple. This may take a few minutes.
5. Adjust your position so that the expressed milk goes into the sterile container. It should flow in steady streams with each compression. You may want to try using a previously sterilized funnel to channel the stream into the container.
6. When the flow diminishes, rotate your hand so that your fingers press on different milk ducts. Repeat this until you have expressed the desired amount or the flow stops. Repeat on the other breast.

With a Pump

Manual breast pumps are fairly straightforward. The suction cup fits over your breast and then you repeatedly squeeze the pump's bulb (or handle) by hand until the desired amount has been expressed. It is possible to pump from one breast while your baby nurses from the other.

Electric pumps generally remove most of the milk within 15–20 minutes. Women who are unsuccessful at expressing with a manual pump find that an electric pump often works well. Just follow the manufacturer's instructions. Set the suction and speed to a comfortable level. Most women pump more milk when it's not on the highest setting. Use a larger-size cup if the lip feels uncomfortably tight, or if nipple and breast tissue are stretched into the cup when pumping.

A breast pump, especially the electric kind, can be expensive. Look for a *gemach* of breast pumps in your area, which would

> ## STORING EXPRESSED MILK
>
> La Leche League International and the American Academy of Pediatrics have published recommendations for storing expressed breastmilk. It is safe to keep mother's milk in a tightly closed sterile container in a regular refrigerator for up to eight days. The breastmilk can be frozen in a regular home freezer for three months and in deep freeze for six months. Fresh milk can be transported in an insulated cooler with ice packs for twenty-four hours.
>
> Thaw frozen milk in your refrigerator overnight, and then warm it by holding it beneath a faucet of warm running water. Or you can place the container of frozen milk in a cup of warm water to defrost. Thawed milk is safe to keep in the refrigerator for up to twenty-four hours, but it should not be refrozen.
>
> Nutritional value is compromised by heating stored breastmilk to the boiling point. It should never be heated in a microwave oven because the milk is heated unevenly and can cause serious burns even when the bottle only feels warm to the touch.

allow you to try different models and choose the best one for your needs.

If pumping is difficult:

- » Try using guided imagery when pumping to help you relax: Imagine a river of flowing water or the sun setting, for example.
- » Look at your baby (or a picture or video, or even yesterday's stretchie, if the baby is not with you) to stimulate the letdown reflex. Some women hold a doll or a bag of flour to help feel like their baby is in their arms.
- » Make sure the pump is positioned correctly; incorrect positioning may cause pain or even cracked nipples over time.
- » If it's difficult to pump for ten or fifteen minutes straight, try doing it in five-minute intervals and rest in between.

Manual vs. Electric Pumps

MANUAL BREAST PUMP	ELECTRIC BREAST PUMP
A good option when you only need to express milk occasionally (one feeding a day, or if you want to go out for a short time)	Best option for frequent daily pumping (for example, if you're returning to work). If you're pumping for a preemie, nursing twins, or trying to increase your milk supply you can rent a hospital-grade pump.
Easily affordable	More expensive than manual pump
No batteries or cords required, so it can be operated anywhere	Operation requires electric outlet or batteries
Easy to assemble and disassemble, with only a few pieces to wash and sterilize after use	Can be complicated to assemble and disassemble for washing and sterilization
Small and lightweight; easy to fit into a diaper bag when traveling	May be heavy and requires a tote or backpack to carry around
Quiet when operating, so it doesn't wake the baby or sleeping husband, or draw attention when used away from home	Makes noise, so it's hard to be discreet when operating it
Requires skill to operate and sometimes both hands are needed	Can usually guide pump with one hand; some even express milk from both sides at once
You control the pace and exact strength of suction (especially important when breasts are sore)	
Most resembles the sensation of the baby sucking	Some women find the vacuum much stronger than the sucking of their baby, so it may be uncomfortable (you can adjust the settings until you're more comfortable)
Hands may get tired the longer you need to pump	Expresses more milk in less time than manual pumps

PUMP ACCESSORIES

» Attachable bottles or bags allowing for pumping directly into the storage container (these can also be used for storing the expressed milk)

» Carry bag for storing the pump

» Some suction cups have comfort features such as cushions or massage cups

» Swivel handle with both short and long sides (to pump rapidly or slowly)

» Container for sterilizing the pump in the microwave

» Stand for holding pump if you need to pause in the middle of pumping (prevents tipping over and spilling the expressed milk)

» An electric breast pump that can be detached and used manually as well

» Some have a double pumping feature that allows you to express from both sides at once

» Carry bag for storage

Chapter Eleven

A Guide to Formula Feeding

There are many reasons why it may become necessary to choose formula feeding over breastfeeding. Whether the mother has to take strong medication, has a health condition, a physical anomaly, or adopted the baby, or because the baby is unable to nurse (due to a physical anomaly or illness), feeding your precious infant formula does not diminish your lofty status as an *eim b'Yisrael* in any way. You may hear implied criticism from insensitive or shortsighted people, but you don't owe any outsiders an explanation for your decision to nourish with formula instead of nursing.

Remember — whatever your choices, whatever your situation, if you're bottle feeding your baby, do it with love! Cuddle her and hold her close to you. Feeding your baby by bottle generally takes less time than nursing, so find other opportunities to bond with your baby. And don't just prop the bottle — this can lead to tooth decay once the teeth come in and it has a small risk of choking. Babies whose bottles are propped may eat more than they need, and studies are finding it may turn off baby's fullness cues and lead to obesity. Most important, it means your baby is missing out on that infant-parent bonding.

Before You Begin

Formula feeding requires equipment. Make sure you have everything you need at hand.

Bottles

The smaller-size four-ounce bottles are meant for very young babies and the larger eight-ounce bottles for bigger babies. Different neck widths are a matter of taste (wide, standard, or narrow) and shouldn't affect the feeding.

There are bottles designed especially to prevent the baby swallowing air while feeding; if your baby is suffering from colic after feedings, this is a good option. Some bottles come with a hole in the middle; these are convenient for older babies to grip but are more complicated to clean.

Glass bottles are an option if you are concerned about the possibility of BPA, a carcinogenic component in some plastics; also plastic becomes stained over time. On the other hand, glass is breakable. Babies tend to drop bottles so you may find plastic more practical in the long run.

How many bottles will you need? Newborns eat six to eight times a day, so you'll need at least six bottles if you want to always have a clean bottle at hand. Not every nipple fits every bottle, so be sure you have nipples that fit all your bottles correctly.

Nipples

Most bottles come with nipples, rings, and caps made by the same manufacturer, but you may favor a different style or material and there is a wide variety of shapes and sizes to choose from. Silicone nipples last longer than rubber (latex) ones, which eventually become sticky and lose their elasticity. Avoid nipples labeled "orthopedic," which can actually harm tooth development.

PACED BOTTLE FEEDING

Whether you are bottle feeding your breastfed baby (for example, if you are leaving her with a caregiver and pumped milk) and want the experience to be as close to breastfeeding as possible, or if you are simply bottle feeding, "paced bottle feeding" is a good way to go. Paced bottle feeding lets baby control how quickly she drinks and lets her recognize when she's full – much like breastfeeding. Here's how it works: Seat baby in your lap (not lying down), and keep the bottle parallel to the floor. In this way, she'll only drink when she sucks, and won't be overwhelmed. To begin feeding, gently stroke baby's lips with the nipple, and let her draw the nipple into her mouth herself, rather than sticking the nipple into her mouth.

Different nipples also come with different-size holes to allow for faster or slower flow of milk. There is no industry standard for labeling the flow, and some will flow much faster than others. Hold the full bottle upside down and see how fast the milk drips out to see if it is suitable for your baby. It's sensible to use nipples that have a slower flow so baby can continue controlling how much he drinks even as he grows. Choking, sputtering, or leakages from the sides of the mouth are signs that the flow is too rapid. Nipple biting, pulling back, and crying in frustration indicate a flow that is too slow.

The rate of flow can also be adjusted by tightening or loosening the bottle ring. If the nipple flattens while the baby is sucking, try loosening the ring that holds the nipple on the bottle. You will see bubbles rising up through the formula as air is drawn into the bottle, and the milk will flow more freely.

Formula

There are several types of formula on the market. Your pediatrician is a good source of advice for choosing the one that is most appropriate for your baby. If your infant does not seem content with one type of formula, consult with your health provider before changing to another.

There are four kinds of formula available today:

1. **Formula derived from cow milk:** Giving a newborn whole cow's milk is not wise. The milk of a cow is perfectly designed for the needs of a calf, but it's missing important nutrients that human infants require, and it contains excessive amounts of potassium and sodium. Baby formulas derived from cow's milk are usually based on modified cow's milk with special formulas for particular circumstances (such as preemies).

   There are two kinds of protein in cow's milk: casein (the curds) and whey (the watery ingredient). Formulas vary in the ratio of these proteins. Primary formulas are based on a 40:60 casein-whey ratio, similar to the relative amounts in breast-milk. These are considered easier for the digestion of infants during the first year of life. There is no reason to change to another product if your baby thrives on this formula.

   Milk for Hungry Babies is manufactured with a higher ratio of casein (80:20). The baby needs more time to digest the curds, so she is satiated longer between feedings. It is best not to give this type of formula to young infants.

   Cow's milk should not be given to a baby during the first year, but when a baby is already eating solid foods (often after the age of six months) foods cooked together with dairy products may be offered (see p. 318).

2. **Formula derived from goat milk:** If your baby is lactose intolerant (sensitive to the sugar in cow's milk rather than the protein content), consult with your pediatrician about using formula based on goat's milk. Goat's milk infant formula is available in some locations and has the same nutritional standards as formula based on cow's milk. (It is used more commonly in Great Britain than in the United States.)

However, goat milk formula is not an acceptable alternative for an infant who has experienced an allergic reaction to the proteins in cow's milk because the proteins in goat's milk are similar and are liable to cause the same reaction; a baby with an allergic reaction to cow's milk is at risk for anaphylactic shock after digesting goat's milk. For this reason, switching from cow's milk formula to formula based on goat's milk should only be done with the recommendation of a health professional.

Goat milk is not recommended for an infant under the age of half a year, but when she begins eating solids, it is possible to give her food that was cooked with goat's milk. By the age of one year, a baby whose formula was based on goat milk can begin drinking goat milk straight.

3. **Hydrolyzed-protein formula:** There are two types of hydrolyzed-protein formula: fully hydrolyzed and partially hydrolyzed. Fully hydrolyzed formula is lactose-free, and the proteins from the cow's milk have been hydrolyzed (broken down for easier digestion) to prevent allergic reactions. Available only by prescription, this formula is designed for lactose-intolerant infants unable to tolerate cow's milk.

Partially hydrolyzed protein formula is produced from whey to make it more easily digestible so it is promoted for colicky babies. It is not recommended for allergy-prone infants because not all the proteins are broken down in the hydrolyzation process. If you suspect that your baby is allergic to milk, consult with your pediatrician before using this type of formula.

4. **Soy-based formula:** This product is designed as an alternative to milk-based formula. It is produced from soybeans and enriched with vitamins, minerals, and other nutrients. Soy-based formula should only be fed to your infant if it is recommended by your pediatrician. Up to 15 percent of babies with milk allergies are also sensitive to soy. Warning: Adding

more formula powder than the producer's recommendation is not better! Doing this carries the risk of constipation and dehydration. Using less than the recommended quantity of formula may save a little money, but it seriously compromises the baby's nutrition. Bottom line: Always follow the product instructions carefully, and use only the measuring scoop that came with the formula.

For premature infants, newborns with low body weight, and children with compromised immune systems, it is recommended to use ready-to-feed formula (which comes in liquid form), rather than powders, which are not sterilized.

Bottle brush

Since bottles must be thoroughly cleaned before every feeding, invest in a bottle-cleaning brush with nylon bristles that reach the bottom and sides of the bottles when washing. Some have a convenient small brush for cleaning nipples on the opposite end.

Keeping the Equipment Clean

Microorganisms are attracted to the remnants of formula in a baby's bottle. These germs can cause diarrhea and stomachaches. For your baby's protection, all the feeding equipment must be cleaned well before each use. Years ago, sterilizing bottles and nipples was standard procedure. Nowadays, though, most pediatricians agree that washing them in a dishwasher, or with hot, soapy water, is sufficient. (Of course, if the formula is dairy-based, use a milchig dishwasher only.)

Use hot soapy water to wash the bottles and nipples, the retaining rings and the caps, or run the dishwasher on a hot setting, as soon as possible after the feeding. You will need a bottle brush to ensure that any dried milk stuck inside is loosened. It's a good idea to force water through the nipple opening with your finger. It's also recommended to wash the measuring scoop that comes

in the formula container. After all the pieces are clean, rinse well with fresh water and leave to air dry upside down.

Formula Preparation

Always follow the manufacturer's instructions printed on the side of the container of formula powder.

1. Boil water and then let it stand to cool for no more than thirty minutes. Bottled water must be boiled before use just like tap water. Remember, boiled water is needed to destroy any bacteria in the powder.
2. Pour the recommended amount of water into the sterilized bottle. Place the bottle on a flat surface at eye level to be sure you have the exact amount.
3. Fill the measuring scoop with formula powder. Level it with a clean knife and add the correct number of scoops to the water in the bottle.
4. Center the nipple on the bottle lip and tighten the ring to secure it before capping. Shake the bottle until all the powder has dissolved in the water.
5. Check the temperature of the formula by tipping the nipple over your inner wrist. It should feel warm but not hot. If necessary, cool the capped bottle under cold running water.

Preparing the Formula in Advance

If possible, make each bottle of formula fresh when your baby needs to eat. Once you have done it a few times, you will find it is not time-consuming at all. If you will be away from home and must prepare a bottle in advance, consider using ready-made formula that doesn't require refrigeration until opened. Wash your hands before opening the container and sterilize the scissors if you need them to cut the package. Any milk remaining in the carton must be used up within twenty-four hours from opening the container, as long as it has been stored in the coldest part of the refrigerator with the opening folded down.

If this is not an option, prepare only one extra bottle for later use. To do this safely, the prepared bottle should be placed into the refrigerator as soon as the formula powder is mixed with the boiled water. When you leave the house, place the bottle in a cold pack or bag filled with ice to keep it cool and use within two hours. When refrigerated from the time of preparation, a bottle of premade formula can be used up to twenty-four hours from the time it was prepared.

When the baby is ready to eat, a bottle of either formula or breastmilk can be placed in warm water up to fifteen minutes. Electric warmers will heat the bottle to the perfect temperature in four to six minutes. Do not warm bottles of milk in a microwave because it heats the liquid unevenly, creating steaming hot pockets that can burn the baby's mouth.

Never save leftover formula after the baby finishes drinking. If you have an unused bottle of formula that has not been refrigerated, it should be discarded after two hours have passed. Bacteria grow even though a bottle is prepared with sterile water because formula powder is not sterile. At room temperature, microorganisms multiply very rapidly. Bacteria grow more slowly in bottles stored in the refrigerator, but the buildup becomes unsafe after a few hours.

The Feeding

Choose a comfortable position to cuddle your baby during her feeding. Having good back and arm support can be very helpful. Support your baby in a seated position, so she's not flooded by the liquid flowing too quickly into her mouth, as it can when she's lying down.

Some babies suck steadily while others eat in bursts with short pauses. If you hear noisy sucking and gulping sounds, it may mean that she is swallowing air together with her milk. Try positioning her slightly more upright and be sure that the bottle is sufficiently tilted so that the nipple stays full of milk and not air.

The quantity of formula a baby eats differs by age, weight, and appetite, and whether he is also nursing part of the time or has started eating solids. For a newborn (up to the age of one month), offer frequent but small bottles of formula every two to three hours. Let her eat as much as she wants and stop when she's ready. As she grows, there will be longer breaks between feedings and she will eat more at a time.

In the beginning, watch for the cues that tell you your baby is hungry. Perhaps he will be searching, opening his mouth while snuggling against you. He may make sucking movements or put his fingers in his mouth. Feedings will be more pleasant for both of you if you offer the bottle before he is so distressed by hunger that he cries.

During the feeding, watch for cues that the baby is full. If he turns his head, remove the bottle. If he doesn't search for more, he's full. It's all right if he occasionally slows down his sucking and rests a few seconds before continuing. Don't insist that the baby finish a bottle if you see that he wants to stop, even if there's only a little bit of formula remaining: let him keep his fullness cues so he doesn't overeat. Don't worry if a baby older than six months who is eating solids doesn't want to drink all his formula. You can give him dairy foods such as pudding and yogurt to make up for the milk he's not getting.

At certain stages a baby will quickly consume the whole bottle and look around for more. This is the time to talk to your pediatrician about increasing the amount of formula for his feeding.

Part Three

Watch Me Grow!

Note About Baby Development

As we watch our little ones move from stage to stage, we are filled with wonder and happiness — and, yes, often with anxiety as well. "We gave birth the same week — why is her Tova smiling and my Shmuel still seems so serious?" "My Yeruchum isn't crawling yet, and Chaim is, though they are almost the same age."

So here's the rule: Watch your baby develop, enjoy it, and don't compare.

On the other hand... there are developmental milestones that babies generally reach within a few weeks of each other. If your baby hasn't reached that milestone, there is usually no cause for alarm, but it should be mentioned to the pediatrician, to rule out any possible problems.

The charts at the beginning of each of the next four sections give a picture of what the "average" child is doing. But remember — no child is really "average" — especially your darling boy or girl!

One to Three Months

From Newborn to Baby

The first twelve weeks of life are a transition period, full of discoveries. You're occupied full-time, learning how to be the best parent you can be (and trying to do it on a few hours of sleep a night!). It may be a lot more difficult than you imagined. At the same time, you're discovering the true meaning of nachas, and the love and joy you're experiencing is far beyond the happiness you felt before your baby was born.

Your precious little neshama'leh learns about the world by the way his needs are met. When you care for him, you're teaching him all about the world he has entered. Before birth, all his needs were met without his even being aware of them. Now he experiences intense sensations: hot and cold, hunger and satiety, hard and soft surfaces, the pain of a tummy ache and the comfort of your arms. By nurturing him and caring for him, you are teaching him that life is good. That the world is a caring place where he can feel safe to grow and develop his unique potential. You're planting the seeds of emunah and bitachon that will, with Hashem's help, sprout beautifully.

PHYSICAL GROWTH AND MILESTONES

By the age of six to eight weeks you will probably see:

DEVELOPMENTAL MILESTONES	BABY...
Motor	Holds his head up for a short time when held upright, though it will still wobble
	Makes disorganized and reflexive physical movements
	Kneads your breast when nursing
	Briefly raises his head when lying on stomach and turns his head freely from side to side
Sensory	Seems more aware of his environment
	Quiets to the sound of your voice
	Enjoys sounds such as wind chimes, the ticking of a clock, singing, and music
Speech and communication	Becomes more expressive with his cries so that you can differentiate a cry of hunger from a wail of distress
	Begins to coo, making soft sounds like "ahhh" and "oooh"
Social-emotional	Smiles
	Makes eye contact
	Responds to sounds
	Recognizes people and things around him
	Shows surprise at an unexpected noise
	Calms when held

If your baby hasn't reached one of these milestones, DON'T PANIC! But be sure to mention it to your doctor at his next well-baby checkup.

Red Flags

After three months, contact your doctor if baby...

» is not smiling yet
» seems either stiff or floppy
» displays a difference in muscle tone between the right and left sides of his body
» still holds his hands in tight fists
» doesn't respond to comforting during daily crying jags
» is exceptionally "good," sleeping most of the time and rarely crying

Chapter Twelve

Smiling, Crying, Moving, Seeing…

In the beginning it takes all your strength just to keep up with your baby's constant need to be fed, bathed, changed, and comforted. But at some point, hardly realizing that it's happened, your confidence and proficiency has grown until you no longer have to consciously think about what you're doing. Your baby has become an integral part of your life, and caring for her is as natural as breathing. You've become a real mommy!

During these weeks your little one is doing much more than merely growing and gaining weight. In those very first weeks, she was totally helpless, controlled by her instincts and reflexes. As the weeks pass, she gradually becomes more organized until she is able to turn her head in the direction of a noise, follow an object in her line of vision, bring her fingers to her mouth at will, and recognize your voice and touch. By one month she is more interested in the world — and more fun to interact with.

The First Smile

The most thrilling event during this early period of life is when your little one suddenly breaks into a great big smile.

Of course, smiling can be observed in the early days too, but they're fleeting and random. The corners of his mouth jerk up in brief smiles in the same reflexive way that his little arms wave about and his legs kick. These reflex smiles disappear by the time the infant reaches the age of eight weeks, and somewhere between six and twelve weeks, his first genuine smile appears, evoking feelings of joy you never dreamed you could experience.

In order to smile on purpose, a baby's brain and nervous system must have matured enough to repress the original reflexive smiles, and he must recognize your face. Real smiles come as a response to something, and you'll notice that his eyes light up with pleasure. When you smile in return, your baby will be delighted, empowered by the discovery that his feelings have a direct influence on others!

> ### Yiska
> My friend's babies all smiled early, but mine just stared at the world and thought deep thoughts. The weeks passed and I couldn't stand it anymore. One day I picked him up in front of me, face-to-face. I talked and smiled and giggled at him. He seemed interested, watching me in wonder with his wide blue eyes. I blew raspberries on his palms and made faces and funny noises, but nothing worked. He continued to stare at me with great concentration for a long time, as if he wanted to tell me something but didn't want to hurt my feelings. I looked at him, wondering if it meant that I was a terrible mother to have a baby that didn't smile. Then...he smiled! A great big openmouthed grin! And I beamed right back, whooping with excitement and blinking away tears of happiness. He was already ten weeks old, but it was worth waiting for!

After the first smile, your baby will repeat his amazing feat again and again.

Oh, the Sights There Are to See!

By six weeks your baby's eyes are moving in tandem most of the time, and she can focus on objects. It will take four months before she has full color vision, but during these first three months your baby will begin to notice toys hanging over her in her crib or carriage. At first she will stare at the object intently. If there are several, such as a mobile, her eyes will concentrate on each individual shape before moving to the next one. Eventually the baby is ready to reach out toward the toy. She'll bat at it with closed fists. Whenever she makes contact, she'll respond excitedly as the toy bounces or moves away. This success stimulates a baby to try again and again.

Many mothers place open board books in the crib or carriage so their babies can look at something. Hold your baby in your lap and "read" to her; the snuggly interaction helps make brain connections that will last a lifetime. Since a baby is born nearsighted (she can only focus on things within ten inches of her face), board books with various black-and-white shapes will hold her attention the longest. She will also stare at photos (tzaddikim or family faces) within her visual range. By the age of four months the range of her vision will be fully developed, and she will be able to see things at a distance.

Hands and Feet: Getting to Know Them

At this stage, your little one is discovering the wonders of having arms and legs. By the end of the first month, you'll notice a great improvement in his control. Instead of quivers and jerks, he cycles his arms and legs in smooth circles. By the second or third month, your baby will often seem calmer, because the common newborn reflexes are fading and he's gaining control of his movements. Every alert moment is spent learning how his body works, so your little one is very busy.

On his tummy, the baby may lift his head off the mattress by pushing down with his arms. He may even make crawling motions with his legs. Most infants are able to lift their heads and turn them from side to side from birth, but their muscles are not strong enough to hold their heads steady. Supporting the baby's head is important up until the three-month birthday.

Likewise, a one-month-old can be gently pulled to a sitting position, but his muscles are not strong enough to keep his head straight and it will flop backward. The back neck muscles grow stronger faster than the front neck muscles; from week to week he can hold his head up higher and longer than before. It may take until his four-month birthday to really be able to lift his chest up and hold his head steady, but this major accomplishment means freedom to see what interests him and opens new vistas of his world for discovery.

Hands are a source of fascination to infants. Your baby flexes his arms and gazes at his hands moving before his eyes, studying them attentively and never getting tired of looking at them. He may be able to get them to his mouth occasionally, and whenever he succeeds you'll hear him sucking with relish.

During the first eight weeks, a baby's fingers are clenched into fists most of the time. If you open his fingers and slip the handle of a rattle inside he will grasp it tightly and listen in wonder to the noise as it moves, but this is not yet a deliberate action. During the third month, his hands seem to relax. He opens and closes them over and over. By the time he is three months old, he should be able to grasp something placed on his palm and purposefully bring it to his mouth to explore before dropping it.

Babies love to kick. Near the end of their first three months, babies can kick forcefully enough to actually flip over from tummy to back. This means you must pay very close attention when you've placed your little one on a surface higher than floor level, because it's impossible to predict exactly when an energetic baby will turn over. Most infants discover how to turn over from the front to back around three months of age, though it will take another three months before he can freely roll from back to tummy.

Look Who's Talking!

Some babies begin to coo and gurgle and squeal as they near three months. Imitating the baby's sounds back to her encourages communication. You'll be surprised at the long "conversations" you can have together!

Even though she's still tiny, speak to your little one. Research shows that speaking to small infants sets a better foundation for communication. Babies who are spoken to consistently from a very young age develop greater intelligence and have larger vocabularies. Tell her the names of family members. Identify objects around you in the house or outside. She can't repeat the words back to you yet, but her brain is processing the sounds she hears and storing them in her memory.

Regularly hearing more than one language spoken benefits infants in the early months when they are learning to form and recognize phonetic sounds. Children in bilingual homes learn to speak both languages, often excelling in general language skills later in life.

Trimming Baby's Fingernails and Toenails

Despite being soft and pliable, a newborn baby's fingernails can become long and sharp. Within the first week, you'll notice the nails' ends beginning to split at the corners and gradually peeling away, and the toenails, which are also soft, curling over the tips of his toes.

To keep baby from scratching his own face when his arm flails, some mothers cover his hands with mittens, soft baby socks, or his sleeves, pulling them down over his fingers. But this sensory

deprivation and the natural discomfort of being confined disturbs some newborns, who need their hands to show hunger cues. Sometimes mothers will catch a loose fingernail or jagged edge with their teeth or fingers and pull it off. Unfortunately, with this method it is easy to accidentally pull the little nail past the quick, causing the baby pain and introducing germs from your mouth through the tiny cut.

Instead, use a baby-size emery board to file down the edges. After about three weeks, the nails will harden, making it less complicated to trim them.

How to cut your baby's nails:

- » Make sure there is sufficient light before you begin.
- » Use scissors with rounded tips made specifically for babies, which won't jab him if your little one jerks his hand away in the middle of the trimming procedure. If you prefer, use baby clippers designed especially for tiny fingers.
- » With your nondominant hand, press his fingertip pad away from the nail. Keep a firm hold! When trimming fingernails, follow the natural curve of the baby's fingers. When trimming toenails, cut straight across.

BABY'S "MANICURE"

A good time to trim a baby's fingernails is after bath time when they are softened from the bathwater, or when she is asleep so she won't wriggle.

You'll find it helpful if another person is present to distract the baby while you work.

» A finger will bleed if inadvertently nicked. This sometimes happens, even with the most experienced parent, so don't let it undermine your confidence. Rinse the finger under cool water and then press a clean tissue against the cut until the bleeding stops. Don't put on a bandage — because babies are always sucking their fingers, it can come off in the baby's mouth and cause choking. Liquid bandage products are also not recommended.

Choosing a Babysitter

Whether you're starting to think about going back to work or you have a family *simchah* to attend (or you're simply craving a night out), at some point you're going to need a babysitter.

If you need to briefly leave a very young baby with a babysitter while you leave the house, it's best to choose someone you already know who has experience caring for infants. Grandmothers and doting aunts are excellent choices. If they're not available, you can often find a trusted neighbor or hire a reliable older teenager, who has experience with young infants, to watch your baby.

If you're a working mother who must soon return to her job, you'll want to take time to do your research when choosing who will watch your baby. The nanny or babysitter you choose will have a big influence on your precious baby, so it's extremely important to find a good match for your family. You can't be too careful. Every prospective babysitter must give you references — whom you should call — and it is your obligation to make a comprehensive background check before trusting her with your treasure.

If you're satisfied with the background check, schedule a personal interview with the candidate. Here are some suggested questions to give a picture of the applicant's personality:

1. Ask about her interests — a creative and imaginative babysitter will be a stimulating influence on your child's development.

> ## THE BACKGROUND CHECK
>
> Call the reference given by the applicant. Explain the purpose of your call, and determine if it is a convenient time for the person to answer your questions. Assure the reference that the information she shares will be held in confidence. Here are some questions you may want to ask:
>
> 1. History: When did she work for you? How long did you employ her? Why did she leave? How much was she paid?
>
> 2. Performance: What did you like best about her work? What are her strengths? Can you give me examples? Is she patient? Is she organized? Is she punctual? Is she flexible? Does she have initiative? Is she energetic? How does she handle stress? Would you say she is a warm and friendly person? Does she prefer working independently or being told exactly what to do? Is she good at following instructions? Did she feed the baby per your instructions? Did your children like her? How would you rate her work (excellent, very good, okay, poor)? Would you hire her again? Do you recommend her?
>
> 3. Responsibility: Did she have any other responsibilities besides child care, such as light housework, food preparation, or bathing the children? Was she prepared to do more when you needed extra help? Briefly outline your own expectations from the babysitter and ask the reference if she thinks it's a good fit or not.
>
> In conclusion, ask the reference if she can offer you any advice on working with this applicant and, of course, thank her for her time.

2. Pay attention to whether she dresses and behaves modestly, in keeping with your family's values.

3. If she dresses with care and seems to be organized, she is likely to be orderly and tidy with your belongings as well. It's a good idea to speak with someone who has been in her home to see that it is well cared for too.

4. Notice if she texts or answers her cell phone during your conversation. You want someone who will focus on your baby, not a screen.
5. Find out if she has taken CPR and first-aid training. If not, is she willing to?
6. What does she do when a fussy baby is not calming down?
7. Ask in general about her family and friends. Be cautious if you sense problems in her close relationships.
8. Ask why she chose to work as a caregiver.
9. Tell her your expectations (including payment for services) and ask if she's comfortable with them.

BUBBY TIP

BABYSITTING

Make sure your babysitter has the following information, easily accessible:

» *Hatzalah or other emergency responder phone number*

» *Your pediatrician, local hospital, and Poison Control contact info*

» *Your cell number, and the number of at least one other family member or trusted neighbor*

» *If she is babysitting in your home, where she can find extra diapers, wipes, clothing, and baby's favorite toy. If baby is bottle fed, where there are extra bottles and nipples.*

» *If baby is already eating solids, and the babysitter provides food, what foods she may, and may not, have, and where to find them*

10. Does she feed by the clock or when baby is showing signs of hunger? If you prefer paced bottle feeding, does she know how to do that?
11. Ask her about her hours and vacations. (Does she take off during Chanukah? How much time does she take off before Pesach? Does she take summer vacation? Will she work on Fridays? Until when?) As a working mother, you won't want to find out at the last minute that you need to hire a substitute. Also, what are her policies if you come home late? Will she be willing to add hours sometimes — either earlier or later — if you need it?
12. If she seems to be the right one, request that she agree to a few hours trial (paid) when you are home so you can see her style and your baby's response to her.

Always trust your intuition if something doesn't feel right. A caregiver's role is too important to take any chances.

Why Is Baby Crying?

As time goes by, you will learn to recognize your little one's nonverbal cues. You will understand whether he is crying from hunger or because he needs to be cuddled or needs a diaper change.

A fussy baby is communicating that something bothers him. It could be that he needs to move his bowels, he might still be hungry after a feed, or a trapped bubble of air in his tummy makes him uncomfortable.

When an infant cries, nearly all people respond with the obvious question, "Is he hungry?" Don't forget to take into consideration the opposite possibility: perhaps his tummy aches because he overate. If you have ample milk and the baby ate for a reasonable length of time at his last feeding, offering more milk can cause the problem to worsen. Small, frequent feeds may help him be more comfortable than large feeds spaced too far apart.

When inconsolable crying happens day after day for no apparent reason at approximately the same time, it is likely to be infant colic.

Infant Colic

No one has successfully explained why so many babies develop the condition known as infant colic. Some professionals conjecture that colic is due to an immature digestive system. Certain experienced mothers believe that colic is caused by the baby's sensitivity to a particular food that Mommy eats (see pp. 191-192 for the types of food commonly held responsible). When she identifies and refrains from eating that food, noticeable improvement is sometimes reported, but this is very individual, even among siblings in the same family.

Colic is characterized by predictable episodes of distress in perfectly healthy infants. It typically occurs between 4:00 and 6:00 p.m. and 1:00 and 3:00 a.m. Some little ones scream for three to six hours or even more. The baby's tummy feels rigid, his fists clench, and his little legs draw up toward his body. Beyond holding him close, rocking his bassinet nonstop, or taking him out for a 2 a.m. stroll, parents are helpless to relieve the discomfort.

Eventually baby will fall asleep, still whimpering. Amazingly, when he wakes up for the next feeding, it's as if nothing happened — until the scene is repeated during the same hours on the following day.

Rarely, colic indicates a serious medical problem. Consult with your doctor to rule out any medical conditions. A baby who consistently cries most of the day with few periods of calm should be examined by his pediatrician.

Symptoms of infant colic usually appear around the age of two to three weeks and continue on and off for about twelve weeks. Enduring this comparatively short-lived period is a real challenge to novice (and sleep-deprived) parents. Fortunately, by the time babies are three months old, most have recovered completely,

even though Mommy and Tatty may still find themselves tensing in anticipation of the usual colic hour.

Recording the hours your baby eats and sleeps during the day will give you a comprehensive picture of his typical routine. Any abrupt change accompanied by obvious distress should be reported to your pediatrician. Otherwise, infant colic is the most common explanation. It may feel like an emergency to you at the time, but there is no cause for alarm as long as your baby calms down within a reasonable period.

As much as you adore your precious baby, this period is very trying. But no matter how frustrating it can be, *never ever shake a baby*, which can cause permanent brain damage. If you find

> **TECHNIQUES THAT CAN HELP A BABY SUFFERING FROM COLIC**
>
> » Walk with him (motion and body contact).
> » Rock his crib or carriage (steady, rhythmic movements).
> » Comfort nurse or offer a pacifier (sucking relaxes infants).
> » Use "white noise," such as the steady droning sound of a fan.
> » Place him on his tummy across your knees and, while gently bouncing or swaying, rhythmically pat his bottom or rub his back.
> » Hold him in your arms in a tummy-down position, similar to a football hold, with his head resting on the crook of your elbow while his legs dangle on either side of your hand. Incline his side against your stomach for support.
> » Go for a drive; the car's motion is often soothing.
> » Wrap him in swaddling (see p. 34).
> » Gently rock baby back and forth or swing him from side to side.
> » Tenderly massage his tummy or heels.
> » Administer over-the-counter drops for easing colic.
> » Drinking natural fennel tea an hour before breastfeeding is often effective.

yourself overstressed, arrange to go out for an hour or so to calm your nerves, and let someone else tend to the baby. If that is not practical, put the baby into his crib and step into another room to calm yourself down.

It's normal to feel overwhelmed sometimes, but if you or your husband experience depression or extreme anger, consult your pediatrician for coping suggestions, speak to a trusted mentor, *rav* or *rebbetzin*, or family member — and get help quickly.

Infant colic is described in ancient history by the Greek physician Galen (who lived in the second century CE), who recommended narcotics to calm fussy babies. It is recorded that in medieval times some mothers applied opium or alcohol to their nipples. Even in comparatively recent history, doctors used to prescribe sedatives, analgesics, and relaxants for colicky babies. This is no longer done due to their potentially serious side effects, but it goes to show that colic in babies is universal. At least it's comforting to know that colic is normal, not dangerous, and temporary.

Self-Soothers: Pacifier vs. Thumb

Comforting your baby when he cries is obviously very important. Some infants are easily soothed when you talk or sing softly to them, cuddle them, or gently rock them in their crib. Other newborns want to suck all the time, even when they're not hungry.

Many infants are born with an extremely strong sucking reflex. In the beginning, your baby will suck anything that touches his lips, without differentiating between a source of food or something else, even Mommy's chin or cheek! This instinct is obviously related to the newborn's need for nutrition, but sucking also brings him pleasure and comforts him. If your baby continues to be fussy and searches for the nipple even after feedings, a pacifier can be helpful.

An important benefit of encouraging your baby to use a pacifier is the recent recommendation by the American Academy of Pediatrics that the use of a pacifier during the first year of life may

help protect infants from SIDS (sudden infant death syndrome). However, pacifiers are possibly associated with increased ear infections in older babies.

The optimal time to introduce a pacifier is during the first two months, when the sucking reflex is strongest. Lactation consultants, as well as the American Academy of Pediatrics, recommend postponing the use of pacifiers until a baby is proficient at nursing. (Sucking on a pacifier releases a hormone that tells baby he's full. If baby is not feeding well, the pacifier can make the situation worse.) When you're sure that your baby is gaining weight well and she is eating on schedule, try offering her a pacifier.

In the past, it was believed that pacifiers and thumb-sucking changed the anatomical shape of the mouth. This is a real concern when the habit continues beyond the age of four or five, but children often discontinue using a pacifier or sucking their thumb by then (though thumb-sucking may last much longer, even up to the age of ten). The risk of complications such as tooth tilting or orthodontic misalignment becomes relevant only at the age when permanent teeth appear — when the child has hopefully left pacifiers and thumb-sucking behind.

The advantage of letting a baby suck his thumb is that it's always available, never gets lost, and the baby doesn't have to cry for you to retrieve it. The alleged advantage of a pacifier is that parents have control and can withhold it to prevent prolonged use past infancy. In reality, most parents find it very difficult to deny a screaming child his Binky.

Not every baby takes to a pacifier. Some spit it out repeatedly or shut their mouths firmly every time it's offered. Today pacifiers come in many different shapes and sizes, so you can try out different kinds until you find the one your little one approves of. Even after all that, though, some babies still prefer to suck on their fingers or thumb.

It's not the end of the world if your baby really wants to suck her thumb or fingers. Many children stop on their own at around the age of a year. Pulling the baby's thumb out of her mouth generally strengthens the thumb-sucking behavior. If you want her to stop, avoid a power struggle by distracting her with something else she can reach for and hold on to.

When looking for the right pacifier, you'll find that there are many varieties, including rubber or silicone, orthodontically-shaped to a sucking infant's mouth, or simple, old-fashioned "dummies" (which babies often seem to prefer over the more expensive versions). Conventional rubber pacifiers feel soft in the baby's mouth, but they wear out quickly and must be replaced more often. Synthetic pacifiers are durable, easier to clean, and don't retain stains or odors from food. However, the silicone remains rigid in the baby's mouth and usually takes more time for the baby to get used to it.

New pacifiers should be boiled for five minutes to sterilize them and remove any chemical residue from the factory where they were made. Try offering the pacifier after feedings to help baby go to sleep, but remember that sucking a pacifier is habit-forming and if overused it will be very difficult to take it away later. After she falls asleep, the pacifier will fall out of her mouth — don't put it back in her mouth so that she won't become dependent on it during sleep.

If your baby resists the pacifier, don't force the issue; try other ways to soothe her. You can find another opportunity to try again later, especially if she starts to suck her thumb. It's much easier to wean a baby off the pacifier when she is a year old than when she is three or four, so don't wait too long to take it away.

Pacifier Dos and Don'ts

» Since cavity-causing bacteria exist in adult saliva, it's not recommended to clean a pacifier by putting it in Mommy's mouth.

» Dipping a pacifier into sweet liquid (juice or soda) can cause decay in the infant's emerging teeth.

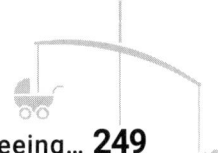

- » Keep the pacifier clean by rinsing it with water, and replace if the pacifier shows cracks or other signs of wear.
- » Coating a pacifier with sugar or honey is not safe for a baby (who should *never* be exposed to honey under the age of a year).
- » You may attach the pacifier to your baby's clothing with a clip designed for this purpose, but *never* tie it around her neck or to the sides of her crib, as this poses a risk for strangulation. Make sure the strap or chain is short and that any decorations won't fall off or tear, to avoid a choking hazard.
- » If your baby loves his pacifier — keep a few identical extras where you can easily locate them, in case it gets lost.

Four to Six Months

A Bundle of Fun

You've nursed, held, and cared for your newborn around the clock. Now, be prepared to fall in love.

By four months, babies start giving back the endless love they receive. No longer just eating-crying-sleeping machines, they will smile, squeal, and giggle, expressing complex emotions and developing meaningful relationships with the people around them. They will "hatch" — emerge from their shells and interact more with the world, revealing rich and unique personalities.

What's more, many parents find relief at this stage: most four- to six-month-olds are calmer, happier, and have settled into a routine, sometimes sleeping for relatively long stretches at night. Now that their digestive systems have matured and gas bubbles have diminished, even colicky babies have usually mellowed.

While no parenting stage is without its challenges, get ready to enjoy a whole new level of sweetness and joy.

PHYSICAL GROWTH AND MILESTONES

Between four and six months, your baby will develop an array of exciting skills. Here's what you *should* be seeing by now:

DEVELOPMENTAL MILESTONES	BABY...
Physical growth	Sleeps four- to six-hour stretches
Motor and sensory	Lifts her head up while on her tummy and shows good head control
	Brings arms forward to reach out
	Visually tracks moving objects
	Shows good neck strength: does not wobble her head when held upright
Speech and communication	Produces vowel sounds like "ah," "eh," or "oh"
	Makes steady eye contact
Social-emotional	Smiles
	Responds to loud sounds and visual cues (like bright lights)
	Shows particular attachment to Mommy's voice — gets excited or alert

If your baby hasn't reach one of these milestones, DON'T PANIC! But be sure to mention it to your doctor at her next well-baby checkup.

Here's what you'll *likely* see in the fourth to sixth month:

DEVELOPMENTAL MILESTONES	BABY...
Physical growth	Is alert and awake for one and a half- to two-hour stretches
	Doubles her birth weight (usually at four to five months)
Motor and sensory	Rolls from tummy to back and vice versa
	Reaches for toys during tummy time
	Uses both hands to explore toys
	Brings hands and objects to her mouth
	Inserts feet into mouth while lying on her back
	Enjoys an assortment of movements
	Notices toys that make sounds
	Holds a bottle on her own
Speech, language, and communication	Begins to babble — usually with *p*, *b*, and *m* sounds Uses babbling to get attention
	Responds to and imitates facial expressions and sounds
	Recognizes her own name
Social-emotional	Begins to distinguish between familiar and strange faces

Red Flags

By four months, contact your doctor if baby...
» seems overly stiff or floppy
» does not try to reach or grasp for toys
» does not bring hands or objects to mouth
» is frequently irritable for no apparent reason
» avoids eye contact
» doesn't respond to loud noises
» does not smile or coo

Chapter Thirteen

Teething, Sleeping, Moving, Playing...

The Tooth Fairy Arrives

Over the next three months, your baby might cut a tooth! That's exciting — except that the teething is often accompanied by significant, prolonged discomfort.

Here are some signs that pearly white number one is on its way:

» Swollen, red gums

» Fussiness, especially at night

» Frequent drooling, which may lead to a rash on the chin, face, or chest

» Changes in feeding: Some babies don't want to nurse or take bottles, as sucking brings more blood to the gums, increasing sensitivity and swelling in the area. Other babies do the opposite: they want to nurse more often, since the breastmilk soothes the gums. Teething can also lead to preferring to nurse on one side only.

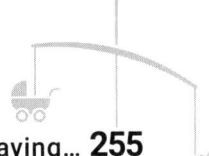

- » Continual biting of toys and fingers
- » Ear pulling and cheek rubbing (the ache from the jaw can transfer to the cheeks or ear canal)
- » Mild fever — under 102°F (the connection between fever and teething is unclear, but some theorize that teething lowers immunity — due to increased stress and decreased sleep — making baby more susceptible to viruses)
- » Diarrhea, due to the excess drool
- » Diaper rash, since teething causes changes in the acidity of baby's stool

Some doctors believe that these symptoms have nothing to do with teething; they're simply the result of typical viruses and infections. For the first few months of life, infants are protected from pathogens by maternal antibodies imbued at birth. By four to six months, these antibodies have mostly depleted, accounting for the sudden increase in aches and pains.

Whatever the true source of these ailments, one thing is clear: These unpleasant symptoms can last for up to several months before the tooth makes its appearance.

What can you do to alleviate baby's pain and discomfort — and maintain your sanity?

- » **Serve it chilled.** Once he's been introduced to solids, try feeding baby cold applesauce or yogurt, straight from the fridge. (For more on introducing solids, see Chapter 15, p. 313.)
- » **Give him something to chew.** Offer safe objects for your baby to chew on, such as teething rings — preferably cold — or a clean, frozen wet washcloth. Consider buying chillable gel-filled teething rings, which are designed just for this purpose. But make sure the ring is BPA-free, with an outer layer that's completely intact and leak resistant. Discard it as soon as you notice punctures; those are breeding grounds

for bacteria and mold. Never freeze teething rings: They can crack from the pressure or become too hard, injuring baby's gums. Rings should be stored in the fridge only.

- » **Massage the gums.** Use a clean finger, moistened gauze pad, or teething ring to rub baby's gums for two minutes. He may balk at first, but ultimately he'll find the counterpressure soothing.
- » **Bring out the bib.** To prevent baby's shirt from becoming soaked with drool, consider outfitting him with a teething bib. Some bibs come with a textured corner that baby can nibble on for relief.
- » **Administer medication.** If baby is still suffering, give him acetaminophen or ibuprofen-based medications — with your pediatrician's go-ahead. (Don't give aspirin, as it can cause Reye's syndrome — a rare but potentially fatal illness — in children under twenty.) Stay away from oral anesthetics — numbing gels sold in pharmacies — the U.S. Food and Drug Administration warns against them, since the gel can numb a baby's throat and make swallowing difficult. The gels can also put a baby at risk for reduced oxygen levels in the blood.
- » **Provide comfort and distraction.** Sometimes an extra snuggle or a new toy is enough to get baby's mind off the pain.

And when the going gets tough, remember that this, too, shall pass!

Dental Development and Care

In most babies, teeth arrive in pairs. The first ivories to debut are usually the lower front teeth, followed by the upper front teeth. By age three, most babies will sport a full set of twenty primary teeth.

To keep those chompers gleaming, start brushing as soon as they arrive. The American Dental Association gives parents the green light for fluoridated toothpaste, but only a rice-grain-size smidgen should be used until three years of age, on a supersoft baby toothbrush. Parents should brush the teeth of breast- and bottle-fed babies, since milk proteins can cause tooth decay. Don't allow baby to fall asleep with her bottle; this can cause significant decay. You can give baby a four-ounce bottle of water after her milk bottle, to wash the milk from her mouth and teeth.

When should baby make her inaugural visit to the dentist? Between one and two years of age, experts say — or whenever he can sit still long enough for a dental examination. Choose a pediatric dentist, or a dentist who has a rapport with kids.

Do you live in an area with fluoridated water? Consider yourself fortunate. Water fluoridation has been proven to prevent tooth decay, and nearly all public health, medical, and dental organizations consider this water safe for baby. While babies exposed to too much fluoride can develop fluorosis — a condition resulting in teeth discoloration — incidence is low, and the condition is rarely caused by fluoridation alone (it's usually the result of unnecessary or excessive intake of fluoride supplements). If you're concerned

MOMMY'S TWO CENTS

Just gave baby a sugary snack in the park or bus, where you're unable to brush her teeth? If you've already introduced her to solids and dairy, slip her a slice of cheese — any kind. Cheese chewing encourages saliva production, which causes a rapid pH increase in the mouth, reducing the risk of teeth erosion.

If you're out of cheese, here's another option recommended by pediatric dentists: Wipe baby's teeth with a soft gauze (like those used in bandaging). This usually gets at plaque that's hard to remove when brushing a squirming baby's teeth.

about your child's fluoride intake, consult with your pediatrician or dentist.

The Mystery of the Disappearing Sleep

After invoking the requisite rainbow of anti-*ayin hara* watchwords, you bragged to your green-eyed friends about six-week-old baby doing eight-hour stretches at night. Suddenly, at four months, she's started waking up every two hours. What happened?

Brace yourself: Three to four months is a common time for sleep regression (the other prevalent sleep-crisis time is eight to nine months). Many babies who've until now slept like — well, like babies — will begin showing regular nighttime fussiness. For some the culprit is teething, which can last anywhere from three to twelve months (see above for survival tips). For others, an increased alertness and curiosity about the world prevents them from sleeping too soundly.

Either way, Mom and Dad have got to get some shut-eye. To minimize any unwanted nocturnal rendezvous, establish and maintain a solid bedtime routine. Don't skimp on daytime naps: An overtired baby will be even harder to put to sleep. When nothing seems to be working, take a deep breath and remember that this stage is temporary. (For more on getting children to sleep well during the night, see below.)

Does baby rise before the sun? Some babies effortlessly fall asleep — and stay asleep — only to wake up bright-eyed and chipper at 5:00 a.m.

Try the following strategies to keep baby sleeping for longer:

» **Make it dark.** It's a fact: sunlight sends a memo to the brain: "Time to get up!" To keep the room dark, consider installing blackout curtains, putting up temporary darkening shades, or even taping up dark garbage bags. If you've got Israeli-style shutters (a *"tris"*), count your blessings!

- » **Block out the noise.** Particularly if you live on a busy street, hang heavy drapes or blankets over the windows. If that's not enough, consider buying a white noise machine — a nifty device that plays soothing, continuous sounds like rolling waves or winds blowing through trees.

- » **Experiment with bedtime.** Remember: With most kids, sleep begets sleep. Saying night-night to baby an hour late may just result in a super-cranky kiddo who woke up at the same time the next morning — minus an hour of much-needed sleep. Fascinatingly, putting baby in *earlier* might actually help him stay sleeping for longer. If this doesn't work after a week, try the opposite: Delay bedtime by ten minutes and see if there's a difference.

- » **Push the nap forward.** Move baby's afternoon nap to a bit later in the day; this way, she'll go to bed later and possibly wake up later.

- » **Upgrade the diapers.** Soaked-through or leaky diapers often cause babies to wake up. Try double-diapering baby or outfitting him with superabsorbent diapers designed for nighttime use.

- » **Provide in-crib entertainment.** Set aside special "early-morning toys" — a rattle or cloth book — and put them into your baby's crib when he shows signs of life at unearthly hours. If they're sufficiently engaging, you might earn yourself a few more minutes of slumber.

- » **Be realistic.** Some babies this age are capable of sleeping through the night, but most will wake up at least once. So if baby hit the sack at 7:30 p.m., don't expect his beauty sleep to last until 9:00 a.m. — even if it's Shabbos. Developmentally, a wake-up time of six or seven is reasonable for most babies. Sorry, Mom!

- » **Don't overreact.** If baby is talking, fussing, or babbling in her crib at 5:30, there's no need to jump out of bed and fetch her. Let her chatter for a while; learning to self-entertain is a fantastic skill. Respond only when she's really had enough — don't worry, she'll make that clear!

» **Hold off on early-morning parties.** Keep it calm, and avoid early-morning stimulating social interaction. If you switch on the lights, turn on the music, and sing animatedly to baby at 5:00 a.m., her circadian rhythm will take note. *Not* what you want.

If none of these strategies work, you may just have to bite the bullet. Clearly, baby's body clock is still adjusting, and his internal alarm clock needs time to reset. Remember, this stage is temporary! Go to sleep early, adjust your expectations, then embrace the fresh morning air. If you're really ambitious, take a post-dawn stroller jog; you'll feel invigorated and energized.

Seeing Eye-to-Eye

Exciting news: Baby's vision is getting sharper each day. By now, baby can see objects that are several feet away, but she still prefers looking at objects close-up. At around five months, she'll acquire depth perception: the ability to see objects three-dimensionally. She'll also learn to distinguish between shades of the same color, so she'll notice, for example, a dark blue rattle on a light blue rug.

Time to break out the colors of the rainbow? Not yet. Baby's newfound visual prowess notwithstanding, stick with bright primary colors for toys and décor. Those are still the most engaging and stimulating for his developing brain. (Baby might show a particular preference for blues and reds.)

If baby is cross-eyed or squinting, this is not cute. Baby's eyes should be moving smoothly and in-sync, following objects and people around the room. If you notice any visual abnormality — crossed eyes, one or both eyes turning in, pupils darting to and fro — consult with your doctor.

Feeding Fixes

Starting at four months, you may find that baby nurses for less time. Not to worry: Your more efficient little guy is getting the same amount each day, just doing it more quickly, and the milk composition is changing to fit his needs. As long as he's gaining weight nicely, you can relax.

If baby is showing a lack of interest during nursing sessions, frequently pulling his head away to check out noises or sights, don't panic: This is the classic four-month "yenta" syndrome. Thanks to increased attentiveness to visual and auditory stimuli, he's simply more curious about the world...and hopelessly distracted! He is *not* yet ready to wean. To facilitate coffee break–free mealtimes, feed baby in a quiet, dimly lit room.

Does baby salivate while watching his parents eat dinner? Some little guys will show interest in solids already at four months. But don't buy stock in Gerber yet: It's best to hold off until your doctor advises you to give solids — generally not before six months. By then, there's a decreased risk of

- **Infection from food** — his digestive tract is more developed;
- **Allergic reactions to food** — his immune system is more developed;
- **Choking** — once he masters the art of sitting upright, he'll be physically ready to ingest food.

If baby still seems hungry, try nursing more often; he may need more during a developmental or growth spurt. You can also discuss starting solids early with your doctor. Depending on the circumstances, some pediatricians will give the go-ahead. (More on feeding in Chapter 15, p. 313.)

Baby's on a Roll

It's going to be a while before baby gets around. But at this stage, you should be noticing that she's got better control of her body: she can lift up her head and bear weight on her arms. When you hold her, her neck stays aligned, and her head barely wobbles.

Thanks to this increased upper-body strength, baby will soon learn to roll over — at first, only from her stomach to back. The first few roll-overs may be scary or startling: Often, babies don't realize that pushing hard on their arms plus leaning toward one side will yield a full-body flip. To calm her and reinforce that this is a *positive* development, offer loads of reassurance and applause.

When will this grand roll-over take place? Generally around four months of age, but some babies do it even earlier, and there are no telltale signs that it's coming. Since it can occur from minute to minute, always err on the safe side: Never leave baby unattended on a changing table or raised surface, even for a second.

Tummy Time

If baby hits the five-month mark and hasn't yet made the twist, it's time to buckle down on...you guessed it: tummy time! In truth, this should have started as early as the first week of life; by three months, experts say baby should be on her tummy for at least twenty minutes a day. By focusing on tummy time from her earliest stages, you can help avoid developmental delays and the need for physical and occupational therapies. More tummy time results in better motor and cognitive development — and the more comfortable baby will feel in the position.

Baby is not particularly fond of tummy time? That's normal at first. (Do *you* love doing push-ups?)

Try the following:

» Ease into it gradually: Start with five minutes, slowly prolonging the duration. If that doesn't help, stick to smaller time-bytes: Set at least four tummy time sessions over the course of the day, five minutes each.

- » Do tummy time on your tummy! Lean back comfortably on your couch and place baby tummy down on your chest. She'll push up to look at your face and not even realize she's getting tummy time!
- » Make sure you've fed and burped baby first. A hungry or gassy infant will not appreciate this workout.
- » Invest in an engaging play mat with strong primary colors.
- » Create a view. If your baby can barely lift up his head, try propping him up on his hands, your knees, a rolled-up towel, or a nursing pillow. When he becomes aware of the interesting sights awaiting him, he might be motivated to keep that head up for longer.
- » Place toys within reach to encourage her to stretch out her arms. (This develops arm strength.)
- » Suspend a colorful toy a bit above baby's head, cajoling her to lift her head and bear down on her arms.
- » Get down on the floor and give her the gift of your company! Your face — or your husband's — is infinitely more interesting than a toy (especially when you're being goofy). Engage your little girl at eye level; then lift your head a bit to encourage her to follow suit.
- » Make it routine. Incorporate tummy time into your routine: Put baby facedown for three to four minutes each time you change his diaper. Just be sure to stay close and keep him secure.

Once baby is more amenable to tummy time, go through the motions: Slowly move her limbs to practice a tummy-to-back roll. Make sure the floor is equipped with a mat or carpet to cushion a high-speed or unexpected flip. Also make sure that facedown baby is always supervised. If she shows clear signs of fatigue, immediately put her to sleep on her back.

What if your baby's become so adept at two-way rolling that she rolls over at night — from her back to stomach? That's fine. Continue putting her to bed faceup, and if she rolls over, there's no need to turn her back. Now that she's mastered this motor skill, most health experts assert that she's far less likely to stay in a position that jeopardizes her breathing. However:

» Make sure the crib mattress is firm, the sheets are tight, the surface is clear of toys and pillows, and that your physician agrees that this does not compromise safety.

Do not swaddle her anymore. Rolling over while swaddled is a suffocation risk.

Diaperless Babe on the Loose

Baby's newfound ability to roll over is exciting — except she may attempt to use the skill during changing time. What's a mom to do when her little one squiggles and wriggles and lurches to one side while being changed?

» **Have everything ready.** Before you launch Operation Diaper, prepare the wipes, a fresh diaper, and any other necessary supplies (baby powder, rash ointment, moisturizer, etc.). Consider keeping one of each in key rooms of the house, to preclude constant trips upstairs to the baby room.

» **Distract with toys.** Hand baby a rattle or cloth book to keep her busy, or suspend a mobile on top of her changing table. For maximum interest, designate these as "diaper toys," and offer them to baby only during diaper changes. Some mommies report that letting baby hold the new diaper keeps him happy — and still.

» **Rotate the scenery.** Try changing baby in a variety of places — the couch, the floor, the bed — so she gets some fresh views. Even placing her head at the other side of the changing table periodically can feel like an adventure!

» **Beat the clock.** This is not the time for Pesach cleaning! Don't obsess. Baby's bottom is no longer soiled? Diaper is fastened? You're a champion.

» **Speak soothingly.** Avoid becoming anxious or harried. Sing, talk, or coo in an even-keeled, calm voice, and baby will similarly relax.

Baby's Up for Grabs

With improved hand-eye coordination (facilitated by none other than...tummy time!), your baby is now empowered to grasp objects. And grasp he will! But his mouth is still his primary means of exploring the world, so our newbie gripper will transfer all finger-held objects straight to his lips.

When holding him, remove dangling earrings or necklaces to prevent painful tugs or broken jewelry. Get rid of all small objects within reach. To minimize germ spread, wash all toys occasionally, especially if other babies have been around.

It will take time for your baby to perfect his grasp. At first, he'll swipe and swipe, consistently missing his target. With time, his hand-eye coordination will become more accurate, leading to a skillful grasp.

Sometimes, during this learning process, baby will hit himself in the face with a toy or book and then look accusingly at you. This is par for the course; take it in stride.

Making Sense of Baby's Senses

From four to six months, you can boost baby's sensory development in lots of ways:

1. **Offer a variety of textures for play.** For example, faux fur, tissue, felt, velvet, and towel. Look for touch-and-feel books that make touching part of the reading experience. This

exposure will help baby when she's introduced to foods with new, unfamiliar textures.

2. **Touch baby as often as possible.** Stroke her, massage her, lift and rock her. Babies love a gentle caress. For more on infant massage, see pp. 267-271.

3. **Turn on the music!** Evidence increasingly supports music's myriad positive effects on baby's emotional, sensory, and language development. Unlike sight, hearing is usually well developed soon after birth, so babies can begin enjoying tunes immediately. (Did your baby dance to the music in utero? She could hear your voice before she was born!) Classical music or songs specially geared to babies are great, but any music can work well. What's important is that you enjoy the music too. This way you'll be more inclined to turn it on often. Benefits of frequent music and song playing can include:

   » **Better language skills**. The baby acquires a solid understanding of rhythm and intonation, both of which are essential components of speech. She'll also learn many new words from the lyrics, as well as the concept of rhymes.

   » **Improved mood and stronger parent-child bond**. Moving to music together produces oxytocin, the same delightful hormone that's secreted when you nurse. So you can expect more smiles and less fussiness when you and your baby enjoy the music together. Lullabies can be particularly calming for both mom and baby during predawn kvetch sessions.

   » **Try to incorporate movement.** Babies who engage in making music or moving to music are found to use more communicative gestures at an earlier age than babies who are passive music listeners. Offer baby a rattle, toy drum, or xylophone and teach him to get into the beat: Clap, bang, and wiggle together. No need to invest money: A pot or plastic container with a wooden stick can be a great merrymaker.

- » For bedtime, choose a particularly soothing tune and play it each evening. This will both cue baby in to the agenda (memo to munchkin: go to sleep) while helping him relax. But don't leave the room and let baby fall asleep to the music; he might become dependent on it, and you'll be stuck on Shabbos, Yom Tov, or anytime the tune is unavailable. Play the song once or twice, then turn it off and say "good night."

- » Finally, **don't limit yourself to recorded music.** Songs starring Mommy are just as stimulating. Don't worry about your pitch; even if you can't carry a tune, baby loves your voice (in fact, it's his absolute favorite!). Songs that have a motor element — like "Itsy Bitsy Spider" — are always winners and have also been shown to aid in cognitive development.

Baby Massage: A How-To Guide

Good news: You can start massaging baby from the moment he's born. What happens when you gently rub those delicious limbs? His central nervous system is stimulated, and it begins to produce serotonin, a feel-good hormone that relaxes the heart rate and breathing, while reducing the production of cortisol, a stress hormone. In the meantime, your body secretes oxytocin, another feel-good hormone that lifts your mood and makes you feel empowered. Final product: a calmer baby — and a happier mom. (Interestingly, some studies show that baby massage can alleviate symptoms in mothers suffering from postpartum depression.)

Research has shown that baby massage can

- » Reduce crying and fussiness
- » Alleviate colic and constipation
- » Boost healthy sleep patterns
- » Promote sensory and tactile development

- » Normalize muscle tone
- » Improve circulation
- » Strengthen the parent-child bond

What's more, some studies suggest that massage even helps baby fight off infections. In light of these boons, consider setting aside ten minutes a day for some easy-to-do movements. Or suggest the idea to Daddy: It's a great way for him to connect with baby.

Some pointers to keep in mind before you get started:

- » **Time it right.** Massage baby between feeds — when he's not too hungry, not too full, and not too tired. Pay attention to his cues: Steady gaze? Content expression? Alert eyes? Those are good signs. It's ideal to integrate the activity into your daily routine so that baby can learn to expect it. Choose an hour when you're relaxed and when baby is usually settled; many mothers find that a soothing pre-bedtime massage hits the spot.

- » **Choose a moisturizer or oil.** Oils and creams allow your hands to glide effortlessly over baby's skin, so they can greatly enhance the experience. If you choose to use oil, be sure to place a towel under baby to avoid stains. Stick with vegetable oils, which tend to be gentler on baby's sensitive skin, and are digestible (in case baby does some post-massage finger sucking). Stay away from nut oils, which can induce allergic reactions, as well as baby and mineral oils, which clog pores. Test any oil or cream first by rubbing a smidgen on baby's skin the day before and looking out for reactions. If baby has eczema, you can use his prescription cream as your lubricant.

- » **Create the setting.** This is special bonding time, so you want to create a calm, soothing atmosphere. Remove all noises and distractions (ahem, cell phone). Turn on relaxing background

music, and speak to baby in a warm, soothing voice. Lay baby down on the changing pad, a bed, a rug — or your lap. You can even put a towel on a spacious kitchen countertop. If you choose a harder surface, place his head on a pillow or padded blanket (he may still have vulnerable soft spots).

» **Keep it warm.** Your baby will only be wearing a diaper, so give the massage in a room that is nice and toasty, without any drafts, and not too near a heater, radiator, or air conditioner.

» **Ease into it.** Touch baby gently at first, gradually building up pressure. The older your baby, the firmer your touch should be. Be sure to remove all hand jewelry before starting, so you don't accidentally hurt him.

» **Follow baby's cues.** Never force a massage; you want to ensure positive associations. If baby resists your overtures, skip it and try again another time. If she seems overwhelmed by the touch, go gentler. She may enjoy some movements more than others, so pay attention. If she starts whimpering after a particular stroke, stop and try something else, or just call it a day and offer a cuddle.

» **Don't give up.** If baby doesn't go wild over the massage at first, don't get disheartened. Some babies need time to get used to the sensations; most babies ultimately love it. So keep trying those moves for a few minutes each day.

Once the stage is set, warm the oil — and your hands — by squirting a bit into your palms and rubbing vigorously. Then gently begin massaging baby's skin. Most experts recommend starting from the legs and working your way up; legs are less sensitive than some other body parts, and your baby is used to people touching them during diaper changes.

» **Legs:** Hold your baby's ankle in one hand; with the other stroke firmly but gently down from his ankle, then up again. Repeat. Then, starting from the thigh, roll the leg with both hands, as if you're rolling a rope of challah dough. Repeat and switch feet.

- » **Feet:** Gently rotate the foot several times in each direction. Use your thumbs to trace circles — on the sole, and around the ankle.
- » **Toes:** Rub each of baby's toes between your thumb and forefinger, gently pulling and squeezing each one. Switch feet and repeat.
- » **Arms:** Roll baby's arm between your hands (the challah dough move), starting at the shoulder and moving down to his wrist. Rotate the wrist several times in each direction. Repeat and switch. Then stroke his arms with the same strokes you used for his legs (see above).
- » **Hands:** Use your thumb to trace soft circles in baby's palm; move in both directions.
- » **Chest:** Place your hands near baby's sternum. Then gently press outward over the ribs, as if you are flattening pastry dough. Using your fingertips, stroke diagonally from each shoulder to the opposite hip, creating an *X*.
- » **Belly:** Move your fingers fluidly around baby's belly button in a circular, clockwise motion. Then bend baby's knees and push them toward his chest for thirty seconds; repeat several times. Then place one of your wrists on baby's belly button, gliding down rhythmically. These movements may help release pent-up gas; they're particularly recommended for colicky babies.
- » **Face:** Place your thumbs on baby's forehead, then gently push outward from the center, as if smoothing his creases. Using both hands, trace a heart shape from forehead to chin. Then do some long downward strokes, from the top of the head all the way down to baby's toes.

» **Back:** Starting from the base of the neck, give long, firm strokes down to baby's bottom, or even down to his feet. Then stroke from side to side.

For colic relief, start with the belly massage, and repeat as needed.

For the inaugural massage, you may want to ease baby into it by doing only a leg and toe rub. When you start massaging more regularly, try to keep to the same movement sequence each time; babies love predictability.

King of the Burble

The time has come: Your little guy is emerging as a silver-tongued orator! No matter that his newfound speech consists of babbles. He certainly sounds and looks as if he's delivering the Gettysburg Address.

By now, your baby should be producing all kinds of vowel sounds (*ah*, *eh*, *ee*, *oh*) and experimenting with the first-to-arrive consonant sounds: *B*, *M*, and *P*. That means he might say, for example, "ma," "pa," or even "mama" (sorry, daddies and *tatties* of the world!).

He'll also start experimenting more with his lips and tongue, discovering that he can employ these limbs to produce all kinds of cool and weird sounds: kissing, clucking, cheek popping, and more. Be prepared for repeat showings of the raspberry (or razzing) — that ever-so-elegant noise.

How to promote baby's speech development at this stage? Just keep talking to him, all day long. You may feel silly offering an endless running commentary, but it's a worthwhile investment. While baby is too young to understand specific word meanings right now, easy, simple conversation will give him essential groundwork for communication: rhythm, tone, and exposure to native sounds. Use varying intonation, respond to baby's coos and gurgles, and ask questions. Make sure to use simple, everyday words in short sentences.

INSTEAD OF...	TRY...
"That station wagon is humongous. It's far bigger than anything I've seen before!"	"Car! So big!"
"I don't see Tatty. Where could he have disappeared to? Did he leave the house?"	"Where's Tatty? Where did Tatty go?"

Think beyond words: Make lots of funny, engaging sounds (we're back to the raspberry!) and see if baby imitates. Read animal books together regularly and produce the sounds.

Remember that the most stimulating experience for a baby is human interaction. No toy or gadget — no matter how state-of-the-art — can compete with human voice and body language.

Play = Learning

When it comes to promoting language development (the ability to understand concepts and understand verbal and non-verbal communication), there are so many games and activities beneficial for this age group:

» **Books.** You can never read too much to baby. At this age, simple picture books with one or two items per page are ideal. Choose large, brightly colored pictures with high black-and-white or color contrast and simply name the items on the page. Babies especially love faces, so board books with baby faces are recommended. Don't feel the need to finish the book from start to end; at this age a baby's attention span is short. Feel free to flip through the book, stopping only at the pages that baby likes. Finally, don't be beholden to the text: Even if you're reading a storybook, skip the story and just name the items in the pictures.

- » **Peekaboo.** Baby is just now starting to learn about "object permanence" — the notion that even if an object is not visible at a given moment, it might still be there. Playing a simple peekaboo with your hands — cover your face or one of his favorite toys — is a great way to start implanting this concept.

- » **Body-part naming.** Body parts are extremely concrete and functional, so if you're looking to build language, they're a great starter vocabulary group. "Where's my nose? Here's my nose!" or "Where are your eyes? Here are your eyes!" This activity works particularly well in the bath, when all the body parts are visible.

- » **Imitation games.** Imitation is a skill that's essential for all areas of development: Children progress by copying the behaviors they observe. When your baby produces a noise, imitate it consistently — this teaches him that what he says makes a difference, and that imitation is something we do. Once you've familiarized him with the concept, try making simple sounds ("bah!" "boo!") and wait a few moments — see if he takes the bait and imitates you.

- » **Cause-and-effect games.** Any game that incorporates cause and effect is excellent for this age group. Start simple: Flick a light, or open and close a cupboard (while saying "open!" "close!"). Then move into more active scenarios: Roll a ball across the floor to baby, or play the dropping game: Baby drops toy, parent says, "Uh-oh!" and picks it up (if baby is not ready for dropping yet, parent can assume this role too — just leave a toy at the edge of the table, then knock it off). These repeat sequences can be wearisome for the grown-ups, but they teach baby important concepts: Actions have effects, and *his* actions can have an effect on this world.

Building Lifelong Bonds

Parents will do everything they can to ensure that their baby develops within the normal range, but they often overlook a powerful, evidence-based truth: A stable, secure relationship with a loving caregiver is the best predictor of normal development in infancy. Translation? A healthy, strong bond with your baby is critical...and the time to cultivate that bond starts at birth.

When it comes to social-emotional connections, *stable* is the key word. Even when baby is restless or cranky or keeping you up for hours at night, try to exhibit unfaltering love and patience. This teaches baby that Mommy will be there for her no matter what, giving her the confidence she needs to explore the world.

The best gift you can give your baby is to convey that you *enjoy* being around her. This comes easily to some mothers, but is harder for others — they might find infant care somewhat boring or unstimulating. If you're finding yourself in the latter group, don't feel bad; you're in good company. Figure out which activities you enjoy doing with baby — a walk outdoors? mommy and me group? book reading? — and go heavy on those. Every mother-baby pair has different preferences, so don't feel pressured by "what's done" or "what's typical."

If baby relaxes when you hold her, shows unease when you leave, or coos when you touch her, then you're probably doing a great job in the relationship-building department.

But your baby is not focused only on her relationship with you. Between four and six months, she'll start interacting more with all the people in her world: smiling, cooing, and making steady eye contact. While she'll still flash smiles freely at total strangers, she's beginning to show preference for the special people in her life.

Try to balance stimulating game time with snuggle time. After a playful afternoon, relax together in a rocking chair, sing soothing songs and lullabies, or just whisper quietly. It's a good idea to designate one calm-down song — one tune that you'll sing

> ### MOMMY'S TWO CENTS
> Don't feel like spending ten dollars on a rattle made in China? It's easy to make a budget-friendly rattle at home. Pour pasta, rice, or beans into a small plastic bottle; seal tightly. Vary with different shapes, sizes, and contents, and create an orchestra of rattles! (But don't forget to sell it with the *chametz* for Pesach!) When baby learns to open the container, it's time for a new toy: Uncooked pasta, beans, and rice are choking hazards.

whenever baby is sad or fussy. With time, she'll learn to associate this song with comfort and attention, and just hearing the first verse will calm her. This strategy is particularly helpful for when you're driving and can't hold her.

Toy Story

For this age group, you'll want to offer simple toys with basic colors. Try to bring out only one or two toys at a time, so as not to overstimulate baby.

Some four to six months favorites:

- » Rattles
- » Soft dolls
- » Toy key chains
- » Sturdy board books (that can withstand baby's relentless gumming)
- » Plastic bowls and measuring cups

Seven to Nine Months

A Half a Year of Baby

You've passed six months of motherhood — a huge milestone. By now, you've gained confidence in yourself as a mother, appreciating that when it comes to intuiting your baby's needs, no one else can fill your shoes. And if your baby was colicky, that's probably tapered off by now — and you're getting a tad more sleep.

But just when you thought you got the nursing or bottle feeding down pat, surprise! It's time to start thinking about transitioning to solids. It's also time for baby to start getting serious about motor development — and for you to make sure baby has plenty of opportunity to creep and crawl.

In this section, you'll get the full lowdown, with plenty of tips and tools for success.

PHYSICAL GROWTH AND MILESTONES

Between seven and nine months, your baby's development will be rapid. Here's what you *should* be seeing by now:

DEVELOPMENTAL MILESTONES	BABY...
Physical growth	has doubled her birth weight
	Sleeps six- to eight-hour stretches, though many still wake up at least once at night
Motor and sensory	Rolls over from back to tummy and vice versa
	Reaches for objects and brings them to his mouth
	Passes objects from one hand to the other
	Holds her head steady
	Sits with minimal support
Speech and communication	Strings vowels together to produce sounds, like "ah," "eh," or "oh"
	Makes sounds to show joy or displeasure
	Squeals or babbles, then waits for a response from you!
Social-emotional	Smiles and laughs
	Makes eye contact
	Responds to sounds
	Recognizes people and things around her
	Shows stranger anxiety around unfamiliar people
	Shows greater interest in socializing; enjoys watching other children

If your baby hasn't reached one of these milestones, DON'T PANIC! But be sure to mention it to your doctor at her next well-baby checkup.

Here's what you'll *likely* see in the next three months:

DEVELOPMENTAL MILESTONES	BABY…
Physical growth	Debuts her first teeth!
Motor and sensory	Is starting to creep on the floor (commando crawl), sliding on her tummy while pushing forward with hands
	Sits without support
	Supports her weight with her legs, so she can bounce when you hold her
	Follows a moving toy closely with her eyes
	Rocks back and forth on her knees
	Grasps small items, like a cheerio, with her thumb and index finger
Speech and language	Produces consonant-vowel combos like "ma" and "ba" and might even babble away with a string of repetitive sounds: "bababa" or "mamama" (if he's a real wunderkind, he'll combine two different sounds: "ba-ma" "pa-ga")
	Uses exclamatory phrases, like "ooh!"
	Understands "no"
	Looks where you point
Social-emotional	Knows his name; turns to look at you when you call him
	Tries to attract your attention through actions
	Shows a preference for certain objects, like a particular pacifier or plush toy

Red Flags

By seven months, contact your doctor if baby…
» Reaches for toys or objects with only one hand
» Refuses to cuddle
» Shows no affection for parents or steady caretakers
» Seems very stiff (tight muscles) or very floppy (like a rag doll)
» Shows poor head control: her head flops back when she's pulled to a sitting position
» Shows difficulty getting objects to mouth
» Conveys eye sensitivity to light, or tears frequently
» Does not roll over
» Is frequently found with both hands closed in a fist
» Doesn't express pleasure (through facial or vocal expressions) when interacting with others

Chapter Fourteen

Your Emerging Social Butterfly

t around seven months, it seems like your baby has suddenly turned into Miss Social. No longer a docile (or not-so-docile) cutie-pie, she now seeks attention and is learning new and varied ways to communicate. And, as you'll quickly see upon removing a particular object or toy, she also lets her opinions be known!

Baby is also learning to enjoy her captive audience. She'll try to keep the attention coming with irresistible tricks like throwing kisses or waving bye-bye. When the music turns on, she might start clapping her hands.

Play with Me!

Baby's brain is ever developing, laying down new neural pathways each day. You can help promote your baby's language and communication skills through your daily interactions and play. Bear in mind that your baby craves predictability (the world is overwhelming and confusing for him!), so though you may be

SPEAKING OF SPEECH

> Are you ready? I'm going to reveal the secret, nearly foolproof formula for jump-starting baby's speaking career. *Talk to him.* All day long, about anything. This recipe sounds ridiculously simple, but in our techno-frenzied world, you may be surprised at how little time you end up communicating face-to-face with your baby.
>
> In the park, in the supermarket, on the way to playgroup — keep the talk flowing. But avoid highfalutin' vocabulary or rapid speech; keep your language slow and frills-free, so your baby can pick up word meanings. And even if she doesn't acquire a single word (some kids need a few more months), she's learning loads about intonation, rhythm, eye contact, and facial expressions — essential elements of communication.

bored to tears, play the games over and over. At this stage, repetition is highly recommended.

Here are some communication and language-boosting games you want to play with your "half a year" baby:

» **Peekaboo.** This classic enthralls baby — and for good reason. Baby is just now beginning to understand "object permanence," the notion that an object (or person) might still exist even if he can't see it. Use a blanket to cover and uncover different objects, as well as yourself, and be amazed by how long this game will captivate your little treasure. Pop-up toys like jack-in-the-box are also great for reinforcing object permanence. If your baby seems frightened by the popped-up figures, allow him to explore the toy while open and become familiar with the grinning animals or clowns before proceeding to the pop-up play.

- » **Play with me.** By now, baby is ready for interactive games. Be his playmate: When he passes you an object or rolls a ball, send it back. This teaches critical skills like turn taking and joint attention (the shared focus of two individuals on an object).
- » **Action rhymes.** Babies love rhymes and singsongs that incorporate motion, like "Patty-Cake," "Round and Round the Garden," and "Itsy Bitsy Spider." There is also a sweet Jewish-themed game that offers great speech sound exposure: Each finger is assigned an *alef-beis* letter; for example, "*Alef* goes... ah-ah-ah" on the thumb, "*Beis* goes...ba-ba-ba" on the index finger, and so on, until the pinky gets "*Hei* goes...ha, ha, ha, ha!" while Mommy's fingers race up baby's arm to tickle his

SPEAKING OF SPEECH

¿Hablas español? Parlez-vous français? Redst a bissel Yiddish? Midaberet Ivrit?

If you or your spouse speak a language other than English, now's the time to use it. In just a few months, baby will start dropping foreign sounds — i.e., sounds not used by Mommy or Tatty — from his vernacular. Later in life, it will be much harder for him to relearn these sounds when attempting to master a foreign tongue.

Don't be afraid to expose baby to multiple languages; he will not find it confusing. Children who most easily achieve bilingualism years down the line are the ones who've heard two or more languages consistently during this crucial period of speech development.

SPEAKING OF SPEECH

LITTLE GUY STILL USING PACIFIER? That's okay, but reserve the dummy for sleeping and chilling time only, so it doesn't hamper baby's speech and language development. (There's a reason it's called a "dummy" — it causes kids to shut down and use minimal communication.)

BABY SUCKS THUMB? Same story: It's okay for tired and cranky hour, but if it's happening all day long, try engaging her with a toy or book to snap her out of the "trance." Don't worry about tooth damage: The American Dental Association says most children can engage in this self-soothing habit without damaging teeth or jaw alignment until permanent teeth begin to erupt (usually around five or six years of age). For more on pacifiers, see pp. 246-249.

underarm. (Double fun: Use the fingers on both of baby's hands, and end with "*Yud* is a *Yiddeleh!*")

» **Mirror, mirror.** By now, baby has begun to understand reflections: She no longer thinks you're actually *in* the mirror. Mirror play is a fabulous way to promote self-awareness, imitation, visual focus, and language. Place a mirror at your baby's height and play copycat, making silly faces and noises. Stick your tongue out, puff up your cheeks, say "ba-ba-ba" — and see if your baby follows. Point to different body parts and name them: eyes, nose, mouth. This is also a great sibling activity — which kid doesn't like looking at himself in the mirror? (Some families have a *minhag* not to let a baby look in the mirror until a certain age; obviously, this is not a game for them to play until baby is older.)

Separation Anxiety

The flip side of your baby's emotional growth spurt is that she now knows that there are people she knows and loves — and there are strangers. At this stage, you might see separation anxiety and stranger wariness intensify, which can be super challenging for the working mom compelled to leave her bundle of love in day care. What can you do to minimize the pangs?

First and foremost, project confidence. Baby will take her cue from you. If your expressions and manner express confidence in your child's caregiver (whom you surely have chosen with much diligence, after extensive research), baby will feel reassured that she's in good hands. (For more on choosing a babysitter or caregiver, see p. 240.)

Finger Play

Congratulations! Baby has now progressed from being a swatter — swiping at objects with open hands — to a gripper! He's likely attempting the "pincer grasp," which uses the thumb and forefinger to grasp small objects. If your baby is safely eating solids, spread plain Cheerios or cooked elbow pasta on his tray; these offer great pincer-grip practice.

Here are some other fine-motor milestones your baby should reach during the next three months:

- » Emptying and filling containers, drawers, and purses (emphasis on the emptying part!)
- » Clapping
- » Dropping and throwing objects (much to his delight! — baby has finally learned to open and close his fingers at will)
- » Self-feeding — that is, independently picking up food pieces (it may take time, though, until he actually gets the food in his mouth)

- » Stacking cups and rings
- » Sorting objects by shape

Say Hello to Sippy Cups

With her newly refined motor skills, your baby might be ready for a two-handled sippy cup. Sippy cups are a great way to transition from bottle or breast to the cup, and they also promote hand-to-mouth coordination.

How to facilitate this changeover?

- » **Experiment.** Every baby is different; some prefer soft, nipple-like spouts, while others fancy a harder feel. Sippy cups aren't that pricey, so try different models to see which one baby likes best.
- » **Remove the valve.** Some cups are so spill-proof that their valves make it hard for baby to extract any liquid. If your baby seems frustrated, try removing the valve. It will make a mess at first, but she'll learn what the cup is there for. Once you put the valve back in, she'll likely make the extra effort to suck out the contents. Alternatively, you can cut a slit in the valve to allow for greater liquid flow.
- » **No cup in bed.** It's better not to let baby take a sippy cup with juice or milk to sleep; the sugars can cause decay. The same goes for letting him coddle the cup and sip all day long (which, incidentally, is also bad for his appetite). If you want to offer juice, limit it to mealtimes. The rest of the day, when baby is thirsty, refill the cup with water. To minimize decay, the American Dental Association recommends transitioning to a regular cup by baby's first birthday.
- » **Clean regularly.** You're busy, you're exhausted, but don't skimp on cup cleaning — bacteria and mold will build up before you can say "Staphylococcus!" If you can't scrub with

soap immediately, at least rinse. If the cup is dishwasher safe, make use of this wonderful invention. And since with time the valves become harder to clean, consider replacing the cups every two or three months.

» **Safety first.** While the jury is still out on the effects of BPA — a chemical frequently used in plastic baby products — take no chances and choose a BPA-free cup. For added safety, don't let baby use a cup with scratched or rubbed-off spouts. These dents invite bacteria.

Toy Story

You want to enrich baby's repertoire, but you're not too thrilled about enriching Toys "R" Us. Which development-boosting toys are really worth investing in?

Here's what you want to own for babies age seven to nine months:

» Stacking cups

» Tower ring

» Colorful blocks and an empty container

» Shape sorter

NOW WHAT COLOR ARE THOSE EYES?

Baby was born with dreamy blue eyes. But wait — what's this? Changes in eye color are to be expected for the first few months of a baby's life, so don't get too attached to those baby blues. By nine months, though, eye color generally stabilizes. So whether she's got piercing blue or chocolate brown irises, by now they're probably here to stay.

If only one eye changes color (a rare phenomenon), or if you notice cloudiness in your baby's eye, contact your pediatrician.

» Pop-up toys (which require fine-motor maneuvering and reinforce object permanence)

In addition to the toys, books, books, and more books! It's never too early to cultivate a lifelong love of literature. Read at least one picture-filled board book together every day.

Sitting Pretty

Learning to sit with minimal support is an exciting milestone: Now your baby can soak up the world from a whole new angle! Plus, it means that he's developed the head control and trunk strength necessary for this skill. Most babies will learn to sit between six and eight months, after learning to roll over. If he hasn't mastered this skill by nine months, speak to your doctor.

Until he becomes an independent sitter, baby might "tripod" — lean forward and support himself with both arms. This in-between position is normal.

But don't fall into the sitting trap. Once he's learned how to sit, your baby may become enamored with the position and turn up his nose at tummy time — essential for development. Don't give in. Keep promoting tummy time with lots of interesting toys and, of course, the biggest attraction of all: Mommy or Tatty's floor-time company.

Creepy Crawlers

Big news: Baby is going mobile! By now, your little nipper is probably using his hands to creep along the floor, attracting every

> **MOMMY'S TWO CENTS**
>
> For that awkward stage when baby is sitting up but not totally steady, place a nursing or sofa pillow behind him to cushion backward or sideway falls.

speck of dust and serving as a highly effective vacuum cleaner. He might even be rocking back and forth on all fours, wondering why he's going nowhere fast (warning: this may continue for a while).

Here's how to facilitate her transition to crawling:

» **Tummy time!** We know it's coming out of your ears, but this one can't be overstressed. Baby can only learn to crawl if given plenty of opportunity to practice! So keep him *out* of bouncers, car seats, ExerSaucers, strollers — and on the floor.

» **Bring out the toys.** Make it exciting. Set aside special toys (rattles, mirror, stacking cups) or intriguing items (a jangling ring of keys; a cup and spoon) to be used only when baby's on her tummy. To motivate movement, put some of them just out of reach — and watch your baby grunt her way to success!

» **Join her on the floor.** Put baby on all fours and make silly faces to keep her engaged. Model crawling or rocking on all fours (if she isn't doing that yet). If baby's trunk keeps collapsing, use a rolled-up towel or receiving blanket placed under her chest to give her the support she needs.

» **Keep it warm.** In the winter, the floor's got to be warm and inviting. If your floor is not carpeted, place a firm rug or mat under your baby — but *not* a blanket, which makes it difficult to creep or crawl. If weather allows, place her on a wood or tiled floor, which is more conducive to crawling.

» **Keep it safe.** Make sure the designated floor space is free of hazardous items, and that baby is always supervised (see pp. 292-300 on baby-proofing your home).

» **Embrace all styles.** In his quest for mobility, your baby might experiment with an assortment of crawl techniques, some of which look highly unusual. Don't fret — it's normal. Here are some of the more common grooves:

Your Emerging Social Butterfly **289**

1. **Classic Crawl** — Baby moves forward on alternating bent arms and legs.
2. **Crab Crawl** — Baby tucks in one leg and extends the other, while pushing with her hands. This yields the unfortunate result of moving backward, which can be highly frustrating for a forward-thinking baby.
3. **Belly Crawl/Combat Crawl** — Baby creeps on stomach, using flat forearms and feet to propel forward.
4. **Leapfrog Crawl/Bunny Hop** — Baby makes a bridge with her arms and feet, then thrusts forward.
5. **Scooting** — Baby bounces on her bottom, bending and unbending her knees while sitting upright. She might also use her hands to propel forward; this is good because it provides hand-eye-leg coordination practice.
6. **Bear Walk** — Baby lumbers along on all fours, arms and legs unbent.
7. **Step-Scoot Mix** — Baby tucks one knee under her bottom, then mobilizes three limbs: She leans forward on one hand to create a tripod of hand, knee (on the same side), and foot (on the opposite side). Baby then swings out the kneeling leg, thrusts forward with her hand, returns the leg to a kneeling position, and repeats the cycle.

» **Be patient.** While most babies are doing some kind of crawl by ten months, chunkier babies — who, ahem, must exert more energy in lugging themselves around — may take a bit longer. Just keep at it with tummy time and toys.

» **Don't rush walking.** Experts agree that tummy time and crawling are highly beneficial for sensory, motor, and visual development. So if she hasn't yet mastered the crawl, don't encourage baby to stand up, and don't "practice" walking by holding her hands.

Is Crawling Essential?

Everyone else's kiddos are effortlessly wriggling around, but your baby is doing this weird bopping thing. Or he just doesn't stop rolling — he's become so good at it, that rolling is now his primary method of locomotion. What will be with his development? His future?

Don't panic yet. The debate about crawling — is it a necessary or okay-to-bypass milestone? — is actually quite heated. Many pediatric occupational therapists assert that babies who skip classic crawling (with alternate arm and leg movements) lose a critical opportunity to develop strong upper body muscles. Years down the line, they contend, these kids will have trouble climbing a jungle gym, pulling themselves out of a pool, or even sitting upright in class. Since crawling also strengthens the finger muscles, they may have trouble grasping a pencil and developing a neat handwriting. What's more, classic crawling promotes bilateral coordination — reciprocal movements of both sides of the body — which is essential for daily activities like getting dressed, feeding, and sports.

Empirical evidence of this position, however, is limited, and many doctors vehemently deny the existence of a long-term developmental consequence.

> **FUN FACT**
>
> Is your little one a summer baby? She's likely to crawl at a later age. A fascinating study showed that babies born in the spring and summer tend to crawl later than babies born in the fall and winter, since they are usually wearing more restrictive clothing when first attempting to crawl. (Of course, the study noted that this also depends on the climate of where the baby lives.)

The takeaway for Mommy? Do everything you can to get baby crawling with alternate movements. But if it still doesn't happen, relax with the knowledge that you did your best, and he'll probably be okay. Just keep your eyes open for upper-body weakness as your baby gets older.

Speak to your doctor if baby...

» uses only one side of his body to advance,

» shows no interest in moving anywhere, or

» skips crawling as well as any other developmental milestone.

Stand-Up Comedy

What's next for baby? Once she's picked up the crawl, she'll likely start trying to stand — pulling herself up via the couch, coffee table, your skirt, and any other graspable surface. Remember that she may not yet know how to get down (she's smart, but not *that* foresighted), so be available to assist in her descent. Show her how to gently bend her knees and lower her legs and bottom to the floor.

With baby now newly vertical, you may be tempted to purchase a walker — the device your mother lovingly bought for you at this age.

Don't. Research has proved walkers to be dangerous, since they allow baby to trip, roll down stairs, trap a finger, or reach for hazardous objects. In some countries, the sale of walkers has been banned. While walkers manufactured after 2000 are a whole lot safer, thanks to tightened safety regulations, they're still not so good for baby. Walkers allow babies to move around freely when they aren't yet physically ready for it, causing unusual movement patterns and poor muscle control. And because those equipped with trays conceal the lower body, they prevent baby from getting visual feedback critical to the learning process: Baby can't see his legs in action, and therefore can't develop a feel for which movements are effective — and which aren't.

Bottom line? Walkers can hamper baby's development. If you're desperate for a contained environment, choose an ExerSaucer, stationary activity center, or play yard. But ideally, let baby play freely on a hazard-free floor.

Baby-Proofing Your Home

Now that your munchkin is on the move, it's time to make his environment safe. While many parents worry about the safety of their infants outside the home, studies show that children between the ages of one and four are more likely to be harmed by accidents in the home than by stranger violence or abductions.

Here's a room-by-room guide to childproofing your home, making it as safe an environment as you can. If for some reason you can't baby-proof a particular room, make sure to place a gate at the doorway or leave the door closed at all times.

Living Room

- » Remove all sharp-cornered furniture, or cover the edges with bumpers.
- » Place cords from shades or blinds out of reach. If possible, install cordless curtains or blinds.
- » Remove lightweight objects that baby might use to pull himself up with (and then fall backward!), like potted plants,

decorative tables, and floor lamps. (Incidentally, there are plants that are poisonous — and many babies *will* try ingesting the leaves if they are in reach.)

» If possible, bolt bookcases to the wall to avoid tip-overs. At the very least, place heavier items on the bottom shelves to minimize top heaviness and promote stability.

» Put all framed pictures out of reach.

Playroom

» Clear the floor from all ingestible objects — think small Lego pieces, board game pieces, marbles. Sweep carefully, paying extra attention to corners and spaces under the furniture. Now that baby can crawl and grasp small items, he can and will insert them into his mouth. If your older children want to play with these toys, have them do it in an enclosed, inaccessible area or when baby is asleep or in a playpen or ExerSaucer.

» Check stuffed toys to make sure the seams are tight and closed. At times, toy stuffing may be inhaled or ingested.

Foyer

» Place safety gates on all stairway landings. Choose JPMA-certified gates that baby won't be able to dislodge, but are easy for you to open and close. (Otherwise, you'll be tempted to leave them open.) Don't use pressure gates at the top of a stairwell; a permanently installed gate is far more secure. Go for straight-slat designs; avoid gates with accordion or V-shaped openings, which can pose a strangulation or entrapment hazard.

Kitchen

» The kitchen is perhaps the trickiest room in the house to childproof because it's filled with inherent dangers. The best way to prevent accidents is continual supervision of baby. If you're cooking and can't keep a constant eye on baby, place him in a play yard or highchair nearby so he can safely be part of the action.

Poison

- » Place all toxic materials — bug sprays, cleaning agents, detergents — on a high shelf, preferably in a locked cabinet. Since the fumes of many chemical products are harmful, consider switching to less hazardous materials like vinegar, beeswax, mineral oil, and non-chlorine bleach — which also should be closed carefully and kept out of reach.
- » Keep the phone numbers for Poison Control and Hatzalah near every phone.
- » Buy products with child-resistant caps.
- » Keep hazardous products in their original containers; never transfer them to generic, unlabeled containers, or, even worse, food containers.

Cabinet Storage

- » Place locks on the doors of all cabinets that contain pointy objects (knives, peelers) or choking hazards (coins, marbles, beads, paper clips). This is particularly applicable to the "junk drawer."
- » To keep baby happy (and prevent him from opening every cabinet), designate one cabinet as the "safe cabinet," preferably far from the oven and stovetop. Fill it with safe but interesting objects like plastic containers, wooden spoons, measuring spoons, and smooth-edged foil pans. Rotate the contents periodically to keep baby engaged.

- » After washing the dishes, don't leave sharp or breakable utensils accessible in the drainboard. Dry them immediately and store.
- » Store glassware and china in high cabinets.
- » Baby can yank at dangling wires and be hurt by falling electronics. If you've got a busy kitchen electric area (think cell phone and MP3 player chargers, electric kettle, toaster), consider creating a drawer for the outlet strip. If space doesn't allow for this, use cord holders to securely keep cords out of reach.

Countertops and Tabletops

- » Store appliances like toaster ovens, urns, and coffeemakers out of baby's reach. When not in use, unplug and roll up the cords. Cords should be as far back as possible on the counter, never dangling below counter level.
- » Never leave glassware, sharp utensils, or hot beverages unattended. And never carry baby while holding a hot drink in one hand, or while frying and cooking at the stove.
- » Take care when using placemats and tablecloths: Baby can pull them and jump-start a dangerous avalanche. Consider buying clips that secure tablecloths to the table. Use placemats only when an adult is sitting at the table and watching for baby's reaching hands.

Ovens and Appliances

- » Try to use only the back burners of the stove. If you must use the front burners, turn pot handles away from the edge, toward the backsplash.
- » Install safety covers on your stove knobs so baby can't turn on the burners.
- » Put latches on your oven and microwave doors.

» If your oven has a safety feature that locks the oven controls, activate it whenever the oven is not in use.

» Consider installing a *dry* fire extinguisher near your oven. Use it only for small electric and grease fires; for bigger fires, race out of the house — of course, alerting everyone in the house and making sure the little ones are with you — and call the fire department (another emergency number to keep on hand). Water extinguishers are suitable only for fires involving ordinary combustible materials such as paper, wood, cardboard, and most plastics; they can be deadly when used for grease or electric fires.

» Never pour detergent into the dishwasher dispenser until you're ready to activate the cycle: Baby can discover the sweet-smelling but poisonous powder and ingest it. Consider using multipurpose straps to secure the dishwasher shut.

Refrigerator

» If baby can open it, install a latch.

» Remove all small magnets. Remember the rule of thumb: Anything that can fit into a toilet paper roll is a choking hazard.

Garbage Cans

» Trash bins make for exciting discovery zones — except that they're often filled with dangerous or harmful materials. Make sure your garbage can has a lid, and secure it with a safety latch.

» Immediately dispose of sharp items, such as cans or broken glass bottles, in the outdoor trash bin.

» Garbage bags and plastic shopping bags can cause suffocation. Make sure these are stored in a locked or inaccessible cabinet.

Highchair

» Be diligent about using the straps. Never leave baby unattended.

Bathroom

» Make sure all medicines are in a locked or inaccessible cabinet. Don't take medicine in front of your baby, as he may want to mimic you. Never call medicine "candy."

» Purchase a first-aid kit. Make sure you — and all babysitters — know how to use the supplies in case of emergency.

» **Practice water safety:**

1. Never leave baby unattended in the tub, even if it's just for a second, and even if he's in a bath seat or ring.
2. Never leave a bucket with water unattended. Babies can drown in as little as an inch of water. After mopping, empty the bucket immediately.
3. Install a safety latch on the toilet to prevent curious babies from falling in. (But make sure parents can open it easily!) Even better: Install a latch on the outside of the bathroom door to protect baby from the bathroom's array of hazards.
4. To prevent scalding, consider adjusting your water heater so that water can't get hotter than 120°F.
5. Most importantly, supervise baby at all times when in the bathroom.

Nursery

» Position the crib away from windows, blinds (the cords pose strangulation hazards), heaters, wall decorations, electric cords (from a lamp, cell-phone charger, baby monitor), or furniture that baby can climb on.

- As soon as baby can push up on his hands and knees, remove baby mobiles and any other hanging toys attached to the crib. Lower the crib mattress to its lowermost position.
- **During changing time:**
    1. Store diaper-changing supplies like baby oil, baby powder, wipes, and creams far from baby's grasp.
    2. Make sure you have all items ready before you start changing baby. Never leave him unattended on the table.
    3. Place a toy or teething ring nearby to keep baby's hands busy and divert his attention.
    4. Consider using a changing mat that includes safety straps to keep baby buckled while his diaper gets changed. Alternatively, make a habit of getting down on the floor with baby and changing his diaper there.
- Keep soft items like bumpers, pillows, and stuffed toys out of baby's crib. Baby can use these to climb out, or he can press his face against them, making it difficult to breathe.
- Avoid toy chests with lids that slam down (putting little fingers at risk) or wicker drawers with easy-to-pull-off pieces (presenting a choking hazard). Purchase a storage container with a light, removable lid, or one that slides. Newer toy chests feature special safety hinges that close gently.

Home Office

- Make sure to fully close file cabinets after using, since one pulled-out drawer can cause the entire cabinet to topple over.
- Little ones love office supplies. Keep paper clips, staples, scissors, and glue in a locked drawer.

Doors

» To prevent pinched or crushed fingers, use doorstops or door holders on hinges to keep the doors from slamming — particularly with heavy doors.

Backyard

» Got a permanent pool? Install an enclosing fence at least four feet high. Lock the gate to the pool after each use. Consider installing an electrified alarm that goes off if the gate is opened.

» Got a wading pool? Drain immediately after use. Store upright.

» Many garden plants and flowers can be poisonous. If you have a green thumb, keep the plants out of reach, or ensure that baby is always supervised.

» Visually scan your garden for hazards, and make them inaccessible. These can include: gardening tools, sharp rocks, barbecue grills, garbage, pesticides, and more.

» Remove all ropes and cords from playground equipment (these can pose strangulation hazards). On hot days, check the temperature of accessible play structures, since they can get hot enough to burn the skin. If you own a wooden playground set, seal the wood at least once a year with standard penetrating deck treatments to prevent splinters.

HAZARDOUS HOUSE GUESTS?

Be vigilant when hosting visitors. *You* may have scrupulously scoured the house for hazards, but Aunt Sadie didn't — and she might accidentally leave her lipstick, purse, perfume, aspirin, or other medications accessible.

Miscellaneous

Electricity

» Shield all electrical outlets with plastic outlet protectors (available in most hardware or baby equipment stores). It's best to use broad covers with a sliding safety latch, since the removable plug-in caps can end up in a determined baby's mouth.

» Consider installing a safety breaker so that if baby sticks a nail (or other electricity-conducting object) into the outlet hole, the electricity will automatically shut off throughout the house.

Detectors

» Smoke detectors save lives. Studies indicate that a smoke detector can reduce the risk of death by fire by nearly 50 percent. If you haven't yet done so, install one in every sleeping area of your home. Once a month verify that it is working, and change the batteries no less than once a year.

» Carbon monoxide is a silent, deadly poison. It can leak from dryers, fireplaces, furnaces, gas space heaters, automobiles, and even air conditioners. Install a carbon monoxide detector on each level of your home. Ideally, a detector should be placed within fifteen feet of every bedroom; most instances of fatal carbon monoxide poisoning occur when the victims are asleep. If you have an attached garage, place a detector next to the internal garage door (a car left running can cause a rapid carbon monoxide buildup). Check the batteries every spring and fall when you change the time on the clocks.

» Don't put detectors within fifteen feet of fuel-burning appliances (like the stovetop, fireplace, or boiler), since those can trigger false alarms and cause you to ignore the signals.

> **JUST SAY...NO?!**
>
> As you may have already gleaned, "no" doesn't work well at this age. Fret not: This is not a portent of doomed parenting. Baby is simply too curious, and she'll often forget you said no. Instead, just distract her from the forbidden fruit and keep it out of sight. Don't discipline or engage in power struggles; just remove temptation.

Also avoid installing them in bathrooms, in direct sunlight, or near appliances that generate heat, since the devices are designed to work within specific tolerances for heat and humidity.

Batteries

» Put electric tape over small battery compartments on bathroom scales or remote controls. Small batteries, if swallowed, can be particularly dangerous to children.

Overwhelmed by this list? It seems like a lot, but many of the items can be done quickly, with minimal hassle. And most are one-timers — once you've installed locks, for example, you won't have to scramble as your family grows. Most of all, remember: While childproofing is essential, nothing is as effective as responsible supervision. Baby-proofing is no substitute for good parenting.

Dreaming About...a Good Night's Sleep

How are you sleeping these days? If you're anything like most parents of infants, probably not great. Depleted for months, you may be at your wit's end.

The good news is that now's the time to regain your z's. At seven months, baby is probably developmentally ready to qualify for sleep training. If the thought of letting baby cry makes you choke up, relax. There are many ways to sleep-train that are neither heartless nor tear-filled. Remember that easing baby into a healthy schedule and encouraging good nocturnal habits is important for her growth and development — and that the longer you wait, the harder it will be to change ingrained routines.

How many hours should baby be sleeping at this age? By now, many babies are capable of doing an eight- to twelve-hour stretch at night. Sounds like a dream? It doesn't have to be.

There are dozens of approaches out there for getting baby to sleep through the night and leaving you to your sweet dreams. We've listed the most common ones, but if you don't resonate with these, look further. Each mother and baby has different temperaments and needs. For each approach, ask yourself:

- » Does this advice sound sensible to me?
- » Does it feel right?
- » Does it suit my baby's temperament?
- » Be aware that any approach that includes skipping feedings may impact on your nursing goals. When milk is removed less often, less milk is made. Consider your nursing goals when choosing a sleep method.

More important than which method you choose is consistency in the implementation, so make sure you're comfortable with the chosen route and be prepared to follow it through. A recent review of fifty-two sleep studies using various methods showed that when applied consistently, almost all proved effective.

The Ferber Method

Dr. Richard Ferber is the director of the Pediatric Sleep Disorders Center at Boston Children's Hospital. His time-tested "ferberization" approach, recommended for babies ages three to five months and used by parents worldwide, is based on the belief that babies must learn how to self-soothe.

In a nutshell:

» Use a warm, loving bedtime routine.

» Put baby to sleep while she is still awake, not letting her fall asleep and then placing her in the crib.

» Allow short periods of crying followed by comforting at prescribed intervals.

» Intervals get progressively longer each night.

» Rub, pat, or sing, but don't pick up baby while comforting.

Ferber's technique is perhaps the fastest way to get baby sleeping through the night, and it has spawned a host of variations. The common denominator of them all is the let-them-cry element.

The No-Tears Approach

This group of methods — perhaps most commonly associated with Dr. William Sears and Elizabeth Pantley, authors of *The Baby Sleep Book* and *The No-Cry Sleep Solution* respectively — promotes a more gradual approach characterized by soothing, rocking, and feeding until baby falls asleep.

Proponents of these programs reject the "quick-fix" notion, asserting that cry-it-out methods erode trust and can leave a baby with negative sleep associations for a lifetime. They stress the importance of a predictable, *substantial* bedtime routine (for example, bath, lotion massage, pajamas, tooth brushing, bidding good night, nursing, and verbal reminders — "we're going to sleep"), and provision of a toy or blanket for cuddling when you're not present.

Some experts encourage parents to "hover": sit next to baby's crib for three nights until he falls asleep, then across the room for three nights, then in the doorway, then in the hallway.

Middle of the Road

A popular read among parents from across the world, Tracy Hogg's *Baby Whisperer* is considered a cross between the cry-it-out and no-tears methods. In her book, the registered nurse introduces the E.A.S.Y. routine, urging parents to implement a strictly structured routine throughout the day, then use the pick-up, put-down method for putting baby to bed — shushing, patting, or picking up baby for two to three minutes maximum and putting her down until she falls asleep. Ms. Hogg also shows caregivers how to identify their baby's personality type and decipher his unique cries, gestures, and facial expressions.

The Five S's

Author of *The Happiest Baby on the Block*, pediatrician Harvey Karp believes the best way to help baby doze off is by recreating the womb environment. He trains parents to do that with the five *S* steps, advising them to begin with the first and add another *S* as needed:

- » **Swaddle.** This recreates the secure, snug feeling baby had in utero.

- » **Side or Stomach Position.** These are the coziest positions for infants, great for pre-bedtime soothing. (Make sure to roll baby onto his back once he's calmed down and ready to conk out.)

- » **Shush.** If you think your baby prefers quiet, think again! Featuring a constant "blood-swoosh" that experts say is louder than a vacuum cleaner, the womb was a pretty noisy place. Loudly say "shhhh" directly into baby's ear. As she calms down, lower the volume. You can also experiment with CDs that play low, rumbly, womb-mimicking sounds.

» **Swing.** Hold your swaddled baby and jiggle him gently, using small, rapid movements — just as he was jiggled in utero. Make sure to support his head.

» **Suck.** Offer baby a pacifier or thumb. Pacifiers are safe for sleeping.

Caveat to Mommy: Karp's five *S* steps are geared to babies under four months. After that age, the behaviors will still be soothing, but may not offer the 98 percent success rate seen with the younger set. Just like a pillow and blanket induce sleep in adults, each of these steps cues baby "now it's time to sleep."

Your Baby's Personality

Rina, mother of two

Chezky was a timid baby from early on. He frightened easily and didn't take well to new faces or places. When he was nine months old and we went to visit my parents overseas, it took him weeks until he'd allow me to leave him on the floor and play. Today, at five years old, Chezky is still a very anxious child. He's a natural worrier, and I work with him to allay anxieties and overcome the challenge of transitions.

Amalia, mother of four

From the minute Shira was born, she didn't stop crying. She was colicky for three months straight, and even once that died down, she was a fussy, needy baby. She never played on her own; she needed me to be sitting on the floor with her at all times. Today, at eight years old, Shira is a bright, super-creative bundle of energy — and she's still pretty needy and high-strung. It's amazing that her personality emerged so early on!

> ### Chaya Sara, mother of five
>
> My baby was born a week before Rosh Hashanah, and we didn't know what to name him. My husband suggested Yitzchak Isaac after my great-grandfather, particularly because the name was appropriate for the time of year — the day we invoke the zechus of the Akeidah. I wasn't sure; my family had a lot of "Yitzchak Isaacs" already. The next day, while I was taking care of him (he was maybe thirty hours old), he gave me a real smile (he's not my first — I could tell it was real). And he hasn't stopped since. He is the only one of my kids that started smiling immediately, so I felt the name Yitzchak was perfect. Today, he is still my happiest kid — sunny and upbeat, just like his name **and** his namesake.

Many newbie moms and dads assume that all babies are alike: They eat, sleep, and cry — offering a smile or laugh along the way. But parents with several kids know better: They've seen firsthand that every baby has a distinct personality, and many start showing their personalities early on.

Identifying baby's personality can help you better match her needs at this stage and adjust your expectations accordingly. But don't label her for life. While many babies remain true to their hardwired profiles, many surprise us (think high-maintenance infant who morphed into content, well-adjusted kid; angel baby now impossible at the age of seven). Never assign a "role" to a particular child, and remember that your *response* to her temperament can significantly shape her personality.

Is your kiddo a dreamy artist or a practical future business entrepreneur? A teeny-weeny busybody, always looking around her, or a deep thinker, busy with his own profound thoughts? A zippy, action-craving *macher-ette* or a beloved, mellow family man?

Here's a quick quiz that can help you pinpoint baby's personality:

1. Is baby soothed or distracted easily?
2. Does he fight bedtime, or drift off to sleep easily?

3. Is baby shy and clingy around new people? How long does it take her to warm up?
4. How does baby handle a change in routine or changes in environment?
5. Does baby move around a lot?
6. Can baby entertain himself? What happens when baby is left alone in the crib, with toys to play with?
7. What happens when baby is trying something new and it's not going easily? Does he persist, or move on to the next toy?
8. Does baby need instant gratification? If baby's hungry, and food is not yet ready, how does she react?
9. Is baby sensitive to sensory stimulation? How does he react to loud noises, strong smells, firm touch, unusual textures, or bright lights?
10. When baby is swaddled, does she feel soothed or constrained?
11. How does baby handle a long car ride? Does he fuss, or seem content?

Evaluate your answers. Then try to determine how your baby rates in each of the following main personality traits:

- » Adaptability
- » Regularity
- » Intensity
- » Sociability
- » Energy level
- » Disposition
- » Persistence
- » Distractibility
- » Sensitivity

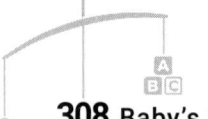

Use the following chart to adapt your manner accordingly.

	YES! BABY IS...	NO! BABY IS NOT...
Super-active?	Offer lots of opportunity for free play. Be mindful about safety and baby-proofing, because this is a kid who will test boundaries. Though you may find yourself doing lots of baby chasing, she'll likely sleep well once she's drifted off — all that activity wears her out.	Encourage physical play, but in a calm, non-frenetic way. Even if she's content to space out for hours in the stroller, don't give in to the temptation — it's no good for her development. Keep her stimulated with engaging toys and constant conversation.
Warms up quickly to strangers? Highly adaptable?	Invite other babies and neighbors often; the new sounds and faces will keep baby stimulated. But don't assume baby will love everyone at first sight. For example, if baby is set to be cared for by a new babysitter, make sure he plays with the sitter in your presence before his first day.	Keep the pressure down; don't force him to interact socially. Hold baby for as long as he needs to feel safe. Introduce new caregivers, sights, and settings very gradually. When on the go, offer familiar objects like blankets, toys, or stuffed animals for security.
Demands constant attention and company?	Provide her with lots of toys and stimulation. Frequent outdoor trips to the park and supermarket can keep her content — and preserve your sanity.	Though she might not protest, don't leave baby playing on her own for too long — your company and involvement is important for her development.
Craves predictability?	Give him those structured routines! He needs it to feel secure and happy. And happy baby = happy mom!	Be more flexible about routines, but keep some elements steady — like how you soothe him, or where he's nursed. And keep to your bedtime schedule: Even the most freewheeling babies get cranky when sleep-deprived.

Always smiling?	Count your lucky stars! It's much easier to care for a sunshine baby.	Disposition is mostly innate — don't blame yourself or assume you're doing something wrong. Remember that with consistent love and care, many babies outgrow their insecurities and become content toddlers. Offer plenty of smiles and affection, even when they're not reciprocated. Accept her as she is, be patient, and you should see more smiles!
Drifts off to sleep easily?	Thank Hashem for this windfall! But don't skimp on the bedtime routine, even though you can get away with it.	Read up on our sleep-training section for the best ways to soothe baby. Implement a structured, predictable bedtime routine.
Highly reactive? Often crying?	Don't get flustered by baby's constant cries. Tend to his needs, but know that his high-pitched wails are usually not indicative of earth-shattering pain; they're simply his way of communicating a want. Take care of yourself, and take a break when at your limit. Remind yourself that intense babies usually grow to become the world's movers and shakers!	Your life will be easier (and quieter!), but you'll have to try harder to interpret baby's cues. Pay attention to his expressions and verbalize his feelings — "Oh, you don't like this food?" This will increase his self-awareness and empower him to better communicate.

Remember that temperament is never inherently negative: With acceptance and support, almost all traits can be channeled in positive directions. Many psychologists believe that "goodness of fit" — the compatibility of a person's temperament with his surrounding environment — is a powerful predictor of the person's success in life. Accepting your baby and reacting well to his behaviors will help shape him into a happy, well-adjusted kid.

Baby's First Year: The Jewish Mother's Guide

Building Your Family by Building Yourself

What's your schedule like these days? If you're a typical working mother of one, it might look like this:

DAILY SCHEDULE

6:00 AM	6:00 AM	Wake up, nurse baby.
	6:30 AM	Attempt to get dressed and apply makeup while entertaining baby.
7:00 AM	7:00 AM	Daven and grab something to eat. Dress baby, pack up workbag and diaper bag.
8:00 AM	8:00 AM	Leave baby with Dad — who will bring him to sitter — and race off to work.
9:00 AM	9:00 AM	Arrive at work. Prove relevance to company by finishing long-overdue work project.
10:00 AM		
	10:30 AM	Pump.
11:00 AM		
12:00 PM		
1:00 PM	1:00 PM	Lunch break. Call sitter to make sure baby is okay.
2:00 PM		
	2:30 PM	Pump.
3:00 PM		
4:00 PM		
	4:30 PM	Leave work.

5:00 PM	5:00 PM	Get to sitter. Hug baby, head home.
	5:30 PM	Cut up salad, fry cutlets, put up rice. Tend to fussy baby all the while.
6:00 PM	6:00 PM	Nurse. Feed baby solids.
	6:30 PM	Dad comes home. Family supper.
7:00 PM	7:00 PM	Give bath, start bedtime routine.
	7:30 PM	Nurse. Good night, baby!
8:00 PM	8:00 PM	Run out on important errand.
	8:30 PM	Bake cupcakes for Shaindy's son's shalom zachar.
9:00 PM	9:00 PM	Wash dishes, tidy house, put in load of laundry. Prepare lunches for tomorrow. Defrost chicken.
10:00 PM	10:00 PM	Shower, freshen up. Call Mom to check in.
11:00 PM	11:00 PM	Nurse baby. Collapse into bed.
12:00 AM		
1:00 AM		
2:00 AM	2:00 AM	Nurse baby. Collapse into bed.
3:00 AM	3:30 AM	Calm fussy baby with pacifier and soothing.
4:00 AM		
5:00 AM		
6:00 AM	6:00 AM	All over again!

Mommy-ing is exhausting. All the more so if you have *several* children! That's why it's so important to take care of yourself — and your marriage.

It's critical to carve out recharge time that's just for you: exercising, reading a book or magazine, going shopping with a friend, getting a manicure — whatever it takes to make you feel energized. If it fits into your budget, buy yourself something new. Make sure you look in the mirror and feel satisfied; if you feel frumpy or haggard, do what it takes to freshen your wardrobe or makeup or wig. You are a mother, not a *shmatte*!

Just as important, every marriage needs constant nurturing. Dedicate at least one evening a week to spend time with your husband, preferably outside the home. On all other days, make sure you catch up and schmooze over supper, or later in the evening. *Eiruv*-permitting, use Shabbos afternoons to take walks and connect.

Feel guilty about getting babysitters or "pampering" yourself? In the long run, your family will benefit. A depleted mom is an ineffective mom, and a starved marriage is no good for anyone — most of all baby.

If allotting time to these priorities means cutting corners on your *klal* activities or dinner menu, that's okay. Your emotional health and your marriage come first.

Chapter Fifteen

Feeding Time: Moving Up to Solids

Happy half-year birthday! Moishe is now a full six months. According to his diligent mommy — who's assiduously studied every book on the topic — it's high time for the Inaugural Spoonful. Purposeful yet teary-eyed (*My baby is growing up...*), she fastens Moishe into his spanking new highchair, strides to the counter, and ceremoniously mixes rice cereal with formula or expressed breastmilk. A beaming but compliant Tatty takes position with his camera, ready to capture the moment and send it on to the doting *bubbies* and *zeidies*.

Mommy is ready. She lifts the ergonomically designed, grip-friendly, soft-tip spoon — lovingly purchased after hours of research — and swoops it elegantly toward Moishe's mouth. The hour has arrived: Her son will finally join the ranks of solids-eating men.

AAAH!

Moishe shrieks in protest and shoots out pellets of beige mush, scrunching his nose until it looks like a Craisin. He grabs the $10.99 spoon and flings it across the room, twisting his *head away from Mommy in case she hasn't gotten the message. Camel-colored drops of drivel speckle Tatty's beloved Canon PowerShot G3X. Mommy looks like she's about to cry.*

What went wrong?

Nothing.

Moving your baby from a liquid to solid diet is not always going to be straightforward. While this chapter will offer an excellent primer, giving you important tools to minimize challenges, know that this transition requires time and patience. Most parents will encounter a bumpy ride, and that's okay. When the going gets tough, realize *this is normal*. Just keep at it.

> ### Tamar
> I remember dreading my baby's feeding sessions. She was completely disinterested. She nursed beautifully for seven months. Why do we have to rock the boat? I thought to myself. Who invented this food business anyway? Looking back, I think she sensed my anxiety. If I had only known to expect less, take it slower, and relax, I think it would have gone more smoothly.

> ### Chaya
> My daughter began accepting solid food at five and a half months, but she wasn't particularly interested in it until seven months. I regret giving in to people who pressured me to start solids early. For the future, I would pay less attention to age and instead start when the baby shows interest.

When to Start

Today, many doctors assert that six months is the ideal time to start experimenting with solids. At this age...

» baby is still open to new experiences and less likely to reject unfamiliar textures;

» baby's iron stores from birth are beginning to deplete, necessitating outside reinforcement;

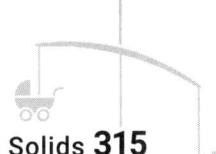

- » baby starts developing the ability to transfer solid food from the front to the back of his mouth;
- » baby is sitting upright, with a digestive tract ready for a non-liquid diet.

Having said that, some nursing mothers (and their babies!) prefer to wait until baby is eight or nine months before introducing solids. Giving up exclusive breastfeeding presents an emotional challenge: It's a breach in the cherished mother-child bond. If you want to push off giving solids for a couple of months, run it by your doctor. As long as your baby is gaining weight satisfactorily and receiving iron drops, the doctor will probably give the okay.

When you do make the leap, allow yourself to feel the pangs of separation. They are normal and healthy. At the same time, remind yourself of real food's nutritional importance at this stage.

Telltale signs that your baby is ready for food:

- » He can sit up (with support) and hold his head and neck upright.
- » His birth weight has doubled.
- » He often mouths his hands and toys.
- » He's interested in what you're eating and tries to grab food from your plate.
- » He can retain food in his mouth rather than letting it dribble out.
- » Even after being breast- or bottle-fed eight to ten times a day, he doesn't seem full. When his bottle is empty, he clamors for more, and wants to nurse more often than in the past. (But remember: During growth or developmental spurts babies often nurse more. The increased nursing increases the milk production. Generally, avoid solids before six months.)
- » He's spitting up more than he used to, because his relatively empty stomach needs food to hold the liquid down.

Prep for Success

As you plan baby's grand initiation to solid food, here's how to set yourself up for success:

- » **Time it right.** Make sure your baby is not ravenous — or too full. Nurse or bottle-feed her a bit before, so she won't be distracted by hunger pangs. On the other hand, she won't be interested in eating anything if her tummy is satiated. If she's cranky or sick, don't even attempt introducing her to solids. Choose an hour when she's happy and mellow — perhaps after a nap.

- » **Watch for reactions.** Keep your eyes open for hives, rashes, or other allergic reactions.

- » **Take her lead.** Baby's rejected all culinary overtures? That's fine. Don't push it, and don't be frustrated. Wait a few days — until she forgets — and try again.

Best Beginner Foods

Many doctors recommend introducing solids with single-grain, iron-fortified powdered cereals like rice or oatmeal. To ease the transition, parents are advised to mix a few tablespoons of cereal with breastmilk or formula — a familiar taste.

MOMMY'S TWO CENTS

If your baby is still guzzling down thirty-two ounces of milk a day, what should be served first — liquids or solids? Because of the comfort element, many mothers like to nurse a bit, feed some solids, then nurse again just before nap time or bedtime. Other moms prefer to offer a full liquid meal first, with solids as dessert. Bottom line? It doesn't matter. See what works for you and your baby.

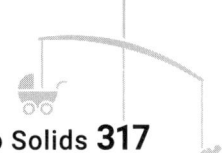

But lots of babies don't go for this entrée. The cereal is bland, and some varieties — especially rice — can cause constipation. If your baby turns up his nose at grains, move on to pureed fruits or veggies.

In the beginning, avoid serving blended fruits or mixed soups. Offer each fruit and vegetable individually and wait three days before introducing the next new food. This allows your baby to process the taste and empowers you to quickly determine the culprit if there's an allergic reaction or other adverse effect, like diarrhea.

If you have a family history of allergies, talk to your doctor about how to introduce solids.

Some great starter foods:

- » Carrots
- » Sweet potatoes
- » Squash — all kinds
- » Applesauce
- » Pears
- » Peaches
- » Bananas

These can be store-bought in jars (fast, easy, pricey) or made at home (time-consuming but economical). Just be sure to puree the cooked veggies and fruits very finely with a blender — removing all seeds, peels, and hard parts — or baby might turn up his nose at the texture.

Once baby has adjusted to the milder orange and yellow veggies above, move on to the stronger-tasting greens:

- » Peas
- » Spinach
- » Green beans
- » Avocado

Which should you introduce first — fruits or vegetables?

You may have been warned that if baby starts with fruits, he'll develop an irreversible sweet tooth and refuse veggies for life. But there's no solid evidence backing that claim. Do what works. If your baby shows disdain for veggies, make fruits her main course but try to get in a few spoonfuls of veggies each day. Many foods are an acquired taste, and repeated exposure will help.

Foods to Avoid

While medical professionals have become more and more liberal in advocating a variety of foods at young ages, there are still several foods that should be avoided:

1. **Milk:** Don't serve pure cow's milk before baby's first birthday. Its high concentration of proteins and minerals, plus non-baby-friendly fats, can irritate his stomach. (In processed dairy products like yogurts, these proteins have been broken down and are more safely digested.)

2. **Honey:** No baby under a year should ever be given honey. Raw or cooked honey is liable to contain bacterial spores which — in a baby's underdeveloped digestive system — can produce deadly toxins. Commercial products (like Honey Nut Cheerios) incorporate honey in a variety of ways, and because the manufacturing processes are so complex, it's difficult to know which products are truly baby safe.

3. **Citrus fruits:** The high acidity of citrus fruits has proven to be stomach irritating for many babies. If your baby expresses interest in your peeled orange, give her a small piece, but keep an eye out for rashes, diarrhea, and other adverse reactions.

4. **Sugar:** Some people spend much of their lives battling sugar addiction — so why start your child on that road? Avoid foods with refined sugar whenever possible. But if you're at a birthday party where everyone is eating cake, and your little one is practically

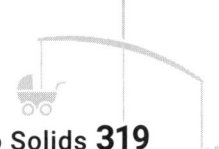

salivating, don't deprive him. For most children, minimal amounts of sugar won't have long-term deleterious effects.

5. **Juice:** Fruit juices don't contribute much to a baby's diet and might cause diarrhea or ruin her appetite for other, more nutritious foods. Plus, excessive juice sipping can cause tooth decay, especially if it's just before bedtime.

6. **High-sulfur foods:** Foods high in sulfur — like cauliflower, broccoli, cabbage, and beans — tend to produce excess gas and cause stomach upset. If you'd like to include a bit of these foods in a recipe, minimize their potency by throwing in a potato or two.

7. **Caffeinated drinks:** You're losing enough sleep as it is — don't give baby more reasons to stay up! This category includes caffeinated soda and iced tea.

8. **Choking hazards:** When it comes to round, firm foods, just say no. Here are some classic hazards that should be avoided until twelve months at least:

    » Whole or chunky raw fruits and vegetables (mash or puree instead)
    » Whole pieces of canned fruit
    » Very sticky food, like peanut butter, marshmallows, and taffies
    » Very hard food, like popcorn (with their hard kernels), meat chunks, hot dogs, or hard candy (not to be given before age four)
    » Nuts (not to be given before age four)

Miri

I once made the mistake of letting my baby snack on cornflakes, which are pointy and rough-edged. She started wheezing at one point; it was clear that a cornflake had gotten stuck in her throat. I didn't do anything because I saw she was still breathing. Those were the longest ten seconds of my life — I felt so helpless! I called Hatzalah just in case, but, baruch Hashem, she managed to propel it out on her own.

CHOKING: PREVENTION AND INTERVENTION

A choking baby is every parent's worst nightmare. Here are some steps you can take to minimize the risk:

» **Sit her up.** Don't feed your baby when she's reclined in the swing or infant seat. Feed her only when she's sitting upright.

» **When in doubt, go smaller.** If you're not sure, slice that potato or bread into finer pieces. The firmer the food item, the smaller it should be cut.

» **Place her face-to-face.** Always feed your baby when you can clearly see her face. If she's sitting on your lap, you'll have a hard time discerning whether she swallowed. She may be accumulating food pieces in her mouth, where they'll ultimately meld into a too-big, unsafe mass.

» **Take a course in child safety** (or a refresher, if it's been a few years). Familiarize yourself with safety techniques. Don't wait until an emergency! Be prepared!

What if it happens?

If you see your baby choking, here's what you need to know and do:

» **Double-check.** Choking is characterized by a complete airway blockage. If your baby is coughing hard or making loud sounds, it means that his airway is not fully obstructed. That's good. As excruciating as it is to watch, don't act. Forceful coughing is the most effective way of dislodging an object. *In the meantime, call 911 or Hatzalah just in case.*

» **No blind finger sweeps.** Never try to extract the food out of your baby's mouth unless you can see it. You may inadvertently push it deeper into his throat. And never tilt baby's head backward so you can see better — this can cause the object to lodge deeper inside.

» **Start the Heimlich.** If baby is not breathing, or if he's turning blue, and if you haven't yet done so, call Hatzalah or emergency services, then begin the Heimlich Maneuver (see next page).

THE HEIMLICH MANEUVER FOR INFANTS

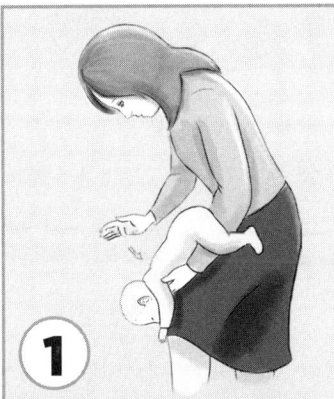

1

If your baby is choking:

» Hold his face down on your thigh, supporting his stomach with the palm of your hand.

» Make sure his head is lower than his chest.

» Thump his back five times between the shoulder blades with the heel of your hand.

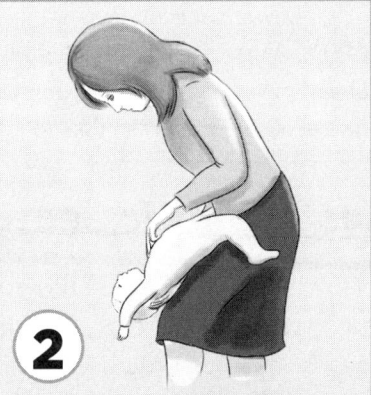

2

If the object is still lodged:

» Support the baby's head and turn him faceup on your thigh.

» Keep his head lower than his body.

» Place two or three fingers in the middle of his chest, just below the breastbone, and give five quick chest thrusts.

  Continue until the object flies out or emergency help arrives:

» Keep alternating between five back slaps and five chest thrusts.

» If your baby becomes unconscious, begin infant CPR immediately (see Appendix III, p. 410).

With Hashem's help, the combination of gravity and physical force will dislodge whatever was in his throat.

Note: *This procedure should only be used for infants under one year. If you suspect your baby's airway is blocked because her throat has swollen shut — due perhaps to an allergic reaction or respiratory condition — do not do the Heimlich; call 911 or Hatzalah immediately.*

> **MOMMY'S TWO CENTS**
>
> Empower yourself as a mother by registering in a CPR and first-aid course — it's worth the investment. If you've already learned emergency-rescue basics in high school, take a quick refresher course in person or online.

Gastronomic Gear

Now that you've depleted your bank accounts on the newborn baby gear, are you ready for a list of feeding essentials? The good news is that this time there's no need to break the bank. When it comes to feeding tools, simpler is often better. Here is the equipment you'll want to have on hand when your baby is ready for the big day:

Soft-tipped spoons

For babies, spoons are hard, foreign objects that you're suddenly trying to thrust into their mouths. To mitigate the adjustment, choose super-small, soft-tipped spoons. Go for flatter and less concave; these demand less effort from baby.

Bibs

Unless you particularly enjoy scrubbing Shout and Clorox furiously into fabrics, these are essential.

- » **Choose bibs with a Velcro or snap in the back**; you don't want to be lifting a filthy bib over baby's freshly washed hair. But make sure the closure is strong enough that baby won't be able to pull it open.
- » **Waterproof or washable?** Determine your preference. Waterproof bibs are ideal for runny foods, but they have to be wiped down well after each use. Cloth bibs must be washed frequently, but they're useful when you're short on time — just launder after each use.

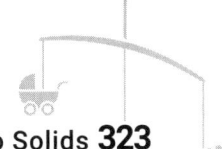

- » **Look for bibs with a handy pocket at the bottom.** They're great for catching falling chunks of food and minimizing cleanup.
- » **Unbreakable utensils.** Now is not the time to bring out Aunt Gertie's heirloom china. If you don't yet own durable plastic plates and bowls, now's the time.

Highchair

Bear in mind that many highchairs' price-upping features are purely aesthetic. When making the purchase, consider the features you'll really need:

- » **Space:** Some highchairs bear an uncanny resemblance to... thrones. If you live in a small apartment, or if your kitchen is cozy, resist the temptation to buy big and choose a compact, foldable model.
- » **Movability:** If you see yourself frequently moving the highchair from kitchen to dining room to den, opt for a model with wheels.
- » **Ease of use:** Does the chair come with a convenient extra tray for fleishig meals? Can you remove the tray with one hand? Is it removable for easy dishwasher cleaning? Does the tray's perimeter encircle baby as closely as possible, for minimal food drops? All these features will simplify your daily routine. Also, the fewer seams and crevices in the design, the less time you'll spend cleaning (you'll certainly be thankful for this come Pesach!).
- » **Comfort:** While too much padding is not recommended — excessive lining can reduce sensory input and hamper a baby's development — the seat should be a place where baby will want to hang out: roomy (especially for a bigger baby) and padded with smooth, non-scratchy material. A footrest is a nice bonus.

» **Safety:** JPMA-certified highchairs reflect the gold standard in safety. The majority of highchair accidents occur due to unbuckled occupants — so make sure the buckle can be easily fastened by adults.

Part of beginning to eat solids is learning to close the lips around the spoon. Because in the beginning baby isn't naturally skilled at this, many well-meaning mothers make the mistake of inserting the spoon at an angle, scraping against baby's upper lip and using it to sweep food off the spoon. This may get the food in his mouth, but it won't teach your baby to close his lips on his own. Instead, gently place the spoon on the lower lip, and wait until your baby brings his lips together.

Moving Forward

Once your baby has mastered pureed fruits and vegetables — usually between eight and nine months — move on to tiny finger foods: cut-up cooked potatoes, carrots (only cooked ones!), or Cheerios, for example. Toothless babies can join the party too: As long as the foods are soft, gumming will be sufficient. At this stage, you can also start serving meat and poultry, eggs, dairy products, and beans. Have fun mixing and matching vegetables, proteins, and grains.

Some great options:

» Blended vegetable and/or bean soups
» Soft meatballs
» Pieces of challah
» Cooked chicken (Watch for small bones.)

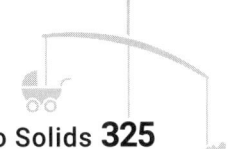

- » Rice, casseroles, and kugels
- » Melt-in-your-mouth crackers
- » Cholent (First, try beans and potatoes separately to make sure baby likes them. Then you can put them together and let him enjoy his first taste of Shabbos!)
- » Cottage cheese and yogurts (sugar-free)
- » Small pieces of banana (A banana cut into rounds is too big. You can use a baby spoon to measure a safe amount.)
- » Eggs (Use a hard-boiled egg chopped into small pieces, or a soft scrambled egg; make sure eggs are completely cooked.)
- » Well-cooked pasta, cut into pieces

In the past, parents were advised to wait before introducing highly allergenic foods like wheat, eggs, fish, and ground nuts. But new research shows that waiting to introduce these foods doesn't reduce the risk of allergies; they can all be introduced at eight to nine months. If you, your spouse, or some of baby's siblings are highly allergic, though, consult with your doctor first — he may advise you to introduce these foods at home with an oral histamine readily available, or wait until the child's second year to introduce those foods.

What about peanuts? The jury is still out. Some parents still hold off on peanuts, peanut products, and peanut butter products, because allergic reactions can be severe. Interestingly, however, research shows that in Israel — where, for many, the time-honored peanut-based Bamba staple is baby's first food — incidence of peanut allergies is one-tenth the rate of Western countries, where peanut consumption in babies is limited. Since research is ongoing and recommendations are often changing, for the most current information on when (and if) to introduce peanut products to your little one, speak to your pediatrician.

Excessive sodium intake can be harmful for babies, whose immature kidneys are not yet equipped to handle it. The daily

> **MOMMY'S TWO CENTS**
>
> Jars of baby food deplete quickly, and the cost adds up. For a more economical route, throw lots of veggies into your Shabbos chicken soup, then blend and freeze them separately (or mixed — depending on the stage your baby's at) in labeled jars. For newbie eaters, freeze the mush in ice cube trays; babies only eat a few spoonfuls a day at the beginning, so one or two defrosted and warmed cubes should suffice. Added bonus of soup veggies: They're packed with flavor.

recommended sodium allowance for children under twelve months is only one gram. Since many processed products (breads, crackers, cookies) already contain sodium, it's best to avoid salting baby's food altogether. Don't worry about giving baby a portion of the family chicken soup or cholent — a teaspoon of salt distributed throughout a substantial dish is not significantly worrisome — but don't add a shake of salt directly onto baby's beans or puree, even if you notice that he likes it. To excite a discerning baby's taste buds, use flavorful herbs and spices instead.

> *Yael*
>
> *Whenever he spotted vegetables on sale, my husband would stock up on sweet potatoes, butternut squash, and carrots. About once every two months, I'd do a peeling marathon and cook them all up, with just a bit of water. We yielded about twenty containers each time, and the puree was simple, healthy, and cheap. My daughter loved it!*

Abort Mission?

You lovingly take out the fruit jars each morning. You choose the optimal time of day and make mealtime fun with books and songs. But baby is not cooperating! What now?

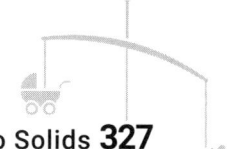

Relax. Keep trying, but don't project anxiety or tension. He'll get there. In the meantime, here are some strategies to facilitate the journey:

- » **Let the kids play.** What *is* this gooey orange stuff? Often, babies need to thoroughly explore food before they feel comfortable ingesting it. Place some food bits or puree on baby's highchair tray with the sole purpose of letting him play with it. As he fools around, he may inadvertently take a lick and discover that this stuff tastes good! Don't mind the mess. Baby *will* run sweet potato through his hair and get pears up his nose, and that's okay. Just place a towel or mat under his highchair to minimize the mess, and get out your camera. What's a childhood without that classic grubby-hands, big-smile photo? Remember: His cholent-laced coiffure is nothing a five-minute bath can't fix.

- » **Variegate textures.** Some babies find smooth, saucy textures revolting. If he's not going for purees, he may prefer more textured finger food. Try offering tiny pieces of soft food like shredded mashed chicken and challah.

- » **Spice it up.** While most experts recommend starting with bland foods, your baby may have a more sophisticated palate. Add as much flavor — with spices and herbs — as needed, but go easy on sugar and salt.

- » **Go social.** We know this from our own diet lapses: social eating (think Shabbos table, dinnertime, shul *kiddush*) encourages us to eat. Set baby up in his highchair during family meals. You may be surprised at his sudden willingness to accept samplings from your plate.

- » **Walk the walk.** If you want your baby to diversify his diet, eat a varied diet yourself. Research indicates that the flavors Mommy ingests transfer to her milk, so anything a breastfeeding mother eats will be more familiar and palatable to her baby.

» **Never force.** Pushing a spoonful of food into your baby's mouth against his protestations is a sure way of creating long-lasting unhealthy food associations. Encourage, facilitate, but never compel. Opened jars of baby food can be safely refrigerated for up to three days, so try again tomorrow. (Always transfer baby food into a separate dish when serving, because once baby's saliva comes in contact with the jar contents, the three-day grace period no longer applies.)

» **Follow baby's lead.** As parents, we should be training kids to eat when they're hungry and stop when they're satisfied. Don't feel pressured because your nephew or neighbor downs three jars in one sitting. There's no fixed amount; as long as your child is gaining weight and thriving, believe him when he conveys, *I've had enough*. Encourage him to listen to his stomach.

» **Keep an eye on the diaper.** Until now, your baby's bowel movements were likely a mustard color. Once he's introduced to solids, you may start seeing darker colors and different consistencies. If the baby seems constipated, or if his stools seem hard, dry, or overly runny, consult with your doctor.

I Can Feed Myself!

Until around nine months, babies grab toys and food using the "raking grasp," where they swipe at objects with fingers open. Between nine and twelve months, babies develop the "pincer grasp," where they use the index finger and thumb to pinch objects. This allows them to start self-feeding with finger foods. Cheerios, well-cooked elbow pasta, and small pieces of banana or chicken offer great pincer-grip practice. Once she's gotten the hang of it, let your baby try eating with a spoon — even if it makes a mess. To ease her into spoon usage, stick a dollop of a gooey substance like cream cheese to the end of a spoon and scatter

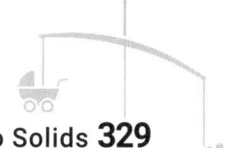

some cereal on the tray. This way, baby's spoon will easily attract and retain food.

Another handy way to train baby to use utensils is to place a spoon in her hand at mealtimes. She'll play with it, and — between bites from Mommy's spoon — occasionally succeed in making mouth contact. This setup takes advantage of every baby's mimicking instinct.

The Scoop on Supplements

Manipulative media ads often urge new mothers to boost baby's diet and give him that "extra protection" with an array of vitamins and minerals. Are these really necessary?

No, indicates current research. Except for unique cases (like premature or malnourished babies), studies show that most vitamin and mineral supplements are not beneficial to healthy breastfed or formula-fed babies during the first six months — and some can even be harmful. As long as nursing Mommy is eating well, her baby will thrive sans vitamins.

There are three notable exceptions:

» **Vitamin K** — This vitamin is essential for blood clotting. Some babies are born with insufficient quantities, and a deficiency can cause a devastating hemorrhagic disease, Vitamin K Deficiency Bleeding (VKDB). To prevent VKDB, standard hospital protocol in most developed countries since 1944 has been to give all babies a vitamin K injection immediately after birth (see p. 27).

» **Vitamin D** — Breastmilk is the ideal food for baby, but it usually doesn't contain enough vitamin D, which is essential for prevention of rickets (a weakening and softening of the bones). Since sun exposure — the vitamin's primary source — is not recommended for infants, babies under six months are at risk of a deficiency. Once baby transitions into a substantive diet of solids, she can get her sunshine vitamin from oily fish, eggs, and fortified foods. But since most babies don't eat these foods consistently before the age of twelve months, the American Academy of Pediatrics advises parents to give vitamin D supplements for at least the first year. Some doctors even recommend continuing until age five.

» **Iron** — Slow weight gain, pale skin, no appetite, irritability? These are all common symptoms of anemia, or iron deficiency, in infants. The good news is that healthy full-term babies have iron stores from the good ol' days when Mommy supplied it in utero. This cache lasts until at least six months, and often even until twelve months. What's more, iron in breastmilk is more easily absorbed than iron in formula, so breastfed babies are at an advantage. Some doctors assert that after six months — when babies start ingesting less breastmilk but are not yet eating solids consistently — infants should receive iron drops each day. Other health authorities say that as long as baby is gradually introduced to iron-rich foods — like meat, chicken, spinach, and iron-fortified cereals — alongside breastmilk or formula, supplements are unnecessary and can be harmful. If you have concerns about your baby's iron levels, speak to your doctor.

Bear in mind that iron from both supplements and plant sources (soybeans, lentils, spinach, and various legumes) is best

---

MOMMY'S TWO CENTS

Iron drops are notoriously messy, and babies rarely swallow them without protest. To avoid stained clothing, give the drops just before bathing, when your little one is totally undressed. Never squirt the drops — or any liquid medicine — into baby's throat! Place the dropper in his mouth and release medicine between his gum and cheek. Mix with a teaspoon of orange or citrus fruit juice to enhance absorption.

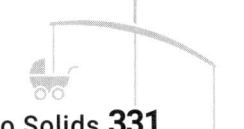

absorbed when consumed together with vitamin C foods (for example, citrus fruits, tomatoes, melon). Absorption is poor when it's eaten together with — or soon after ingesting — caffeine-filled substances like tea, or calcium-rich foods like dairy products. In those cases, the iron binds to the food components and isn't well absorbed.

A Diet for My Darling?

Childhood obesity is rapidly on the rise, now affecting one in six American children and precipitating a host of negative emotional, psychological, and physical effects. Does this mean bulging *pulke*s baby should start watching his weight?

Not quite. At each of your baby's well checkups, your doctor will measure his height and weight and calculate his BMI (body mass index). Generally, a BMI above the eighty-fifth percentile indicates overweight; a BMI above the ninety-fifth percentile points to obesity. But since babies depend on high-fat diets to grow, caloric restrictions are not recommended for children under two. That means no Atkins for a while! The problem is, being too heavy can delay crawling and walking — essential aspects of physical and cognitive development. And while super-chunky babies are cute, they're at risk of becoming obese kids — not so cute.

So how to prevent a worrisome BMI in your bambino?

» **Watch your weight.** Excessive weight gain during pregnancy can increase your baby's birth weight, and high birth weights are heavily linked to childhood obesity.

» **Breastfeed.** Research suggests that breastfed babies are less likely to become obese.

» **Think beyond the bottle.** Baby is shrieking? Don't assume he's hungry. Sometimes a new position, a soothing environment, or a gentle stroke is all he needs.

- » **Don't rush it.** According to recent Harvard research, babies fed solids before four months were significantly more likely to be obese by age three. Best time to introduce solids? Between four and six months, and fourteen to sixteen pounds of body weight — but only if baby shows signs of readiness.
- » **Junk the juice.** Sweetened drinks and juices don't contribute much to a baby's nutrition and should be assiduously avoided. When your baby is ready for real food, offer nutrition-rich fruits and vegetables instead.
- » **Respect baby's signals.** During mealtimes, watch your baby carefully for signs that he's full. Avoid the temptation to "get down another spoonful." Overfeeding can quash natural body signals, wrongly teaching your baby that satiated means stuffed.
- » **Get moving!** Ever seen a bouncer-bound baby? Those are the kiddos content with chilling in a seat for hours, watching the mobile spin. This may be good for Mommy, but it's not good for baby. Turn on the music, put your baby on his tummy, and get on the floor too. Encourage movement!
- » **Say no to videos.** Babies who watch media are far more likely to become overweight or obese. Don't let baby watch videos or smartphone clips before age two. They're much better off moving than watching images on a screen! And it's not only about obesity: Toys with flashing lights provide an overload of visual stimuli. Baby's brain is not yet ready for it. Avoid giving baby any toy with flashing lights before age one, and say no to videos or iPhone playing before age two. (And, of course, there are a host of other problems associated with smartphones for children, which are not in the scope of this book.)

Ten to Twelve Months

From Baby to Toddler

Time to stop and enjoy the nachas! Baby development between ten and twelve months is less pronounced than previous months, but you can still look forward to plenty of milestones.

PHYSICAL GROWTH AND MILESTONES

Here's what you *should* be seeing by now:

DEVELOPMENTAL MILESTONES	BABY...
Physical growth	Will have grown about ten inches in length since birth
	Continues to gain weight, albeit at a slower pace
Motor	Moves around by creeping, crawling, or cruising
	Sits without support
	Self-feeds finger foods and attempts the pincer grasp
	Holds a bottle on her own
	Stands with support
Speech and language	Produces longer, repetitive strings like "mama," "dada," and "ma-ba-ba-da"
	Responds to simple verbal requests, like "give me the spoon"
	Uses gestures to communicate: points to objects, waves bye-bye, shakes head for "no"
Social-emotional	Cries when you or another beloved caregiver leaves
	Has definite opinions; may protest during activities like diaper changing or nap time
	Mimics your actions — may brush hair, for example, or talk on the phone
	Displays copious affection with hugs, cuddles, and smiles

If your baby hasn't reached one of these milestones, DON'T PANIC! Be sure to mention it to your doctor at her next well-baby checkup.

Here's what you'll *likely* see in the next three months:

DEVELOPMENT MILESTONES	BABY...
Physical growth	will have tripled her birth weight by one year
Motor	pulls up to a standing position
	walks while holding an adult's hands
	crawls up stairs (get those gates installed!)
	places one block on top of another
	transitions from a standing to a sitting position
	pulls off socks and hats
	holds large markers and makes marks with them
Speech, language, and communication	repeats single words after you
	fully understands object permanence, for example, even if he can't see Mommy, she's still there
	understands basic cause and effect, for example, if he cries, Mommy will come
	matches shapes, for example, putting a cube in the square hole
	points to correct body parts when asked
	holds out arms and legs when getting dressed
	uses two to eight words
Social-emotional	shows distress when she does something wrong
	imitates other children
	enjoys being the center of attention
	shows empathy, like starting to cry when another baby cries
	shows a like or dislike of people and objects
	expresses new fears about situations that were previously okay

Red Flags

By ten months, contact your doctor if baby...
» does not move around
» does not show an interest in his surroundings
» does not show a preference for Mommy and Daddy

Chapter Sixteen

Walking, Thinking, Talking, Feeling...

Just Cruisin' Along

She creeps, she crawls — what's next for baby? Once she's mastered the art of getting around, she'll likely start trying to stand — pulling herself up via the couch, coffee table, your skirt, or any other graspable surface. Remember that she may not yet know how to get down (she's smart, but not *that* smart), so be available to assist in her descent. Show her how to gently bend her knees and lower her legs to the floor.

Baby's gotten the hang of standing up. Before you know it, she'll be on to "cruising": shuffling along while holding on to furniture. While not particularly graceful, this step is exciting, because it's one of the last stages before bona fide walking. As baby builds confidence, she'll dare to let go of the furniture and attempt to cross narrow gaps without holding on (think table to Tatty).

Now here's a caveat: Some babies will cruise for a long, long time. You'll be all geared up, ready to capture her first unassisted

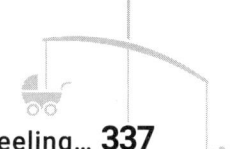

step on camera, but your baby will show no signs of loosening her grip on the couch. Is this normal? You bet.

Weeks or months may pass until baby is physically and emotionally ready to make her move. During that time, she might focus on other areas of development, like language, acquiring new words each day. So just sit and wait patiently — and in the meantime, here's what you can do "behind the scenes" to facilitate overall motor development:

- » **Let him roam.** It's a tempting, convenient option, but don't over-confine baby to the playpen or stroller. Make your home as safe as possible, then let baby ramble to his heart's content. Give him the chance to practice his skills!
- » **Put him down.** Resist the urge to carry your baby everywhere. Let him try to independently cover short distances on his own.
- » **Don't slip up.** Tumbles and tears are part and parcel of the learning process — but a painful fall can be traumatic, discouraging baby from trying again. Let baby totter around barefoot for maximum grip (this also helps to build arches and strengthen ankles). If the floor is cold, outfit him with nonskid booties or socks.
- » **Invest in push toys.** Once your baby is cruising well (read: minimal topples!), offer stable toddle toys — such as wide-based doll strollers and activity walkers — in an enclosed environment to further build confidence and competence. Don't use baby walkers; these support baby on all sides, which can be detrimental to development (see p. 291).
- » **Pile on the praise.** Applaud your baby for even the tiniest independent step. Bring on the cheering squad! Make a big deal! (Okay, you didn't need to be prompted for this one...)
- » **Create an obstacle course.** Use pillows, play tables, and phonebooks to prepare a short trail for baby. Whether he traverses the course by crawling or cruising, it's a great way

to keep him moving and experimenting. Note: Tired parents lying on the floor are also great obstacle options.

» **Baby blanket ride.** If he is sitting steadily on his own, put baby onto a blanket on his bottom and pull it to give him a gentle ride! This activity encourages balance and helps develop proprioception — a sense of where you are in space. Both elements are essential for walking.

» **Sound the music.** Music gets kids moving — it's a fact! Show baby how to clap his hands, shake his head, bounce, and sway. With time, he'll get into the groove instinctively. Music is also great for reinforcing the intonation and rhythm needed for speech.

In the early stages of cruising, you might notice that baby puts weight only on his tiptoes. This is normal; with time, he'll learn to use the entire foot. But don't be deceived: Tiptoeing cruisers can cover ground quickly, so make sure the stairs are blocked and the environment is safe. (For more on safety, see pp. 292-300.)

Walk the Walk: Getting on Two Feet

The moment has arrived! She crawls, she stands, she cruises like a pro — and now, baby has taken that first step. Walking is the most major move toward independence, so don't be surprised if you find yourself becoming emotional: Your precious infant has just graduated babyhood and is ready to conquer the world!

Does your baby walk like Frankenstein, with outstretched arms and awkward, wide steps? Don't be alarmed. These elements help her maintain balance in the beginning; in no time, she'll be doing the *kazatzke*.

Most babies start walking between nine and twelve months, but some children don't start before sixteen or seventeen months. So don't feel pressured if your baby is taking her time to get walking. If baby isn't toddling by fourteen or fifteen months, though, bring it up with your doctor. This is still within the normal

> **MOMMY'S TWO CENTS**
>
> To encourage walking, set baby down in a walking position instead of a sitting or crawling position.

range of development, but it's a good time to rule out anything that might be delaying the milestone. Remember that babies who bottom-shuffled tend to walk later than babies who crawled.

And give your little walking cutie time to get around — most babies take about one thousand hours of practice from the time they pull themselves up to the time they can walk unassisted.

Goody Two-Shoes: Baby's First Shoes

Now that baby has taken his first step, is it time to rush out to your local shoe boutique? Not just yet. Here's the scoop:

When? Shoes can impede baby's developing mobility, so wait until he's taking steady, consecutive, independent steps before making the purchase. And for the first month of his walking career, use shoes only when walking outside or on rough, uneven surfaces. Even once baby is practically jogging, it's always beneficial to let him go without shoes on safe, clear surfaces like carpet, grass, or sand. Toddling around in bare feet (or even with socks) builds intrinsic muscle strength and coordination in the legs.

Where? Choose a shop that specializes in fitting babies. And since babies' feet swell during the day, it's better to shop in the afternoon.

What? First footwear should...

» have flexible, nonskid soles (usually rubber) and a substantial upper;

» be made of leather or mesh, so baby's feet can breathe comfortably;

> **PIGEON-TOED? NOT *MY* BABY!**
>
> Have you noticed that your baby's toes turn overly outward or inward? This can be disturbing, but don't panic. Gait differences are very common in babies. In-toeing and out-toeing are not painful and, in most cases, disappear during the toddler years. But it's worthwhile to monitor progress: Speak to your pediatrician, who might refer you to a pediatric orthopedist.

- » have ample space at the front and back — you should be able to squeeze your pinkie between baby's heel and the heel of the shoe, and you should be able to fit the entire width of your thumb between the end of her longest toe and the tip of the shoe;
- » feature sides and top that aren't too tight (use your fingers to check).

Before sealing the deal...

- » Let baby walk around for five minutes, then remove the shoes and check his feet. If you see irritated spots, nix the pair.
- » Make the choice between Velcro and laces. Velcro fasteners are easy and fast, but they're also easy for baby to open — when you least want it! If you go for laces, make sure the strings are long enough for double knots (not on Shabbos!), so they won't frequently come undone.

How often? Baby's feet can grow rapidly at this stage, so check his shoe fit monthly at home. Be prepared to invest in new footwear every two to three months.

Bye-Bye Butterfingers?

By now, baby can grasp small objects with his thumb and index finger (the pincer grasp). This means that parents need to be

extra careful with choking hazards: Baby's mouth is still Explorer-in-Chief, so small objects will go straight in.

But with all her picking-up prowess, it's important to remember that baby can't yet put things down in a controlled manner; she'll likely drop the object when she's had enough. (Keep this in mind if your baby is high up, or holding an object near an infant.)

Baby is also showing signs of an auspicious career in engineering: She's learning to place blocks on top of each other. Chunky magnetic blocks are great for this stage, since the tower won't topple easily.

Here are some activities to further promote fine-motor development:

- » **Good things, small packages.** Invest in *menschies* or Fisher Price Little People or other smaller, age-appropriate toys, so that baby can experiment with different finger grasps.
- » **Make a mark on this world.** Baby can't hold paper down yet, so tape a sheet to a table or highchair tray and provide large washable crayons or markers. See if baby can make some marks! Don't worry about a perfect pencil grasp; that develops much later. If crayons prove too challenging for your munchkin, stick with markers — they require less pressure.
- » **The Cheerio challenge.** Place a Cheerio or animal cracker inside a small plastic jar and challenge baby to get it out by dumping it.
- » **Finger paint.** This activity is great for both motor and sensory development; you're exposing baby to new, different textures. For minimal cleanup, try this outdoors. Make sure you buy or make baby-safe, edible finger paints, since lots may go into baby's mouth!
- » **Have a blast in the bath.** Bring on the toys! Offer cups for pouring, sponges for squeezing, and funnels for cool water watching. Make a homemade watering can by poking holes in a flat-topped bottle cover. No need to spend money on tub

> **FUN TO EAT AND YUMMY TO TASTE**
> **EDIBLE FINGER PAINTS**
>
> 1 cup cold water
> 4 tablespoons cornstarch
> 4 cups boiling water
> Different colors liquid food coloring
>
> 1. Mix cold water and cornstarch together, until smooth.
> 2. Add boiling water, one cup at a time, mixing after each cup. Stir until it's a smooth paste.
> 3. Pour into four unbreakable cups. You can also pour them into a muffin pan.
> 4. Stir in food coloring, a different color for each cup.
> 5. Have fun!

toys; baby will be delighted with plastic cups, yogurt cups, and any other thoroughly rinsed plastic container. For added excitement, switch the selection (read: new containers) every month or two.

» **Extraction exercises.** Challenge baby to pull tissues from a box or pegs from a board. If you don't want to waste Kleenex, fill an old tissue box with colorful scarves. To moderate the challenge, tie the scarves together. (But don't leave baby alone with the scarves — it's a choking hazard.)

» **Let 'er rip!** Offer baby several magazines and let the ripping begin! For further stimulation (and to preclude a big mess), provide a big basket and challenge baby to place the shreds in the basket.

» **Mad scientist at work.** By now, baby's a pro at stacking, filling, and emptying containers. Present a shoe box filled with random (safe!) items; let her lift the cover, empty the contents, and put them back. If you're really brave, head

outdoors (or to an area where mess is okay) and show baby how to pour cornmeal, salt, or water from one container to another.

» **Package play.** In the bath, present baby with a "present" — a bath toy wrapped well in one or two wet washcloths or diaper cloths. Challenge baby to unwrap the package and discover the contents. No matter that it's the same toy she's played with for months; she'll relish the surprise! This activity is also good for reinforcing object permanence.

» **All stuck up.** Use masking tape or Velcro strips to stick some of baby's toys to the floor. Then challenge her to unstick them. Baby will hone her hand-eye coordination, strengthen her arm muscles, and feel like a million bucks!

Brain Builders

What's new in baby's brain? A whole lot. Baby now has a good understanding of object permanence, and he'll try to find objects you've hidden. He's become more creative and flexible: If something is not working, he'll try new methods to attain his goal. He might be a little copycat, imitating the actions or words of people around him. And he'll probably show awareness of parents as people separate from himself; when asked, "Where's Mommy?" he'll point to Mommy.

Your little Einstein is also beginning to understand basic cause and effect: *When I drop the block, it falls. When I cry, Mommy comes.* (It never fails!)

Here are some great ways to promote cognitive development:

» **Count the buttons.** Babies love buttons and snaps, so each time you get him dressed, use the opportunity to promote skills and count those buttons out loud. (Don't count loose buttons at this age; they are a choking hazard.)

» **Make it real.** Give baby toys that are safe miniatures of real-life objects: phones, kitchenware, brooms, and tools. This will encourage him to observe and imitate, laying the foundations for early imaginative play.

Speak Up

At ten months, baby is no longer the strong, silent type — he's definitely got plenty to say! Most of his oratory consists of long chains of incoherent babble that he seems to find very profound. Amusingly, you'll also notice that he's begun varying intonation: He alters pitch and volume, making him sound emphatic and dramatic.

Baby has also learned that speech is meaningful: He can differentiate between speech sounds and other sounds, attending more to the speech sounds. And when you turn on the music, he may try to sing along.

Some babies have produced their first real words by now — "Mama," "bye-bye," "no" (that's a favorite!) — but if your baby hasn't, there's no need to worry. As long as he's babbling well and showing a good understanding of basic objects (for example, he points to Tatty when asked, "Where's Tatty?"), he'll probably get there soon.

Here's what you can do until then to facilitate speech and language development:

» **Be a good listener.** Research indicates that mothers who listened and responded to their babies' spontaneous sounds saw increased vocal production from baby. In plain English, this means that listening is just as important as talking. Set aside some listening time each day. For example, during story time, let baby turn the pages and "comment" on the pictures. Don't translate or interpret; just listen, make eye contact, and periodically repeat baby's exact sound — without correcting it.

» **Capitalize on animal sounds.** Short, easy, and intriguing, animal sounds offer great starting points for beginning linguists. Buy inviting animal books or stuffed animals that make noise. Practice and reinforce the sounds together: *Meow! Mooo! Woof-woof!*

» **Continue the conversation.** Babbling is the precursor to meaningful words, so it's something you want to encourage. When baby excitedly emits a long-winded burble, take him seriously! Respond as if he said something intelligible and talk back.

» **Name it.** Point to and name the people and objects in baby's world: Zeidy, book, bird, dog, chair, car.

SPEAKING OF SPEECH

> At this age, baby will likely use the *B*, *P*, *M*, and *D* sounds most consistently. Why? Because those are the easiest. *B*, *P*, and *M* are called "bilabials"; they require complete closure of the lips (labials) — a very visual, easy-to-learn movement. *D* is also one of the first acquired sounds because all that's involved is bringing the tongue behind the front teeth (or gums, for still-toothless fellows) and then letting out some air.
>
> If baby is still not enunciating these speech sounds clearly, model them in an exaggerated way whenever you imitate his babbling. For example, say "Ba-ba-ba" while opening and closing your lips in a very pronounced way.
>
> At this age, baby begins to discriminate between foreign speech sounds and native speech sounds. In other words, he'll start dropping the unfamiliar (weird!) sounds he's been producing until now, and use only sounds that are part of his native language — what Mommy and Tatty speak. If the babysitter speaks to him in another language, he'll retain those sounds too.

- » **Acquaint with anatomy.** During bath time, diaper changes, or while dressing baby, point out and name different body parts: hands, tummy, nose, eyes. Eventually, ask "where" questions for each part: "Where is your nose?"
- » **Ask simple questions.** Pull out a bright, simple board book and ask baby "where" questions on each page. "Where is the duck?" "Where is the bottle?" If baby doesn't respond, model the answer by pointing to the picture.
- » **Give simple commands.** Tell baby, "Please bring me your cup!" or "Put it down," and wait to see if he responds accordingly. If he doesn't, offer visual and intonation cues (for example, point to the cup, point downward, or use a stern voice when saying, "Stop that!"). When all else fails, model the correct response.

Baby Has Feelings Too

During these three months, baby's emotional awareness increases dramatically. She's more aware of herself as an individual person, and she's more aware of her feelings. It's important for Mommy and Tatty to acknowledge these developments.

- » **Help her handle her feelings.** If baby cries or shows fear, comfort her. If she expresses frustration, acknowledge it ("You must be frustrated!") and help her calm down and try again. This support helps baby learn to recognize and regulate strong emotions.
- » **Follow her lead.** The best kind of play is child directed. Instead of telling baby what's on the agenda, lay out three toys or activities and just wait quietly until she gravitates to one. Letting baby lead the show encourages independence and teaches her a critical lesson: She can impact this world with her choices and actions. (Sadly, babies who are not given this opportunity can become passive and detached.)

What's more, the more baby "owns" the game, the more motivated she is to keep at it and learn more.

TOY STORY

There are zillions of toys out there, but you want to be an educated consumer. Here are the development-boosting toys worth buying for babies ten to twelve months:

- **Rolling toys** — This category includes cars, balls, trains, and anything that moves. By now, baby is more mobile and dexterous, and she'll soon learn to roll them on her own, and eventually chase after them.
- **Button toys** — Baby can now use her index finger to point, poke, or prod, so invest in toys with buttons, pop-ups, or dials (for example, a train that chugs when you press the button). These are great for developing fine-motor skills — finger strength and precision — while reinforcing the concept of cause-and-effect.
- **Wooden puzzles** — Baby won't be able to place the pieces independently just yet, but he'll get familiar with the concept. Choose bright, clean puzzles with jumbo-knobbed pieces that match to corresponding pictures on the board.
- **Toys with movable parts** — Look for toys with doors that open and shut, ladders that go up and down, or shapes that go in a chute. Baby now has the fine-motor skills to manipulate these objects.
- **Simple picture books** — You can never have enough books — *good* ones, that is. Look for durable books with bright, real-life pictures (ideally photos) on clean pages. Visuals that are too busy will prove overwhelming for baby.
- **Push and pull toys** — to encourage standing and cruising.
- **Real-life miniatures** — like phones and keys. These classics are great for imitating skills and imaginative play, which is starting just about now.
- **Blocks** — Start with large, unpainted wooden blocks. When baby gets very good at building towers (usually thirteen to fifteen months), move on to plastic blocks that snap together, like Duplo.

Chapter Seventeen

Weaning: Making the Break

In the Torah, Avraham and Sarah held a special party for three-year-old Yitzchak on the occasion of his weaning. Nowadays, though, most babies stop breastfeeding well before age three. In fact, 75 percent of initially breastfed babies in the United States are no longer nursing by age one.

If you and baby are both enjoying nursing, keep going! There's no need to stop. But between nine and eighteen months, many mother-baby pairs do gradually end the breastfeeding relationship.

Who initiates the weaning process? There are only two choices:

1. Baby
2. Mommy

Child-Led Weaning

In many cases, baby shows a decreasing interest in breastfeeding. He might want to nurse only once or twice a day, and his sessions will get progressively shorter: He'll nurse for a minute or

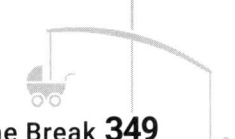

two, then get distracted and run off to play. This can be painful for Mommy. *Already too big for my milk?* she wonders sadly, watching her big boy scamper off. *No more cuddly time with Mommy?*

These emotions are normal. Weaning is one of the first major steps toward separation and individuation, and you'll likely find it hard to let go of the special nursing relationship. Your child no longer needs you exclusively for sustenance. Validate these feelings, and seek support from friends. Try to remind yourself that, ultimately, this is what every parent davens for: independent, self-sufficient children.

When you see baby's signals that he wants to be weaned, ready yourself to wind down, but don't stop nursing overnight — that can cause painful engorgement. Encourage baby to take small "sips" for several nights consecutively, lessening the amount each night. If he's easily distracted, sit together in a dark, quiet room just before he goes to sleep.

If baby goes "cold turkey" on you — refusing to nurse at all — you may need to manually pump for a week or two. This will relieve your discomfort until the milk supply has dried up. Make sure to express only as much milk as you need to feel relief. Each day, try to extend the time between pumpings. A hot shower can also provide enormous relief.

Offer your expressed milk to baby — he might enjoy the nutrient-rich fluid from a cup or bottle. If he still turns up his nose at your liquid gold, consider donating it to a milk bank.

Mother-Led Weaning

Sometimes it's Mommy who initiates the weaning process. By the time baby is nine or twelve months, you might...

» find the breastfeeding lifestyle too stressful, restrictive, or time-consuming to maintain;

» feel that breastfeeding causes hormonal side effects that adversely affect your intimate life;

» discover that you are expecting another baby and receive doctor's recommendations to cease nursing. (Note: La Leche recommends nursing even while expecting.)

Many mothers who don't particularly enjoy nursing will "stick it out" until this stage, knowing the extraordinary benefits of mother's milk. But now that baby is older and eating solids well, they're ready to move on.

If this describes you, there's no need to feel guilt. Breastfeeding is most beneficial during the first six months of a baby's life. Past that point, it's a valuable but less crucial experience. Applaud yourself! You gave your baby nine to twelve months of unparalleled nutrition; you gave her the healthiest start possible. That's a huge accomplishment.

But take some time to consider your real needs. Do you want to wean baby completely, or will cutting out several feedings a day do the trick? Even just two breastfeeding sessions a day — once in the morning and once at night — can often be enough to satisfy a baby who is also eating solids, while giving Mom the flexibility she needs.

If you do decide to wean completely, the process must be very gradual. A sudden stop in breastfeeding can be traumatic to your baby.

Here's how to do it carefully and sensitively:

» **Cup or bottle?** Depending on baby's age, decide if you'll be weaning to a cup or bottle. Many doctors recommend going straight to the cup after nine months, to avoid the stress of eventual bottle weaning. But some babies find the breast-like bottle nipple familiar and comforting.

» **Least favorite feeding.** Identify the feeding your baby seems least interested in and offer her a bottle or cup at that hour instead. Until your baby turns twelve months, compensate with formula (don't offer cow's milk before baby's first

birthday). If it's close to baby's first birthday, increase solid food as you decrease breastmilk feedings.

- » **Drop one at a time.** Slowly, depending on your comfort level and baby's willingness, cut out another feeding every few days or once a week.
- » **Nighttime last.** The nighttime feeding is usually the last to go. Create a soothing bedtime routine — book reading, cuddling, songs — so that baby will still have comfort mechanisms once the nursing is dropped.
- » **Find substitutes.** If baby refuses to take a bottle from you, delegate the job to Daddy or another caregiver and leave the room — she might be more amenable in your absence.
- » **Switch routines.** If you normally nurse in the bedroom, offer a bottle in the living room. Avoid sitting in your favorite nursing chair, and hold baby in a different position when giving her the bottle.
- » **Take trips.** For maximum distraction and stimulation, try to get out of the house as much as possible during this stage. Head out with baby to the playground, supermarket, or a friend's house.
- » **Go heavy on TLC.** Give plenty of hugs, cuddles, and massages (see pp. 267-271) throughout the process to ensure that baby feels loved and to retain your mutual closeness. Don't abstain from hugs because you're afraid baby will pine for the breast; she needs the physical touch now more than ever.
- » **Be patient.** Allow yourself time. If you start weaning with a full milk supply, it may well take a full month, and sometimes even longer, to finish the weaning process.

Gradual weaning is emotionally beneficial for *both* nursing partners. It's also healthier: Your body will sense the imminent weaning and produce milk with increased immunity levels to give baby one last "hurrah" of protection against infection, as your milk production slowly decreases, preventing engorgement, blocked ducts, or mastitis.

No-Go Weaning

Mother-led weaning is often a bumpy process.

Here are some signs that the weaning is going too fast:

» New or increased separation anxiety

» Biting — when it wasn't a problem before

» Increased fussiness and tears

» Baby seems more withdrawn than before

» Heightened aggression

» Refusal to eat; stomachaches or constipation

If baby is having a hard time, slow down on weaning and pile on the affection. If that still doesn't improve symptoms, you may want to wait it out. Often, time is the best remedy. When baby is emotionally ready to say farewell, he'll do it effortlessly.

Alternately, you can try the "don't offer-don't refuse" approach. In this tried-and-true method, Mommy doesn't offer to breastfeed, but happily acquiesces at baby's request. This method takes time but is often effective, because baby feels in control. Plus, it's the least emotionally draining option.

Cold-Turkey Weaning

Abrupt weaning can be terribly distressing for both mother and baby, while causing physical complications and drastic hormonal plunges. If a health care professional directs you to wean baby immediately, seek a second opinion. If the consensus is that you must wean, consult with an experienced lactation consultant or La Leche League leader to avoid pain and minimize emotional angst.

> ### Malka, mother of eight
> When I was pregnant with my fourth, I fell into a deep depression and required medication. Looking back, I'm sure that my sudden weaning of baby number three — who was only seven months at the time — contributed. My doctor advised me to stop nursing, and I did, overnight. Today, I know I'd only make such a move with careful consideration and planning.

Help! Baby Got Sick

Sick babies need lots of fluids — and often, they'll refuse to drink from a bottle or cup. If your baby starts feeling ill during the weaning stage, consider pausing for now and restarting the process another time. Breastfeeding your baby during his illness will provide her with essential fluids, and antibodies to fight the illness, while offering unmatched comfort.

In general, avoid weaning during stressful situations. If baby is starting with a new babysitter, if you're moving to a new home, or if he just began teething, sit tight and wait for a more opportune time.

Extended Breastfeeding

Baby is pushing three, but you and she are crazy about nursing? Good for you! Don't feel pressure to stop. The World Health Organization (WHO) recommends breastfeeding up to a child's second birthday "or beyond."

As baby grows, family members who are uncomfortable or unfamiliar with the phenomenon may make comments or tease you about breastfeeding, but don't capitulate. Do what you feel is right for you and your baby. Amazingly, breastmilk evolves with a baby, so as your little one gets older you'll be nourishing him with milk that provides nutrition and immunities — exactly what he

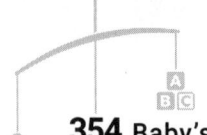

needs at this stage. Studies also show that breastfeeding beyond a year brings numerous benefits:

» Continued immune protection

» Better social adjustment — because baby feels a deep, constant sense of security

» Availability of a sustainable food source in case of emergency

What's more, research indicates that the longer women breastfeed, the lower their risk of breast and ovarian cancer.

Chapter Eighteen

Everyone Loves Baby

As you delight in the giggles, babbles, and exciting milestones that your baby seems to be reaching every day, your extended family will join the chorus. Between adoring grandparents, protective aunts, smitten cousins, and, yes, slightly bewildered siblings, your baby will get love and affection from every direction.

But the blessing of relatives can come with challenges. What happens when Bubby oversteps bounds? When ten-year-old Tzvi insists on holding baby — in his awkward, less-than-secure arms? You might feel torn between your family's wishes and your baby's well-being.

In this chapter, we'll focus on ways to facilitate positive, healthy interactions between your baby and his doting *mishpachah*.

Abba Attachments

Apart from you, the next family member whose life will be irrevocably changed by the baby's arrival is Daddy (aka Tatty,

Abba, Pappa; it's your choice — no, actually, it's *his* choice!). If this is your first child, Daddy may be experiencing mixed emotions: He's thrilled to become a new father, but struggling to create a unique relationship with baby. As he watches you bond with your newborn through breastfeeding and cuddling, he may feel excluded and even superfluous: *What's my role here? Who needs me anyway?*

What's more, since you'll be exhausted and physically on the mend, quality spousal time may be limited — another downer.

How to avoid this common postpartum drag?

» **Involve Tatty as much as possible.** Find opportunities for your husband to become an active participant in baby's care, like bath time or bedtime. If Tatty takes on the daily bath, for example, he'll gain invaluable one-on-one bonding time while providing you with a few minutes of quiet time to yourself.

» **Discuss the challenges openly.** Don't be afraid to broach the subject. Speaking openly about challenges helps minimize the angst. Ask your husband how he's feeling about the new baby, validate his emotions, and acknowledge that these sentiments are normal. It takes time for all the players to comfortably settle into a new dynamic.

» **Develop a household system that works.** Are your household responsibilities bogging you down, leaving you drained? This depletion may deny you the physical and emotional wherewithal needed to set aside and enjoy time with your husband. If that's the case, respectfully raise the issue: How can your workload be reduced? In what ways can your husband pitch in, empowering you to be a happier, calmer wife? With improved mutual understanding and joint effort, ultimately you'll both emerge as winners.

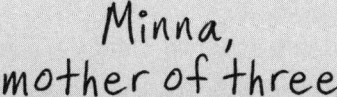

> ### Minna, mother of three
>
> I'll never forget the scene when our first child was born. I nursed her, then handed her over to my husband, whose exposure to infants had been minimal. He panicked. "How am I supposed to hold this thing?" he cried, frantic. "Where do I put my arms?" Oh no, I thought to myself. We're in for a looong haul. Thankfully, the journey was shorter than I thought. It took time and patience, but eventually my husband did learn the ropes. I worked hard to model well, give clear directions, and make no assumptions of previous knowledge. Three children (and some mishaps) later, he's still not naturally "geshikt" but he's a great nurturer — both physically and emotionally. Lesson? There's hope for everyone!

> ### Miriam, mother of four
>
> I got a serious virus and wound up in the hospital when our firstborn was less than a week old. Though they let me keep the baby so I could nurse him, I didn't have the koach to do much else for him. My husband, David, who was the youngest in his family and had very little experience with babies, rose to the occasion beautifully, holding our beautiful boy, changing his diapers, dressing and cuddling and generally taking care of him while I recovered. Men can't take care of babies? As far as I'm concerned, that's just a myth!

Skeptical Siblings

You pull up in the driveway. Abba gingerly lifts the baby's car seat and schleps it to the door, which is plastered with colorful signs and balloons. You enter your home, and baby's three siblings — a toddler, preschooler, and first grader — are utterly baby-struck! From the moment they see that pink bundle, they shower love and warmth and goodness her way, never touching or teasing or hurting her (G-d forbid!). And Family Klein lived happily ever after.

Sound like a fairy tale? Guess what — it is! This scenario rarely happens. Sibling rivalry is as ancient as the very beginning of creation. It's particularly understandable when a child's life has just changed dramatically. A new sibling is a joy, but his arrival also presents a major upheaval to the family. If your child is showing resentment — or even aggression — toward baby, that's totally normal. Feeling threatened and insecure, many children tend to regress somewhat: They'll demand increased attention, want bottles, need cuddles, speak baby talk, or become kings and queens of the tantrum.

Now for some good news: There are many ways to minimize the inevitable adverse reactions.

Prep for Success

The first step to a smoother transition is eliminating the shock factor. Experts generally advise parents to prepare their children before a new sibling is born. But choose your moment wisely. Preschool-age kids don't have an established concept of time and may exhaust you with constant questions of "When is the baby coming already?" It might be ideal to tell a young child about the upcoming arrival only a month or two in advance. Alternatively, you can refer to a specific season: "Baby will be born before Pesach, when it starts getting warm outside." (If your community does not tell children about an upcoming birth, refer to others in your community as to how this should be handled.)

How much detail should you offer? This depends on your personal preferences and what is accepted practice in your community.

Some ideas for involving the children before the baby's arrival:

» Look through albums of the older sibling's baby photos (even more fun — share your own baby pictures!). This will not only make the child feel special, but also give her a concrete idea of what to expect when baby comes.

» Read books about greeting a new baby sibling. Ideally, choose books that explain newborn behavior and describe

the ambivalence a sibling will typically feel, offering validation and acceptance for real, common emotions.

» Visit friends who have infants.

» Pack a bag for the hospital together.

» If Moishy insists that you bring home a specific gender ("If you don't give me a brother, I will pack my bags!"), don't dig in your heels and insist that sisters are just as wonderful. Acknowledge the feelings, but stress that only Hashem decides if it will be a boy or girl. If you've decided to find out the baby's gender, and it will *not* be to Moishy's liking, make sure to prepare him for the disappointment — either by sharing the information (recognize, though, that your child will probably tell everyone else), or simply stressing that a sister is *very likely*.

What if he remains inconsolable? Take comfort in the fact that most babies don't show boyish/girlish sides until they're much older, so after the initial letdown, Moishy might forget that the new baby is (yuck!) a girl.

» When planning arrangements for your children during your hospital stay, aim to enlist familiar, beloved family members. Discuss these plans with your kids so they know what to expect.

» In the days and weeks preceding baby's arrival, try to keep the routine as consistent as possible. Want to redecorate the nursery or shift the furniture? Do this well in advance, so your other children have time to acclimate. Involve them in the process. Want to toilet-train toddler or help him transition from crib to bed? Tackle these projects at least two months before the birth, or push them off until post-baby.

» Don't forget to clue in your child about the realities of a newborn. Gently explain that the baby may cry and Mommy will have to hold her a lot: "Tiny babies really need their mommies." Emphasize that one day your children will be great friends, but in the beginning, baby won't be a very exciting playmate.

» Consider allowing your child to visit you in the hospital soon after the birth, ideally when no other family members are around. This reinforces the birth as an intimate family event, and makes your older child feel like a *"mechutan"* in the milestone.

"Baby's" Presents

Before giving birth, it's a great idea to buy a special toy for each child — something significant over which they'll be ecstatic. As soon as you come home from the hospital, break out the toys and have the new baby "give" them as gifts. Aside from offering great distraction and entertainment, continued linking of the gift to the baby ("Wow! Look what Shalom gave you! Are you playing with the truck from Shalom now?") will create deep, positive associations.

Another good idea is to stock up on child-safe *tchatchkes* from the 99-cents store. Keep them on a high shelf, to be used one at a time during crises: When toddler wants to go to the park and you have to nurse, when toddler refuses to attend playgroup, or when toddler keeps pulling at baby's hair.

When it comes to sibling jealousy, breastfeeding sessions are often the most challenging time. Older sibling watches as Mommy and baby bond in a way that's exclusively baby's. To avoid nursing struggles, set aside three or four toys as "nursing" games. Choose items that can be played with independently, like Lego, coloring books, or *menschies*. Alternatively, if you're a masterful multitasker, you may want to designate nursing time as "reading time." Allow your toddler to choose a book, and read it to him while nursing baby. This keeps him happily engaged, while offering a Mommy-snuggle-equivalent activity. If you are comfortable nursing on the floor, leaning against the sofa, you can even join him in playtime!

> ### Esti, mother of four children under six
> When I came home from the hospital, I presented my two-year-old daughter with a beautiful doll. The doll came with a small bath, bottle, and changing pad. Whenever I had to nurse, bottle-feed, or bathe the baby, I reminded her to get her doll, and we each "took care" of our babies. She loved imitating me and felt very important. Best of all, she was entertained when I needed it most.

Settling In at Home

When you step through the doorway for the grand posthospital reunion, remember that your older children need you most. Your newborn — probably dozing — does not need to be cuddled right now. Let Daddy carry in the baby while you zero in on the other kids. Pile on the hugs and kisses, offer your full attention, and only then introduce siblings to their new brother or sister.

Capitalize on toddlers' inherently narcissistic natures and relate everything about the baby to him, the older sibling:

- » "Look at these tiny toes! Do you know that *you* used to have tiny toes like these?"
- » "You are so good at building Lego towers. Will you teach baby how to do that when he gets big?"
- » "I love the way you are so kind to baby. I hope baby grows to be kind like you."

Articulate each child's unique strengths: "You are so responsible and reliable" or "I love the way you make me laugh." Emphasize that each child has a special role to play in the family.

If your older children express an interest in the baby, do your best to involve them in caring for baby. Bathing, dressing, or diapering will take much longer with their "help," but the trade-off is worthwhile: You're giving opportunities for positive interactions with the baby.

Here are some innovative ways they can help:

» Choose a stretchie or diaper for the baby (many diapers come with different picture patterns).

» Dab moisturizer on baby's toes with a cotton ball during diaper changes.

» Gently rub baby's back during tummy time (with a parent supervising closely to prevent overzealous muscle action!).

Make a big deal about this invaluable "assistance" in front of others. With the older sibling in earshot, detail to Bubby and Zeidy exactly how he helps, and why baby loves him so much. The idea: Cast him in role of caretaker rather than rival. But don't overdo it — you don't want the older sibling to feel burdened by this new role. Take your cue from his reactions.

If your child expresses zero interest, perhaps even ignoring the baby and pretending he's not there, don't be alarmed — and don't force it. This is a normal reaction that will hopefully pass with time. Until then, avoid making everything about the baby. Instead of "I'll help you when I finish changing baby's diaper," try "I'll help you as soon as my hands are clean." Instead of "We'll go to the park when baby wakes up," try "We'll go to the park when I finish making supper."

Whether your toddler is gaga or pareve about baby, never leave him — or any preschool-age child — alone with the baby, even for a few seconds. If you notice your child getting rough, quickly move baby away and distract the older sibling with a book, toy, or song. Avoid admonishing where possible. Realize that this child (especially if she is the oldest) is experiencing a period of grief: She's mourning the exclusive relationship she once had with her parents. Make it clear that hurting is *not* allowed, but empower her by suggesting other ways to express her feelings: She can draw an angry face on a paper, or roar like a lion.

Schedule your day wisely: Take advantage of baby's nap times to give one-on-one attention to siblings. A child who knows he'll get his share of Mommy time will usually feel less resentful, and even just five undivided minutes can go a long way. Consider using a baby sling or carrier so that you can keep baby close while freeing two hands to play with the other kids (see p. 135). Have Abba take the older child to the supermarket or pharmacy, and emphasize that these are "big boy outings."

Solicit help from relatives. Remind grandparents and aunts that your children may want to schmooze about topics *other* than baby. If relatives ask how they can help, suggest they take an older sibling out for a fun outing or spend time together over a special activity. If you sense that your child specifically craves Mommy time, ask a relative to watch or hold the newborn while you play a game with big sister.

When Baby Goes Mobile

Often, siblings seem to adjust beautifully to baby — until baby gets moving, learning to crawl and destroy carefully constructed games, towers, and Playmobil scenes. Preempt the upset by discussing the new reality with your older child. Acknowledge that baby has now reached a new stage, and stress that he may sometimes get in the way because he's excited, curious, and too little to understand.

Advise your older child to set himself up for success by confining all destructible games and projects to a high surface, like a table. Suggest that he build a "special" tower that baby can freely knock down and rebuild to distract him from toppling more important items. Emphasize that on the whole, this new stage is exciting, because it means baby is becoming more interesting and engaging.

Grandparent Goodness

Of all extended family relationships, there's one that stands out for its life-changing impact: the grandparent-grandchild bond. Grandparents have been crucial players in the lives of *eineklach* since time immemorial. And despite the twentieth-century disintegration of multigenerational households, research indicates that grandparent involvement is still pretty significant.

According to an AARP analysis of the U.S. 2000 census, at least 5.8 million American grandparents live in homes with their (under eighteen) grandchildren. Thanks to increasing divorce rates and rough economic patterns, parents are increasingly relying on grandparents.

The benefits of fostering a tight Zeidy-Bubby-*einekel* bond are manifold:

» **Relationship modeling.** Every relationship a person maintains in childhood will serve as a subconscious model throughout life. Grandparent relationships are generally awash with love and lacking the tensions common in parent-child counterparts. Result? Child emerges with yet another ingrained model of healthy, normal connection.

» **Sense of history.** A child who enjoys a strong grandparent relationship will feel part of something bigger. He'll have earned a priceless link to the family legacy and, yes, to the *mesorah* that goes all the way back to Har Sinai.

» **Development of independence.** Grandparents often serve as stepping-stones in the process of a child's healthy separation and individuation. An overnight stay at Bubby's, for example, will be far less traumatic than a sleepover at neighbors.

» **Support for parents.** Grandparents — free from the day-to-day parenting grind — can provide loving care when the parent feels depleted and drained (yes, you *will* feel depleted and drained at times!).

Amazingly, these benefits last throughout adulthood. Research indicates that adults who enjoy a close relationship with grandparents show significantly better psychological health.

Are we surprised? Not really. Some of our deepest, most cherished memories involve our grandparents: Zeidy scooping us up

from the couch, tucking the blanket around our arms. Bubby removing hot cookies from the oven, piling them high on a plate. The warm and fuzzy feeling that surfaces — decades down the line — upon seeing Savta's favorite recipes showcased on the table. Shopping with Grandma for Yom Tov outfits, or just having fun on a snowy day with Zeidy.

The takeaway is clear: Facilitating a loving attachment between grandparent and baby is a worthwhile investment. Now how to go about making it happen?

There are three elements required, the experts say, to create an impactful connection:

- » Creating a sense of emotional closeness
- » Ensuring regular contact
- » Encouraging children to view their grandparents as a source of social support

Transcending the Distance

"Regular contact" is the trickiest element on the list. In today's global community, it's become increasingly common for grandparents to live far from their grandkids. Here are some tools to overcome the often-difficult physical separation:

- » **Visit as often as you can.** Tickets may be pricey and logistics overwhelming, but try to bite the bullet: Consider the expenditures an investment in your child's future.
- » **Employ technology.** Your children can talk to Bubby and Zeidy on the phone or watch them on Skype, and just seeing their faces and hearing their voices regularly can make a huge difference.
- » **Capitalize on song.** Allow baby to listen to Bubby singing on the phone; play audio tracks with Zeidy singing in the background. Empower baby to familiarize herself with these voices and form a connection through music.

» **Ensure a presence.** Refer to Bubby and Zeidy frequently in your home. Create an album featuring photos of them and flip through it frequently. Hang a clear photo on the wall, and before putting baby to bed at night, encourage her to say "good night" to her grandparents.

» **Send pictures.** Maintain the connection by regularly sending photos of the grandchildren to Bubby and Zeidy.

» **Choose a regular "visiting" time.** In today's hectic, overscheduled world, it's a good idea to have a regularly scheduled time when Grampa and Grandma either call or Skype. That ensures the kids will be home and gives everyone something to look forward to.

Leah, mother of six

When the kids were young, my mother-in-law would call them every Thursday night. They would line up to talk to her; it was the highlight of their week. She knew who was taking a test, who had a gan party, whose best friend was moving away. She was incredibly involved in their lives — even though we lived in Eretz Yisrael and she was in Flatbush! I think it worked because it was done so regularly, and because my mother-in-law understood that to build a relationship with a child, it has to be about their lives.

Visiting Grandparents

Whether you live near or far, hopefully you'll get to visit Bubby and Zeidy during significant times of the year. Some grandparents instinctively know to childproof their home ahead of visits, but many — especially first-time *sabas* and *savtas* — take longer to cross this hurdle. Be prepared to tackle this job yourself and also come equipped with lots of toys in case Bubby hasn't yet stocked up.

If your baby has attained newfound mobility, take a walk around your parents' and in-laws' homes and remove all hazards (refer to our childproofing section, pp. 292-300). If you'll be staying for a while, consider bringing and installing child locks for the cabinets. This will lighten Bubby's load and help avoid tension.

When Bubby (or Zeidy) Is the Babysitter

Do you work many hours outside the home? If you are fortunate enough, you might have a retired parent or parent-in-law who is happy to care for your baby. At first glance, this arrangement seems idyllic: grandparent develops a close bond with baby, and parent gets to leave her angel in the most loving hands possible. If the grandparent is offering the service at no cost, there's yet another enormous financial plus.

But the setup has its snags. What happens if Bubby engages baby in an activity that Mommy considers unsafe? What if Zeidy starts feeding baby honey-smeared challah, insisting that the health precautions are excessively restrictive? What if Savta refuses to accept payment, but you sense that she needs some kind of compensation?

Before even considering this kind of arrangement, make sure your relationship with this parent is overall a healthy one. Consider doing a trial week before you start.

If you decide to give it a try, make sure expectations are clear from the beginning.

Sit down with the grandparent and come up with answers to the following:

- » Will you pay the grandparent for child care? If so, how much and how often?
- » Where will the care take place — in whose home?
- » What if the child or grandparent gets sick?
- » Who will be a backup if the grandparent cannot babysit that day?
- » Who will provide and pay for the food, formula, diapers, and wipes? Keep in mind that it may be simpler to pay for the food instead of preparing and lugging meals over each day.

It's never appropriate to criticize a parent (and halachically forbidden!). To avoid awkward situations, prepare a written list detailing baby's eating, sleeping, and playing patterns. Include info on baby's habits: his favorite toy, blankie, and bedtime routine.

Acknowledge that you may go overboard in your dos and don'ts, and ask your parent or parent-in-law to humor you.

Once the arrangement begins, be careful not to sweat the small stuff. Even if things aren't exactly as you would have done (baby's hair is streaked with food; toys were put away in the wrong places), think twice before speaking up. Nitpicking can generate resentment. You may have mentioned it to a typical, paid babysitter, but with a parent, only bring up issues that seriously hamper routine, development, or safety. And remember, your parents brought you up, and your in-laws brought up your spouse, and they may know a thing or two! (Of course, Bubby and Zeidy, if you're reading this, remember, you raised your kids your way, let your kids raise their children in the way they want!)

Your baby's habits and moods will change frequently, so make sure to update Bubby regularly.

Examples of items to mention:

Baby...

- » is teething,
- » skipped a meal or snack,
- » has not been sleeping well,
- » is showing signs of an imminent cold,
- » developed a diaper rash,
- » is becoming wary of strangers,
- » developed new fears, such as of loud noises or certain toys,
- » developed an attachment to a blanket or security object, especially if needed for sleep.

In some ways, you should treat the grandparent as you would any other babysitter. Don't assume she'll just "manage." Arrive with enough diapers, supplies, and food for the time allotted. Don't come late for pickup, and don't overstay your welcome — your parent may need some space.

If the babysitting takes place in the grandparent's home, make sure all medications and sharp items are put away. Purchase a child gate or child locks if necessary.

Remember to keep the roles separate. Grandma watches baby all week, but let her be just "Grandma" at family functions. Don't expect her to take care of baby while you catch up with cousins or dance with the *kallah*.

Most of all, express appreciation frequently and thoughtfully. Even if the grandparent refuses payment, try to give gifts periodically (think vacations, restaurant meals, housewares, books, flowers — something that is in your budget but shows your gratitude). And make sure to cover all food and transportation expenses.

It Takes a Village

"It takes a village to raise a child," the axiom goes. As you grow older and more experienced, you'll probably begin to appreciate the profundity of this statement. Parenting is a tough job, and having the support of loving family can transform the "impossibly exhausting" into "challenging but doable."

What's more, research has shown that when children are cherished by many people — not just their parents — they develop a deep sense of security and protection, as well as a bolstered self-esteem. They acquire broader world knowledge, gaining exposure to ideas and interests besides those of their parents.

Few things are as delightful as family gatherings — occasions where you can share your *nachas* with people you love. If you have many younger siblings, cousins, nieces or nephews, your baby will likely become the center of attention, a novelty to be admired and passed around.

But what should you do when baby is being handled roughly or carelessly? At what age is an older child considered a reliably safe baby holder? And how to handle visitors who insist on holding your four-day-old baby, whose immune system is decidedly immature?

You can feel comfortable allowing adult visitors to hold your newborn infant, but to be safe, make sure they wash their hands with soap first. If a relative has a fever, cough, cold, or other sickness, politely ask them to visit another time; your baby's health comes first. Make sure no one is coughing or sneezing near baby.

If a relative is a smoker, make sure he or she hasn't smoked for at least twenty minutes before holding the baby. The toxins from nicotine — which remain on the smoker's clothing and breath — can be harmful.

Try to keep visits on the short side. If you sense your baby is becoming overstimulated, or if you feel the oohing and aahing is disrupting her feeding and sleeping schedule, gracefully extract her from the crowd while thanking her fan club for their adoration.

Older Siblings

Once your baby is six weeks old, and weighs ten pounds, you can let yourself relax a bit about germs in the air: His immune system is likely far stronger at this point. But you should still insist that visitors scrub their hands well before holding him.

What about older siblings? Most proud big sisters and brothers will nag parents endlessly for the privilege of holding the baby. Experts don't pin down a particular age for this skill; they recommend that parents look at each child individually and follow their gut: Do I trust him? Is he capable of following instructions carefully? Often, a mature, nurturing nine-year-old can be more reliable than a flighty thirteen-year-old. If you're not sure, allow baby-holding only while the child is sitting and under your close supervision. See how that goes. If a child is devastated by a "No, you can't dance around with baby," you might want to suggest that he transfer baby short distances while she's strapped in her infant seat.

Afterword

From the Day of Birth ... to a Happy Birthday

And now baby is one year old ....

It's been a magical, wondrous, sleepless, challenging, miraculous year.

Look at your little boy, wandering all over the house, crawling or perhaps even wobbling to and fro on unsteady feet. Look at your little girl, smiling, babbling, bubbling over with the excitement of discovery. Remember the wonder of her tiny, perfect features right after birth? How he nestled in your arms for the very first time, seeking nourishment and his mommy?

In these 12 months, your baby has grown so much and learned so much. And guess what? So have you!

In the months and years to come, both you and baby (soon to be big boy or girl!) will grow and learn even more. We wish you a safe and happy and meaningful journey, you and your baby together, with the strength to overcome the challenges, the *siyata d'Shmaya* to guide your way, and the love that makes everything possible.

Mazel tov!

Appendix I

Selected Halachos of Baby Care

This section involves common situations that are likely to arise with babies up to one year of age. It is not meant to be a comprehensive treatment of the subject. Consult your *rav* when dealing with older children or special circumstances.

— Selected Laws of Shabbos —

Treating Illness or Injury on Shabbos

Halachah differentiates between various degrees of severity of an illness; as the severity and danger to life increases, more activities normally forbidden on Shabbos are permitted — and often mandated. In these halachos, children are viewed differently from adults, in terms of what may and may not be done medically on Shabbos. Generally, the younger the child, the more medical intervention is permitted, since younger children are considered to be weaker and in more danger from illness.

Umbilical cord care

» Cotton swabs dipped in alcohol, sometimes used for treating the umbilical cord of a newborn baby (see p. 78), should not be used on Shabbos because of the *melachah* of *sechitah* (squeezing). Instead, sprinkle alcohol onto the area and then rub it with your hand, or very lightly with a cotton swab, being careful not to squeeze the liquid out of the cotton.

» If the area around the cord becomes red, or if there is excessive bleeding or a foul odor from the cord, consult a doctor.

From birth until twelve weeks

» A newborn or infant who has fever or any unusual symptoms is considered to be a *choleh sheyeish bo sakanah* (a sick person whose life is in danger). Time may be of the essence, and a doctor must be contacted immediately. If possible, minimize *chillul Shabbos* by performing the necessary actions with a *shinui* — that is, in an unusual manner. For instance, when calling the doctor, use the pinky instead of keying in the numbers in the usual way.

NOTE: If there is any doubt about how urgent the emergency is, err on the side of caution and do whatever is necessary to get the child medical attention as soon as possible.

Q *If I'm right-handed and do the necessary action (such as calling a doctor), with my left hand, is that considered an "unusual manner"?*

A The general rule is that anything that requires an extra amount of energy or concentration to accomplish the task is considered "unusual" for these purposes.

» If the baby must be transported to be examined or treated and the medical professional consulted says a short delay is acceptable, it is preferable to find a non-Jewish driver.

However, in an obvious emergency or if the doctor says that a delay may pose a danger, a Jew may drive the baby to the doctor or hospital.

> **Q** *If the hospital is close by, may the child be carried in an area where there is no eiruv?*
>
> **A** It is preferable to have a non-Jew drive than to carry the child.
>
> In a case where a Jew may drive, if a Jew carrying the child would get the child to treatment sooner than driving, he may be carried. If time permits, make certain the child has nothing in his hands or pockets.

» If the driver is Jewish, when the driver arrives at the doctor's office or hospital, he is not permitted to shut off the car's engine, since that has nothing to do with caring for the sick child.

> **Q** *If the car would be left running, children are liable to go play with it. Is this itself considered to be a danger?*
>
> **A** Yes, if there is a possibility that children would start driving the car, it is a danger. If one cannot find a non-Jew to turn off the engine, a Jew may do so himself.

» If you take a taxi or a non-Jew is driving, ask him to open and close the car doors to avoid turning the interior lights on and off yourself.

» If the baby has been treated and released on Shabbos, it is preferable to wait until after Shabbos to return home. However, if the baby will be uncomfortable and needs to go back home, a non-Jewish driver may take the infant and his parent home. If both parents accompanied the child, a halachic authority should be consulted regarding what the second parent may do.

After the age of twelve weeks

» After three months, a child is considered stronger and is not considered to be in danger because of a slight rise in temperature or minor symptoms. However, if the child has high fever, problems breathing, severe diarrhea or vomiting, dehydration, is not reacting, or has any other serious and unusual symptoms, the child is considered a *choleh sheyeish bo sakanah* and a doctor must be contacted immediately. (For how to contact a doctor on Shabbos, see above, p. 374.) If there are any doubts about the seriousness of the symptoms, contact a medical professional or take the child to a medical facility immediately.

» A child under the age of three (or even older, depending on the child and the situation) who is suffering any illness or injury that is causing him serious discomfort is considered a *choleh she'ein bo sakanah*, a sick person whose illness is not life-threatening.

» A Jew may not transgress a Torah law for the benefit of a *choleh she'ein bo sakanah*. However, a Jew may perform such an act with a *shinui*, if there is no permissible way to treat the child.

» A non-Jew can be asked to perform any act, even a Torah prohibition, on behalf of such a child.

Treating rashes

» Applying creams and ointments falls under one of the prohibited *melachos* of Shabbos: *memarei'ach*, smoothing. The Torah (*d'Oraisa*) prohibits smoothing over the surface of any firm substance; this includes thick diaper ointments, such as Desitin.

» It is also forbidden rabbinically (*d'rabbanan*) to smooth over a substance whose consistency is thinner, such as Vaseline.

- » Substances that are liquids do not fall into the category of *memarei'ach*. This includes fluids such as baby oil, baby lotion, alcohol, calamine lotion, etc.
- » If a baby has a slight rash or irritation that generally causes no discomfort, no ointment should be used on Shabbos.
- » If a baby has a rash (including diaper rash) that is causing substantial discomfort, the child is considered a *choleh she'ein bo sakanah*. Therefore, a person may apply medication to heal the infant. However, the person must try to avoid violating the prohibition of *memarei'ach*, as far as possible without compromising the child's health.
- » Because a child with a rash that causes distress is a *choleh she'ein bo sakanah*, a Jew may do a *melachah* that is prohibited rabbinically, if necessary for the child's health. The *melachah* should be done with a *shinui*. If violating a Biblical prohibition (*d'Oraisa*) is necessary (such as boiling water), a non-Jew should be asked to do it.
- » If the baby's rash developed before Shabbos, smear the ointment onto diapers or bandages before Shabbos and store them in a clean plastic bag, so there is no problem of *memarei'ach*.
- » If cream or ointment must be applied, if possible use liquid medication. If that is not available, use lotion that is not thick, as that is a *melachah d'rabbanan* only.
- » If a very thick ointment is necessary, do not smear it onto the rash itself. Remove it from its jar with a *shinui* (such as using a spoon handle) and drop the amount necessary onto the rash. A diaper or bandage may be put over it, even though that will smooth out the ointment.
- » Alternatively, you can take the ointment out of the jar in an unusual manner and place it onto a diaper or bandage, and then put the diaper or bandage on the affected area.

- If the ointment is in a tube rather than a jar, squeeze it directly onto the rash and place the diaper or bandage on the area. Alternatively, you may rub the ointment into the skin with a *shinui,* such as using the back of your hand.

Treating other medical conditions of children

- If a house is not properly heated, a person may become ill. Therefore, if the house is unusually cold, it is considered a situation of *choleh she'ein bo sakanah*. This is true even if no one is sick at that moment. In such situations, you can ask a non-Jew to turn on or raise the heat, even if it is warm enough for adults, but not warm enough for the children in the house. If it becomes too cold, it is permissible to tell a non-Jew to lower or turn off the air conditioner.

- If a child gets a splinter, you can remove it with a needle. Although you cannot sterilize the needle in a flame, you may sterilize it with alcohol. When removing the splinter, be careful not to draw blood. If you think the child will bleed, but he is in pain, you can remove it in any case.

- If a child gets a bump, you can put ice on it. To avoid the *melachah* of squeezing, put the ice into a plastic bag and not directly into a towel or cloth bag.

Using a vaporizer or nebulizer

- If a baby needs to use a vaporizer that was not turned on before Shabbos, and the situation is not life-threatening, you should ask a non-Jew to turn it on.

- If a hot-water vaporizer has been on since before Shabbos, you may add hot water from a thermos or hot-water urn. If no hot water is available, you may ask a non-Jew to heat it. Add the water through the vaporizer's spout, or in some other way that will not cause the motor to turn off.

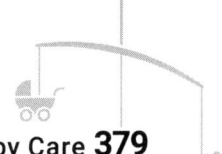

- » If a cold-water vaporizer has been on since before Shabbos, you may add cold water through the vaporizer's spout, or in some other way that will not cause the motor to turn off.
- » If a child is wheezing and the situation is potentially life-threatening, you may turn on the hot water in the bath or shower to relieve the child's wheezing (of course, if a non-Jew is available without delay, one should ask a non-Jew to turn on the water. If the situation is certainly not life-threatening, you may have a non-Jew turn on the hot water; if a non-Jew is not available, you may turn on the hot water with a *shinui*. If the water is heated by the sun (*dud shemesh*), you may turn on the hot water yourself, without any *shinui*.
- » If a child needs medication regularly administered through a nebulizer, the device can be put on a Shabbos clock.
- » If the child is having trouble breathing and needs a nebulizer, if time is of the essence a Jew should turn it on, if possible with a *shinui*. If it is not absolutely urgent, either a non-Jew should be asked to turn it on, or, if the child is capable, she should turn it on herself with a *shinui*.
- » **As with all illnesses, if there is any doubt as to the urgency of the case, whatever is necessary for the child's health should be done with no delay.**

Treating a wound

- » If a child gets a scrape or cut, you should try not to apply pressure to the wound in a way that will draw more blood. But if the only way to stop the bleeding is to apply pressure that will draw more blood, it is permitted.
- » If the bleeding is heavy, it is considered a case of a *choleh sheyeish bo sakanah,* a life-threatening emergency, and all measures must be taken to stop the bleeding.
- » A scrape or cut may be cleaned with water, alcohol, hydrogen peroxide, or other liquid. To avoid the *melachah* of *sechitah*,

squeezing, pour the liquid onto the wound and then rub lightly with a cotton swab or tissue.

» If you want to place an adhesive bandage, such as a Band-Aid, on the cut, try to open the wrapper of the bandage by gently pulling the ends apart. If you must tear the wrapper, try to do so without tearing any letters.

» Permanently connecting two items may violate the *melachah* of *tofer*, sewing. Therefore, when you put on the bandage, especially when bandaging around a finger, make sure the two ends of the bandage don't stick to each other, but are on the skin.

» If the only bandage available is too long, it should not be cut.

» If you are wrapping a dressing around a wound, it should be tied with a single knot and bow (and not a double knot or double bow), avoiding the *melachah* of *kosher*, tying.

» It is best not to secure a dressing with tape or a Band-Aid. Safety pins or clips may be used.

Thermometers

(For more on thermometers and fever, see p. 380.)

» It is permitted to use a non-electronic device to measure temperature or blood pressure on Shabbos.

» It is preferable to use a fluid-filled thermometer if available.

» There are differing opinions on whether or not one may use a strip that changes color when the child has fever. If letters or numbers appear on the strip, is should not be used, except if there is no other non-electronic thermometer available.

» Digital thermometers and sphygmomanometers (that measure blood pressure) may not be used on Shabbos, except in potentially life-threatening situations.

» Rectal thermometers may be dipped in Vaseline.

» Before using a mercury thermometer, you may shake it to lower the mercury. If you will not be using it again on Shabbos, do not shake it down after use, as that is preparing for after Shabbos. But if you expect to be using it on Shabbos again, you may shake it down.

Food Preparation on Shabbos

Preparing a baby's bottle

» If a bottle contains pasteurized liquid (such as milk), or if it contains a previously boiled liquid that has cooled off, you can pour hot water from a *kli rishon* (such as a kettle on the stove or an electric urn) onto the bottle containing pasteurized or previously boiled liquid.

» Alternatively, the bottle may be heated by putting it into a utensil containing hot water. That utensil must be a *kli sheini* — that is, the water was poured from a pot on the stove or an electric urn (*kli rishon*) into the utensil (*kli sheini*). To avoid violating the prohibition of *hatmanah*, insulating, do not cover the bottle completely with water.

» If the liquid was not pasteurized or was never cooked, the bottle can be immersed only in a *kli shelishi* (that is, the hot water is poured from the vessel in which it was heated, to a second vessel, and then a third vessel, in order to cool it down somewhat).

» When preparing formula for an infant, you may mix the powder and liquid on Shabbos in the same way as during the week. If necessary, the exact amount of formula or liquid can be measured, but it is preferable to estimate. If an exact measurement is necessary, it may be weighed on a scale that does not use electricity or batteries.

- » You may not puncture a bottle's nipple in order to make an opening or enlarge an existing hole. If there is no other nipple available, you may ask a non-Jew to do it. If no non-Jew is available, you may make the hole with a *shinui*.
- » A hole in the nipple that became clogged may be cleaned for use.
- » A bottle brush may be used on Shabbos, as long as the bristles are spaced apart and don't trap the water.

Preparing food for babies

- » You should try to have everything you will need for Shabbos in your home before Shabbos. In the event that on Shabbos you do not have formula or food for a child, since a young child is considered a *choleh she'ein bo sakanah*, one with an illness that is not life-threatening, it is permissible to ask a non-Jew to buy formula or cereal for an infant on Shabbos if there is none in the house. Similarly, in the event that the need suddenly arises, the non-Jew may be asked to boil milk or cook for a child.
- » The proper way to prepare baby cereal on Shabbos depends on the thickness of the mixture. If the mixture is thick enough to be seen as one mass, yet will flow when poured from one bowl to another, it is considered halachically to be a "loose mixture."
- » It is preferable to use a "loose mixture" rather than a "thick mixture." However, if no loose mixture is available, or if the child must have the thick mixture, it is permitted to prepare such a mixture on Shabbos.
- » **To prepare "loose mixture" cereal:**
    1. Combine the ingredients in reverse order. If the liquid is normally placed in the bowl and then the solid ingredients added, on Shabbos place the dry ingredients in first, and

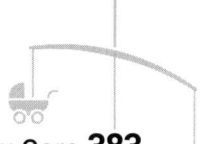

then the liquid. If during the week the dry ingredients are put in first, on Shabbos place the liquid in first.

2. If you do not know the usual procedure, read the instructions on the box and reverse the order of those instructions.

3. If you have no usual procedure, and there are no specific instructions, place the dry ingredients in first. Then add the liquid quickly, so that the mixture becomes soft as soon as possible.

4. Since mixing the liquid and solid can constitute the *melachah* of *lash*, kneading, mix the ingredients in an unusual manner, such as using your finger or the handle of a spoon or fork.

» **To prepare "thick mixture" cereal:**

1. Thick-mixture cereals may be prepared on Shabbos only in cases of necessity (for example, if the baby will not eat a loose-mixture cereal, and the thick-mixture cereal cannot be prepared before Shabbos). If possible, some liquid should be added to the dry cereal before Shabbos and mixed so that it is absorbed.

2. When preparing a thick-mixture cereal, combine the ingredients in reverse order, as described above with regard to a loose mixture. In addition, the mixing must be done in an irregular manner, as described above. However, using a knife or the handle of a utensil to stir the ingredients of a thick mixture in a regular manner is forbidden, but it may be done by moving the handle in a crisscross pattern.

» Because of the *melachah* of *tochein*, grinding, we may not grind fruits and vegetables. This prohibition includes shredding, grating, chopping, mashing, and cutting the produce into very small pieces. Because parents routinely cut foods into small pieces for children, care should be taken not to cut the produce into very small pieces on Shabbos.

The prohibition does not apply to foods that do not grow in the ground, such as meat, chicken, and eggs.

- » The produce should be cut immediately before the meal.
- » If a baby can only eat very tiny pieces, they can be cut immediately before feeding the baby, but a grinder, even a manual one, may not be used.
- » Rabbi Moshe Feinstein maintained that the prohibition against grinding does not extend to mashing foods, such as bananas, which do not break down into particles, but rather form a soft paste because of their natural moisture. However, Chazon Ish was more stringent and required bananas to be mashed in an unusual manner, such as using the handle of a utensil. Even Rabbi Feinstein suggested being stringent when possible.

Cleaning a Baby on Shabbos

Bathing a baby

- » A baby who got dirty may be washed on Shabbos with water that was heated before Shabbos. Some *poskim* are lenient and permit the use of sun-heated warm water (e.g., from a *dud shemesh*), while other *poskim* disagree.
- » The baby should be washed by hand, and not with a sponge or washcloth, because of the *melachah* of *sechitah* (squeezing).
- » The use of a bar of soap is prohibited, but loose liquid soap is permitted. Some recommend preparing diluted liquid soap before Shabbos.
- » It is preferable not to wash a baby's hair on Shabbos. If it got very dirty it can be washed, but it should not be rubbed with a towel.

Baby wipes

» There are differing opinions on whether the use of baby wipes is permitted or forbidden on Shabbos, and it is recommended that you ask your rav or *posek*.

Children's Clothing on Shabbos

» If a child's clothing becomes dirty, it is not permitted to spray or pour water or detergent on them or to soak them, because of the *melachah* of *kibus*, laundering.

» A shoelace may be tied with a single knot and bow. However, this is permitted only if the intention is to untie the knot within twenty-four hours. Therefore, when removing the shoes, you should untie the lace, rather than just slip off the shoes.

» It is forbidden to tie a "double bow" — to tie a knot and bow and then knot the bow itself. Some *poskim* rule that if it is common to open the knot within twenty-four hours, it is permitted to tie such a double bow.

» If the knot and bow became tangled into a double knot, it is permitted to untie it on Shabbos.

» We may not dress a child in pajamas on Shabbos afternoon, so that the parents will have more time *motza'ei Shabbos*. However, if that is the child's regular time for getting ready for bed, it is permissible to dress him then.

Disposable diapers

» Disposable diapers may be opened up for use on Shabbos.

» Some *poskim* rule that it is permitted to open the adhesive tapes of the diaper on Shabbos. Other *poskim* require that the tapes be opened before Shabbos.

- After putting the diaper on the child, one may tape it closed. One may then open the diaper to remove it from the child. It is best not to tape the diaper closed when disposing of it.
- Nowadays, many diapers close with Velcro tabs, and these may be used on Shabbos.

Breastfeeding on Shabbos

- A woman may nurse her baby normally on Shabbos.
- However, expressing milk is a *toladah* (sub-category) of the *melachah* of *dash*, threshing.
- A woman may express a few drops of milk into her baby's mouth in order to encourage nursing.
- If the mother must express milk for her baby who cannot breastfeed, a *rav* or *posek* should be consulted.
- If a woman's breasts are engorged and she is in pain, she may pump the milk with a manual pump, but the milk must be discarded. According to some *poskim*, the milk should be expressed directly into a sink or toilet, rather than into the chamber of the pump or a utensil. If the woman is expressing the milk into the chamber of the pump or a utensil, she should first put in something like salt or vinegar, so the milk immediately becomes unusable.

Carrying a Child on Shabbos in an Area Without an *Eiruv*

- A child may not be carried in an area without an *eiruv*.
- This applies both to children who can't walk and those who can.
- If you are in the street and a child refuses to walk, it is preferable to ask a non-Jew to carry him.

- » If this is impossible, and there is more than one person to help, each person should carry the child for less than 4 *amos* (approximately 6 feet), then put the child down and have someone else carry him. This should be done until the child reaches his home or an area in an *eiruv*.
- » It is always permitted to walk holding a child's hand to help support him.
- » A carriage may not be pushed in an area without an *eiruv*.

Cribs, Carriages, and Swings

- » One may not attach a cover to the top of a carriage to protect the baby from sun or rain, or to take this type of cover off on Shabbos, because of the *melachah* of *asiyas ohel*, erecting a tent.
- » One may open and close the hood or mosquito net of a carriage — or a mosquito net or cover of a crib — that were in place on the carriage or crib before Shabbos. However, it is best to have them spread over at least 3-4 inches of the carriage or crib before Shabbos.
- » It is permitted to unfold or fold a crib, playpen, baby carriage, or stroller on Shabbos, provided one does not tighten any screws or bolts to hold them open. Cribs with legs that must be bolted or screwed may not be assembled on Shabbos.
- » It is permitted to change a baby carriage into a stroller and vice versa, provided the stroller is placed into the frame and latched into place. Similarly, one may add a seat to a baby carriage, if the changes or additions do not require adjusting screws.
- » According to some *poskim*, it is permissible to wind up a baby swing on Shabbos, provided no music plays while the swing is in motion.

Selected Laws Concerning Soiled Diapers

Saying Berachos in the Presence of Soiled Diapers

- » A person should not say a *berachah* in the presence of waste substances (feces or urine), even if the substance is not giving off a discernible odor.

- » A wet or soiled diaper, not covered by other clothing, of a baby older than three months, is considered a waste substance. Therefore, a person should not say a *berachah* near a child older than three months if the child is wearing a soiled diaper not covered by other clothing.

- » If the baby is wearing clothing over the soiled diaper, and there is no bad smell, a person can say a *berachah*.

- » If the soiled diaper is behind the person who wants to say the *berachah*, or to his side, and there is no odor, he may recite a *berachah*, if he is at least 7.56 feet (2.3 meters) away from the soiled diaper. However, a *berachah* may not be said while the person reciting it is facing the soiled diaper, even if he cannot smell the odor, unless the diaper is so far away that he can't see it.

- » A person should also not say a *berachah* in the presence of a bad smell. If the diaper is giving off an unpleasant smell, the person saying the *berachah* must be at least 7.56 feet (2.3 meters) away from the point where the smell ends.

- » If the soiled diaper was placed into a plastic bag, a person may say a *berachah* even while standing next to the bag, if it does not give off an odor.

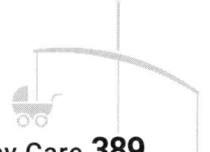

» If a person wants to say a *berachah* in the presence of a child wearing an uncovered diaper, he does not have to check the diaper to see if it is soiled (assuming the diaper is not giving off a bad smell).

Changing Diapers in the Presence of Kedushah

» A person may change a child's soiled diaper in a room with *sefarim*. However, it is better not to place a child on a potty in a room that contains *sefarim*; if another room is available, the child should be taken there.

» One should not change a diaper or have a child use a potty in a room with a clear mezuzah case unless one closes the door and the mezuzah is then outside the room.

Selected Laws of Kashrus

» One may not feed a child of any age non-kosher food. A child should not eat non-kosher food even if he is below the age of *chinuch* (i.e., trainable; approximately six years old, depending on the child's intelligence), even if he feeds it to himself. This is because it is liable to have a negative spiritual effect upon the child.

» A young child does not have to wait between eating meat and dairy. Before giving him dairy, wipe the meat particles off the child's mouth.

» If the mother has to consume non-kosher food because of health issues that are life-threatening, she should not nurse her baby.

> **Q** Before I became religious, I ate non-kosher food. Does this disqualify me forever from nursing my children?
>
> **A** The day after stopping the non-kosher diet, a woman is allowed to nurse a Jewish child, since enough new and kosher food will have entered her digestive system to render the milk as coming from a kosher source.

» A child over the age of two who has stopped nursing for three days should not nurse again, unless there is a health problem and he needs to do so.

Selected Laws of Yom Tov

Rosh Hashanah

» If a woman cannot hear all the shofar blowing, she should hear at least the first 30 blasts.
» Women may eat before they hear the shofar blowing, but should make *Kiddush* beforehand.

Yom Kippur

» It is customary for parents to bless their children, whatever their age, before going to shul on Yom Kippur eve.
» A child may not be bathed on Yom Kippur, even by a non-Jew. If a child is dirty, the dirt can be washed off.
» A mother who has given birth to a child within a week before Yom Kippur should consult a rav about her obligation to fast (or eat).
» Generally, pregnant and nursing mothers must fast on Yom Kippur. However, if there are extenuating circumstances, a rav should be consulted.

Chol HaMoed

» Though one may not wash clothing on *Chol HaMoed*, if children don't have enough clothing for the Yom Tov their clothing may be washed.

» Even if they have enough clothing, but the clothing that is dirty is more appropriate for the holiday, the clothing may be laundered.

» Clothing that is not needed for the Yom Tov may not be laundered.

Purim

» Young children who cannot stay quiet for an extended length of time should not be brought to the Megillah reading. In many communities there are special Megillah readings for mothers after the primary reading.

» If a mother cannot hear the Megillah read, she should read it for herself from a kosher Megillah. However, the blessing before reading it is slightly different. She should say "… *lishmoah mikrah Megillah*" (to *hear* the Megillah reading). She does not have to read it with the *ta'amim* (cantillations).

Pesach

» A firstborn male fasts on Erev Pesach, to mark the salvation of Jewish firstborns during *Makkas Bechoros*. The father of a firstborn male child customarily fasts on behalf of his son, until the child reaches bar mitzvah.

» Alternatively, the firstborn — or the father of the firstborn, until he reaches bar mitzvah — can take part in a *siyum* (celebration of someone who finishes a Talmud tractate) and then he may eat normally.

- The father does not fast or attend a *siyum* on behalf of a child below the age of thirty days.
- Children who can understand the story of the Exodus should not eat matzah on Erev Pesach, so that the matzah should be new to them in the evening,
- The *Sedarim* should not be delayed. When the father comes home from shul, the *Seder* should start immediately, so that the children do not fall asleep. It is advisable to have them nap on Erev Pesach in the afternoon, so that they can be up for the *Seder*.

The Nine Days and Tishah B'Av

- Children who are dirty may be bathed during the Nine Days.
- If children need specific clothing, they may be washed until the week in which Tishah B'Av falls. During the week of Tishah B'Av, clothing can be laundered only for children who constantly soil their clothing.
- Children who do not understand the mourning of this time may eat meat or chicken during the Nine Days.
- A nursing woman whose milk will be affected if she does not eat meat may even eat beef during the Nine Days.

Appendix II

Tefillos and Techinos

A Prayer Said on Behalf of a Woman in Labor

May it be Your will, O Hashem, great, powerful, and awesome, that there be recalled before You the merit of this poor woman who is in travail, and cries out from her pangs. If she has any sin, pardon her and purge her sin by virtue of her suffering from the pain of her travail, and may the sound of her cries ascend until Your Holy Throne. Block up the mouths of those who prosecute her, and may all her advocates enter Your presence, as it is Your characteristic to be beneficent to those who are worthy as well as those who are not worthy. May Your mercy over her be aroused, for You respond in times of distress. Compassionate King, Who has compassion for all, He Who redeems and rescues, hears and responds.

יְהִי רָצוֹן מִלְּפָנֶיךָ הַשֵּׁם הַגָּדוֹל הַגִּבּוֹר וְהַנּוֹרָא שֶׁיִּזָּכְרוּ לְפָנֶיךָ זְכוּת הָאִשָּׁה הָעֲנִיָּה הַזֹּאת אֲשֶׁר תָּחִיל וְתִזְעַק בַּחֲבָלֶיהָ, וְאִם יֵשׁ בָּהּ שׁוּם עָוֹן, מְחַל לָהּ וּמָרֵק אוֹתוֹ בְּמָה שֶׁנִּצְטַעֲרָה בִּכְאֵב הַחֲבָלִים וְתַעֲלֶה קוֹל צַעֲקָתָהּ עַד כִּסֵּא כְבוֹדֶךָ וּסְתוֹם פִּי הַמְקַטְרְגִים עָלֶיהָ וְיִכָּנְסוּ לְפָנֶיךָ כָּל הַמְלִיצִים בַּעֲדָהּ טוֹב כְּמִדָּתְךָ לְהֵטִיב לַהֲגוּן וּלְבִלְתִּי הָגוּן וְיִכָּמְרוּ רַחֲמֶיךָ עָלֶיהָ כִּי אַתָּה עוֹנֶה בְּעֵת צָרָה, מֶלֶךְ רַחֲמָן וּמְרַחֵם עַל כֻּלָּם, פּוֹדֶה וּמַצִּיל, שׁוֹמֵעַ וְעוֹנֶה.

A Prayer Said by a Woman Going into Labor

May it be Your will, O Hashem, my God and the God of my forefathers, that You have mercy on me among all the pregnant women giving birth of Your people Israel, and rescue me from that which was written concerning Eve. When I give birth, ease my travail so that I give birth easily without any pain, before birth pangs come to me.

May the child come out into the world in an instant, with ease and with no harm — neither to me nor to the child — and may he be born in an auspicious time with good fortune, for a good life of peace and health, finding favor and grace, with wealth and honor. May my husband and I raise him to Your service and Your holy Torah, and to a good and peaceful life.

May neither I nor the fetus be harmed — neither in the body, nor the limbs, nor the veins, nor the sinews, nor the skin, nor the flesh nor any of the rest of the makeup of a human being — neither in the inside of the body nor on the outside of the body.

If I have sinned, pardon me through what I have suffered in my birth pangs, and may the sound of my cries ascend until Your Throne of Glory. Block up the mouths of those who prosecute me, and may all who advocate on my behalf enter Your presence, as is Your characteristic, to be beneficent to those who are worthy as well as those who are not worthy.

May Your mercy over me be aroused, and may You rescue us from all pain, confusion, and futility, and may the placenta emerge in its proper time. May I be healthy and fitting for Your service, for You respond in times of distress, O Compassionate King Who has compassion for all, He Who redeems and rescues, hears and responds.

יְהִי רָצוֹן מִלְּפָנֶיךָ ה' אֱלֹקַי וֵאלֹקֵי אֲבוֹתַי, שֶׁתְּתָרַחֵם עָלַי בְּתוֹךְ כָּל עֻבָּרוֹת הַיּוֹלְדוֹת מֵעַמְּךָ יִשְׂרָאֵל. וְתַצִּילֵנִי מִפִּתְקָהּ שֶׁל חַוָּה. וּבְעֵת לֵדָתִי תָּקֵל מֵעָלַי צַעַר הַלֵּדָה, וְאֵלֵד בְּנָקֵל בְּלִי שׁוּם צַעַר, בְּטֶרֶם יָבוֹא חֵבֶל לִי.

וְיֵצֵא הַוָּלָד לַאֲוִיר הָעוֹלָם בְּרֶגַע קָטָן בְּקַלּוּת בְּלִי שׁוּם הֶזֵּק לֹא לִי וְלֹא לַוָּלָד, וְיִהְיֶה נוֹלָד בְּשָׁעָה טוֹבָה וּבְמַזָּל טוֹב, לְחַיִּים טוֹבִים וּלְשָׁלוֹם וְלִבְרִיאוּת, לְחֵן וּלְחֶסֶד, לְעֹשֶׁר וְכָבוֹד. וַאֲנִי וּבַעֲלִי נְגַדְּלֵהוּ לַעֲבוֹדָתְךָ וּלְתוֹרָתְךָ הַקְּדוֹשָׁה, וּלְחַיִּים טוֹבִים וּלְשָׁלוֹם.

וְלֹא נִהְיֶה לֹא אֲנִי וְלֹא הָעֻבָּר נִזּוֹקִים, לֹא בַּגּוּף וְלֹא בָּאֵבָרִים וְלֹא בָּעוֹרְקִים וְלֹא בַּגִּידִים, וְלֹא בָעוֹר וּבָשָׂר וּשְׁאָר כָּל בִּנְיַן בְּנֵי אָדָם, לֹא בְּתוֹךְ חֲלַל הַגּוּף וְלֹא חוּץ לַחֲלַל הַגּוּף.

וְאִם יֵשׁ בִּי עָוֹן, מְחַל לִי בַּמֶּה שֶׁנִּצְטַעַרְתִּי בִּכְאֵב הַחֲבָלִים, וְתַעֲלֶה קוֹל צַעֲקָתִי עַד כִּסֵּא כְבוֹדֶךָ. וּסְתֹם פִּי הַמְקַטְרְגִים עָלַי, וְיִכָּנְסוּ לְפָנֶיךָ כָּל הַמְלִיצִים בַּעֲדִי טוֹב, כְּמִדָּתְךָ לְהֵטִיב לַהֲגוּן וּלְבִלְתִּי הָגוּן.

וְיִכָּמְרוּ רַחֲמֶיךָ עָלַי, וְתַצִּילֵנוּ מִכָּל כְּאֵב וְטֵרוּף וּבֶהָלָה, וְתֵצֵא הַשִּׁלְיָה בִּזְמַנָּהּ, וְאֶהְיֶה בְּרִיאָה וְטוֹבָה לַעֲבוֹדָתְךָ, כִּי אַתָּה עוֹנֶה בְּעֵת צָרָה, מֶלֶךְ רַחֲמָן וּמְרַחֵם עַל כֻּלָּם, פּוֹדֶה וּמַצִּיל, שׁוֹמֵעַ וְעוֹנֶה.

A Prayer of Thanksgiving Said by a Mother After Childbirth

May it be Your will, Hashem, my God and the God of my forefathers, O merciful and compassionate King, just as You have rescued me from this great distress and from this intense danger, so may Your mercy be aroused to rescue from this danger all the daughters of Abraham, Isaac, and Jacob, offspring of those who are beloved by You. Just as You have saved me now, so too, make a sign of goodness for me whenever I give birth.

יְהִי רָצוֹן מִלְּפָנֶיךָ ה' אֱלֹקַי וֵאלֹקֵי אֲבוֹתַי, מֶלֶךְ רַחֲמָן וּמְרַחֵם, כְּשֵׁם שֶׁהִצַּלְתַּנִי מֵהַצָּרָה הַגְּדוֹלָה הַזֹּאת וּמִן הַסַּכָּנָה הָעֲצוּמָה הַזּוֹ, כָּךְ יִכָּמְרוּ רַחֲמֶיךָ לְהַצִּיל מִן הַסַּכָּנָה הַזּוֹ לְכָל בְּנוֹת אַבְרָהָם יִצְחָק וְיַעֲקֹב זֶרַע אֲהוּבֶיךָ. וּכְשֵׁם שֶׁהִצַּלְתַּנִי עַתָּה, כָּךְ עֲשֵׂה עִמִּי אוֹת לְטוֹבָה כָּל פַּעַם שֶׁאֵלֵד.

A Prayer Said by a Mother Just Before Her Son's Circumcision

May it be Your will, Hashem, my God and the God of my forefathers, that just as he is desirable before You now, when he has neither sin nor iniquity, that he always be thus before You. May his covenant not become flawed, and may You not bring him into the power of challenge, nor into the power of scorn.

May he be of sound vitality, but only for Your service, and may Your awe always be set before him. May his intention and will never be withdrawn from studying Your Torah and from performing Your commandments, and may He continue with You in this manner until the day of his death. Prepare for him his sustenance from Your hand, and do not bring him to rely on the power of flesh and blood, for that is a dividing curtain preventing him from serving You, being covered with shame and disgrace by longing for the hands of

יְהִי רָצוֹן מִלְּפָנֶיךָ ה' אֱלֹקַי וֵאלֹקֵי אֲבוֹתַי, כְּשֵׁם שֶׁהוּא רָצוּי לְפָנֶיךָ עַכְשָׁו שֶׁאֵין בּוֹ לֹא חֵטְא וְלֹא עָוֹן, כָּךְ יִהְיֶה תָּמִיד לְפָנֶיךָ, שֶׁלֹּא תִפָּגֵם בְּרִיתוֹ, שֶׁאַל תְּבִיאֵהוּ לִידֵי נִסָּיוֹן וְלֹא לִידֵי בִזָּיוֹן, וְיִהְיֶה בָּרִיא אוּלָם לַעֲבוֹדָתֶךָ, וְתָמִיד יִהְיֶה נֶגֶד פָּנָיו יִרְאָתֶךָ. וְלֹא יָסוּר דַּעְתּוֹ וּרְצוֹנוֹ מִלִּמּוּד תּוֹרָתֶךָ וּמֵעֲשִׂיַּת מִצְוֹתֶיךָ, וְיִהְיֶה כֵן עִמְּךָ עַד יוֹם מוֹתוֹ, וְתַזְמִין לוֹ פַּרְנָסָתוֹ מִיָּדֶךָ, וְאַל תְּבִיאֵהוּ לִידֵי בָּשָׂר וָדָם, דְּזֶהוּ מָסָךְ מַבְדִּיל שֶׁלֹּא יוּכַל לְעָבְדְּךָ, בִּהְיוֹתוֹ מְכֻסֶּה בּוּשָׁה וּכְלִמָּה לְצַפּוֹת מִיַּד בָּשָׂר וָדָם נָבָל וְקַפְדָן וּמַתְּנָתוֹ מְעַט, זְעֵיר שָׁם זְעֵיר שָׁם. וְכֵיוָן שֶׁמְּצַפֶּה לַאֲחֵרִים,

flesh and blood — vile and impatient — giving meager gifts, a bit here and a bit there. Because he longs for others, his wisdom becomes putrid, his soul is saddened and his flesh hurts him. Such is not the case for one who receives from Your beneficent hand, which is open, broad, and full. May he never be dependent on people until the day he dies, and when he is privileged to reach old age, may it be [Your] will that no suffering befall him, neither serious nor light, may illness not happen upon him, and rescue him from mishap and evil occurrences so that he will always be ready to do Your will. Make it his will to intend to do Your will, and may nothing in the world become an obstacle before him — not in Torah matters and not in matters of personal needs — and may no blemish befall him because of illness or blow. Grant that he reach old age with sons and daughters whose bridal canopy he will see, and who will be involved in Torah and commandments. May he not die from serious or unusual illness, and may he come to his grave complete in all his limbs, Amen.

Your word is a lamp to my feet and a light for my path. For a commandment is a lamp and Torah is light; and reproving discipline is the way of life. A man's soul is the lamp of Hashem, which searches the chambers of one's innards.

חָכְמָתוֹ נִסְרַחַת וְנַפְשׁוֹ עָלָיו נֶעֱצֶבֶת וּבְשָׂרוֹ עָלָיו יִכְאָב, לֹא כֵן הַמְקַבֵּל מִיָּדְךָ הַטּוֹבָה, הַפְּתוּחָה וְהָרְחָבָה וְהַמְּלֵאָה. וְלֹא יִצְטָרֵךְ מִן הַבְּרִיּוֹת עַד יוֹם מוֹתוֹ, וּכְשֶׁיִּזְכֶּה לְזִקְנָה יְהִי רָצוֹן שֶׁלֹּא יָבוֹאוּ עָלָיו יִסּוּרִים לֹא כְּבֵדִים וְלֹא קַלִּים, וְלֹא יֶאֱרַע לוֹ חֳלָיִם בְּחַיָּיו, וְתַצִּילֵהוּ מִכָּל פְּגָעִים וּמִקְרִים רָעִים, כְּדֵי שֶׁתָּמִיד יִהְיֶה מוּכָן לַעֲשׂוֹת רְצוֹנֶךָ. וְתֵן בִּרְצוֹנוֹ לְכַוֵּן לַעֲשׂוֹת רְצוֹנֶךָ, וְאַל יָבֹא לִידֵי שׁוּם מִכְשׁוֹל דָּבָר בָּעוֹלָם, לֹא בְּדִבְרֵי תוֹרָה וְלֹא בְּדִבְרֵי צְרָכָיו, וְלֹא יִפֹּל בּוֹ מוּם מֵחֲמַת חֳלִי אוֹ מַכָּה. וְתַגִּיעֵהוּ לְזִקְנָה בְּבָנִים וּבְבָנוֹת שֶׁיִּרְאֶה בְּחֶפְתָּם עוֹסְקִים בַּתּוֹרָה וּמִצְוֹת, וְלֹא תִהְיֶה מִיתָתוֹ מֵחֳלִי כָּבֵד וּמְשֻׁנֶּה. וְיָבֹא אֶל הַקֶּבֶר שָׁלֵם בְּכָל אֵבָרָיו, אָמֵן.

נֵר לְרַגְלִי דְבָרֶךָ וְאוֹר לִנְתִיבָתִי. כִּי נֵר מִצְוָה וְתוֹרָה אוֹר וְדֶרֶךְ חַיִּים תּוֹכְחוֹת מוּסָר. נֵר ה' נִשְׁמַת אָדָם חֹפֵשׂ כָּל חַדְרֵי בָטֶן.

The Shelah's Prayer for Children to Go in the Way of Torah

You are Hashem, our God, before You created the world, and You are Hashem, our God, after You created the world, and from this world to the World to

אַתָּה הוּא ה' אֱלֹקֵינוּ עַד שֶׁלֹּא בָּרָאתָ הָעוֹלָם, וְאַתָּה ה' אֱלֹקֵינוּ מִשֶּׁבָּרָאתָ הָעוֹלָם, וּמֵעוֹלָם וְעַד

Tefillos and Techinos

עוֹלָם אַתָּה אֵל, וּבָרָאתָ עוֹלָמְךָ בְּגִין לְאִשְׁתְּמוֹדָעָא אֱלָהוּתִךְ בְּאֶמְצָעוּת תּוֹרָתְךָ הַקְּדוֹשָׁה כְּמוֹ שֶׁאָמְרוּ רַבּוֹתֵינוּ זִכְרוֹנָם לִבְרָכָה, "בְּרֵאשִׁית", בִּשְׁבִיל תּוֹרָה וּבִשְׁבִיל יִשְׂרָאֵל, כִּי הֵם עַמְּךָ וְנַחֲלָתְךָ אֲשֶׁר בָּחַרְתָּ בָּהֶם מִכָּל הָאֻמּוֹת, וְנָתַתָּ לָהֶם תּוֹרָתְךָ הַקְּדוֹשָׁה, וְקֵרַבְתָּם לְשִׁמְךָ הַגָּדוֹל.

וְעַל קִיּוּם הָעוֹלָם וְעַל קִיּוּם הַתּוֹרָה בָּא לָנוּ מִמְּךָ ה' אֱלֹקֵינוּ שְׁנֵי צִוּוּיִים: כָּתַבְתָּ בְּתוֹרָתְךָ "פְּרוּ וּרְבוּ", וְכָתַבְתָּ בְּתוֹרָתְךָ "וְלִמַּדְתֶּם אֹתָם אֶת בְּנֵיכֶם", וְהַכַּוָּנָה בִּשְׁתֵּיהֶן אַחַת, כִּי לֹא לְתֹהוּ בְרָאתָ כִּי אִם לָשֶׁבֶת, וְלִכְבוֹדְךָ בָּרָאתָ יָצַרְתָּ אַף עָשִׂיתָ, כְּדֵי שֶׁנִּהְיֶה אֲנַחְנוּ וְצֶאֱצָאֵינוּ וְצֶאֱצָאֵי כָל עַמְּךָ בֵּית יִשְׂרָאֵל יוֹדְעֵי שְׁמֶךָ וְלוֹמְדֵי תוֹרָתֶךָ.

וּבְכֵן אָבוֹא אֵלֶיךָ ה', מֶלֶךְ מַלְכֵי הַמְּלָכִים, וְאַפִּיל תְּחִנָּתִי, וְעֵינַי לְךָ תְלוּיוֹת עַד שֶׁתְּחָנֵּנִי וְתִשְׁמַע תְּפִלָּתִי לְהַזְמִין לִי בָּנִים וּבָנוֹת, וְגַם הֵם יִפְרוּ וְיִרְבּוּ הֵם וּבְנֵיהֶם וּבְנֵי בְנֵיהֶם עַד סוֹף כָּל הַדּוֹרוֹת, לְתַכְלִית שֶׁהֵם וַאֲנִי כֻּלָּנוּ יַעַסְקוּ בְּתוֹרָתְךָ הַקְּדוֹשָׁה, לִלְמֹד וּלְלַמֵּד לִשְׁמֹר וְלַעֲשׂוֹת וּלְקַיֵּם אֶת כָּל דִּבְרֵי תַלְמוּד תּוֹרָתֶךָ בְּאַהֲבָה, וְהָאֵר עֵינֵינוּ בְּתוֹרָתֶךָ וְדַבֵּק לִבֵּנוּ בְּמִצְוֹתֶיךָ לְאַהֲבָה וּלְיִרְאָה אֶת שְׁמֶךָ.

אָבִינוּ אָב הָרַחֲמָן, תֶּן לְכֻלָּנוּ חַיִּים אֲרֻכִּים וּבְרוּכִים, מִי כָמוֹךָ

Come You are God. You created Your world to reveal Your Divinity by means of Your holy Torah, as our Sages, of blessed memory, explain [the first word of the Torah] "Bereishis," for the sake of the Torah and for the sake of Israel — for they are Your people and Your heritage whom You have chosen from all the nations, and to whom You have given Your holy Torah and whom You have brought closer to Your great Name.

Two commandments have come from You, O Hashem, our God, concerning the continued existence of the world and the continued existence of the Torah. You wrote in Your Torah, "Be fruitful and multiply," and You wrote in Your Torah, "You shall teach them to your children." The intention of both is the same: For You did not create [the world] for emptiness, rather to be inhabited. It is for Your glory that You created, fashioned, and even formed, so that we and our offspring and the offspring of all Your people, the House of Israel, know Your Name and study Your Torah.

And so, too, O Hashem, King Who reigns over kings, may I come to You and cast my supplication. My eyes are fixed upon You until You are gracious to me and hear my prayer to present me sons and daughters, who, in turn, will also be fruitful and multiply — they, their children, and their children's children, until the end of all generations — for the purpose that they and I — all of us — will occupy ourselves in Your holy Torah to learn, teach, safeguard, perform and fulfill all the words of Your Torah's teaching with love. Enlighten our eyes in Your Torah, and make our hearts cleave to Your commandments to love and fear Your Name.

Our Father, O Merciful Father! Grant us all long life [filled] with blessing. Who is like You, Merciful Father, Who recalls His creatures mercifully for life, remember us for eternal life. As our forefather Abraham prayed, "O that ... might live before You," which our Sages, may their memory be blessed, explain as [living] "in Your awe."

For therefore, I have come to ask and beseech You that my offspring, and their offspring forever after, be proper. Let not be found in me, my offspring, and their offspring forever after any disqualification or filth; rather, only peace, truth, goodness, and uprightness in the eyes of God and in the eyes of man. May they be masters of Torah: masters of Scripture, masters of Mishnah, masters of Talmud, masters of secrets, masters of mitzvah, masters of charitable deeds, masters of sterling character; and may they serve You with love and true awe, not [merely] external awe. May You grant with honor each and everybody among them all their needs; grant them health, honor, and strength; grant them height, beauty, graciousness, and kindness; and may there be love, fraternity, and peace among them. Prepare for them worthy mates — the offspring of Torah scholars and the offspring of the righteous — and their mates should be like them in all that I prayed for them, for one memory applies to this and to that.

You, O Hashem, are the Knower of all mysteries, and before You that which is hidden in my heart is revealed; [You know] that my intention in all this is for the sake of Your great and holy Name, and for the sake of Your holy Torah. Therefore, answer me, O Hashem, answer me for the sake of the holy forefathers, Abraham, Isaac, and Jacob, and for their sake bring salvation to the children, that the branches be similar to their roots, and for the sake of David Your servant, the fourth leg of the Chariot, who wrote Psalms with Your Holy Spirit.

אַב הָרַחֲמִים זוֹכֵר יְצוּרָיו לְחַיִּים בְּרַחֲמִים, זָכְרֵנוּ לְחַיִּים נִצְחִיִּים, כְּמוֹ שֶׁהִתְפַּלֵּל אַבְרָהָם אָבִינוּ "לוּ יִחְיֶה לְפָנֶיךָ", וּפֵרְשׁוּ רַבּוֹתֵינוּ זִכְרוֹנָם לִבְרָכָה, "בְּיִרְאָתֶךָ".

כִּי עַל כֵּן, בָּאתִי לְבַקֵּשׁ וּלְחַנֵּן מִלְּפָנֶיךָ שֶׁיְּהֵא זַרְעִי וְזֶרַע זַרְעִי עַד עוֹלָם זֶרַע כָּשֵׁר, וְאַל יִמָּצֵא בִי וּבְזַרְעִי וּבְזֶרַע זַרְעִי עַד עוֹלָם שׁוּם פְּסוּל וָשֶׁמֶץ, אַךְ שָׁלוֹם וֶאֱמֶת וְטוֹב וְיָשָׁר בְּעֵינֵי אֱלֹהִים וּבְעֵינֵי אָדָם, וְיִהְיוּ בַּעֲלֵי תוֹרָה, מָארֵי מִקְרָא, מָארֵי מִשְׁנָה, מָארֵי תַלְמוּד, מָארֵי רָזָא, מָארֵי מִצְוָה, מָארֵי גּוֹמְלֵי חֲסָדִים, מָארֵי מִדּוֹת תְּרוּמִיּוֹת, וְיַעַבְדוּךָ בְּאַהֲבָה וּבְיִרְאָה פְּנִימִית, לֹא יִרְאָה חִיצוֹנִית. וְתֵן לְכָל גְּוִיָּה וּגְוִיָּה מֵהֶם דֵּי מַחְסוֹרָהּ בְּכָבוֹד, וְתֵן לָהֶם בְּרִיאוּת וְכָבוֹד וְכֹחַ, וְתֵן לָהֶם קוֹמָה וְיֹפִי וְחֵן וָחֶסֶד, וְיִהְיֶה אַהֲבָה וְאַחֲוָה וְשָׁלוֹם בֵּינֵיהֶם, וְתַזְמִין לָהֶם זִוּוּגִים הֲגוּנִים מִזֶּרַע תַּלְמִידֵי חֲכָמִים, מִזֶּרַע צַדִּיקִים, וְגַם זִוּוּגָם יִהְיוּ כְּמוֹתָם, כְּכָל אֲשֶׁר הִתְפַּלַּלְתִּי עֲלֵיהֶם, כִּי זִכָּרוֹן אֶחָד עוֹלֶה לְכָאן וּלְכָאן.

אַתָּה ה' יוֹדֵעַ כָּל תַּעֲלוּמוֹת, וּלְפָנֶיךָ נִגְלוּ מַצְפּוּנֵי לִבִּי, כִּי כַוָּנָתִי בְּכָל אֵלֶּה לְמַעַן שִׁמְךָ הַגָּדוֹל וְהַקָּדוֹשׁ, וּלְמַעַן תּוֹרָתְךָ הַקְּדוֹשָׁה. עַל כֵּן עֲנֵנִי ה' עֲנֵנִי בַּעֲבוּר הָאָבוֹת הַקְּדוֹשִׁים אַבְרָהָם יִצְחָק וְיַעֲקֹב, וּבִגְלָלָם תּוֹשִׁיעַ בָּנִים לִהְיוֹת

הָעֲנָפִים דּוֹמִים לְשָׁרְשָׁם, וּבַעֲבוּר דָּוִד עַבְדְּךָ רֶגֶל רְבִיעִי בַּמֶּרְכָּבָה, הַמְשׁוֹרֵר בְּרוּחַ קָדְשֶׁךָ.

שִׁיר הַמַּעֲלוֹת אַשְׁרֵי כָּל יְרֵא ה' הַהֹלֵךְ בִּדְרָכָיו. יְגִיעַ כַּפֶּיךָ כִּי תֹאכֵל אַשְׁרֶיךָ וְטוֹב לָךְ. אֶשְׁתְּךָ כְּגֶפֶן פֹּרִיָּה בְּיַרְכְּתֵי בֵיתֶךָ בָּנֶיךָ כִּשְׁתִלֵי זֵיתִים סָבִיב לְשֻׁלְחָנֶךָ. הִנֵּה כִי כֵן יְבֹרַךְ גָּבֶר יְרֵא ה'. יְבָרֶכְךָ ה' מִצִּיּוֹן וּרְאֵה בְּטוּב יְרוּשָׁלָיִם כֹּל יְמֵי חַיֶּיךָ. וּרְאֵה בָנִים לְבָנֶיךָ שָׁלוֹם עַל יִשְׂרָאֵל.

אָנָּא ה' שׁוֹמֵעַ תְּפִלָּה! יְקַיֵּם בָּנוּ הַפָּסוּק וַאֲנִי זֹאת בְּרִיתִי אוֹתָם אָמַר ה' רוּחִי אֲשֶׁר עָלֶיךָ וּדְבָרַי אֲשֶׁר שַׂמְתִּי בְּפִיךָ לֹא יָמוּשׁוּ מִפִּיךָ וּמִפִּי זַרְעֲךָ וּמִפִּי זֶרַע זַרְעֲךָ אָמַר ה' מֵעַתָּה וְעַד עוֹלָם. יִהְיוּ לְרָצוֹן אִמְרֵי פִי וְהֶגְיוֹן לִבִּי לְפָנֶיךָ, ה' צוּרִי וְגֹאֲלִי.

A song of ascents. Praiseworthy is each person who fears Hashem, who walks in His ways. When you eat the labor of your hands, you are praiseworthy, and it is well with you. Your wife will be like a fruitful vine in the inner chambers of your home; your children will be like olive shoots surrounding your table. Behold, for so is blessed the man who fears Hashem. May Hashem bless you from Zion, and may you gaze upon the goodness of Jerusalem, all the days of your life, and may you see children born to your children, peace upon Israel.

Please, Hashem, Who hears prayer! May the following verse become fulfilled for us: '"And as for Me, this is My covenant with them,' said Hashem, 'My spirit that is upon you and My words that I have placed in your mouth shall not be withdrawn from your mouth, nor from the mouth of your offspring, nor from the mouth of your offspring's offspring,' said Hashem, 'from this moment and forever.'" May the expressions of my mouth and the thoughts of my heart find favor before You, O Hashem, my Rock and my Redeemer.

Appendix III

Medical Care

Centers for Disease Control Recommended Vaccination Schedule

BIRTH	1 MONTH	2 MONTHS	4 MONTHS	6 MONTHS	12 MONTHS
HepB	HepB			HepB	
		RV	RV	RV	
		DTaP	DTaP	DTaP	
		Hib	Hib	Hib	Hib
		PCV	PCV	PCV	PCV
		IPV	IPV	IPV	
				Influenza (Yearly)*	
					MMR
					Varicella
					HepA**

Shaded boxes indicate the vaccine can be given during shown age range

*Two doses given at least four weeks apart are recommended for children age 6 months through 8 years who are getting an influenza (flu) vaccine for the first time and for some other children in this age group.

**Two doses of HepA vaccine are needed for lasting protection. The first dose of HepA vaccine should be given between 12 months and 23 months of age. The second dose should be given 6 to 18 months later. HepA vaccination may be given to any child 12 months and older to protect against HepA. Children and adolescents who did not receive the HepA vaccine and are at high-risk, should be vaccinated against HepA.

Vaccine-Preventable Diseases and the Vaccines that Prevent Them

	VACCINE	DISEASE SPREAD BY	DISEASE SYMPTOMS	DISEASE COMPLICATIONS
Chickenpox	Varicella vaccine protects against chickenpox.	Air, direct contact	Rash, tiredness, headache, fever	Infected blisters, bleeding disorders, encephalitis (brain swelling), pneumonia (infection in the lungs)
Diphtheria	DTaP* vaccine protects against diphtheria.	Air, direct contact	Sore throat, mild fever, weakness, swollen glands in neck	Swelling of the heart muscle, heart failure, coma, paralysis, death
Hib	Hib vaccine protects against Haemophilus influenzae type b.	Air, direct contact	May be no symptoms unless bacteria enter the blood	Meningitis (infection of the covering around the brain and spinal cord), intellectual disability, epiglottitis (life-threatening infection that can block the windpipe and lead to serious breathing problems), pneumonia (infection in the lungs), death

	Vaccine	Transmission	Symptoms	Complications
Hepatitis A	HepA vaccine protects against hepatitis A.	Direct contact, contaminated food or water	May be no symptoms, fever, stomach pain, loss of appetite, fatigue, vomiting, jaundice (yellowing of skin and eyes), dark urine	Liver failure, arthralgia (joint pain), kidney, pancreatic, and blood disorders
Hepatitis B	HepB vaccine protects against hepatitis B.	Contact with blood or body fluids	May be no symptoms, fever, headache, weakness, vomiting, jaundice (yellowing of skin and eyes), joint pain	Chronic liver infection, liver failure, liver cancer
Influenza (Flu)	Flu vaccine protects against influenza.	Air, direct contact	Fever, muscle pain, sore throat, cough, extreme fatigue	Pneumonia (infection in the lungs)
Measles	MMR** vaccine protects against measles.	Air, direct contact	Rash, fever, cough, runny nose, pinkeye	Encephalitis (brain swelling), pneumonia (infection in the lungs), death
Mumps	MMR** vaccine protects against mumps.	Air, direct contact	Swollen salivary glands (under the jaw), fever, headache, tiredness, muscle pain	Meningitis (infection of the covering around the brain and spinal cord), encephalitis (brain swelling), inflammation of testicles or ovaries, deafness

	Vaccine	Transmission	Symptoms	Complications
Pertussis	DTaP* vaccine protects against pertussis (whooping cough).	Air, direct contact	Severe cough, runny nose, apnea (a pause in breathing in infants)	Pneumonia (infection in the lungs), death
Polio	IPV vaccine protects against polio.	Air, direct contact, through the mouth	May be no symptoms, sore throat, fever, nausea, headache	Paralysis, death
Pneumococcus	PCV vaccine protects against pneumococcus.	Air, direct contact	May be no symptoms, pneumonia (infection in the lungs)	Bacteremia (blood infection), meningitis (infection of the covering around the brain and spinal cord), death
Rotavirus	RV vaccine protects against rotavirus.	Through the mouth	Diarrhea, fever, vomiting	Severe diarrhea, dehydration
Rubella	MMR** vaccine protects against rubella.	Air, direct contact	Children infected with rubella virus sometimes have a rash, fever, swollen lymph nodes	Very serious in pregnant women — can lead to miscarriage, stillbirth, premature delivery, birth defects
Tetanus	DTaP* vaccine protects against tetanus.	Exposure through cuts in skin	Stiffness in neck and abdominal muscles, difficulty swallowing, muscle spasms, fever	Broken bones, breathing difficulty, death

* DTaP combines protection against diphtheria, tetanus, and pertussis.
** MMR combines protection against measles, mumps, and rubella.

Medical Care **405**

Fahrenheit and Celsius Temperature Chart

C°	F°
40	103.9
39.8	103.6
39.6	103.3
39.4	102.9
39.2	102.6
39	102.2
38.8	101.8
38.6	101.5
38.4	101.1
38.2	100.8
38	100.4
37.8	100
37.6	99.7
37.4	99.3
37.2	99
37	98.6
36.8	98.2
36.6	97.9
36.4	97.5
36.2	97.2
36	96.8
35.8	96.4
35.6	96.1
35.4	95.7
35.2	95.4
35	95

NORMAL RANGE: 36.2–37.8 °C / 97.2–100 °F

World Health Organization Growth Charts

Birth to 24 months: Boys
Head circumference-for-age and Weight-for-length percentiles

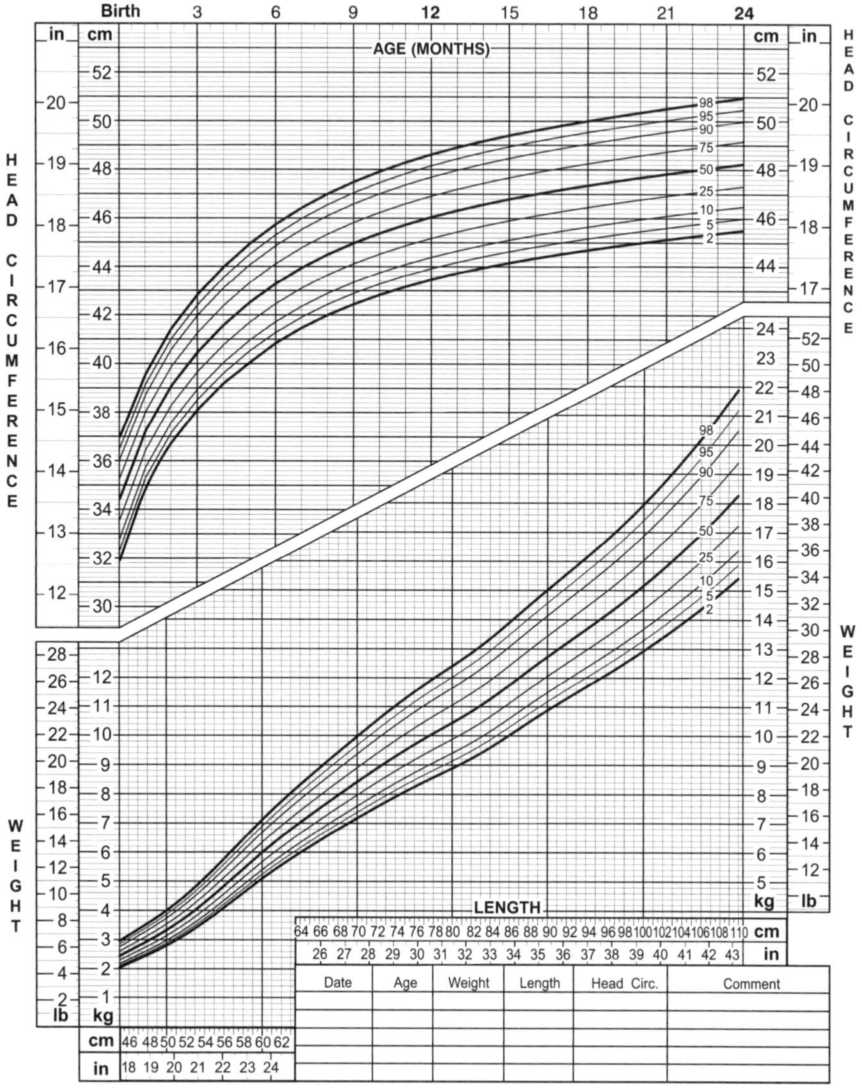

Published by the Centers for Disease Control and Prevention, November 1, 2009
SOURCE: WHO Child Growth Standards (http://www.who.int/childgrowth/en)

Medical Care **407**

Birth to 24 months: Boys
Length-for-age and Weight-for-age percentiles

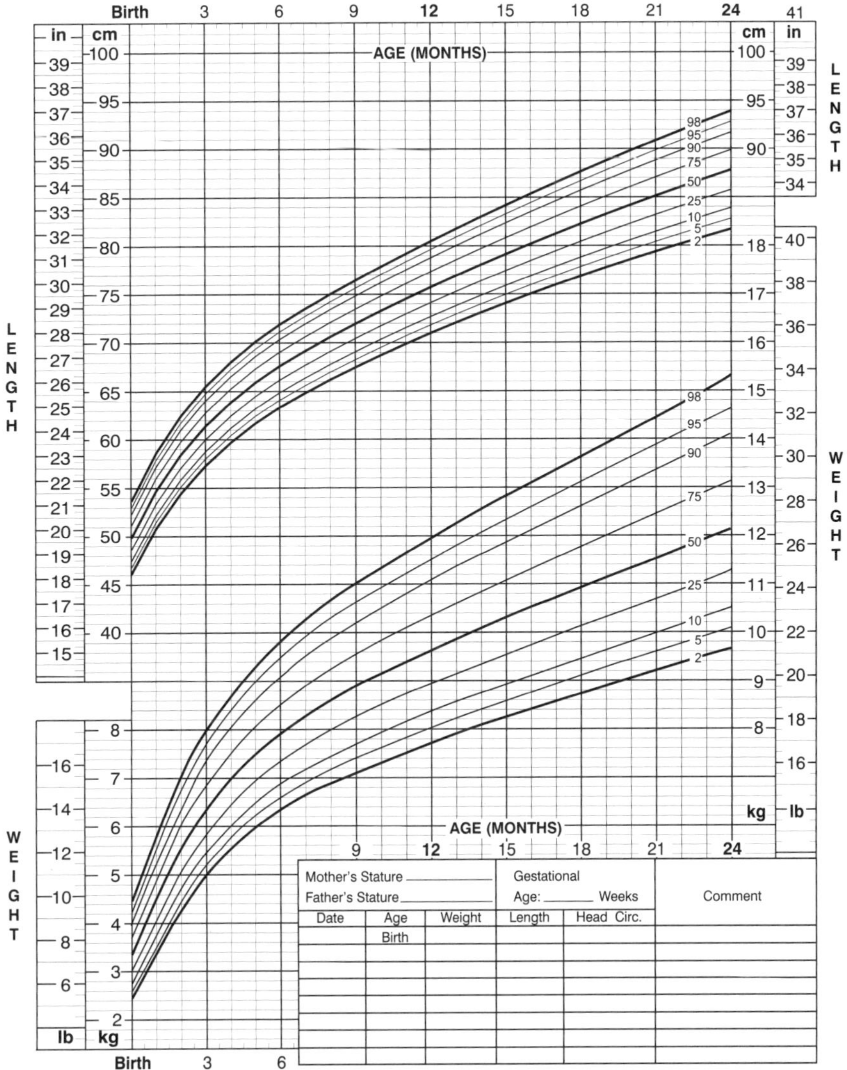

408 Baby's First Year: The Jewish Mother's Guide

Birth to 24 months: Girls
Head circumference-for-age and Weight-for-length percentiles

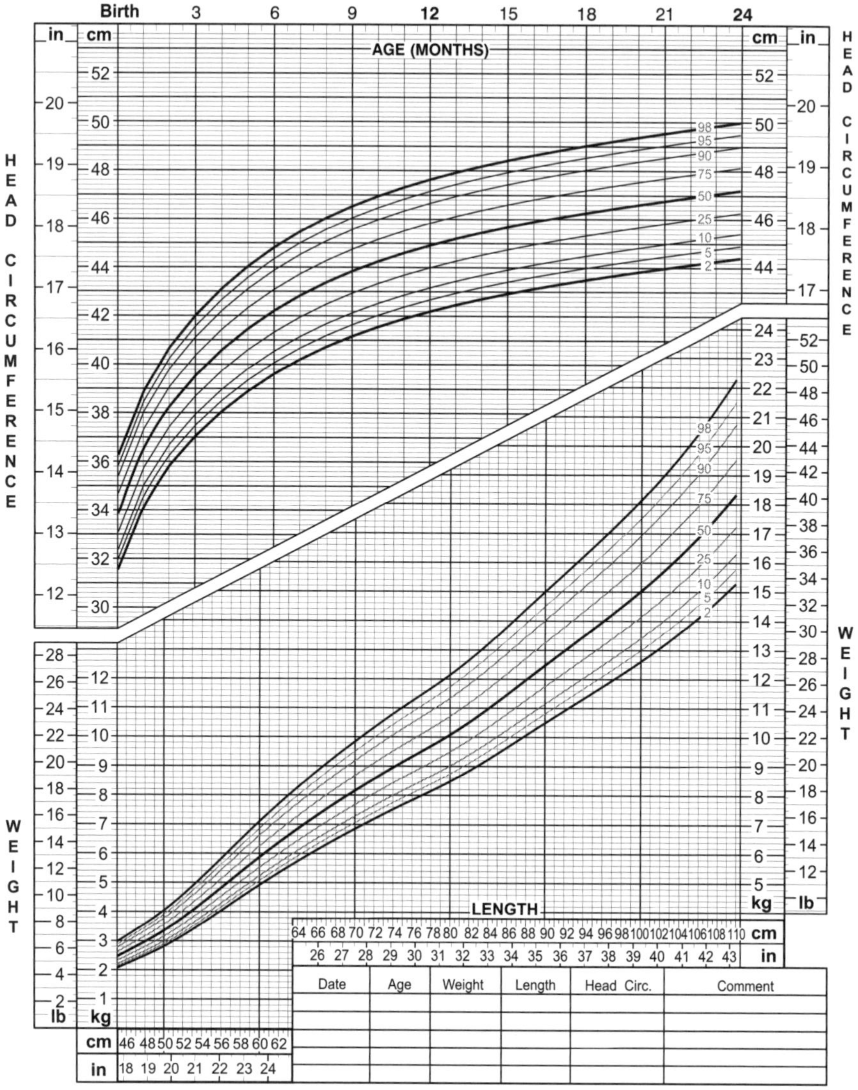

Published by the Centers for Disease Control and Prevention, November 1, 2009
SOURCE: WHO Child Growth Standards (http://www.who.int/childgrowth/en)

Medical Care **409**

Birth to 24 months: Girls
Length-for-age and Weight-for-age percentiles

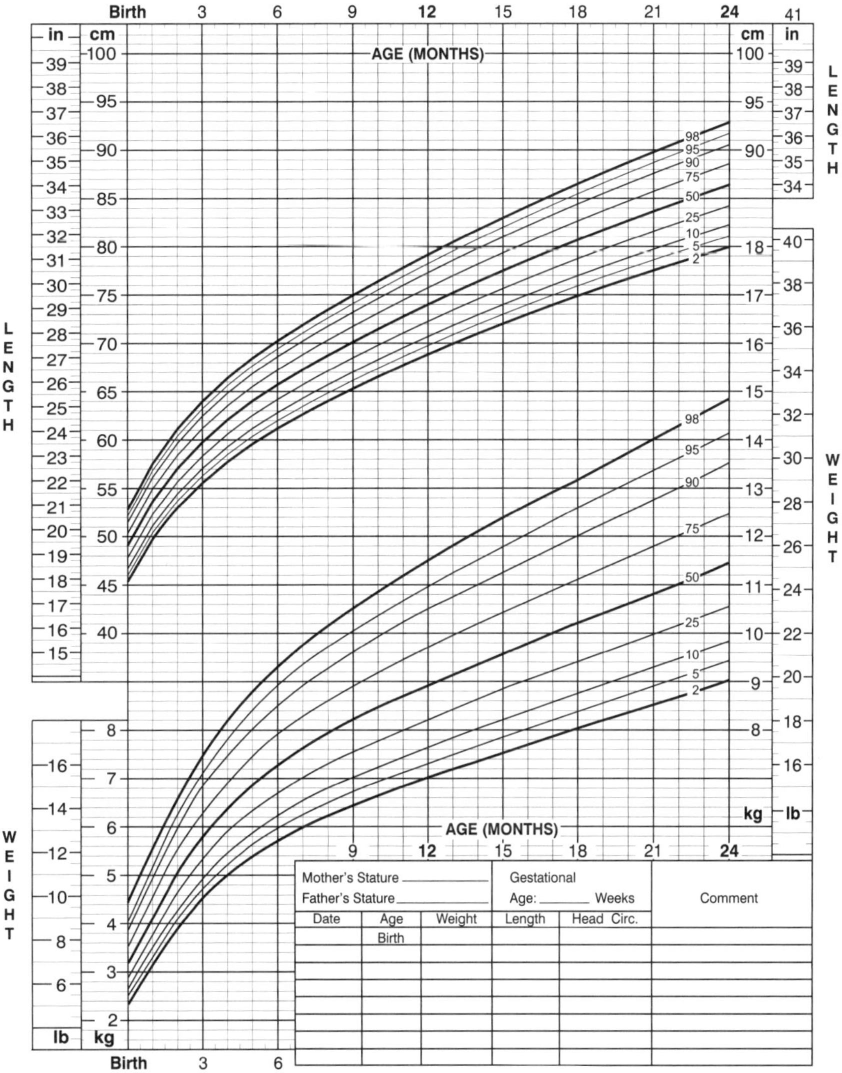

Published by the Centers for Disease Control and Prevention, November 1, 2009
SOURCE: WHO Child Growth Standards (http://www.who.int/childgrowth/en)

CPR for Infants
(up to age 12 months)

Don't wait for an emergency! All parents (and caretakers) should take an infant CPR course if at all possible.

If the baby is choking but conscious, see p. 320.

If the baby chokes and loses consciousness, or is found unconscious:

- » If you are alone, do two minutes of infant CPR (see below) and then call Emergency Services. If you don't know how to do CPR, call Emergency Services and they can guide you. Use a speakerphone if possible, so your hands are free.
- » If there is someone with you, one should begin CPR while the other calls Emergency Services.
- » When you or someone else calls Emergency Services, be sure to immediately give the baby's name, age, and condition, the address where you are located, directions on how to get there, and any other pertinent medical information.

Step-by-Step CPR for Infants

Step 1: Check to see if the baby is conscious
(This should not take more than 10 seconds)

- » Shout at the baby loudly and see if he responds, or call his name.
- » For an infant, flick the soles of his feet. For an older baby, tap his shoulder.
- » Place your ear near the child's mouth and nose, facing towards his feet. Can you feel his breath on your cheek? Is the child's chest moving? Put your hand on the baby's chest — can you feel it moving?

- » If the baby does not respond and is not breathing, go on to Step 2.
- » If the baby is not responding but seems to be breathing, even with difficulty, ask Emergency Services for guidance, but do not continue with CPR unless instructed to do so.

Step 2: Open the airway

- » Place the baby on his back on a firm surface such as the floor, table, or desk.
- » Gently tilt the baby's forehead back slightly with one hand, while using the fingertip of your index finger to lift the chin slightly, so that the face tilts downward from chin to forehead.
- » Pick out any visible obstructions from the mouth and nose. Do not grope deep inside with your finger because it can push obstructions deeper into the throat.

Step 3: Give two "rescue breaths"

- » Inhale, place your mouth over both the infant's mouth and nose. Press your mouth over the baby to make a seal, and blow in for one second. You should see the chest rise. Remove your mouth and let the chest fall.
- » Deliver two of these "rescue breaths."
- » Don't breathe too forcefully into the infant, since a baby's lungs are small and don't need a full breath to fill them. If you are doing this correctly, you will see the baby's chest rise with each breath.
- » If the baby does not start breathing, go on to Step 4.

Step 4: Begin "compressions"

- » Put two fingers in the center of the infant's chest (the center of an imaginary line running between his nipples).

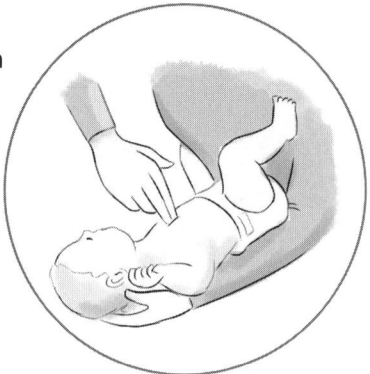

- » Push down about ⅓ of the depth of the chest (about 1.5 inches).
- » Release the pressure so that the chest returns to its normal place.
- » Repeat 30 times, at a rate of at least 100 compressions a minute (about ½-second each).
- » Compressions should be done smoothly and quickly. Let the chest rise between pushes.
- » Count the compressions out loud so that the compressions are steady and spaced apart evenly.
- » After 30 compressions, repeat Steps 2 and 3.

Continue CPR (30 compressions, 2 rescue breaths) until the baby starts breathing on his own or until trained help arrives.

Index

A

AAP. *see* **American Academy of Pediatrics**
ABO incompatibility *83*
abscess *203*
acetaminophen, for infants *152*
afterbirth contractions, Advil or Tylenol for *182*
alcohol to clean thermometer *117*
alfalfa sprouts and milk supply *187*
allergenic foods *325*
allergic reaction. *see also* **allergies**
  oral histamine *325*
  throat swollen shut *321*
  to newly introduced foods *317*
  transitioning to solids, look for *316*
allergies
  breastfeeding and allergenics *188*
  dairy and soy *223*
  family history of *191, 325*
  introducing new foods with *325*
  peanuts *325*
American Academy of Family Physicians, recommendation *28*
American Academy of Pediatrics
  antibiotic eye ointment, recommendation for *28*
  back sleeping, recommendation for *63*
  breastfeeding, recommendation for *159*
  breastmilk storing, recommendation for *216*
  certified pediatric practitioners *137*
  cough medication, warning *154*
  pacifier, postponing use of *247*
  pacifier, reduces risk of SIDS *246*
  pediatrician follows guidelines of *137*
  safety guidelines for cribs *123*
  sleep sack or wearable blankets, recommendation for *113*
  sunscreen, safe for infant skin *117*
  vitamin D supplements, recommendation for *330*
American Dental Association
  bottle feeding *285*
  fluoridated toothpaste, use of *257*
  thumb-sucking, safety of *283*
amniotic fluid
  excreted after birth *196*
  immunological benefits *31*
  nasal passages, in *38*
  swallowed *30, 191*
  vomited after birth *36*
antibiotic eye ointment, at birth *28*
antibiotic ointment, after bris *117*
antibiotic, prescribed for abscess *203*
antibodies, maternal *255*
anti-D injection *83*
antifungal ointment, for thrush *205*
apathy, sign of inadequate nutrition *197*
Apgar Test *23*
  activity *24*
  appearance *24*
  Dr. Virginia, developed Apgar test *23*
  evaluates newborn's condition *23*
  grimace response *24*

performed 23
pulse/heart rate 24
respiration 24
score checked twice 24
appearance, newborn's 29
appetite, changes with teething 254
aspirin
  not to be given to infants and children 153
  other names for 153
  Reye's syndrome, may cause 256

B

babbling 345
Babinski reflex 45
Babkin reflex 45
baby bathtub 86
baby blues 71
baby carriage. see also **stroller**
  Shabbos, using on 387
baby carrier. see also **baby sling**
  age limit, baby's 132
  breastfeeding friendly 132
  convenience of 131
  fit 132
  overview 135
  styles 132, 134
  suffocation risk, avoiding with 135
  sunscreen, use with 134
  supports baby's weight 132
baby clothes
  comfortable, should be 54
  new, wash before using 54
  snaps or Velcro instead of zippers 55
baby food
  baby cereal, preparing on Shabbos 382-383
  homemade vs. purchased 326
  safely refrigerating 328

baby gym 118
baby lotion, not for newborn use 32
baby massage
  benefits 267
  setting for 268
  technique 269
baby monitor 119
baby nurse 66
babyproofing 292-300. see also **babysitter**
babysitter
  background check 241
  choosing 240
  personal interview with 240
  update about changes in routine 368
baby sling 135. see also **baby carrier**
  adjusting 135
  comfort using 132
  pointers, for purchase 135
  using while playing with toddler 363
  using with newborn 52
baby swing 118
  Shabbos, using on 387
baby walker, hazards of 291
baby wipes, use on Shabbos 385
baby wrap. see **baby carrier, baby sling**
back sleeping 63, 264
BAER test 29
bassinet 112, 121-122
bathing
  illustration 86
  newborn, sponge bath 85
  Nine Days, during 392
  Shabbos, on 384
  step by step 87
bathtub
  bath ramp, use for support 115
  bath seat, safety 115

Index

newborn 115
bedtime
  increase sleep time 259
  routine 70, 258, 351
behavior, when tired 70
berachah
  bad smell, saying in presence of 388
  soiled diaper, saying in presence of 388
bib 118
bilingualism 282
bilirubin 26, 82–85
birthmarks 32–33
birth weight, losing in first week 62
blanket, baby 114
blocked airway 321
blood
  bowel movement, in 42
  clotting and Vitamin K 329
  diaper in, baby girl's 79
  fetal flow reverses direction 23
  fetal, high in oxygen 82
  hepatitis B 28
  newborn spits up 36
  reabsorbed after forceps delivery 31
  releases glucose 56
  Rh factor 83
  strawberry marks; hemangiomas 33
  tests in hospital 25
  test, to determine cause of fever 145
  Vitamin K and 27
  vomit, in 147
BMI 331
Body for Life, for nursing mothers 193
bonding 67, 266, 274
books
  board, read to baby 236
  picture, for cognitive development 347
  picture, four to six months 272
  stimulate development 287
bottle feeding
  paced 183, 221
  propping, danger of 219
  sleeping and tooth decay 257
bottles and nipples
  bacteria in unwashed 224
  brush, for cleaning 224
  brush, using on Shabbos 382
  formula feeding, types of when 220
  nipple, enlarging holes of on Shabbos 382
  nipples, differing milk flow with 221
  number recommended 116, 220
  Shabbos, preparing on 381
bouncer 120
bowel movement 42–43, 83–84, 328
BPA carcinogenic
  plastic bottles, in 220
  sippy cup, in 286
brain damage
  HDN and Vitamin K 27
  shaking baby, causes 245
breastfed baby
  rapid weight gain in 196
breastfeeding
  abscess, with 203
  accessories 175
  advantages for mothers 161–162
  after epidural 168
  allergenic foods while 188, 191
  alternating sides 181
  baby carrier, with 132
  benefits 160, 354
  bilirubin, if insufficient to pass 84
  bonding 74, 181, 356
  bottle-feeding breastmilk 165
  breastmilk storage capacity 182
  colic, fennel tea for relief of 245
  color of baby's stool 42

contraindications *163–165*
correct positioning *168*
coverups *175, 194*
dieting during *192*
discomfort during first days *195*
discuss with pediatrician *138*
engorged, if *203*
engorgement, while *179.* see also **engorgement**
ephedra, avoid during *194*
establishing a routine *62*
exercise during *193*
expressing and pumping breastmilk *214*
expressing breastmilk, with inverted nipples *198*
feedings, gauging intake *177*
first experience *157*
first six months, exclusively for *159*
first six months, most beneficial for *350*
flat or inverted nipples, with *197*
flavors of mother's food transfer to milk *327*
frequency after third day *46*
gas-causing foods during *191*
health advantages for infants *160–161*
health advantages for mothers *161–162*
hormonal discomfort while *164*
hormonal side effects and intimacy *349*
hydration during *190*
illness, during baby's *353*
immunological benefits of *31*
incorrect positioning *62*
increase mother's fluids *38*
increasing milk production *186–187*
lactation consultant *172*
latching on *168, 170, 172, 179, 195, 198*
leaking milk, nursing pads for *176*

letdown reflex *171, 180*
milk blister *204*
milk production, decreased *186*
milk production, increased *178, 182*
natural *159*
nipples, everted, flat, inverted *196–197*
nipple shield *197*
nipples, large, compressing *195*
nipple soreness *172, 205*
not always an option *47*
nursing bra *175*
nutritional needs increase during *189*
obesity, reduces risk of *160, 331*
oxytocin and prolactin *180*
pain during *199*
pointers *172*
popularity, return to *159*
postpartum depression, lowers risk of *161*
professional help in hospital *167*
rooming-in *176*
Shabbos, on *386*
shallow latch *172*
shorter feeding after milk comes in *46*
shorter intervals between feedings *185*
sibling rivalry *360*
stopped, age two *390*
stopped until high bilirubin resolves controversial *84*
supplementing *26, 186*
supplements not necessary with *329*
support from pediatrician *139*
timing *183*
tongue tie and *62*
transitioning from *315*
traveling while *194*
valued and encouraged *159*
vitamin supplements during *189*
weaning *348–350*

Index

weight gain during 193
while traveling 194
breastmilk
comes in on third day 46
dieting, negative effects of 193
digested in 90 minutes 39
evolves with baby 353
expressed, storing 216
expressed, transporting 216
expressing and pumping 214
expressing, by hand 214
foremilk and hind milk 180
frozen, discard if contaminated by thrush 206
iron in, more readily absorbed 330
leaking, nursing pads or shields 198
mixing with cereal 316
mother's diet 188
nasal mucus, loosening with 149
natural food for baby 160
perfectly formulated for newborn 45
production 187-188
sufficient supply 46
superior to formula 162
supplement with solid food 184
thawing stored 216
vitamin D, usually not enough in 329
warming stored 216, 226
breast pump
electric vs. manual 217
helps establish milk supply 197
bris 96-103
antibiotic ointment needed at 117
healed by second week 81
healed, checked at well baby visit 141
jaundice resolved before 83
postponed due to jaundice 26, 84
sponge bath until healed 86
Brit Yitzchak 95
burping
illustration 38

releases air bubbles 37
techniques 37
burping, during breastfeeding 68

Caesarean section
amniotic fluid in baby's lungs 30
breastfeeding after 171
engorgement after 201
head not molded 30
no pidyon haben after 107
caffeinated drinks, avoid giving baby 319
calcium, sources of 190
caput succedaneum 31
carbon monoxide 300
caregiver. *see* **babysitter**
car seat 114, 125-126, 130
when leaving hospital 52, 57
cause and effect
ten to twelve months, understanding 343
CDC. *see* **Centers for Disease Control and Prevention**
Centers for Disease Control and Prevention
recommendations 28, 161, 401
vaccines for preventable diseases 402
changing pad 124
changing table 124
changing position during diapering 264
dressing and undressing baby on 55
fall from 150
leave baby unattended, do not 55, 75, 262
mobile over 264
chickenpox 402

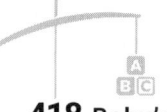

childproofing, *see also* **babyproofing**
  grandparent's home *367*
chillul Shabbos *374*
choking *320*
choking hazards
  foods *319*
  objects *54, 118, 275, 296, 298, 342–343*
  propped baby bottle *219*
choleh she'ein bo sakanah *376–377, 382*
choleh sheyeish bo sakanah *374, 376*
Chol HaMoed, washing clothing on *391*
circulation, cut off *40*
citrus fruit, may cause stomach irritation *318*
clothing, caring for on Shabbos *385*
cognitive development, encouraging *343*
cold virus and newborn *38*
colic *244–246, 267*
  bottles to prevent when formula feeding *220*
  digestion, and *160*
  gas-producing foods, caused by *191*
  relieving symptoms of *244–245, 271*
colostrum *33, 36, 174, 177–178*
compresses, to relieve engorgement pain *202*
constipation *190, 267, 328*
contraception *162–163*
convulsions *56*
cortisol, reduced by massage *267*
co-sleeping *63, 122*
coughing *146*
cough suppressants *154*
cow's milk, avoid *318, 350*
CPR, infant *321, 410*
cradle cap *151*

crawling and creeping *288–290*
  reflex *45*
crib
  convertible to toddler bed *122*
  mattress, safety issues *124*
  safety issues, guidelines *123*
  secondhand, safety issues *121*
  Shabbos, folding or unfolding *387*
cross-eyes *260*
croup *146*
cruising *336, 338*
crying
  during diapering *75*
  food sensitivities, caused by *191*
  inconsolable, colic may cause *244*
  late hunger signal *174*
  less when hungry *186*
  long periods, do not leave baby alone while *39*
  newborn communicates through *39*
  newborn, reasons for *39–40, 243*
  reduced by baby massage *267*
  respond to baby to stop *69*
  sign of distress *168*
  spicy food in mother's diet, caused by *188*
cuddling, newborn *52*

D

dehydration *56, 80, 147–148*
demand or scheduled feeding *73*
dentist, first visit *257*
developmental milestones
  four to six months *252–253*
  seven to nine months *278–279, 284*
  six to eight weeks *233, 236, 238*
  ten to twelve months *334, 346*
developmental or growth spurt, *see* **growth spurt**

diaper bag *115, 133*
diaper changing *75, 77-78, 264, 389*
diaper pail *120*
diaper rash *75, 79, 255, 368*
diapers
 cloth or disposable *76-77, 114, 121, 385*
 dry *56, 186*
 liners, flushable *115*
 number daily *114*
diarrhea *147, 224, 255, 317*
dieting, not recommended *331*
digestion *191*
diphtheria *402*
diseases and vaccines *402*
doula. see **postpartum doula**
drooling, with teething *254*

E

ear infection *150, 247*
eczema, prescription cream for *268*
electric bottle warmers *226*
electrolyte solution, with diarrhea *148*
Elijah's/Eliyahu's chair *101*
emotional awareness, ten to twelve months *346*
emotional issues, mother's *64*
engorgement *201-202*
 avoided with rooming-in *26*
 nipples seem flat due to *197*
 nursing on both sides *179*
 prevent by timing feedings *183*
 recurs during ineffective nursing *201*
 relieving pain of *202*
 restricting liquids unnecessary *191*
 weaning, with *349*
 when milk comes in *182*
ephedra, avoid *194*

erythema toxicum *32*
essentials *113*
 diaper bag *133*
 feeding, for *322*
 furniture and equipment *112-113*
 medicine chest *116, 153*
establishing a schedule *69*
establishing father's relationship *74*
establishing milk supply *182*
exercise, mothers *68, 193*
expressing and pumping breastmilk *214-216, 386*
eye color, changes in *286*
eye contact with baby *281*

F

facial expressions, essential for communication *281*
failure to gain weight *47*
failure to thrive *56*
falls and fractures *150*
father and baby *74, 108*
feeding cues *39, 168*
feeding essentials *322*
feedings
 become less frequent, more efficient *261*
 changing position during *196*
 consulting an expert *62*
 dry diapers between *186*
 formula cues *227*
 frequent due to rapid growth *69*
 GER, with *40-41*
 hospital nursery; scheduled *25*
 increased small feeding for jaundiced infant *85*
 newborn *25, 174, 227*
 reducing number of *350*
 routine, developing *185*

second day, baby more alert *46*
setting for *117*
small, frequent *26, 178*
solids, transitioning to *326–328*
solids, when to start *184, 261*
spoon-feeding *324*
supplies, bottles *116*
third day, breastmilk comes in *46*
thrush, with *205*
vomiting after *199*
weight loss in breastfeeding mother *193*

fennel tea, for colic relief *245*
fenugreek *187*
fetal blood flow *23*
fetal/maternal blood *83*
fever *142–145*
fine-motor development *341, 347*
finger foods, pincer grasp with *328*
finger foods, starting *324*
fingernails *52, 239*
finger paints, edible *341*
fire extinguisher *296*
first step *338*
flu *403*
fluid intake, increase for dehydration *80*
fluoridated water *257*
fontanel *29–30*
  fusing properly *140*
foods to avoid, for baby
  caffeine *319*
  choking hazards *319*
  citrus fruits, may cause stomach irritation *318*
  cow's milk, before one year *318*
  fruit juice, may cause diarrhea and tooth decay *319*
  high sulfur foods, may cause gas *319*
  honey, before one year *318*
  sugar, when possible *318*
forceps delivery *31*
foremilk and hind milk *181*
formula
  adding to excrete bilirubin *84*
  amount fed per weight *183*
  bacteria in unwashed bottles *224*
  bottle-feeding *221*
  bowel movement with *42*
  cereal, adding with GER *41*
  cereal, mixing with *316*
  choosing to use *47, 219*
  colic more common in *160*
  feeding, advantages of *163–165, 185*
  feeding equipment *220*
  feeding schedule *68*
  feeding technique *226*
  hunger cues *227*
  incomplete feeding, supplemented *227*
  iron in, not readily absorbed *330*
  leftover *226*
  night nurse feeds *67*
  preparation of *225–226*
  prepared, use within 24 hours *226*
  quantity fed *227*
  ready-to-feed, recommended for use of *224*
  Shabbos, preparing on *381*
  spitting up *40*
  supplementing with *26, 196*
  supplements not necessary with, for healthy baby *329*
  supplement with solid food *184*
  types of *222, 223*
  weaning from breastfeeding, when *350*
fruit juice, may cause diarrhea and tooth decay *319*
fruits and vegetables, preparing on Shabbos *383*

furniture and equipment.
see essentials

G

games *273, 281–282*
gastroesophageal reflux. see GER
gemachim, for breastmilk *165*
genitals *80*
GER *40–41*
glider *117*
goat milk *222*
grandparent *363–369*
grasping reflex *55*
grasp, pincer, at seven months *284*
growth charts *140, 196, 406–409*
growth spurt *48, 183, 261, 284*
gynecologist *49*

H

hagomel blessing *91*
hand clapping, at seven months *280*
hand-eye coordination *265*
hatov v'hameitiv *92*
Hatzalah, keep number handy *294*
head, newborn *29–30, 51*
hearing *141, 266*
Heimlich maneuver *320–321*
help for new mother *65*
hemangiomas *33*
hepatic cancer and Hepatitis B vaccine *28*
hepatitis A *403*
hepatitis B *403*
Hepatitis B *28, 142*
herbal remedies, to increase milk production *187*

Hib *402*
hiccups, newborn *38*
highchair *297, 323*
high-sulfur foods, may cause gas *319*
hip dysplasia *29, 141*
honey, not safe for infants *249, 318*
hormonal changes and postpartum depression *70*
hormones, maternal in newborns *79*
hospital, leaving *48–49, 52, 57*
hospital nursery
  discharge from *49*
  feedings, scheduled *176*
  hunger cues, in *176*
  treatment and observation in *27*
hunger cues *168, 176*
hydration, during breastfeeding *190*
hydrocele *80*
hydrogen peroxide *117*
hyperthermia and dehydration *56*
hypoglycemia *56*
hypothermia *56*

I

ibuprofen, age appropriate *152*
identity bracelets, hospital *49*
imaginative play *344, 347*
immune system, newborn *370*
immunity, through mother's milk *72*
increasing milk supply *186*
infant seat *120*
influenza *403*
injections, shortly after birth *27*
interactions, family *355–363*
International Board-Certified Lactation consultants *47.* see *also* lactation consultant

iron absorption *330-331*
iron deficiency *330*
IV fluid *46, 196*

J

jaundice in newborns *26, 82-85, 141*
journaling *245*

K

kvatter and kvatterin *101*

L

lab test, to assess bilirubin *84*
lactational amenorrhea *162*
lactation consultant
  breastfeeding education 172
  breastfeeding support 62
  engorgement, consult about 202
  inverted nipples, consult about 197
  latching on, consult about 179
  pacifier use, consult about 247
  pain, consult about 195
  recommend supplements 187
  tongue tie, consult about 199
  weaning, consult about 352
La Leche League. *see also* lactation consultant
  breastfeeding support 62
  breastmilk storing guidelines 216
language development *272-273*
lanolin oil, for nipple soreness *200*
lanugo, on newborn *32*
latching on *168, 170, 172, 178-179, 195, 198*
letdown reflex *171*
lifting newborn, safely *62*

M

marriage, needs nurturing *312*
massage, baby *267*
mastitis *202-203*
measles *403*
meconium *42, 177*
medication
  administering by weight, not age 152
  anti-nausea, inappropriate for babies 154
  check with pediatrician before administering 145
  expiration date, dispose of by 154
  fever, for reducing 145
  infant drops, concentrated 152
  liquid, administering 330
  over the counter or herbal 146
medicine chest essentials *116, 153*
medicine dropper *116*
Megillah, reading on Purim *391*
melanin cells, excess *33*
menstruation *162*
microwave, not for warming bottles *226*
midwife *22-23, 31, 43*
milk bank *165, 202*
milk blister *204*
milk duct, blocked *203-204*
mirror play, promotes self-awareness *283*
MiShebeirach, on the birth of a girl *90*
mobile *61, 119*
mohel *96, 99*
moisturizer or oil *32, 268*
Mongolian spot *33*
Moro startle reflex *43, 44*
Mother's Milk tea *187*

mother, stressed *310, 312*
motor and cognitive development
  tummy time aids *262*
motor and sensory development
  finger paints, edible, aid in *341*
mucus, in infant's bowel movement *42*
mumps *403*
muscle tone
  floppy *24*
  well baby visit, checked at *141*
music
  bedtime, soothing at *267*
  moving to, increases communication skills *266*
  positive effect on emotional, sensory, and language development *266*

N

nail scissors and nail clippers *116*
nails, clipping *239*
naming your baby *90, 102–104*
nasal bulb or aspirator *116, 148–149*
nasal discharge *38–39*
navel, discharge from *82*
nebulizer, using on Shabbos *378*
neural pathways, developing *280*
neurological development *61*
newborn
  activity, stages *170*
  alertness *23*
  assessed at birth *23*
  baby gym and play mat *118*
  baby lotion and *32*
  baby sling and *52*
  back sleeping recommendation *63*
  bathtub *115*
  behavior *33, 70*
  bilirubin, elevated *26*
  blood, spits up *36*
  bonding with father *43, 74, 356*
  bonding with mother *21, 67*
  breastfeeding after birth *168*
  breastfeeding difficulty *196*
  breastfeeding schedule *68*
  calming after birth *23*
  carrying *50*
  car seat for leaving hospital *52*
  clipping nails *52*
  clothing, linen, and accessories *52, 113*
  colostrum, perfect food for *177*
  communicates through crying *39*
  co-sleeper *122*
  cow's milk not recommended for *222*
  crying due to discomfort *39*
  cuddling *52*
  daughter, blessing after birth *90*
  diaper changing *78*
  diapers *114*
  dress in layers *54*
  erythema toxicum in *32*
  examined in hospital *29, 49*
  eyes, puffy *23*
  feedings *47, 176, 178, 184*
  fever *143, 145, 374*
  fingernails and toenails *52, 238*
  fluid, inhaling *36, 37*
  formula-fed *227*
  head *29, 51, 55–56, 62, 134*
  hemorrhagic disease (HDN) *27*
  hiccups *38*
  holding *50*
  hospital, leaving *48*
  hunger cues *168*
  hypoglycemia in *56*
  hypothermia *56*
  ill, call pediatrician *146*
  immature circulatory system *55*
  immune system *370*

injections after birth 27
jaundice 26, 82, 83
lanugo 32
lifting 50-51, 62
midwife 22, 31
mittens to prevent scratching 52
mobile, use of for 119
naming 90, 102
night nurse for 67
nursing pillow with 117
oxygen deprived after delivery 23
pediatrician, first visit to 57
postpartum depression and 71
protecting health of 73
reflexes 43
rocking chair, use of with 125
schedule, adjusting parent's 64
second day, sucking 46
siblings and 359
skin 23, 31-32, 54. see also **skin, babies; skin, newborn**
sleeping 33, 61, 70
sponge bath 85
stomach, size of 177
stroller 129, 130
sucking reflex 246
temperature, cannot regulate 54
third day, nurse less frequently 178
vision, still developing 61
visitors, handwashing and 370
wardrobe 52, 54
weight loss, normal in first few days 47
well baby checkup 139
night baby nurse 67
night light 119
nighttime fussiness 258
Nine Days, selected halachos of 392
nipples
 blood, baby swallows from 201
 breastfeeding, compressing large 195
 cracked 36, 198, 200-201
 flat or inverted 196-197
 pain, caused by dryness 200
 pain, caused by milk blister 204
 pain, caused by thrush 205
 soreness 172, 200
nipple shield 197
non-kosher food 389
nourishment, sufficient 47
numbing gels 256
nursing bra 175
nursing cues 199
nursing garments 175
nursing pads or shields 198
nursing pillow 112, 169, 175, 287
nursing shawl 175
nursing shells 197
nursing station, home 174
nutrition 136, 163, 197, 224, 332
nutritional needs, mother's 189
nutritionist, consult about weight loss 194

obesity 160, 331
object permanence 273, 281, 343
oil or medicinal powder, after bris 101
ointment, for diaper rash 115
oral histamine 325
oral surgeon and tongue tie 62
otitis media 150
overheating in newborn 56
overweight 331
oxygen deprived in newborn 23
oxytocin 161, 181, 267

Index **425**

P

paced feeding *183*
pacifier *246-249*
  colic, may relieve symptoms of *245*
  discuss with pediatrician *138*
  for additional sucking *183*
  hospital nursery, use in *26*
  shows preference for particular *279*
  speech development, may hamper *283*
pain, during breastfeeding *198, 204-205*
pain relievers, infant *116*
Pedialyte with diarrhea *148*
pediatrician
  advises treatment *141*
  antifungal ointment, prescribes *205*
  bathing recommendation *85*
  billing and insurance *139*
  board certified *137*
  choosing *136-137*
  examines newborn before discharge *49*
  first visit to *139*
  GER, prescribes acid suppressor for *41*
  guidance, turn to for *74*
  hepatitis B vaccine, gives *142*
  interview with *138*
  office environment *138*
  routine visits *57, 136, 140*
pediatrician, consult about
  back sleeping *63, 264*
  birthmarks *32*
  bleeding or inflamed scalp *152*
  bowel movement, changes in *42*
  breastfeeding *138-139*
  cereal, adding to formula with GER *41*
  choking *37*
  colic *244*
  crawling problems *291*
  cross-eyes *260*
  dehydration *80*
  depression or anger *246*
  developmental milestones not reached *230, 233, 252-253, 278, 287, 334-335, 338*
  diaper rash *79*
  diarrhea, bloody *147*
  ear infection *151*
  eye, cloudiness or change in color *286*
  eye, discharge from *150*
  fever *144-145*
  fluoridated water *258*
  fontanel, unusual appearance of *30*
  food allergies, starting solids with *317*
  formula *222-223*
  formula feeding *139, 221*
  fracture, possible *150*
  gait abnormalities *340*
  medication *145, 152*
  nasal discharge, yellow or green *39*
  pacifier use *138*
  petechiae *148*
  pinkeye (conjunctivitis) *150*
  poisoning, suspected *146*
  postpartum depression *142*
  schedule, change in *245*
  SIDS, risk of *138*
  teething, medicating for *256*
  tied tongue, correcting *62*
  umbilical cord stump *78, 81-82*
  vaccinations *138, 141*
  vaginal discharge *79*
  visual abnormalities *260*
  vomiting *154*
pediatric orthopedist, consult about
  gait abnormalities *340*
peekaboo and object permanence *273*
personality, baby's *306, 308*
pertussis *404*

Pesach, selected laws of *391–392*
petechiae *148*
phototherapy for jaundice treatment *85*
pidyon haben *107–108*
pigeon toes *340*
pincer grasp *328, 340*
pinkeye (conjunctivitis) *150*
plantar grasp *45*
play *346–347*
playpen. see **play yard**
play yard *119, 122, 292, 294, 337, 387*
pneumococcus *404*
Poison Control *146, 294*
polio *404*
postpartum depression *71–72*
   relieved by baby massage *267*
   risk lowered with breastfeeding *162*
   severity reduced with breastfeeding *161*
   speak to pediatrician about *142*
postpartum doula *66*
postpartum period *356*
potty *389*
PPD. see **postpartum depression**
PPD organizations *72*
prayers, selected *393–396*
premature infants, formula-fed *224*
prescription medications, to increase breastmilk *188*
proprioception *338*
protein, sources of *189*
pumping breastmilk on Shabbos *386*
Purim, Megillah reading on *391*

R

recovery from birth *64*
rectal thermometer *116, 143–144*

reflexes
   rooting *168*
   smile *235*
reflexes, newborn *43*
   Babinski *45*
   Babkin *45*
   biting *44*
   blinking *44*
   crawling *45*
   grasping *44*
   Moro startle reflex *43–44*
   neurological development *43*
   Planter grasp *45*
   rooting *44*
   stepping *44*
   sucking *44*
   swimming *45*
   tonic neck reflex *45*
reflux, continues with GER *41*
relationship with grandparents *364*. see also **bonding**
Reverse Pressure Softening *196*
Reye's syndrome *256*
Rh-factor *83*
rocking chair *117*
rolling over *262*
rooming-in *25–27, 174*
Rosh Hashanah and shofar-blowing *390*
rotavirus *404*
RSV (respiratory syncytial virus infection) *72*
rubella *404*

S

safe sleeping. see **sleep**
safety gates *293*
saline nose drops *116, 148*
sandak *102*

scale, baby 46
scrotum 80
self-awareness, promoted by mirror play 283
self-esteem 369
self-feeding 328
self-soothing, pacifier vs. thumb 246
sensory deprivation, disturbs newborns 239
sensory development 265. see also developmental milestones
separation and individuation 364
separation anxiety 26, 284, 352
serotonin, increased by massage 267
Shabbos, selected laws of 373–387
shaking baby, dangerous 61
shalom zachar 72, 92–94
shehecheyanu 90, 109
shoes 339–340
shofar-blowing 390
sibling rivalry 357–358, 362–363
siblings 357–361, 370
SIDS
  back sleeping may reduce risk of 63
  discuss risks with pediatrician 138
  lower risk in breastfed infants 161
  pacifier may reduce risk of 247
singing, increase communication skills 282
sippy cup 285–286
sitting, by nine months 287
skin, babies
  burn protection 299
  cradle cap 151
  irritated 76
  petechiae 148
  sensitive to chemicals in disposable diapers 76
  sunscreen used sparingly 117
  turning blue, emergency 147
skin, newborn 23, 31–32, 54, 83
  absorbs vernix 31
  red bumps 31
sleep
  AAP recommendations 62
  deprivation, mother's 68
  regression 258
  safe 62
  strategies 258
sleep sacks 113
sleep training 301–304
smile, baby's 235
smoke detector 300
smoking, near baby 370
sneezing 38
social-emotional connections 274. see also bonding
socialization, begins 280
sodium intake, excessive 325
speech and language development 271, 280–281, 344–345
spinal tap 145
spitting up 37
splinter, removing on Shabbos 378
sponge bath and newborn 85
squinting 260
standing 291, 336
stimulating senses 61
stimulation 61
stitches 49
stomachache, caused by bacteria 224
stranger anxiety 368
strangulation, with pacifier clip 249. see also choking hazards
stress and keeping baby safe with 246
stroller 128–129, 387
sucking reflex 246
sucking, weak 186

suffocation hazard
  crib, in 123, 298
  plastic bags 296
  reduce risk of 113
  risk during swaddling 34
sugar, avoid when possible 318
sunscreen 117, 134
supplementing breastmilk 45, 186, 329-330
swaddling
  calms newborn 34
  colic, may relieve symptoms of 245
  helps prevent startling 61
  illustration 35
  not during feedings 172
  receiving blanket for 114
  reduces startle reflex 43
  stopping 34
  suffocation risk with 264
  technique 34
swollen testicles, after breech birth 81

T

tear ducts, discharge from 150
teeth 256-257
teething 254-256
  caregiver, update about 368
  engorgement, causes 202
  sleep regression, causes 258
  weaning, delay with 353
teething rings, BPA-free 255
telephone, emergency numbers 68
temperature conversion chart 405
temperature, newborn cannot regulate 54
testicles
  checked at well-baby visit 141
  swollen after breech birth 81
  undescended 80
tetanus 404
thermometer 143, 380, 405
thrush 205
thumb-sucking 247
toilet training 77
tongue tie 62, 141
toothbrush, for baby 257
toy chest 298
toys
  bath 341
  crib, not kept in 63, 123
  developmental encouragement 286, 337, 347
  early age 275
  early morning 259
transitioning to solids 313-316
tummy time
  developmental aid 64, 253, 262, 265, 288, 290
  establishing routine for 263
  exercises for 263
  frequency of 262
  infant seat, limit use 120
  rejected after baby sits, but still essential 287
  siblings help with 362
  techniques 262
Tylenol, for infants 116

U

ultra-blue light, to treat jaundice 83
umbilical cord, umbilical cord stump 78, 81-82, 374
unconditional love 67
undescended testicles 80

Index **429**

United States National Institutes of Health, back sleeping recommendations *63*
upper respiratory infection *147-148*
urinary tract infection *77*
urine
  clear or pale yellow *47*
  dehydration, sign of *80, 190*
  jaundiced baby's *83*
  test, to determine cause of fever *145*

V

vaccinations *138, 141, 401*
vachtnacht *95*
vacuum extraction *31*
vagus nerve and hiccups *38*
vaporizer, using on Shabbos *378*
Vaseline, for lubricating rectal thermometer *116*
vernix *31*
vision, babies
  checked at well-baby visit *140*
  color differentiation *260*
  developing *61*
  four to six months, at *260*
  newborn *23, 61*
  screening test *29*
  six weeks, focusing at *236*
  three-dimensional *260*
visitors *72-73*
  holding baby *370*
  in hospital *25*
  safety concerns with *299*
vitamin D *329*
vitamin K *27, 329*
vitamins and minerals, supplementary *49*
vocalizing, at three months *238*

vomit, blood in *147*
vomiting *147, 199*

W

waking baby *61, 70*
walkers, baby *291-292*
walking *290, 337-338*
wardrobe, newborn basic *52*
water safety *297*
weaning *193, 348-353*
wearable blankets *113*
weighing baby *46, 186*
weight gain, baby's *193*
weight loss, baby's *196*
Weight Watchers *193*
well-baby visit *140*
wheezing, life-threatening on Shabbos *379*
white noise *245, 259*
whooping cough *404*
wipes, baby *115*
World Health Organization
  growth charts *406-409*
  recommendations *28, 196, 353*
wound, treating on Shabbos *379*

Y

yeast infection *205-206*
Yom Kippur, selected laws of *390*

Z

Zeved HaBat *90*
zinc oxide, for diaper rash *79*

This volume is part of
THE ARTSCROLL® SERIES
an ongoing project of
translations, commentaries and expositions on
Scripture, Mishnah, Talmud, Midrash, Halachah,
liturgy, history, the classic Rabbinic writings,
biographies and thought.

For a brochure of current publications
visit your local Hebrew bookseller
or contact the publisher:

Mesorah Publications, ltd
4401 Second Avenue
Brooklyn, New York 11232
(718) 921-9000
www.artscroll.com